# John Jenkins

## The Reluctant Revolutionary?

**ABOUT THIS BOOK:**

'The descent of an otherwise normal person into the realms of terrorism: is it fascinating? Well, I suppose it is. Wyn Thomas is a beaver after the truth... With the skill of a probing and astute historian, he is not afraid to ask the difficult question. His research skills are second to none, with no stone left unturned.'

**John Jenkins**

'To have a complete picture of someone who I only met briefly in particular circumstances [as a member of the Shrewsbury Unit] is particularly interesting to me. It is a story which is not only of interest in the Welsh context, but also helps in the general understanding of the psychological development of the person and a certain justification for his actions. I only ever considered Jenkins' actions in terms of the criminality; the man himself and what fuelled his decision to affiliate with the MAC campaign, until now, I knew nothing about. As a result of Dr Wyn Thomas' excellent biography, I now have a much clearer understanding.'

**Raymond Kendall QPM, former Interpol Secretary-General**

'An important historical document, which has manifestly been meticulously researched. It is surprising that so little has been written about this very interesting period of Welsh history. This is not only a book for a student of history, but also for anyone with an interest in the history of Wales, as it is compelling to read and easy to follow.'

**Elfyn Llwyd, member of the Privy Council**
**and former Plaid Cymru MP**

'This book is fascinating. The subject matter is, of course, contentious, and Dr Thomas' somewhat sympathetic tone and approach will upset some people. But the material is very rich and consistently intriguing. This is a powerful, dramatic tale – and a poignant one.'

**Professor Richard English, historian specialising**
**in Irish nationalism and the IRA**

# John Jenkins

## The Reluctant Revolutionary?

### Dr WYN THOMAS

*For Chloe and Cora*

First impression: 2019

© Copyright Dr Wyn Thomas and Y Lolfa Cyf., 2019

The publishers wish to acknowledge the support of
Cyngor Llyfrau Cymru

Cover photograph and design: Robat Gruffudd
Back cover photograph: John Jenkins' collection
Author photograph: Wyn Thomas' collection

Photographs from the Jenkins family
collection unless otherwise stated.

ISBN:
hardback  978 1 912631 07 0
paperback  978 1 912631 14 8

Published and printed in Wales
on paper from well-maintained forests by
Y Lolfa Cyf., Talybont, Ceredigion SY24 5HE
*website* www.ylolfa.com
*e-mail* ylolfa@ylolfa.com
*tel* 01970 832 304
*fax* 832 782

# Contents

# Acknowledgements

I would like to thank everyone who has contributed to the writing of this book. All contributions, large or small, have helped me to record accurately this fascinating, enigmatic and over-looked period in recent British history. But I would like to extend my especial gratitude to Carolyn Hodges at Y Lolfa for her painstaking and exacting approach to the editing process, and most of all to John Jenkins. Without John's frank and disarming honesty, this book would not have been possible.

Dr Wyn Thomas
May 2019

# Foreword

This is a warts-and-all account of my life, which is quite correct for an historian renowned for his honest and courageous approach to historical enquiry and writing.

A subversive bombing campaign against the State never makes for easy analysis, because the subject and its protagonists are by nature secretive. While maintaining a useful sense of the ongoing MAC campaign, Dr Wyn Thomas mixes a telling detail with narrative verve to convey both the seriousness and the force of the MAC offensive.

Written in Dr Thomas' elegant style, this book lifts the lid on the campaign of *Mudiad Amddiffyn Cymru* and reveals in extraordinary and factual detail how the protest was undertaken. There has been much rumour and innuendo about MAC, but with unflinching tenacity, Dr Thomas has tackled all such areas of speculation comprehensively. While methodical, he is no propagandist or apologist. Rather, he is motivated by that governing principle that all respected and erudite historians should be guided by – getting their facts right.

Asked by Dr Thomas what I feel the MAC campaign achieved in propagating Welsh political interests in the eyes of the British State, my response was simple: 'We showed them we could do it... Never again will the UK political establishment take Wales for granted.' I would like to congratulate Dr Wyn Thomas on the passion and the relentless commitment he has shown in getting this history correct and making it available to a much wider audience.

John Jenkins
May 2019

# Introduction

In the summer of 1968, in a blaze of noise and colour, the marching band of the Royal Welch Fusiliers played its way through Wrexham. Among the crowd which applauded loudly as the procession made its way down Hope Street were plain clothes police officers. They were assigned to protect the marching servicemen from a group which styled itself *Mudiad Amddiffyn Cymru* (the Movement to Defend Wales). Better known as MAC and responsible during the preceding months for a series of bomb attacks on government installations in Wales and water pipelines both in Wales and over the border in England, the leader of the group was one of Britain's most wanted men.

Having been formed a few months earlier, the Fusiliers' Territorial Army Band was growing in popularity; and with the Royal Investiture of Prince Charles less than a year away, bookings were flooding in. As a proud member of the marching band, and a married man with two small boys, life was going well for John Jenkins, the band's senior drummer. An exemplary soldier, both admired and respected, Jenkins' career was in the ascendant. Nonetheless, unknown to all but the smallest group of associates, Sergeant John Jenkins of the Royal Army Dental Corps had a secret. The eventual detection of John Jenkins as the brilliant strategist behind *Mudiad Amddiffyn Cymru* some 18 months later would rock the British establishment. John Jenkins' arrest and conviction ensured that never again would a member of Her Majesty's Services be viewed as above reproach and suspicion. This is his story.

# CHAPTER 1

# An idyllic childhood

## Northlands and an official letter

John Barnard Jenkins was born on Saturday 11 March 1933, in Cardiff. Since he was a child, John has had the impression that he was born in St David's Hospital, in the Canton area of the city. During a period when home births were common, it is feasible that the complications which John believes prompted a hospital delivery were not merely confined to medical concerns for his mother. Because although John Jenkins is unsure of the detail surrounding his earliest years, according to his birth certificate (on which he is recorded as John Barnard), John was actually born in Northlands in the Gabalfa area of Cardiff.[1] Today a shelter for the city's homeless, at the time John was born, Northlands was a residential home run by the Salvation Army to provide accommodation for unmarried and expectant mothers during the latter stages of pregnancy and for a temporary period following the birth.[2] Furthermore, it is likely, John believes, that on leaving Cardiff, he and his mother, Minerva Barnard, went to live with her sister and her husband in Pontypool, rather than returning to Minerva's parents' home in Aberfan.

John Jenkins' supposition that the circumstances surrounding his birth may have been complicated is supported by the fact that when aged about ten, while 'doing a naughty boy' and 'rooting around and looking in all these drawers for toys', John discovered an official letter which was addressed to his mother.[3] 'It was,' he recalls, 'from some local governmental organisation, or the Home Office, or somewhere.' It outlined, to Jenkins' great surprise, that he was illegitimate and included the 'putative' identity of his father. In a state of confusion, John consulted the family dictionary to ascertain the meaning of the word 'putative'. It was defined as meaning 'taken for granted'. This, he reasoned, indicated that his mother knew the identity of his father. When later discussing the matter, John recalled that the mysterious figure was following 'the normal and correct routine in these matters' and providing for his care by 'paying child maintenance costs on a regular basis' to his mother and her husband, Tom Jenkins – the man whom John had always unquestioningly regarded as his biological father.

At some point during the 18 months after John was born, Minerva Barnard met John's stepfather, Thomas (Tom) Jenkins. Living together at the home of Tom's father in Llanfabon, near Nelson, they married 'in the district of Pontypridd' on 10 November 1934, and soon established the family home in Treharris.[4] On 21 July 1936, they had a son, Keith. John is unsure where Minerva and Tom met, but of one thing he is certain: the couple provided him with 'an idyllic childhood. I was brought up properly,' he proudly professes. 'It was caring and all the rest of it… We never went short of food, or anything like that.' Tom Jenkins may not have been 'the most brilliant of persons – he spent his life working below ground in the local colliery as a labourer,' but he was, Jenkins added warmly, 'a nice chap; and he never treated me as anything other than the son he loved.' In tribute to this 'decent and hard-working man', John insists on referring to Tom Jenkins as 'my father.'

## Minerva's Domestic Service and the Dodingtons

It is testament to the 'wonderful' childhood that John Jenkins experienced that there was never any indication from either his mother or father that all was not perhaps as it seemed. His birth certificate states that his mother, Minerva, is registered as a 'Servant Domestic of White Hart Inn in Quakers Yard' and, when John's birth was registered on 4 April 1933, was living in Northlands, Cardiff. On learning this, John revealed that when he was a boy, Minerva once let slip that before he was born, 'she briefly worked for a family called the Dodingtons somewhere in the Cardiff area.'[5] As the identity of his father is unrecorded on his birth certificate, John was asked to throw light on what he believes may have transpired and whether he was perhaps the result of a sexual liaison between his mother and a member of the Dodington family. John replied that while he could not be certain, he *could* 'just imagine what kind of horrors they were.'[6] Nevertheless, on reflection, he was more inclined to believe that his father may have been a domestic servant too. To clarify the point, John did not think that the name given on the letter he saw when aged ten was Dodington, but rather Underhill, or Underwood. In addition, according to the official letter his mother received, the man paying his child maintenance costs 'either came from Bournemouth, or was now living there.' John's assertion as to the series of events may well be correct. Yet, this avenue of conjecture does leave a lot of tantalising and unanswered questions. Asked by John to look into the matter and to consider the options, there appear to be four distinct possible scenarios: 1) that John is the son of a domestic servant, as John believes; 2) that he is the son of a member of the Dodington family; 3) that John is the son of a well-to-do guest of the Dodingtons who was staying with the family while John's mother, Minerva, worked for them; or 4) that John's biological father was entirely unconnected to the Dodington family, and was someone whom Minerva met during her limited free time.

To examine the first theory: would a domestic servant, in receipt of a notoriously meagre wage for his duties, have been able to afford childcare costs, however small? Indeed, might a domestic servant have felt inclined to pay at all, when despite an apparent legal obligation upon the father to pay child maintenance costs at this juncture,[8] the temptation to simply 'disappear' would have negated the judicial responsibility to do so. This argument is particularly compelling given that John's father would have been aware that Minerva lacked the necessary financial clout to pursue the matter through the courts. In addition, if in domestic service along with John's mother, Minerva, why had the couple not simply bowed to societal pressure, 'done the decent thing' and stayed together; particularly when considering that Minerva was aged 29 when John was born, a somewhat advanced age for a first-time mother during this period? If also in domestic service, was John's biological father married, with a wife and children to support? If so, while it does explain why he and Minerva did not marry, it also renders the fact that he was prepared to pay for John's care and upkeep for ten years even less plausible. Furthermore, would a domestic servant have been willing to pay for John's care, especially if he had been born from a relationship based on affection, but neither want, nor expect to have, any access to his son? It does seem unlikely. Finally, if perhaps a valued member of staff within the Dodington household, was John's biological father sent back to Bournemouth after getting Minerva pregnant, thus assuring that the good name of the Dodington family was not embroiled in unsavoury rumour?

To examine the second theory, that a member of the Dodington family was John's father: might it be that a member of the seemingly wealthy Dodington family was secreted quietly away to affluent Bournemouth to avoid a scandal[7]; and that the family prestige was restored through the father paying regular instalments of money to meet the costs of the infant John's care for an agreed period; for instance, ten years? In addition, was this arrangement brokered on the understanding that Dodington would not be expected to have a relationship with John, and that his name would not be registered as the father on John's birth certificate? As for the third theory: was the same relocation and financial agreement reached with a former prosperous house guest of the family by the name of Underhill or Underwood? Or indeed, as suggested by the fouth theory, was John's biological father named Underhill or Underwood someone unconnected to the Dodington family, whom Minerva met when *not* in work?

An intriguing aspect of the narrative surrounds the fact that John suspects that his mother was not happy while working for the Dodingtons; despite Minerva not having said anything derogatory or pejorative about the family. On the face of it, why should Minerva be unhappy, when employment in supposedly warm, spacious, middle-class suburbia would seem preferable to employment in less comfortable surroundings? Was Minerva the victim of some degree of intimidation? Might it be that Minerva was subject to sexual pressure and for one reason or another, coerced into sexual activity? Possibly, but Minerva may have been unhappy owing to more mundane reasons. Being employed some distance from her family, friends and the familiar surroundings of her childhood, was Minerva lonely? Did she lack the financial resources to visit family and friends as often as she wanted to? If employed to carry out the tasks expected of a domestic servant, did she find the work physically demanding and the hours long? Did Minerva resent being bossed around, and/or take umbrage when she was looked down upon by those also employed by the Dodingtons who were placed higher up the servants' hierarchy?

Finally, Minerva Barnard, as John is proud to testify, was a formidable, rather no-nonsense character. This is a personality trait she appears to have inherited from her father. Consequently, she may not have wanted to incur the wrath of her parents by failing to marry John's biological father, unless there existed an especial reason not to do so, but it is also possible that being apparently strong-willed, Minerva decided against getting married because she believed the marriage was unlikely to work – a decision which then resulted in her being ostracised by her parents in Aberfan.

Whatever the truth, and unaware that John had read the letter when aged ten, Minerva 'never discussed it. Never,' said Jenkins firmly, when asked if his mother had thrown light on the identity of his natural father, or how he came to be conceived. That is 'not to say,' Jenkins ruminated, 'that she didn't discuss the situation with her sister, or someone else she was close to.' Why did John not confront his mother with news of the letter's discovery – for example, when embroiled in a heated exchange during the uncertainty of adolescence? Jenkins replied disarmingly: 'The thing is, you see, if I had brought the matter up, my mother might have taken it as a direct attack on her. And I wasn't going to risk upsetting my mother, so I saw no point. What would be the point of me knowing a name?' But had he not felt the right to know his father's identity? Jenkins laughed and replied eloquently: 'There are rights and there are rights, and some rights are more right than other rights.' He then added, more soberly: 'My mother's peace of mind came first. Her feelings came above my own.' Besides, while the Jenkins family did experience family rows, they 'did not have many'; and they 'didn't have any *nasty* arguments, with people storming off and all that.'

Asked how the relationship with his mother had continued, having learned of his illegitimacy, John disclosed that it was unaffected. He said that he had learnt at an early age to compartmentalise his feelings, and this was something he had compartmentalised so that he could carry on as normal. It was this ability to place his affections in separate boxes, while wearing an emotionally protective suit of armour, which Jenkins was later to rely on heavily. As for who might also have been aware of the Jenkins' family secret, John felt it unlikely that their friends and neighbours knew that Minerva had carried him 'out of wedlock'; with it probably assumed within the community of his childhood home that Tom was John's biological father. Tom Jenkins was certainly aware of the situation; and it says much about the kindness and thoughtfulness of both Minerva and Tom that only in the past few years while sifting through his late mother's correspondence, did John learn that Tom Jenkins had adopted him as his own when John was aged ten. On doing so, it seems that the financial arrangement with John's biological father ended.

Has Jenkins ever contemplated his biological father's personality? 'Well,' he joked, 'he must have been an awkward sod, that's all I can say. And as my mother was an awkward sod as well, between the pair of them that makes me a doubly awkward sod!' By way of closing the matter, Jenkins declared resolutely, but with a typical mixture of candour and humour: 'I don't know who my real father was; and I don't want to find out either; he might be English!' The circumstances surrounding the birth of John Jenkins remain shrouded in mystery. It is an enigma, and one of a number which characterise this intelligent and somewhat complex and intriguing man.

## Life in the Rhondda Valley during the inter-war period

While much of the detail which envelops the story of John's illegitimacy is speculation, its importance must be noted. This is because it may well throw light on the character of John Barnard Jenkins and provide an explanation as to his later decision to spearhead the campaign of militancy in the name of Welsh political freedom. Why? Because it is not inconceivable that John's discovery, when aged about ten, that he was illegitimate might have resulted in feelings of uncertainty and indeed anger, and a subsequent need to control his emotional environment. His desire and determination to protect the things he held dear may well have been transferred later to Wales, and the nation's unique cultural identity.

But if this is indeed true, what other factors *also* shaped and moulded John's personality during his formative years? John was raised within the industrial belt of the South Wales Valleys. The area's fortunes were transformed when coal, which was used in smelting and so initially an aspect of the iron industry, began to be used in London as a domestic fuel in the 1830s. The coal found in abundance in the two Rhondda Valleys was discovered to be anthracite, and so almost smokeless and of a particularly high quality. As demand for coal mined in the Rhondda increased rapidly on a global scale for both military and domestic consumption, the region, once renowned for its rolling green hills and wooded valleys, was soon unrecognisable as the first wave of pits were sunk in the early 1850s to exploit the area's rich mineral wealth.

As those in search of work poured into the area, especially from south and west Wales and the western counties of England, the population soared. In 1851, the population of the Rhondda Valley was less than 1,000. In 1891, it exceeded 88,000 and by 1911, it was more than 150,000. On the eve of the First World War in 1914, 1,100,000 people lived in the south Wales coalfield. The Rhondda Valley's population reached a peak in 1924 of 167,000, as rows of terraced homes sprang up in their hundreds to house the workers and characterise the area. Steady increases in output and manpower saw coal production in Wales peak in 1913, when 46 million tonnes were produced by 232,000 men working in 620 mines.[9] From a cultural standpoint, opinion is divided as to the impact this population explosion had on the use of Welsh in the area. Though many see the massive influx from outside the area as diluting the Welsh language, others argue that had it not been for industrialisation in south-east Wales, many Welsh-speakers both from the Rhondda Valley and from other areas of Wales would have been forced to emigrate in search of work.[10]

While some colliery owners soon enjoyed financial wealth beyond the dreams of avarice, it proved to be hot and perilous work for those employed to remove the coal from the bowels of the earth. The ever-present threat of danger, as exemplified by a litany of mining disasters, resulted in the deaths of hundreds through gas explosions and other routine hazards. It inspired a collective regional mindset characterised by resilience and a scepticism towards authority, and which, in turn, was balanced with a deep sense of community spirit and cohesion. But the good days for the nation's coal industry – at least in terms of coal production – were not to last. From the end of World War I in 1918, the industrial belt of the South Wales Valleys witnessed a period of precipitous economic decline. Where once King Coal ruled supreme and fuelled the British Empire, the years between 1921 and 1936 saw 241 mines close in south Wales. It resulted in the number of those employed in the pits falling from its 1920 peak of 271,000 to 130,000. The main reason for the fall in demand was the development of coal industries overseas, advances in mechanisation and the increasing use of other sources of energy. For instance, by 1939 the navies of almost every country had changed from coal to oil.

The inter-war years of economic depression, characterised by mass unemployment, food shortages and the despised and dreaded Means Test – whereby every aspect of a family's earning ability, including the value of their possessions, was examined in minute and humiliating detail to determine the amount of financial assistance to be received from the State

– coincided with the Labour Party's ascendancy in the political and social life of Wales. Nowhere was the party's political dominance more evident than in the nation's industrial belt. As the Labour Party consolidated its political grip on the industrial heartland of south-east Wales, the increasing threat of war ensured the area received *some* upturn in its fortunes, as Britain stockpiled resources and steadied itself for the grim battle ahead.

Nonetheless, it is hardly surprising, when considering these factors, that such an emotional atmosphere would impact on John's developing personality, go some considerable way to shaping his outlook on life – particularly when faced with perceived injustice – and instil a determination to protect the cultural and environmental identity of his home.

## Day-to-day life during the War

John Jenkins' day-to-day life was not impacted negatively even by the years of economic austerity and the storm clouds gathering over Europe which culminated in the radio announcement at 11 a.m. on Sunday, 3 September 1939 by Prime Minister Neville Chamberlain, sombrely informing the listening nation that Britain had declared war on Germany. Yet such is the importance of this seismic event in British history that John, despite being only aged six and a half at the time hostilities began, and 'not knowing what the declaration of war meant' and so 'unable to foresee what the effect of it would be on us', remembers Neville Chamberlain's radio broadcast. More notably, however, John recalls the 'look of fear and trepidation' on the faces of his parents. Not least because Tom's brother had been killed in the First World War and John has no doubt that his mother, Minerva, also 'had relatives killed during it as well. So, they knew,' John added gravely, 'what world war meant.' Only time would tell what the impact of this war on the Jenkins family would be.

Asked to throw light on notable ancestors, however, John replied that he was unaware of any, because he had not done any research into his family. He was 'not terribly interested' in his background. Perhaps this can be attributed to the fact that of his grandparents, John only knew his stepfather's father, as he later revealed:

'I regarded *him* as my grandfather. He and I were quite close and so I used to go around and see him every Sunday. But he wasn't a blood relation, because my "father" wasn't my father, though I didn't know that until some years later… and I didn't know his wife because she had passed away earlier.'

Jenkins then went on to explain that 'she had a wooden leg, apparently', following an accident at the local colliery where she worked. It had been quite common in south Wales during this period for women to work in the pit. Nevertheless, Jenkins added with a smile, 'it was rather funny', because his grandfather ('who liked his pint'), as a means of ensuring that he could enjoy a few undisturbed beers in the pub across the road, had resorted to unscrewing her wooden leg and taking it with him. She would, Jenkins continued, 'wake up and start thrashing around… She knew where he had gone,' but had been prevented from entering the pub and haranguing him to return home. 'So,' Jenkins chuckled ruefully, 'very notable ancestors indeed!'

Yet, more seriously, other than suspecting 'German or continental' ancestors on his mother's side, hence the name Barnard, Jenkins has limited knowledge of either his mother's or his stepfather's heritage. For instance, he is aware that his mother was aged 29 when he was born; that she was the youngest of 13 children; and that all of them 'lived to a ripe old age', having 'all died in their nineties'. But although the family kept in touch with his mother's brothers and sisters, there was no contact with Minerva's parents or members of the extended family. Asked to expand on this, John disclosed that during the pre- and immediate post-war period, life in the industrial region of the South Wales Valleys was closely knit, but often judgemental. Within this community, characterised by a tendency for oppressive pride and stifling chapel-society recrimination, pregnancies outside marriage were often a source of whispered shame. It is perhaps unsurprising, therefore, having brought the family name into disrepute, that there was no contact with Minerva's parents in Aberfan. Reflecting on the situation and what his mother must have endured, John was vehement: 'I have got to admire my mother's guts,' he proudly declared. 'To have an illegitimate child in 1933 was a hell of a stigma. She put up with all of that. She was a very strong lady.'

However, despite the apparent rejection of Minerva by her parents, on the basis that Aberfan was Minerva's home and where she was born and brought up, throughout his life John has continued to regard Aberfan, somewhat protectively, as 'my home too'. Although Minerva's family home on Cottrell Street was not affected, and John never discussed the disaster with his mother's parents, John's emotional attachment to Aberfan only served to later compound his raw sense of betrayal, anger and desolate frustration as he and the world watched in horror when on 21 October 1966, the small Welsh mining town suffered the greatest industrial disaster in modern British history. It occurred when spoil tip number 7 at Merthyr Vale Colliery thundered down a mountainside in a tidal wave of coal waste and rock, onto the village. It first destroyed a farm cottage, killing all the occupants, before at 9.13 a.m. engulfing some 20 houses and Pantglas Junior School. Among the 144 killed were 116 schoolchildren, all under the age of 11.[11]

But the harsh realities of what the future held in store seemed a world away to the young John Jenkins. Protected by his doting and diligent parents and so knowing nothing about the apparent breakdown in family relations, it was Minerva's sister, John's aunty, that he in fact believed was his grandmother. Referring to her as 'nan', it was her home, a family-run pub in Pontypool, where John and his brother Keith would spend weekends and periods during the school holidays. Asked to describe the relationship with his brother Keith, John replied pensively: 'My brother? Um, well, what can I say? He had ginger hair – and that would sum him up. He was always very feisty,' Jenkins chuckled. 'Well, it's in his background,' he reasoned. 'Both me and my brother inherited that side of our nature from our mother.' He went on to add, affectionately: 'When he was a lad, he adored his cat, Tibby, and was heartbroken when he passed away. He was a very nice chap and we were close growing up; and we still are very close, even though he lives in the south and I live up here in the north.' Contacted and asked for his opinion of his older sibling and their relationship, Keith was equally as effusive: 'I thought the world of my brother,' he stated. 'I would have done anything for him.' Yet, perhaps surprisingly, despite their obvious love and respect for one another, John admits that while he assumes that Keith is aware of his illegitimacy and adoption, they have never spoken of it. 'Funny old family, isn't it?' John declared rhetorically. Perhaps, but are not all families possessed of secrets and intrigues? Nonetheless, when speaking of the bond between them, Jenkins was at pains to point out that while 'we weren't a family accustomed to communicating all sorts of things to each other, we were a close and a tight unit: myself, my father, my mother and my brother.' It was an appraisal shared by Keith Jenkins; who on being asked whether the circumstances surrounding his brother's birth had in any way impacted on the family dynamic, declared the matter of John's illegitimacy to be 'not important'.

Asked to identify both the positive and the negative aspects of the close relationship with his mother, despite Minerva's failure to tell John much about her background, John confessed that the relationship had indeed been subject to somewhat conflicting emotions. 'We were similar,' he explained, 'and when you have two people who are similar, there is usually some contention.' In addressing the positive aspects of their relationship, John remarked: 'Being the first-born provides something that you only have with the first born. But no, I never saw any difference in the way me and Keith were treated, except that I was regarded as the older one and therefore I was supposed to set an example to my brother, and so on.' Was Keith ever jealous or resentful of John's relationship with his mother? 'Not to my knowledge,' John said. But as the first-born, had Minerva confided in him? 'No, she wouldn't confide in me,' John answered. 'There wasn't a great deal that we could talk about except domestic issues. I wouldn't want to engage my mother in politics and all that other stuff. In those days, I wouldn't have known enough about it anyway.' As for the more negative aspects of their relationship, John revealed that this centred on the fact that both he and his mother were 'both touchy', with each prone 'to jump up at the slightest thing, more or less; we were always ready for an argument.' On further developing the point, John continued: 'If it was politically necessary, we would have an argument. If it was psychologically unnecessary and counter-productive, then we wouldn't.' Invited to throw light on the relationship between his mother and his father, John discerned that despite the absence of a wedding photograph in the house, they 'got along well'. This was because, he then asserted, 'My mother ruled the roost... She had a strong personality and so was the dominator, and my father accepted it and was happy to go along with it.'[12]

The matriarchal Minerva Jenkins was a woman of exacting expectations and standards. She saw to it that John and his brother Keith were well-dressed, motivated and, in her presence, well-behaved. It was from this stable, contented and comfortable environment that Minerva, a proud stay-at-home mother and homemaker[13] and known fondly to all in the area as 'Minnie', acted as the local 'Bopa'. This, John revealed, was the local lady revered within south Wales communities of the time for being possessed of a caring and nurturing nature and the person to go to for advice and support.[14] While the youthful Jenkins derived pride and pleasure in seeing his much-loved mother respected in such a manner, it did not come without a price, as John soon became somewhat irritated by the regular interruptions to a family evening, or by returning home to discover another member of the community 'pouring out their heart over yet another cup of tea'. He disclosed, with typical humour:

'There were always people popping in and out to discuss different things. For instance, the lady next door had a family, and nobody in that family could read or write, so they used to bring all their letters for my mother to sort out. And, of course, in the village nobody knocked on doors. Usually they just opened the door and walked in and this was a bit awkward because when you were quite young – seven or eight – and you had a bath in front of the fire, you had this admiring circle of neighbours all around you! "Oh, getting a big boy now isn't he?" That is one of the reasons why I went to the army – I got fed up with the lack of privacy! But I didn't discover until much later how popular my mother was. I would meet people from miles away who would speak very warmly about her.'

Yet, despite his adolescent frustrations, the ability to impart guidance was a skill that John Jenkins was also to exercise later in life, having been called upon to do so by friends and colleagues. 'People have always turned to me for advice,' he admitted, 'and in some ways, it is a strong thing. On the other hand, though,' he stated candidly, 'it can be a bloody nuisance as well.' Nonetheless, despite it sometimes being a burden, the ability to empathise and offer counsel was a talent Jenkins believes he inherited from his mother.

Irrespective of the mystery surrounding his own ancestral heritage – or indeed perhaps *because* of it – John places stock on the importance of a person's genetic profile and strongly maintains that it reveals much about a person's character. Having pondered down the years what makes a person who they are, particularly when he later qualified and worked as a social worker, John professed:

'It's a combination of nature and nurture. It's how one impinges on the other. Because they've been saying for years, or some have said: "It's all about nurture" and others have said: "It's all about nature". But now the more middle-of-the-road people are saying that one affects the other. That's *really* what makes a person who they are. They're both *vitally* important... That is why some people are so very unhappy: because their nature tells them to do something, but their nurture tells them "that's all wrong".'

The debate surrounding what characterises the complex construct of human personality is a subject not lost on a man as intelligent and analytical as John Jenkins, as events in the 1960s would prove.

## John goes to school; Treharris, Penybryn and Winston Churchill

When later discussing the matter of his early education, John revealed that while the family lived in rented accommodation in Treharris, 'right across the road' from the house where Keith was born was a school. It was here, even though John was only two-and-a-half, that because it was both 'so handy and the teachers were quite friendly', he 'was allowed to go to school every day – although it was *really* against the rules.' The importance of what John Jenkins heard while attending, however, made a lasting and profound impression. 'It was in that school,' Jenkins declared, 'that I first got to hear Welsh spoken.' John explained that hearing Welsh for the first time coincided with the period just before his brother Keith was born. And so, as an 'only child and spoilt rotten', he had no one with whom to share the stage. Consequently, the happy home and school life he experienced enabled John to develop a lifelong association of feeling a sense of security *with* the Welsh language. 'So when I hear Welsh now,' Jenkins concluded, 'it gives me that same feeling, to the same extent as it did then.' This sense of emotional attachment was compounded by the fact that 'a lovely Welsh-speaking family called the Fosters' then moved to the same property in Treharris where the Jenkins family lodged, and rented rooms above them. Consequently, on top of the 'happy introduction' to the Welsh language that John received in school, every Sunday the Fosters would take John to the Welsh chapel up the road. It was while attending the chapel services that he listened transfixed as the congregation 'belted out one rousing Welsh hymn after another'.

But as John was to discover, not all expressions of Christian religious observance were as joyous or as uplifting as those he shared with the Fosters. The extent to which 'the 1905 Methodist Revival still resonated throughout much of Wales' was exemplified to John one weekend when he stayed with his uncle and aunt in Llantrisant. Having decided not to accompany his Uncle Charlie to chapel one Sunday, the six-year-old John later witnessed his uncle energetically scrubbing his shoes when he returned home. Feeling a little discomforted and curious as to why his uncle had set about his task with such zeal, John sought an explanation from his Aunt Hester. The impressionable Jenkins was informed that his uncle was 'trying to rid himself of the sin of those he had been amongst that morning'. The power of the pulpit, typified by its ability to instil fear with its message that deliverance could only be achieved through heightened earthly sufferance, affected many in Wales, an incredulous John later opined. It was certainly powerful, he conceded; though somewhat disturbing.

When John was seven or eight, the Jenkins family relocated to Penybryn. It followed a brief period 'living in a little area off the beaten track called Penpwll' and at the home of his paternal grandfather near Nelson, until a house in Penybryn became available. Like Treharris, Penybryn is nestled in the industrial heartland of south-east Wales, amid the middle reaches of the Rhymney Valley. Their new house in Penybryn included such novel amenities as a back garden and an indoor toilet.[15] It was to remain John's home until he left to join the British Army on 4 January 1951. Nonetheless, despite the initial unease which greeted news that just 21 years after the conclusion of 'the War to End all Wars', Britain was again embroiled in military conflict, while later discussing the war period, Jenkins explained that other than the nightly radio broadcast of the BBC news, the war had not 'in any significant way' encroached on his life either before or after the Jenkins family moved to Penybryn. In fact, during a period renowned, perhaps understandably, for an outpouring of jingoism, the people of industrial south Wales had not *altogether* been swept along on this tide of national war fervour. Asked if he had embraced the celebrated heroes of the day such as Field Marshal Bernard Montgomery or Prime Minister Winston Churchill, Jenkins replied staunchly, 'No. Churchill was hated in the valley.' Explaining that Winston Churchill had not been forgiven for ordering soldiers to fire on striking miners in Tonypandy in 1910, when Home Secretary, Jenkins added:

'I remember being somewhat surprised when going to the cinema on a Saturday morning – to the "matinee", they used to call it – and when Hitler came on the news everybody would boo, only for Churchill to then come on the screen and they would boo bloody louder! I was trying to work this out. As far as the public was concerned, Churchill was a bigger lout than Hitler was! But there you are. Perhaps it was common for someone in his position to get the troops to fire on striking miners. But that was a terrible thing as far as they were concerned. To them, he was an out-and-out devil.'[16]

The single-mindedness of the south Wales coal-mining community was again evident early one Sunday morning not long after the Jenkins family moved to Penybryn. With Britain still in the grip of invasion fever, members of the Territorial Army, while conducting an unannounced investigation, began knocking on doors and asking to see the Identity Card of each occupant. What the Territorial Army didn't anticipate, John revealed with no small degree of amusement, was that the miners of Penybryn had not long been in bed, having worked the night shift. The TA did 'not get a very warm welcome', Jenkins laughed, before adding that he even witnessed 'one or two being thrown bodily' from a doorstep. Even more comical, however, was the fact that most of the strong-arm tactics were deployed by the miners' wives! These tenacious women, who proudly stood shoulder-to-shoulder with their husbands, were instrumental in providing the community with much of its character and colour. By way of example, John continued:

'In those days, part of the miners' wages was paid in coal, but they didn't come around with sacks of coal. Oh no. They came around with coal lorries, and on the back was the coal. But the coal had come straight out of the pit, so you would look up the street and all you would see was great heaps of coal outside the front of every house. These women had to go out and shift it. Not the men, because the men had been in work all day down the pit digging it, so they weren't expected to come home and carry it all in. So, the women would all come out with a sledgehammer, bloody muscles like that, and break these great lumps of coal up to make it manageable to put on the fire.'

Little wonder then, in a community fiercely independent and comprised of men almost exclusively excused military service owing to their reserved occupation of coal mining – Tom Jenkins among them – that the rousing radio broadcasts by Prime Minister Winston Churchill and the morale-boosting efforts of the Ministry of Information, which for the duration of the war generated propaganda to influence the population of Britain towards support for the war effort, sometimes fell on stony ground. The sense of detachment from the wider struggle and a lack of neighbours away at the war go some way towards explaining why the conflict did not impact too greatly on John's childhood. What John does remember, however, is how the 'happy and close-knit' mining community of Penybryn[17] contributed to the defeat of fascism in its own indomitable way and how it also closed ranks during times of family difficulty. At no time was this support better expressed than following an accident underground. Few families were spared the trauma of such an event, as John movingly describes:

'When I was about nine, my father suffered an accident in the pit. It wasn't a bad accident, but it was an accident, and all the neighbours came around to the house. I couldn't understand what all these people were doing there. But I quickly realised that they were coming in to show their solidarity with us as a family. It was typical of the community to show its support. A funeral service was very popular and involved the whole community. It was wonderful – and it created such a strong feeling that the community was united.'

The accident suffered by his father coincided with an increase in John's intellectual awareness, as he became more interested in listening to the nightly BBC news on the radio. Doing so, because 'everything in Penybryn was run by gas as there was no electricity', involved taking the radio battery 'down to the town every week or so' where it was exchanged 'at the electricity shop' for a battery already charged. But it was not merely news of national and international developments which John was increasingly drawn to. Although too young perhaps to appreciate the subtler nuances of the humour, John would gather with his parents, along with thousands of other families throughout Britain, to listen to the BBC comedy programmes of the 1940s. One such programme was *It's That Man Again*, which was presided over by Liverpudlian Tommy Handley. To the delight of its 16 million listeners, *ITMA*, as it was commonly called, poked holes in the social fabric of wartime Britain. The programme epitomised the self-reliant, assertive and somewhat ambivalent spirit that the Valleys people prided themselves on. Such people make for good drama: a fact recognised by the BBC, which – in delivering its commitment to broadcast regional wartime programming – launched *Welsh Rarebit*. Billed as 'a programme of variety and topicalities', a feature of the show, through a combination of drama and humour, was a lighthearted portrayal of everyday life in the Valleys. Not surprisingly, *Welsh Rarebit* received a significant listening audience in Wales, most notably throughout the industrial region, where the Jenkins family – and especially Tom and Minerva – were avid listeners.[18] But for all the pleasure that Tom and Minerva derived from *Welsh Rarebit*, its 'obvious poking of fun at Valleys folk' and tongue-in-cheek mimicry initially affronted the more protective aspect of their eldest son's nature. The programme left John 'scandalised that Welsh people could laugh at portrayals of themselves acting in such a backward manner'. It was not an appraisal of the show, however, set to last. 'I got to thinking,' John admitted, '"Well, what else have they got down here, for God's sake? Nothing! Life is bloody grim enough as it is, so why begrudge them a bit of a laugh?" Even if it did mock their weaknesses, it was only a spot of fun.'

It was also during this period that John developed a lifelong love of Welsh choral music. With happy memories of attending both Welsh religious services with the Fosters and the St David's Day celebrations at primary school in Treharris still fresh in his mind, John discovered 'a real joy' of 'going to the front room – or the parlour, as we used to call it' on a Sunday morning, and with a fire lit and the radio battery newly charged, 'tuning the radio to the Welsh-language channel'. Despite being 'able to understand one word in about ten', John was soon enraptured by the impassioned oratory of the vicar conducting the service. But it was 'the absolutely magnificent singing' that truly captured John's febrile imagination. While the hymns were routinely impressive, John declared: 'every now and again you had a real old *hwyl* feature – the sort of singing which would really build up and up. It used to excite me so much that I couldn't believe it.' It was an appreciation of both Welsh choral music and classical music which saw the youthful John increasingly at odds with his primary school classmates, who regarded such styles as 'rubbish'. While he refused to respond to the gentle teasing and merely allowed himself a wry smile by way of reply, the clash of musical interests left John pondering why he derived so much pleasure from the music, and the emotions it provoked, while his classmates were utterly unimpressed.

While living in Penybryn, John and his brother Keith attended the local primary school in Gelligaer. It was inexplicably known to all in the area as 'White City'. 'I have no idea why everyone called it that,' John chuckled. Moreover, 'for reasons known only to the locals, Penpedairheol is just up the road from Penybryn, but everyone calls it Cascade – and nobody knows why!' Although an inquisitive and bright pupil while in primary school, John was not, he admits, particularly studious. Having learnt to read at a very early age, he was, however, good at English and read an awful lot – mainly 'the usual things that kids read, such as comics like *The Dandy* and *Thor*.' Although John would sometimes go on nature walks alone when aged nine and ten, he usually explored the surrounding countryside 'with a gang'. As the leader of the gang, John and his young adventurers would 'go off at dawn and come back at dusk, covered in bruises, scratches and bumps, having spent the day climbing up trees and jumping in rivers.' John remarked – reflecting sadly on the today's 'stranger danger' mindset and obsession with health and safety – 'The freedom we had in those days to just roam and explore was wonderful. We *never* seemed to consider the risks.' Not that the aching and returning heroes were greeted warmly on their return, John laughed, as 'our mothers would be screaming and shouting at us.' Might he have developed this natural ability to lead others and inspire their confidence from his mother? John replied, 'Well, it never occurred to me at the time, but that may be right.'

Despite the Rhondda having witnessed a huge increase in population as migrant workers arrived from far and wide in search of employment, the area had still maintained something of its Welsh character, as John reveals:

'In primary school, there was a certain amount of Welsh spoken because the teachers were all from, I think, Ceredigion. And they used to have a chat with the local milkman, who was also from Ceredigion, and so I used to hear quite a bit of it there. But there was a lot of it around, although I never noticed it as such. I mean, people greeted each other with *shwmae* (hello). That was common. And they would talk about *chwarae teg* (fair play). As for Penybryn, the man who lived next door to us was called Ifan Price and his wife's name was Blodwen. And across the road were a family called the Wigleys. I don't know where the father came from, but the mother's name was Ceinwen, so she obviously wasn't from far away. Just up the road lived my mother's sister, and her daughter was called Bronwen. So I was surrounded by all these lovely Welsh names. I never actually heard Welsh spoken in conversation in that area, but the use of Welsh phrases and Welsh names was normal as far as I was concerned. My father, for instance, referred to a gardening implement as a *caib*, which only many years later did I discover was called a hoe in English.'

## John's personality forms and his compassion is recognised

It is perhaps unsurprising that at this point, as the youthful John absorbed his emotional landscape, that Tom and Minerva – having no doubt recognised the sensitive aspect of his nature – called upon their much-loved eldest son to resolve a delicate family matter. Jenkins later explained how events unfolded:

'My (paternal) grandfather was becoming quite ill, but he wouldn't shift. He was living on his own in a cottage and he could no longer look after himself. But despite my father's efforts to get him to come and live with us, he would not respond. As far as I can tell, my father and my grandfather had a good relationship, but he refused to listen to my father. My mother wanted to look after my grandfather, so they sent me down to talk to him because he was fond of me – and I liked him as well, of course. I was only about ten, but I went and I talked him into it.'

How did he achieve this?

'I pointed out that he would be cared for and that it would be nice for us – and better for him – if he came to live with us. We weren't given to being all lovey-dovey in our family, but as best as I could, I made him see that we cared for him and that we wanted to look after him. He agreed then to join us. You see, he was proud – and that generation *hated* the idea of being a burden. So, realising this, I made him accept what we were offering. That we *wanted* to help because we cared. Anyway, finally he agreed. My father put a double bed in our sitting room for him. And he stayed there until he died, some weeks later. My mother did a wonderful job and only now do I appreciate it. Because there was no National Health in those days – you are talking about 1943. So no NHS, and yet my mother nursed my grandfather through cancer of the stomach – and that is a very messy disease. I was amazed to think of it afterwards. Because, I mean, our home was a simple home. We didn't have any of the amenities and facilities that a hospital ward would have had. Yet, my mother nursed him there, through the final stages of this dreadful illness.'

Having persuaded his grandfather that the time had come to accept the care being offered by the Jenkins family, John was also left to break the sad news of his grandfather's passing to his father. While it was not uncommon for John to later be given the task of breaking the news of a community member's death to friends and neighbours, the day John told his father, Tom, that his father had died remains etched on his memory. 'I remember it like it was yesterday,' John declared.

'It was at the end of January 1943, on a very cold day, and my father was coming down from Gelligaer. I could see him approaching as he walked down the road, having just finished work. I tried not to show it, as it wouldn't have been the done thing, but I think he knew from the expression on my face. Anyway, we met and I told him the news about his father. He was clearly upset, but stoic with it. Because, being a miner, he was used to death in all its forms, and accidents underground and things like that. These things wouldn't have come as so much of a shock to him as it would had he lived in a comfortable, middle-class area, where these things never impinged on the consciousness of those living there.'

It was not just 'a gift for communicating' and changes in John's personal surroundings which were beginning. With the war entering a critical stage, John's parents' initial fears that the conflict would drastically affect their lives had not materialised. For even if wartime rationing led to privations nationwide, John was not aware of any. Having been told when war was declared five years earlier that he couldn't have sweets any more, he had, in fact, 'not missed out on anything'. Minerva had ensured a ready supply of homemade peppermint sweets, and 'the bread she baked, and vegetables were all homegrown.' Nevertheless, his parents had perhaps made sacrifices which neither John nor Keith was aware of. 'For years after the war ended,' John recalled, 'my father was putting condensed milk in his bloody tea to sweeten it.' Whether instructed to do so by their formidable mother, or whether a sacrifice Tom was willing to make voluntarily, he passed his sugar ration to Minerva, 'which,' John explained, 'she used to make sweets for me and Keith – so that we didn't miss out.' John had another reason to be happy during the early summer in 1944, when he passed the Eleven Plus examination and was awarded a place at the prestigious Bargoed Grammar School. Now shown by the exam to be among the most intellectually able 25% of the UK's school population, John was one of only two students from Glyn-Gaer Primary School in Gelligaer to pass the exam that year.[19]

## Bargoed Grammar School and life-changing discoveries

Four months later, having enjoyed the school summer holiday, John Jenkins enrolled as a student at Bargoed Grammar School. In keeping with Britain's grammar school tradition, Bargoed placed emphasis on the importance of self-improvement. Seeking to replicate the studious and aspirational atmosphere found in Britain's older grammar schools, it too was intent on educating the nation's future professional class. John arrived at Bargoed Grammar School fresh-faced and eager to learn. It was not long, however, despite his love of reading now extending to 'adventure novels like *Treasure Island*, travel books and most notably, the *National Geographic*'[20], that John began to question the relevance of a grammar school education, which he increasingly determined was stifling, unimaginative and loftily oppressive. This was typified, he believed, by the school's regular morning ritual of singing the hymn 'Jerusalem,' and its strict adherence to only teaching aspects of British history.

Increasingly frustrated, despite the fact that there was '*some* Welsh being taught by a supply teacher',[21] the youthful John Jenkins began to question his own cultural heritage and Wales' unique historical identity. Speaking later, he revealed that:

> 'On arriving at Bargoed Grammar School, I expected to learn about Welsh history. But it wasn't taught. We were taught about King Alfred and the blackened cakes and Bruce and the spider, all these lovely things, but we weren't taught about the things that really *mattered* to us, such as where we lived and how we got to where we were. And then, somewhat strangely, the penny dropped. The area which I considered to be my stamping ground was bordered by three pubs: at the northern end was The Cross, halfway down was The Harp and a little bit further down was The Plough. And I thought: "This is it. This sums up the place perfectly: The Plough, The Harp and The Cross. That's what my history here is *really* about."'

It was not the only epiphany that John experienced at this point. Drawn increasingly to both places of Christian worship and the natural world, Jenkins began to explore the surrounding countryside. It was during one of his now routine weekend treks over the surrounding hills that John discovered the remains of Capel Gwladys, a fifth-century religious enclosure, on the common land above his home. At the site, John read an inscription which commemorated the founding of the chapel around 430 AD. This discovery of Capel Gwladys near the Roman fort at Gelligaer coincided with John's awareness of an inscribed stone *from* Capel Gwladys which is preserved within Gelligaer parish church. The connection of these two sites proved to have a significant impact on John's emotional and intellectual development. Asked if he could trace his Welsh nationalism to an event or to an occurrence during his childhood, Jenkins was emphatic:

'It was history that started me off. Like my contemporaries, I was taught in grammar school that Christianity was brought to Britain by Augustine in 597. The so-called Venerable Bede, no less, writing in the eighth century, claimed it was the arrival of the Anglo-Saxons in Britain which coincided with Christianity being brought to these shores. Well, no. As I began to ponder both the Christian faith and Welsh history more and more, I became strangely drawn to a very early Christian Church, dedicated to Saint Gwladys, which was founded near the Roman fort above Gelligaer. At this early Christian church was a more recently-erected cross and a memorial stone. Both the cross and the memorial stone were placed within a rectangle of stones. And this rectangle of stones was *surrounded* by a ring of stones, which, as I discovered later, was the mark of an early sacred site. But on this stone was a memorial to a lady named Gwladys and an inscription which claimed that this chapel to her was built around the year 430. At the same time, I was aware that within Gelligaer church, there was a large stone, *from* Capel Gwladys, which was inscribed with a very early rendition of a cross. And so, over the next few years, I began to put the two together in my mind. I began to think: 'Well, this is strange. I've been told that Augustine brought Christianity to the natives in 597, but the natives already had a Christian cross in 430. How can this be?' It was then that I learned that Christianity was brought to Britain not by Augustine in 597, but by the Romans some 300 years earlier.[22] Later I learned that a Christian conference was held in Europe in 314, and that three bishops from Britain attended.[23] But what did the Venerable Bede, who is classed as a reputable historian, do? He simply ignored the facts.

31

As much, if not *more* of, a propagandist than a historian, Bede's intention was to prove that it was the arrival of the Anglo-Saxons which coincided with civilisation – and with it Christianity – being brought to this country. He would have discovered through his own research that there was already a Church in Britain *and* that a conference in Europe in 314 was attended by three British bishops. But Bede simply ignored these facts. And why? For reasons of political power. To promote the idea that the barbarous British natives had been tamed by the invading Anglo-Saxons.'[24]

Having therefore determined that the Christian faith in Wales – and indeed the Christian Church – was both progressive and established in Britain long before Augustine's mission in 597, what was the significance of these events to Jenkins, particularly with regards his blossoming appreciation of life's complications? He stated:

'It made me question the whole idea of history and what history is all about. Does it tell us the truth, or does it tell us certain selected facts? And if they *are* certain selected facts, what are these facts aiming to prove? And what were the facts that were taken *out* aiming to prove? Furthermore, why aren't we given access to *all* these facts, so that we can make our minds up in an informed manner? I quickly realised that this comes under the realm of politics, which is the reason these things happen anyway.'

The lesson that history could be manipulated to serve a political objective was one that John Jenkins was never to forget. It was also at this point, while increasingly unhappy in school,[25] that John began to feel that he was different from the classmates with whom he shared much of his time. Although always approachable and popular, John soon determined that he was 'something of a loner'. It was an insularity, fuelled by a contemplative personality, which has led to a lifelong inability to be swept along with the crowd and be awed by trivia and incidentals. On the bus to school, as discussion invariably turned to the football results, Jenkins would witheringly avert his gaze towards the window and the scenery rushing by. Somewhat lost in his own thoughts, John would think to himself:

'What the hell difference does that make? I knew about the things that the other kids were talking about, but I didn't care about it as much as they did. So I thought then, "There must something wrong with my upbringing or something," because I don't seem to like the same things that they like and they don't like the things that I like. This didn't suddenly come to me like a bolt from the blue, but it did, over a period of years, intensify.'

While the point reveals much about John Jenkins and his increasing adolescent feelings of being an outsider, it seems the die was cast permanently with regards to mainstream attitudes:

'I have heard about the Beckhams. I know he used to play football in some capacity or other. But that's all I know. I don't want to know anything else. I don't care where they buy their bloody clothes and I don't care where they go for their summer holidays. I am simply not interested.'

The apparent emotional rollercoaster that John was on coincided with the final period of the war. Barely able to remember the distant sound of aircraft, only the 'arrival in the village of one or two evacuees from Birmingham and places like that, during the doodlebug back-end stage' had acted to remind the youthful Jenkins that the country was indeed at war. 'Of course, I was aware of El Alamein and the D-Day Landings,' John added, 'but I wasn't terribly interested in the war for much of it.' Nevertheless, with the Jenkins family settled happily within the community at Penybryn and the end of the war finally in sight, the young, intelligent John Jenkins began to develop an interest in politics. 'I was becoming aware of it,' he later explained, 'because the war *made* you aware of things like that. It made you question everything.' He added thoughtfully:

'For instance, when the war ended in 1945, I was aged 12 and so I can remember the awful business about Dachau and Belsen and places like that on the radio.[26] You also saw a certain amount on the Pathé news at the cinema. I went to see these places when later stationed in Germany.'

For a nation denied much cause for celebration over the past nearly six years, the street party to celebrate Victory in Europe on 8 May 1945 was another occasion which John Jenkins recalls with clarity. For the older members of the Penybryn community, it was an especially happy and joyous moment. Asked to recollect the day's events, John remembered 'the smiles on the faces' and that 'there was a sort of a table put out and blancmange and things like that [to eat].'

## The end of the war as a new era dawns

The five-and-a-half-year period of hostilities both transformed Great Britain and precipitated a new world order. In 1939, Britain still ruled over the greatest sovereign empire the world had ever known, and the British people retained a sense that Great Britain was the most powerful and prestigious nation on earth. In 1945, Britain emerged from the war victorious, but exhausted, battered and bankrupt. With large areas of its cities reduced to rubble and its vitality sapped by the efforts of securing victory, Great Britain abdicated its status as the global Great Power; while the United States, its economy booming and its confidence soaring triumphantly, assumed the mantle of world leadership. The United States sat at the table of global political influence and stared uneasily across at the world's other political heavyweight, the Union of Soviet Socialist Republics. Divided by a gulf of ideological and military mistrust, the two vast superpowers eyed each other suspiciously. With this reshaping of the global political map, an icy Cold War descended. The period, characterised by an ever-present fear of nuclear annihilation, ensured a dark shadow loomed over any sense that, with the fascist threat all but removed, the world was now a safer place.

The social and cultural background, conditions and developments that had shaped John Jenkins' early life in the Rhondda Valley coincided with a period of rampant social and political change in Britain and the wider Western industrialised world. In the UK, this transformation began with the landslide victory by the Labour Party at the General Election in July 1945. The Government, headed by the taciturn Clement Attlee, was committed to dismantling the British Empire, reforming the British class system and providing for the health and education of the populace through the creation of a socialist 'welfare state'. The policy of social improvement continued during the 1950s, when the re-elected Conservative Party promoted an American-style consumer economy stimulated by the enticements of an American-style consumer culture.

John Jenkins was both a creature of this new social and cultural milieu and a product of this surge in popular culture and influence – which intensified sharply in the post-war period. The blind deference to one's social superiors which had until recently characterised British society seemed anachronistic in the new industrial age of steel, electricity, widely-available motorised transport and consumer goods that rose from free-market capitalism. The democratisation of post-war British society gave rise to new generation which was no longer content, or willing, to merely observe and await instruction. Although independent by nature and not given to histrionics, as a member of this generation, John Jenkins' character and outlook on life was increasingly shaped by the socio-political landscape to which he was exposed. Not that evening meals in the Jenkins household involved debating the political issues of the day. 'My father wasn't terribly interested in politics, or anything like that; he was only interested in his work as a miner,' said John. Yet, despite John's father's lack of any interest, his political allegiance was staunchly Labour. 'Well, in south Wales everybody is a socialist,' Jenkins ruminated, adding:

> 'I mean, that's the way it works. I never came across a Tory until I was 12 years of age. It occurred one day at Penybryn, when unusually for that area, a car drove into the village and these people started trying to hand out Tory pamphlets. I was amazed, because these people had two eyes and a nose like everybody else, and I couldn't believe it. After all, I'd been told that Tories were all monsters and they weren't fit to live and they should be done away with, and these people seemed just as normal as anybody else. So, I thought, "Um... This is interesting." It was then that I began to question people's attitudes. They were saying that the Tories are this and the Tories are that. Well, I never saw anything which disproved it. But on the other hand, I never saw anything which proved it either. Anyway, they came around, but it was a waste of time them canvassing in Penybryn, or the Rhondda really – they were all socialists to the last man.'[27]

In the summer of 1946, when John was 13 years old, he decided to leave Bargoed Grammar School.[28] Asked how his parents reacted to the news that he would not be returning to school after the summer holiday, John revealed that his mother, while 'not exactly pleased', had left the decision up to him. When considering his actions some time later, John reasoned that as 'something of a late developer academically' and so 'bottom in all subjects except for English literature', it had been the right thing to do. In addition, as it 'coincided with the last days of the old regime', during which parents were expected to pay so much for their offspring to attend grammar school and with his father the sole financial provider, it was time, he maintained, 'to go to work and get some money to help the family out.'

Having begun to question his religious, political and cultural environment, it proved to be the start of a chapter in John's life which also saw him embark on a relationship which was to have a profound effect on his emotional outlook on life. It coincided with the discovery that while employment put money in his pocket, it fell some way short of providing the intellectual stimulation he required. Increasingly resigned to his situation, however, it was the breakdown of his first love which would see John leave Penybryn and the South Wales Valleys for a career in the British Army. This, in turn, would open John's eyes ever wider, as the adventurous boy from Penybryn witnessed the dying embers of Britain's colonial past as they flickered enticingly before his eyes.

# CHAPTER 2

# 'Oh, you're a Welshman!'

John enters employment, reads Welsh history, is fascinated by the Nuremburg Trials and 'pulls back' from the Chapel

Within days of leaving Bargoed Grammar School in July 1946, John Jenkins began work as a blacksmith's apprentice. Having secured the position before leaving education, John's employer – a 'reasonably tempered' Indian gentleman called Mr Pandhi – instructed his junior employee in the art of moulding and manipulating molten steel and iron at his workshop in Bargoed. The firm's principal market lay in replenishing the area's farm gates and their accoutrements, owing to many having been provided for the war effort during the early years of the conflict. On perfecting the skill of making hinges for the gates, Jenkins soon found himself tasked with instructing a trainee, who had been taken on due to the increase in business. Having spotted this demand and niche in the market, the resultant upturn in fortunes resulted in Pandhi opening a shop selling items such as the gates, which were manufactured in the adjacent workshop.

If the mental blow of discovering the letter outlining his illegitimacy had apparently been absorbed by Jenkins with equanimity some three years before, the shock of receiving a work-related injury provided evidence of another facet of the youthful John's personality: namely, that he could take the impact of a physical blow with the same emotional fortitude. Jenkins revealed that while drilling through a gate hinge in the workshop, the piece of metal with which he was working suddenly swung around and hit him in the throat. Initial thoughts that his throat had been cut and that the injury might prove fatal were calmly rejected, as with presence of mind, John walked across the workshop to observe the injury in the mirror.

On doing so, despite the amount of blood, Jenkins calculated that it was 'only a heavy graze', which ultimately resulted in a 'less than significant bruise'. Nonetheless, the episode served to convince John that he could deal with bad and unexpected situations without showing outward signs of stress and anxiety. This ability to hide his true emotions behind a mask of inscrutability was utilised by Jenkins on the day of the Royal Investiture in Caernarfon some 23 years later, when he was cheerfully informed by an acquaintance in the military that two apparent members of MAC had been killed while laying an explosive device which *he* had assembled.

The two and a half years that Jenkins worked for Mr Pandhi were, John recalls, 'very enjoyable – if a little tedious'. However, Jenkins' sense of overall contentment was heightened when, keen to further involve himself in community matters, John joined the Penybryn marching band. Comprised of members who lacked the resources to purchase brass or woodwind instruments, the kazoo and percussion marching bands were a feature of Valleys life in the pre- and post-war periods. As with most villages and towns in south Wales, Penybryn had two such marching bands: a junior band, which catered for those up to the age of sixteen, and a senior band, for those above that age. On discovering a natural flair for drumming, John was a leading light in the junior marching band.

Drumming in marching bands was not the only interest that Jenkins embraced in this period. He also developed an enduring love of Welsh history; and both drumming and history proved pivotal to the story of John Barnard Jenkins. Having managed to beg, steal and borrow books on the history of Wales, Jenkins discovered that immersing himself in Welsh history books provided the perfect antidote to his rather mundane working day. Yet if John found reading his nation's history an effective way to unwind, he also quickly realised how intellectually stimulated he felt, and both impassioned and then subdued, on discovering facts regarding Wales' often troubled historical journey. As his knowledge of Welsh history increased, John began to feel that he was 'a member of a nation which had been downtrodden and which was suffering from the result.' For instance, he was pleased to learn about the industrial expansion of Merthyr, 'once the wealthiest area in the British Isles, where vast quantities of steel and coal were produced and sold all over the world.' But any sense of pride in what had been achieved was soon dispelled when John subsequently discovered that while the owners of mines and steel production plants had enjoyed prodigious wealth – most notably the Crawshay family (of English descent) who built Cyfarthfa Castle – those employed to produce the materials had done so routinely at great personal risk and for meagre financial return. It struck John that this exploitation was 'typical of the situation' that Wales had endured – and he 'regretted it bitterly'.

Jenkins also detected 'a vague feeling that the supine attitude of the Welsh under their English colonial masters was something that they had brought upon themselves.' Wales, he believed, had been 'bled dry of its assets and its resources – and this included its best and sharpest minds.' The 'only option left available for those of spirit,' he reasoned, 'was emigration.' What was the opinion he arrived at, on considering the plight of Wales? John replied pensively:

> 'I began to feel, even at this early age, that there existed a low threshold of understanding of the situation in Wales among Welsh people. Now, whether this was a direct consequence of being suppressed and subjugated for so long, I was at this stage unsure. But for *whatever* reason, it seemed to me that the Welsh people could no longer appreciate how precarious their position was. As I read these books about Welsh history, I couldn't help but think – especially as I looked around me – that the people of Wales were blind to the fact that their *own* country, which was uniquely blessed in so many ways, was facing extinction. As the years went by, my feelings intensified; leading me to believe, more and more, that it was up to me to do something about it.'

Having begun to consider the historic position of Wales within a UK context – particularly in relation to England, its all-powerful neighbour – these proved to be not the only scales falling from John Jenkins' eyes at this point, as a series of events further served to sharpen his focus.

John's tentative questioning of the Christian faith – which had begun when he visited Capel Gwladys and discovered the discrepancy as to when Christianity arrived in Britain – continued and coincided with the Nuremburg Trials.[29] Beginning in November 1945 and concluding in October 1946, leading figures within the Nazi Party and the defeated Axis Powers were tried by the International Military Tribunal for crimes against peace, crimes against humanity, or war crimes. Conspiracy to commit any of these crimes was also considered a criminal offence. In addition to these charges, organisations – such as the SS – could also be declared to be criminal by their very nature, removing any question as to their legal status. To consider the charges levelled at these individuals more closely: crimes against peace involved acts of aggression in violation of treaties or agreements. Charges of crimes against humanity were levelled at anyone thought to be involved in mass deportations or genocide. War crimes were simply those acts committed in violation of laws of war. Tried by members of the victorious Allied judiciary, the defendants were afforded more or less the same legal rights as any defendant in a more conventional, non-military criminal court.

Dismissed by some as 'victor's justice', Jenkins followed the events through watching Pathé news at the cinema – the only source of visual news at the time. John also read printed press coverage of the Nuremburg Trials. It proved another milestone in his emotional and intellectual flowering; providing – albeit initially – the belief that justice and legal redress should be both expected and served. 'It was an emotional time in my life,' he explained.

'This is when you are forming ideas and opinions. And it is these attitudes which determine how you embark on the future. I was still rather naive, I suppose. I still believed in fairness and justice. But I found in that period, around the time of leaving school, that I became very disenchanted with the general way of doing things – very disenchanted.'

Asked to develop the point, Jenkins continued:

'Well, I began to see the difference between what people promised and what they delivered. And what the Bible promised and what it delivered. And how selective people could be in what they picked out of the Bible and what they ignored in the Bible. "Thou shalt not kill", for instance. The way they get around that by saying: "Ah, yes. But the original word didn't really mean 'kill', it meant 'murder'. That is what the *original* word meant." But of course, you can always squirm out of things by saying that a person hadn't read and understood a word or a phrase correctly... That this word was incorrectly interpreted and so on and so forth. The point is, having watched these events almost transfixed, I was very impressed by the Nuremburg Trials; which were insisted on by America, who were – at the time – politically very naive about all this. You see, the Western world realised that the way these things worked was that if you gave a man a uniform, in return, he gave you his conscience. You effectively controlled his actions. And there was no such thing as an incorrect order; an order was an order. But what happened at the Nuremburg trials? Those on trial would get to their feet and in response to being accused of killing people and torturing people, they would produce a document signed by their superiors telling them to do just that. And so their testimony comprised of them saying, individually and collectively, "Well, I acted the way I did because I was *ordered* to do so. We were in the army. We *had* to do it." So how did the court declare its ruling? It maintained that although these individuals *were* ordered by the authorities to commit these acts, their conscience should have told them that it was wrong. And therefore, "You are going to be taken out and hanged for what you did."

Now, this was the time-honoured tradition in the military, anyway. A soldier had *always* been expected to follow an order and not question it, and they knew it. But the judges at Nuremburg had to justify their ruling to hang them. So here we were, being told that an individual could, or indeed, *should* refuse to follow an order that they considered morally or ethically questionable. Basically, what the Nuremburg Trials promised was that, henceforth, no man need act upon an order which he considered to be against his conscience. And what's happened? Well, ever since the Nuremburg Trials, they have been trying to forget this. It is seen as an obstacle; an inconvenience. Most organisations have been trying to ignore the ruling at Nuremburg, because it gave those people under their control a "voice". It provided a legal means of saying: "No. I am not going to do this!" Suddenly, these people are a challenge; they have rights. It is not necessarily the government in charge. And as governments do not *like* such a situation at all, they have simply ignored it.'

Was the Nuremburg Tribunal, therefore, a turning point in how he viewed authority and its use, or indeed, abuse of power? By way of reply, Jenkins was quick to recognise the importance of the Nuremburg Trials to his subsequent concept of justice. 'Oh yes, of course,' he proclaimed.

'One example of what the Nuremburg tribunals established was a ruling which said that if you happen to be a driver of an army vehicle and you are driving along and you come to a red light, even if the officer sat behind says, "Never mind about the red light, drive through", you are entitled to say, "No. Because it is against the law of the land and it is against my conscience." But that is about the only thing that came out of it. But since the trials, they have completely ignored this ruling anyway – and others of a similar nature. Whereas they set great store by what is called "legal precedent", they don't set great store by the precedent set by the Nuremburg trials. And why? Because it goes against their unlimited power to give orders. And that is the sort of thing which sticks in one's mind, I think. Look, let me get this straight: do I believe that these men should have received the harshest of penalties for what they did? Absolutely. Of course I do. The crimes they committed were repugnant. But it was the sheer hypocrisy of the whole thing – or *more* specifically, what then unfolded, as the months and years went by. And these feelings about the hypocrisy and the abuse of power only intensified when I later joined the British Army.'[30]

Nevertheless, with the judicial landscape as established by the trial at Nuremburg yet to be circumvented, or ignored, the sun appeared to be shining on John Jenkins at this juncture because of his first paid employment and his role within the marching band. But the good times were over when, in January 1949, John decided to leave Mr Pandhi's employment for 'a much better-paid job' at Lysaght Steelworks in Newport. Despite the improvement in his financial position, Jenkins did not altogether enjoy the experience. This was in part owing to the length of any working day. Living in Penybryn, some 30 miles from the steelworks in Newport, ensured that a shift beginning at 6 a.m. involved being collected by the work's bus at 4.30 a.m. To ease her son's discomfort, Minerva would get up at 3.30 a.m. to light a fire so the house was warm when John got up. 'This,' he declared with affectionate pride, 'was the sort of mother I had. Nothing was too much trouble.' Nonetheless, despite his colleagues being 'affable enough', the return journey to Penybryn, 'which also took a decent hour-and-a-half', resulted in Jenkins not returning home until 7.30 p.m. It left little time to enjoy an evening before retiring to bed and the process beginning again. Yet, if the day shift was bad enough, 'You can just imagine what the night shift was like!', as John remarked sardonically. The situation was not enjoyable, but the money was good, so Jenkins 'put up with it'.

It is perhaps unsurprising that owing to this unremitting work schedule and the psychological fatigue that such a predicament produced, John decided to 'pull back' from his commitment to the Baptist Chapel at this point. Having regularly attended chapel since primary school – sometimes with his brother, Keith, but usually alone – John now believes that the decision to emotionally withdraw was because the whole of his 'lifestyle was a preparation for MAC'. Invited to illustrate the statement, Jenkins declared:

'The village I lived in, Penybryn, was quite a Christian area. There were lots of very committed Christians around. The sort of people who, on a Sunday, would come out of their door and play holy hell because you were kicking a ball about on the Lord's Day – that sort of thing. So I grew up in that sort of atmosphere. It was, I now think, as stifling as the atmosphere within the grammar school. But the point is, you see, they turned their heavy guns on me. They thought I would be a Minister, and I almost was. They took me to all these different meetings and I was in chapel three times on a Sunday and once in the week. When I look back on it, the pressure that was put on me was enormous. But it was very, very effective. For instance, I was being encouraged to get baptised. And once, I remember, they ran a trip from our chapel to some chapel in Neath and when I got in there, it was packed to the rafters. When the service got going, somebody shouted "Hallelujah" and then somebody else answered, and somebody else, and somebody else, until the entire congregation was chanting "Hallelujah". They were even singing in a different pitch, but it all went together. It was lovely. I really, really enjoyed it and I thought then, "Well, this is part of the pressure – and it's brilliant." It was a strong part of my growing up and an *essential* part – and I could feel the pressure on me to give in; for me to submit myself and become a total Christian. I have no doubt that both my feelings and the feelings of those within the Chapel were genuine enough; and as I say, I felt the strength of it. I thought how nice it would be to have no worries; to "give it all to the Lord in prayer" sort of thing and to be surrounded by people of like mind, and to be safe and secure in your home, and all the rest of it. But then I couldn't. I couldn't do it and I was never able to analyse *why* I couldn't do it, until much, much later. I think the trouble is, I was aware that if I did commit myself to the Chapel, I would give my *everything* to it, which is what I do. I don't know if that is a gift or not, but it could be. On the other hand, it can drag you down too. And every time I was almost persuaded to "pick up the cross", it was as if something stopped me. It's almost as though I was thinking to myself, "You can't go in for this, because if you do, it will stop you from what you are *going* to do".'

Did he mean 'born to do'? That he was born to lead the MAC protest? 'Yes,' John replied, adding:

'I thought "There is something wrong here. I desperately want to commit myself to Christianity, because it obviously gives great comfort... [devout] Christianity enables people to be happy." But something stopped me. I didn't *consciously* say to myself, "No. If you go in for this it will stop you doing what you're supposed to be do." But I thought it. And so I never became a Christian as such: a committed Christian. I mean, I still attended chapel after this point. I didn't physically pull back. But I did pull back mentally. You see – as with my Uncle Charlie, several years earlier – I began to think, "These people are mad." The more they tried to explain to me about the "cross of enlightenment", and how you should take everything to the Lord in prayer, the more I felt it was an attitude I was simply up against! It can't purely be a matter of sufferance! It's about deeds and actions. Kindness, yes, but also standing up against wrong and saying: "No. Enough is enough." So, I began to question this narrow Chapel interpretation. Because it [religion] doesn't affect everyone like that – thank God. But it's also true that having done so, attending chapel didn't have *quite* the same effect on me. It was as if I'd decided in my mind that while much of what the Chapel has to offer is wonderful, it isn't for me. There is something *else* for me. I don't know what it is, but there is *something* else.'

Could it perhaps be argued, to look at the situation from a purely spiritual perspective, that the 'gods' had something else planned for him? 'Um, well,' Jenkins declared cautiously:

'Some would say that spearheading MAC is what the devil wanted me to do. But there you are. I think we're all here for a purpose – and orchestrating the MAC protest was obviously my purpose. Much as I didn't even know it at the time. But we are now talking about predestination, and we are talking about people being born to do things, and destiny and all that. And I don't want to go into that as such, because it makes it sound too airy-fairy. But the fact is, I could easily have been converted then, and had I done so, it would have tied me down for the rest of my life. I would never have been able to do anything after that, because it would have been against the convention.'

By way of closing the discussion, Jenkins was asked if his parents shared his faith and attended chapel services also. 'No, they didn't practise it,' John replied. 'But they were Christians as such. They did good things, rather than preach about it.' Had Minerva and Tom, and particularly his mother, harboured a certain cynicism towards those who express their religious conviction in such a manner? 'There was always a *certain* amount of sniping going on,' John replied chuckling, 'because they would say: "He's up in the pulpit shouting about the evils of drink – well, you should have seen him last night coming out of the pub!"'

It is perhaps understandable why the Chapel earmarked Jenkins as an asset with a future position within the Chapel structure: because Chapel elders recognised in John a natural ability to empathise, impart pastoral care and extend the spiritual hand of friendship to those who required it. Asked whether he had understood this apparent gift to be trusted and to use diplomacy and discretion – particularly during moments of human frailty – at the time, John replied that he had not; before continuing, however, that he 'should have seen, or noticed the indication' that he possessed 'a special gift for being both confided in and listened to'. Exemplifying the point, Jenkins revealed that when 'only a 15-year-old boy', the wife of a neighbour passed away. To John's surprise, it was he to whom the somewhat distraught husband turned to discuss his sense of bereavement. While Jenkins confessed to thinking it 'strange' that the widower, 'a grown man; a working man', should want to tell 'only a kid' his innermost feelings of loss, the experience had left John humbled and to *some* degree pondering why – especially when Jenkins learned that his unfortunate neighbour had decided against approaching someone from his *own* large Christian family to discuss his distress. But if John failed to fully appreciate what the situation revealed of his character, a pattern was emerging. This ability to be empathetic and trusted proved a quality which John Jenkins utilised to great effect some twenty years later when he marshalled the militant offensive of *Mudiad Amddiffyn Cymru*.

Nonetheless, it was also at this juncture that John experienced an event which he maintains had a profound effect on his character and emotional understanding. In 2018, having finally decided to reveal what transpired, John declared tentatively:

'When I was aged about 15, I walked up from Penybryn to Capel Gwladys; and when I was quite near – not next to it, but in the same area – I sat down in this little copse of trees and fell fast asleep. Fast asleep – for about three hours! When I woke up, I rushed off home and I thought,

"Well, I'm damned; fancy falling asleep." It had never happened before. I'd never fallen asleep like that before. Well, the next day, I thought I'd walk back up to this copse of trees – and I couldn't find them again. But I knew where it had to be, because then – as I do now – if I go somewhere, I always make a point of linking where I am to other points in the vicinity. So I knew where I was, and I knew where the trees should be. But they weren't there. And as much as it leaves me feeling uncomfortable to say this, I have always believed that there was something spiritual about this, about what happened. I could say that from that point on, it [my life] was a bit different. I felt different; I looked at life differently. But it has taken me all these years to say this, because I am aware that I am playing right into their [critics'] hands. You know what the reaction will be: "What sort of political activist is this? Spiritual experiences! He's bloody mad." And yet, there are no copses anywhere near to Capel Gwladys. So, I couldn't have got my location mixed up with anywhere else, or another copse. Nothing like that. Apart from which, I knew that mountain like the back of my hand. I had been up there many, many times by then. But I just looked and looked and this copse of trees just wasn't there. And yet I know that by talking about this, they will say, "Here he goes, off with the fairies again!" Perhaps some people will understand, but not everybody will.'

## John meets his soulmate

If the decision to withdraw from Chapel society left a void in Jenkins' life, the resolution to do so coincided with the contemplative John, by now aged nearly 16, falling in love with the girl whom he still maintains was his soulmate and his only 'true love'. Refusing to disclose her identity, other than revealing that her first name was Joan, John recounts what happened.

'I first met her when I was walking my dog, Prince, funnily enough. This was not in Penybryn, but in her village, Cefn Hengoed, which was across the valley. I was still enjoying long walks and exploring the local area. As much as anything, because my shifts at the steelworks didn't leave much time for socialising. Not that I was interested in going to pubs anyway, although I was still attending the marching band practices frequently. But as I walked with our dog early one Saturday evening, I bumped into her and her friend. They were enjoying a walk together. We struck up a conversation and we arranged to meet each other again. And so began a relationship which lasted about nine months. She was a lovely-looking girl, blessed with a nice figure, blonde hair and these big blue eyes.'

Did they enjoy a typical courtship of dancing and going to pubs together? By way of reply, John laughed, before stating:

'It must be remembered that I am from a small village and she was from a small village, so we didn't meet in pubs and all that sort of stuff. It wasn't done for a woman to wait in a pub, anyway. To provide an idea of the mindset of the time – and the community had a good laugh about this – one of the lads from Penybryn went away and married a girl from London. They returned to Penybryn and one afternoon, while he was at work, she thought she would nip to the pub for a drink, as she had done in London. Anyway, she walks in and is greeted with dead silence; before being told, in no uncertain terms, that "women don't go to pubs". As far as these men – and others in the area – were concerned, it was against the rules, really. Women did not *go* to pubs, even with their husbands!'

Questioned as to the extent of their relationship, Jenkins conceded that despite the age difference – he was approaching 16 and she 14 – the relationship was sexually intimate. In fact, despite the couple's youth, the relationship was 'total' and intense. So much so that the romance – to *some* degree – has cast a long shadow over Jenkins' life. In developing the point, John disclosed that they 'just hit it off'. More revealingly, however, Jenkins was 'comfortable in her company'; they were respectful of one another; and while neither legally able nor emotionally inclined to frequent pubs, the couple spent their Saturday evenings walking while engrossed in conversation – discovering, in doing so, that they shared a good deal in common. Unsurprisingly, this emotional and intellectual connection amounted to John believing that he could relax and be himself. Jenkins' young paramour did not meet the indomitable Minerva, but as John later clarified, 'My mother's love for me was unconditional. I could do no wrong. So whatever I decided was the right thing.' Had he met her parents? 'No,' John replied, before adding comically:

'Well, not officially. Her father almost caught me once; not exactly in a 'compromising position', but... thankfully I could run faster than him! I knew her brother though, because he worked in the same place I did

– the steelworks in Newport. He was collected on the same bus as I was, so, he knew me and I knew him. He knew we were in a relationship, but he didn't approve. Well, he was the sort of chap who didn't approve of anything, anyway! He was alright, but... I don't blame him actually... It was his sister, after all, wasn't it?'

Having established the seriousness of the relationship, albeit while recognising its lighter side, John nonetheless regards this fledgling liaison as pivotal to his emotional flowering. He, at least, recognised its potential and hoped the relationship would develop. So why, despite the couple's obvious affinity, did the relationship end? 'The reason I lost my first love was because I allowed duty to come in the way of it,' Jenkins revealed, before adding pensively:

'Here we were in the middle of a ferocious courtship; and one very important Saturday, I was to meet her. It was her birthday, or some special occasion, and all sorts of things had been planned. Just before I was due to leave, to walk as arranged to meet her, there was a knock on the door. It was the leader of the senior marching band. They were due to appear in some important competition somewhere, but one of the two senior drummers had just gone off sick. And as there existed a rule that a minimum of two drummers were required, all the practising they'd done for weeks would be for nothing if they didn't have them. And so I was placed in this dilemma: would I go in this man's place? What was I supposed to do? That was duty, pleasure was the other thing.

Well, I couldn't contact her. There was no means to contact her. There were no mobile phones. We'd never even heard of ordinary phones! There was *no way* I could contact her. So, I just had to leave that and go off with the band. They appeared in this competition and came second. But, naturally enough, she took this as a slap in the face. And that was us finished. Although she never met me again to tell me this. But it was obvious. That was a case of me doing my usual thing and putting duty before anything else.'

How was it 'obvious' that his soulmate now wanted to end their romance? 'For many weeks,' he replied, 'I went back to our designated meeting spot at what was our usual meeting time, but she didn't turn up.'[31] Had the fulness of time allowed Jenkins to arrive at perhaps a more rounded perspective of his first love? By way of reply, John smiled and proclaimed that when experiencing such emotions for the first time, 'everything is fresh and sweet and new'. He then laughed and continued: 'Ah, the sweet smell of honeysuckle. It lingers long in the nostrils. It is still there now.' Jenkins then paused in silent reflection, before adding:

'Look, we are talking about events of 70 years ago. These days I take a more objective view of it: in that I realise [that] what I was in love with was *not* a person, but a concept. And being in love with a concept is the most powerful thing of the lot. It is more powerful than people. People can be destroyed by reputation and by actions, but concepts remain the same. They are "up there" and you look up to them. But they are concepts; and if you fall in love with a concept, you are lost. I was 15 – and at that age *everything* is idealised.'

But did he not try to contact her, to explain his reason for having failed to turn up? Surely someone so in tune with John would have been open to an explanation concerning his failure to attend their appointment? 'These were very different times,' John declared resolutely.

'We'd arrange to see each other at the end of every meeting. We would say, "I'll see you next Saturday at the usual spot, at such and such a time." That was how we communicated. So, once that communication was broken, it was broken. And there was no way I could get in touch with her again. She was only a young girl and I was only a young boy. In those days, you couldn't go banging on people's doors. It was not the done thing. Not by a long chalk. It wasn't the done thing to write letters either. I mean, she was only a young girl. If she'd received a letter addressed to her, it would have caused uproar. That's how things were at the time. It's different now altogether. But it was a bit different in those days – especially in the villages. I wasn't afraid of what her father, or the family, could do to me, but what they could do to her. Because my sending a letter would have bounced back on her – and she had no way of writing back. Young girls – I mean, they didn't have a voice at all, not in those days. We're talking about the late Forties now. The big point I must make about this is that my soulmate was 14 years of age. I was only 15 myself. So it is hardly at an age where you can make a reasonable decision, or appeal to the father of the person. Besides, you didn't know her father! It would never have done to go to her house and just wait for her to appear. Nor to wait outside her place of work, or school. Or to give her brother a letter to hand to her. He and I never discussed the matter. Times were different. I thought it all out, and in the end, I just left it. I just let it go.'

Did he blame her? Did he not feel that she had overreacted by refusing all further contact? 'Well, funnily enough, I didn't blame her for what she did, or what she didn't do,' Jenkins replied.

'It was my fault for putting duty before pleasure. If I'd refused the chap at the door, if I'd explained why I couldn't play with the band that evening, he would have understood. Had I said, "Listen lads, I'm sorry, but I've got a prior engagement which I can't turn down." If I'd said that, they would have understood. But *I* wouldn't have understood. It would have been weighing on my conscience – that I'd actually stopped the band from going out. Because that's what it would have amounted to.'

Has there been any contact since? 'Well, yeah,' John remarked gingerly.

'We had brief contact years later. It was very brief. We spoke, but nothing was discussed. I didn't try to explain what had happened all those years before. I didn't want to drag all that up, because it may have developed into some sort of an argument. I left it for her to bring up and she didn't, so I didn't bother. I haven't seen her for quite some time. She still lives there, in the same place. And of course, I've moved on since then. I've lived in many different places. I have only seen her once or twice in thirty years, and she is not impressive now. But I still see her as she was. It would be nice to discuss our past... I would like to sometime.'

Another fascinating aspect of any future discussion between John and his first love would surely involve whether Joan had recognised Jenkins, when he was arrested in November 1969 for spearheading the militant campaign of MAC, as the *same* John Jenkins she had fallen in love with some twenty years before. Having pondered the question, John declared thoughtfully: 'Yeah. It would be interesting to find out.'

As is perhaps a recurring theme in his life, the end of this relationship – which, though idealised, was no doubt sincere – leaves unanswered questions. Most notably, did Jenkins believe that had he married his soulmate and had a family, his affiliation to *Mudiad Amddiffyn Cymru* might *not* have happened? Having again considered his reply, John postulated:

'Well, it would have distracted me, wouldn't it? It would have given me something else to focus on. At the time, it was the only thing. When I did go for MAC, *that* was the only thing I could go for really. By then I was married, living in a house and I had children, but it wasn't quite the same thing. It wasn't quite the same all-embracing commitment that a first love and a marriage would have brought. That said, how many first loves go to the next stage? Some do, but very, very few. What do they say? "Oh yes, but then you grow up." That's true enough as well, and that's really part of the problem: why this relationship affected me so adversely. Because had it run its normal course, we would either have ended it, or, more likely, it would have gone to the next level. But neither of those two scenarios happened. It just ended abruptly, and I took this very much to heart.

I'm quite sure that other people would have just dismissed it with a shrug of their shoulders and quickly moved on, but I'm not able to be so frivolous. Everything I do has to be done properly and taken seriously. I don't know if that's because I'm obstinate, ruthless or fervent... but I won't stop when most people feel it's advisable, or appropriate, to stop. I will only stop when something is concluded. And so, in one sense, because there was no definitive or natural conclusion, I've been in a sort of limbo with regards this woman and this first love ever since. But do I think I would have got involved with MAC had I married this girl? On balance: yeah, I think it *is* likely, because I latch onto things like that in a way. What I mean is, I would still have been drawn to the political aspect of what was going on. I would have been well aware of the political events which later unfolded – such as Tryweryn. And possibly she would have felt as *I* did about Tryweryn, etc. But if not... Well, I did love this girl. And so our marriage would have been a very close second. A *very* close second. Actually, I think I would have been torn. And that's no good, you can't be torn. It's all or nothing. So, just *maybe*, this relationship wasn't meant to be either.'

## Jenkins joins the Army, helps Minerva with the Festival of Britain celebrations and refuses to watch the coronation

Whether John's relationship with his first love was meant to be or not, Jenkins admits to feeling rejected, confused, and 'in a huff' when it ended. Having decided that he was 'not going to stay around here any more', John weighed up his options and deduced that the 'best way to get away' was to join the British Army. Had joining the British Army featured in his plans prior to this, perhaps while at school? 'Oh no,' he replied emphatically.

'It was owing to this unfortunate love affair, and things not working out. Had this relationship intensified, I wouldn't have left. But having said that, there were other factors at play, I suppose. For instance, I didn't see much future working in the steelworks and so I wanted to get away anyway. I wanted to see the world. But I didn't join the Army for reasons of being "drawn to the colours" or anything. And I can't recall viewing the Army as preferable to the other services. I saw joining the Army as purely a way of earning a living and seeing the world. In those days, the British Army occupied a lot of the world. You could be posted to places like Egypt, Austria, Australia, Belize, Cyprus. All these different places were open to postings. So you could get around and see the world. I'm not sure that exists any longer.

Having made up his mind that his future lay in joining the British Army, John – along with his friend, Trevor Crew, from Blackwood – visited the Army recruitment office in Cardiff. Told to return a month later, on 30 November 1950, Jenkins and Crew sat the standard entrance exam. The mark they received ascertained what careers, within the service, would be available to them. John explains what transpired.

'The exam was intended, I suspect, to determine both your intellectual and emotional state. Anyway, at the end of the exam, they called us in to receive our marks and to discuss what options were available to us. They said to me, "You're eligible to join the Dental Corps," and Trevor said, "Oh, I'll come as well." They said, "No, you won't. Sorry, but you didn't quite reach that standard. You'll have to go in the Medical Corps." Unbeknownst to me, you needed a higher mark to join the Dental Corps than the Medical Corps. Well, that was their impression, anyway. Up until that point, I hadn't particularly considered the Medical Corps as an option. So I signed on. A few weeks later, I received a letter telling me to report to the barracks at Aldershot at such and such a time.'

And so on Thursday, 4 January 1951, some three months short of his eighteenth birthday, John Barnard Jenkins joined the British Army as a trainee member of the Royal Army Dental Corps. Did he enjoy the twelve weeks of basic training? 'Yes,' John affirmed.

'Funnily enough, I did enjoy what is laughingly known as basic training. Because it wasn't like I had been led to expect. There was no shouting and bawling. But the corps I was in, the Dental Corps, wasn't like the rest of the Army, particularly. The Dental Corps doesn't pride itself on that type of approach. It has a very individual outlook on things – and things in that corps are not quite the same as they are in the rest of the Army. It's like the Medical Corps, only better. The Medical Corps is armed; we were not armed. We didn't have guns. Nothing like that. We didn't go near guns during our basic training. So, yes: I enjoyed it.

To give an idea of the corps' ethos: during the war, this staff sergeant and this private decided that life in the Dental Corps was too comfortable and easy, and they wanted to do something really good for the war effort. So, they went across to the continent in a small rowing boat and tried to blow up a German cookhouse, before rowing back across the channel! A bloody film was made about it![32] Well, this was a source of great pride to the Dental Corps, and on being told the story on arriving, I thought: "So now I have joined the ranks of the funny buggers. Oh well, there you are!" It was good fun, the Dental Corps. After basic training, you get posted from the depot in Aldershot to a Dental Centre; and from there you get posted to a surgery, where you receive more training while you work there.'[33]

Had he experienced any recognition for being a Welshman? For example, did his strong Valleys accent prompt any response from his comrades, in either a friendly or not-so-friendly capacity? John laughed and replied:

'Well, it's funny you should say that. Because when I first joined the Army, my first posting was Warminster, which was where they trained infantry soldiers. Well, the RSM there – the senior non-commissioned officer, a very important person and a very strong and outgoing sort of person – was a chap called Rees. P D Rees. Now, he was quite a large chap and we had never met, as such. I'd seen him about the place once or twice, but he certainly hadn't noticed me. But one day he was walking down the road and I was walking down the other side and he shouted across to me, "I can see you're a Welshman." I was delighted. Just by looking at me, he could see that I was a Welshman. He hadn't heard me speak or anything, because I'd never met the fellow, but straight away he could tell. I thought "What a compliment." He just looks at me and says: "a Welshman". I thought, "That is lovely." It made my day. It made my year. It made my

life! Because there are people and you look at them and you say, "You're
Irish," or whatever.'

Does he look back on this stage of his Army career with a sense of fondness?
'Yes,' John confirmed.

'I enjoyed being in the Army from the moment I joined. I'd never met
a cockney before and when we first arrived in Aldershot, we were told
that the RSM was going to address us. And out comes this bloke and he
starts talking about "pie pride". And I think "pie pride?" Oh, they must
be making cakes or something. They are celebrating their new cake, or
whatever it is. I discovered later that what he was trying to say was "pay
parade". But him being a cockney, I was like, "What?" I had never met any
of these people before. It took me some time to get acclimatised.'

If it appears that John had landed on his feet and that he was among
friends, it was not long before regional differences began to impact on his
view of those with whom he now stood shoulder to shoulder. While those
from diverse cultural backgrounds had mixed well, the only trouble had
been provided by those servicemen from London. Asked to develop the
point, Jenkins continued:

'We had some trouble with the cockneys. They were good in Aldershot,
but they were a bit selfish. For instance, when you went on holiday, or
a weekend's leave – which you didn't get very often – you had to book
back into the guardroom no later than midnight on Sunday. But they
recognised that some of us were from Wales and Scotland and places like
that, and that as soon as we got home on the Friday, we would have to
start getting ready to come back on the Saturday evening, to comply with
this regulation concerning being booked back in by midnight on Sunday.
This was because there was never any transport on a Sunday morning.
And in recognition of this, they said, "Well, if some of you won't make it
back by 12 o'clock on the Sunday night, as long as you're all on parade
next morning by 7 o'clock, we'll overlook it." So, fair play. To get back by
7 a.m. on a Monday morning, I'd leave home during the late afternoon on
the Sunday, and walk to Ystrad Mynach. From there, I'd catch the train
to Cardiff. From there, a train to Bristol. I would then wait in Bristol for
about three hours, and get another train to Reading. After another long
wait there, I'd catch another train to Ashgrove, I think it's called, and from

there, the 6 a.m. bus back to the depot in Aldershot. All in all, about twelve bloody hours! But the Londoners, because Aldershot is only about thirty minutes from London, could get down to Waterloo Station at 6 a.m. on the Monday morning and be in Aldershot by 7 a.m. And what happened? A couple of them went out drinking one night, didn't they? And whether they forgot, or they didn't put their alarm clock on, or they couldn't be bothered to get out of bed – whatever the reason, they didn't make the bloody morning parade. So, the authorities had to step in. We recognised that they had no choice. Things couldn't go on like that. So everyone had to be in by midnight on Sunday, which meant it was a waste of time us going home for the weekend. Because we would leave Friday at 4 or 5 o'clock, and not get back home until perhaps midnight. This left only all day Saturday at home, before leaving Saturday evening in order to be back by midnight on Sunday. So, all you got was one day out of a two-day pass, really.'

Despite his irritation, however, Jenkins had learned a valuable lesson – and one which he later utilised to considerable effect when orchestrating the militant campaign of *Mudiad Amddiffyn Cymru*.

'I realised then that it only takes a few to disrupt it for the many. And I have noticed this to be true many, many times. There was, I think, only two of them who got back too late for the Monday morning parade, but that was enough, of course. The authorities made a note of it; and that was the end of this special privilege. I mean, they had to end it. We understood their reason: we'd been given a favour and we kicked them in the face. Well, *we* hadn't. These two Londoners had.'

Having rejected the suggestion that the matter might have developed into a physical confrontation, Jenkins added:

'No, it didn't come to fisticuffs, but there was ill-feeling over it. People knew what had happened. Oh, they were sorry, but it didn't affect them as such, because they could catch the 10 p.m. train from Waterloo and be booked back in quite easily by midnight. We couldn't. And they must have known this when they did it. And so I thought, "I wonder if all cockneys are like this?" They're not, of course, but the experience did leave a bad taste in the mouth. But I realised then how important discipline, organisation and unity were to any such outfit.'

Prompted to describe a typical working day, John explained that he was involved in 'normal, everyday dentistry. The dentists,' he continued, 'were, of course, officers; and we, the other ranks, were employed as the administration and the surgery assistants and all the rest of it. We were a tight little unit. It comprised less than a thousand.'

Renowned for his fastidious appearance, John also revealed that his reasoning had more to do self-preservation and maintaining the upper hand than overt pride. 'I really wasn't that fussed,' he stated.

> 'I mean you do things like that to keep people off your back. That's what it's *really* all about. Otherwise, if you don't do it, there are people shouting and bawling. So to keep them away, you always turn out well. Then they can't complain.'

If weekend visits home had been curtailed owing to the actions of a few, John nonetheless returned to Penybryn during longer periods of leave. One such holiday coincided with the commencement of the Festival of Britain celebrations in May 1951.[34] The Festival of Britain was held over five months and intended to mark the end of post-war austerity and the centenary of the Great Exhibition. At the heart of the festival, constructed on derelict ground on London's South Bank, was an exhibition celebrating British achievements in science and the arts. Although John didn't attend the exhibition in London, he did help, he later comically recalled, to decorate the outside of his parents' home in Penybryn; as the village, along with countless other communities across the UK, celebrated the event. Laughing as he remembered that his parents' house won the local contest, his willingness to lend assistance to his mother had not been motivated by an overt sense of pride in being British, but was rather, Jenkins maintained, born of a desire not to let his family down.

> 'They wanted help with these decorations, so I gave them a hand... I had no thought about helping the Queen or saluting the King and all the bloody rest of it. A little later, in 1953, I was really irritated by the coronation and I refused to watch it. Even by then, I wasn't interested in the Royal Family as such.'

The crowning of Elizabeth II in 1953 broadly coincided with the end of rationing in Britain and the arrival of electricity in Penybryn.[35] With the household cooking no longer 'done by way of gas, or in the ovens by the side of the fire', the advent of electricity led to the eventual arrival of television in the village – although at first this was restricted to one household in Penybryn, John chuckled, resulting in 'people crowding around it, fighting to see the damn thing'. In an area renowned for its fierce adherence to socialism, had the coronation struck a chord? 'Well, it did,' he responded indignantly.

'Because they're a funny lot down there. It's supposed to be "socialist south Wales", but these are the same people who voted for Brexit, aren't they? Nah, they've got a strange dichotomy in that area. They say one thing and they do something else. They're supposed to be socialists and yet a lot of them believe in the Royal Family and accept their OBEs and knighthoods and all the bloody rest of it. By doing that, of course, they imply approval of the existing system.'

## John goes to Austria and Germany

Towards the end of 1952, following a period spent 'happily in Warminster', John Jenkins was posted to Austria. Revealing that his posting was initially to Egypt, Jenkins threw light on what transpired.

'When I got to the depot in Aldershot, from where we were being despatched, there was a bloke there going to Austria, and he didn't want to go to Austria. He wanted to go to Egypt, so I just swapped with him. Now, you couldn't do this in the Army normally, but with us, the Dental Corps, we just went up and said to them, "He wants to go Egypt, and I want to go to Austria. Can we swap?" And they were like, "Yes. Righto." Done! They were very understanding. I still have a great regard for the Dental Corps. They just weren't *like* the rest of the Army... And what a time of year to arrive. It was lovely spending Christmas in Austria; with the trees all decorated and the snow. It was magical – fantastic to experience.'

In Austria on 11 March 1954, John Jenkins celebrated his 21st birthday. Contrary to what might be expected, John's coming-of-age was not greeted in a traditionally raucous way, but rather in a manner which was typically low key. It was a 'reasonable birthday', he later remarked. 'But it wasn't a typical bachelor's do, with everybody getting drunk... It might have been suggested, but I never believed in anything like that.' It was not the only occasion when John's preconceived ideas clashed with those around him. While in Austria, and as something of a surprise, Jenkins discovered that within the British Army 'this ingrained class thing' was still prevalent. In quantifying the point, John declared:

> 'Well, one day, while I was working in the Dental Centre, the Colonel brought his wife in. Anyway, she and I were chatting away – it was all very cordial – and she said to me, "Oh, you must come over for lunch one day." But then she looked towards the Colonel, who let it be known by the manner of his returned eye contact what he thought of the invite, and she went, "Oooh. No, you can't do that." Somebody as lowly as me, going to a colonel's house for lunch? Never heard of such a thing. But there you are. I was a lance corporal at this point, not a sergeant as I later became. But even so. It wouldn't have mattered if I *had been* a sergeant. It wouldn't have mattered if I'd been a sergeant major.'

More revealingly, however, John soon determined that the term 'British Army' was a misnomer, and that this wing of Her Majesty's Armed Forces, at least, proudly regarded itself – even if it was unstated – as the *English* Army. Questioned as to whether being in Austria had fostered anything of note with regard his perception of Wales within in a wider European context, John stated:

> 'Well, one thing of import that happened during the time I was in Austria was that I met a number of people belonging to the Wends race. These people are small, round-headed, black haired… And on meeting them and learning about what they as a people had experienced, I began to feel that the sort of oppression that they had experienced over hundreds of years was *very* similar to the sort of thing that the Welsh had suffered also. Like the Wends, the Welsh people had also been the victims of cultural and economic oppression. This was the feeling I had, and it only intensified when the Tryweryn controversy occurred in Wales a few years later.'

But if the treatment that the Wends people suffered at the hands of their Germanic neighbours caused disquiet, what John experienced while visiting Nazi concentration camps – Dachau near Munich and, later, Bergen-Belsen near Hamburg – still serves to shock. Having followed Pathé news coverage of their liberation by Allied forces as a schoolboy, to what extent had visiting the location of such unparalleled human misery impacted on his emotional well-being? Before replying, Jenkins closed his eyes, as if reliving the experience. 'It was terrible,' he finally declared quietly:

'Terrible. But what really had an impact on me was the day I went to Dachau. A large charabanc full of Germans arrived, and these German people alighted from the bus and were all sitting around on the mounds, laughing away at something or other. And then, coming down the pass in between them, was this old rabbi. And this old rabbi looked at them, and the look on his face! Phew. I've never forgotten it.'

Encouraged to describe the expression on the face of the rabbi, John continued:

'It wasn't hatred exactly. It was as if he was looking at a troop of monkeys picking nits off each other, or whatever, you know? A lesser breed. "These people are bloody bonkers" – something like that. I don't think it was loathing as such. It wasn't far from it, mind. But he couldn't understand how they were sitting on a mound, on which was a noticeboard declaring, 'Here lie ten thousand dead people' – because there are lots of these notices there. And they were, like the Germans do, just sitting down enjoying themselves; discussing this and that, and drinking out of flasks and all the rest of it! It was remarkable.'[36]

Shortly after visiting Dachau, John Jenkins was posted to Berlin. With memories of the concentration camp still fresh in his mind, did he encounter a collective German sense of guilt for what had occurred during the war? 'Well,' he proclaimed incredulously, 'I never saw any.' He continued:

'What I did see was that they were trying to *portray* a sense of guilt. But it wasn't really guilt. It was a disguise. If they were guilty about *anything*, they were guilty for having lost the war, rather than guilty for what they had done. Funnily enough, most of them blamed Hitler. They said he should have left the conduct of the Army to his generals. Which is true, because Germany would have won the war then. But of course, he interfered every step of the way, like a good commander in chief! And he lost them the war. There was a move afoot by the Allies during the war years to assassinate him. But the plan to assassinate him was stopped at a high level, because it was considered that Hitler was the Allies' greatest aid, with all the stupid decisions he was making. So they decided not to kill him. It was far better to keep him there, and demand that Germany surrender unconditionally.'

John's arrival in Berlin coincided with the city undergoing a massive reconstruction and redevelopment programme, as outlined in the Marshall Plan. It was named after George C Marshall, the former US Secretary of State who proposed the measure, and was designed to rehabilitate the many devastated European economies. The strategy behind this huge financial injection, named the European Recovery Program, was to bring about the conditions under which democracy could thrive throughout Europe. With great swathes of the city resembling little more than a building site, Berlin, Jenkins opined, was 'hell on earth'. John was stationed at the Olympiastadion, which became the headquarters of the British military occupying forces. Some 5 miles west of Berlin, it was at the Olympiastadion in 1936 that black athlete Jesse Owens had humiliated Nazi doctrine, which advocated white Aryan supremacy, by winning four gold medals. It had also provided the setting for Nazi rallies: where, in spectacles of spellbinding obedience, Hitler's totalitarian control was affirmed.

The experience of seeing the city recover 'was amazing', John remarked. He was particularly struck by the speed at which war-torn and damaged Berlin was transformed and put back on its feet. 'You would drive along one day in civilian transport and there would be people marking out the ground on this big area of scrub grass. You would drive past two months later and a bloody Woolworths or something would be operating and flourishing there. I couldn't believe it.' To provide an idea of the privations still evident, however, 'anything and everything,' he remarked pointedly, 'was available for a few cigarettes.'

Yet it was not long before the financial fortunes of Germany began to flower. This coincided with John, already enjoying the benefits of a subsidised military lifestyle, earning a salary which ensured his every modest bachelor need was met. The situation improved further when John then passed the exams to become a sergeant. John's newly-acquired financial status provided him with the opportunity to help the Jenkins family, still subject to the ongoing hardships at home. Asked to outline his thoughts at this time, Jenkins declared ruefully:

'When I was in Germany, I was earning lots of money. There was still rationing in Britain and the shops were empty. The shops in Germany were well stocked by comparison, and so I used to send food parcels back to the family in Wales. When I later returned to Germany in the early Sixties, I used to send clothes back for my niece Siân, because there was much more choice in Germany than at home. The redevelopment of the German economy made it seem like a different world over there – almost as soon as the war ended. I used to think, "Who won the bloody war?"'

But as Germany began to prosper in the early 1950s, was there an official policy outlawing fraternisation with the local German populace – if only to ensure resentments were kept in check? 'Well,' John replied trenchantly:

'I think most of the Germans were aware that this *was* the policy, but it hardly took first place in the list of priorities. For the most part, there was a good relationship between the British military and the Germans because the German people are aware that the English, anyway, are direct descendants of Germans. So they take a more relaxed view of them than they would of people from, say, Siberia, for instance.'

The working relationship between the occupying forces of France, the UK, the US and the USSR, constructed from having united to defeat fascism during the war, was now subject to increasing ideological tension. On the western side of Berlin, capitalist France, Britain and the United States were committed to a free market, capitalist economy. In East Berlin, under the control of the USSR, communism was the political system with which the citizens were governed. Determined to showcase the benefits of a 'free' capitalist society, the US ensured that financial investment poured into regenerating the Western Sector of Berlin. It greatly overshadowed the monies being spent on revitalising the eastern area of the city. The difference in both the conditions and the facilities available in the two different sectors soon became dramatically apparent. 'Even the nightclubs in the eastern half were horrible,' declared John; adding:

'They were old, dreadful, soulless places. I socialised in East Berlin up to a point. I wanted to look around and to see what was going on there. West Berlin had a different attitude completely. It is like trying to compare East Chester with West London. It was far more liberal, far more cosmopolitan in the West. By contrast, the East was much more austere and grim. Yeah, that's the word for it: grim.'

Nonetheless, the experience provided by being in Berlin was not devoid of mirth, as Jenkins blithely recounts.

'There was this badge that you wore on your arm. A big round black circle and a red rim all around it, which represented the Russians, of course, because Berlin was in the middle of the red Russian zone. And so the troops nicknamed this bloody badge "the flaming arsehole"! But I didn't know this. So, on arriving at the Dental Centre, this captain says to me, "Have you got your flaming arsehole?" I just stared at him. I wondered what the hell I'd joined!'

Despite the excitement of being in Berlin, the novelty was beginning to wear thin. Jenkins' escalating feeling of sensory overload was further heightened when one day, while visiting a German female friend in her upstairs apartment, he 'heard all these drums and banging and crashing coming down the road'. On peering out of the window, Jenkins observed rows of German men wearing 'combat – almost jungle regulation – uniform'. More alarmingly, however, each carried either a rifle or a machine gun. Feeling distinctly uneasy, if somewhat impressed by the discipline of the display's orchestrated aesthetic, John enquired of his host if the cause of the commotion was the German Army on parade. It was, he was casually informed, not the Army, but rather 'the police coming back from their annual manoeuvres.' I thought, Jenkins concluded sardonically, 'What the hell am I doing here?' It proved the culmination of John's Berlin adventure; one which Jenkins still regards as enriching and an honour to have experienced. Within weeks, John was posted from Berlin back to Aldershot. From Aldershot, on 29 November 1955, having requested a voluntary discharge after having served the full term of his five years' military service, John Jenkins was demobbed.

## Tryweryn

In the autumn of 1955, while preparing to leave the British Army, John became aware through 'letters and newspapers sent from home' and discussions when returning to Wales, of plans by Liverpool Corporation to construct a reservoir and flood the beautiful Dolanog Valley in Montgomeryshire. Monitoring the story, Jenkins later read that Liverpool Corporation had shelved its proposal, having magnanimously bowed to those in Wales opposed to the Dolanog project. This was ostensibly because in this fertile vale of farmsteads and woodlands stood the home of Ann Griffiths, often credited with having done 'most to enrich the Christian tradition of Wales.'[37] But if those who opposed the Dolanog scheme toasted their success, it was a short-lived victory as Liverpool Corporation, having 'considered' ten other sites, turned its attention to flooding Cwm Tryweryn in Meirionnydd instead. In December 1955, the *Liverpool Daily Post* carried the headline: 'Big new dam near Bala planned.'[38] It then outlined Liverpool Corporation's plan to augment the city's water supply by promoting a Parliamentary Bill to obtain the legal authority to dam the Tryweryn River and Valley. This story in the *Liverpool Daily Post* was the first time that the inhabitants of Cwm Tryweryn heard of Liverpool Corporation's proposal. Along with many Welsh nationalists – and others in Wales politically opposed to or suspicious of Welsh nationalism – John Jenkins was alarmed and quickly angered at the callous way the English authority intended to drown the valley. Cwm Tryweryn was home to a thriving community of some 70 people. It comprised several farms, the village of Capel Celyn, and – like Dolanog – was an area similarly renowned for its rich and vibrant cultural heritage. Jenkins also suspected, as did many in Wales, that the Dolanog project had been nothing more than a smoke screen, and that Liverpool Corporation had secretly coveted Cwm Tryweryn as its *true* target site all along. This was owing to the *increase* in the supply of water which the authority's formulated reservoir plans revealed. Although irritated by the way Liverpool Corporation had embarked on resolving its water shortage issue, John still retained a belief that the democratic British political system would prevent the Bill passing into law – and that justice for *all* concerned, both Liverpool and Tryweryn inhabitants, would prevail. With the Parliamentary procedure expected to last many months, only time would tell.

John returns to civvy street, develops a 'personal grievance,' watches the Tryweryn Bill become law, questions the world of politics and meets Thelma Bridgman

On leaving the Army in November 1955, John returned to live with his parents in Penybryn. During a Social Enquiry Report for the Probation Service, compiled in the weeks prior to his trial in 1970, Jenkins stated that he had left the Army because he had received an assurance of 'a good job' at a local factory. Yet the job failed to materialise, owing to the plant being closed due to the economic downturn. The situation was to result in what Peter Absir, Jenkins' Probation Officer, discerned to be 'a personal grievance' for John. Asked to outline his thoughts during the interview, Jenkins opined that 'whenever economic upheavals occur, Wales is the first to suffer.'[39] As a consequence, John worked briefly at the steelworks in Cardiff. Although happy to be back, despite his employment frustrations, it was not long before Jenkins was reminded of the less appealing aspects of life within the close-knit community of Penybryn. 'One night I got lucky,' he explained.

> 'And so I crept back in at 3 a.m. I came down in the morning and there, sat opposite my mother, was the old lady who lived in the house across the street from us. Now, she loved everybody's business, including her own, and she said, "Oh yes, I saw him putting his bedroom light on at 3 o'clock this morning. I thought, oh, where can he have been until now?" It was a bit overwhelming... the attention of neighbours *could* be stifling. But on the other hand, being a part of such a community could also be very handy when you needed a shoulder to cry on.'

Having weighed up the pros and cons of Valleys life, including the region's existing economic limitations, John Jenkins considered his position and decided that his long-term future lay in emigrating to South Africa, and made enquires as to the opportunities available. On determining that employment in the country's gold mines might prove lucrative, John was informed that he needed to meet two criteria: 1) he must be skilled and experienced in mining, and 2) he must be white. With apartheid the political doctrine observed in South Africa at this point – under which the country's indigenous black community was subject to strict and discriminatory control – had the widely-vilified situation featured in his thinking at that stage? 'I wasn't too bothered about the politics of the matter,' John replied candidly. 'In those far-off days, it was a job as far as I was concerned.' Nevertheless, able to meet the second criterion, Jenkins went to work for 12 months in the coal pit at Penallta in the Rhymney Valley to comply with the first. As the months passed while working at Penallta Colliery, Jenkins underwent a change of attitude. It was partly because of his involvement in a minor motorbike accident. Asked to describe what happened, John declared ruefully:

'I came around this corner far too fast, and there were cars coming the other way which were encroaching a bit on my side of the road. So I pulled in, and as I went past this gate, there was a piece of iron sticking out, and that caught my arm and destabilised me. Anyway, I crashed!'

John suffered damage to the back of his right wrist, which required treatment in the form of a supporting splint being applied at the local Casualty unit – although an overnight stay was not considered necessary. More significantly, however, Jenkins' change of heart derived from a greater understanding of the political situation in South Africa. 'I suddenly realised what South Africa was *really* all about,' John declared, 'and so I decided not to bother going after all.'[40] Having again considered his position, Jenkins began work as a student general nurse in the East Glamorgan Hospital, near Pontypridd, instead. There, John met the woman who would become his wife, Thelma Mary Bridgman. Thelma was also a student general nurse. She was aged 18, Welsh (from Treharris) and the sister of a policeman. Were they soulmates? 'Oh no,' he replied firmly. 'Only Joan was my soulmate. She [Joan] is the only person I have ever fallen *heavily* in love with.' Had he and Thelma discussed their past? Again, Jenkins replied in the negative.

'I think it was a conscious decision when we met: that we would leave the past behind and get on with living for the future. And you can't move forward if you are too busy looking back. People who look back and move forward fall over a cliff! Having said that, this relationship with my first love continued to have a big effect on me. It still does. Because first love is the most intense emotion anybody can ever feel any time – and I can certainly guarantee that is a fact.'

Nonetheless, did Thelma suspect there was someone of importance in his background? Had she felt, perhaps, 'second best'? 'No, I don't think she thought that,' returned John.

> 'Because I never made a thing about it. I never, sort of, threw it in her face – nor have I thrown it in anyone's face. But it was always there. In my mind. It's very powerful. It overrides everything, forever. I don't want to compare one person to another, and I don't think I'm able to, anyway. Because my soulmate was based on a concept. When you're in love with a concept, or an ideal, you see things that *aren't* there. It blinds you to some things and alerts you to others. I certainly felt more comfortable in the company of my first love than I did with Thelma. But of course, the relationship was entirely different. Thelma and I had the responsibility of raising a family and paying the bills and keeping the place warm and all the other. You don't get that when you're in the middle of a first love. You have no worries; you just get on with it. But Thelma and I got along well enough, and so we began a courtship.'

With that in mind, what had attracted one to the other? 'Well, someone later asked Thelma what she saw in me, and she said I had lovely, pretty eyes,' John chuckled.

> 'As for me, I really couldn't tell you. She was a nice-looking girl... I was thinking more with my balls than with my brain – as young men do. It happens to a lot of people. We did all the normal things that young couples do. We went dancing. Rock 'n' roll had even reached Penybryn! I suppose it was quite a romantic courtship. But of course, I'd had many flings by this time, so I thought it was about time to settle down. It's called growing up. We began to talk more and more about marriage. And so, having given the matter some thought, I decided that the best thing to do was to rejoin the Army, because we wanted somewhere to live and the Army provides a house. That was the plan, you see: I would rejoin the Army; soon after which, we'd get married.'

The plans that John and Thelma were making to get married and start a family coincided with John joining the Territorial Army in Pontypridd – where, along with more combative duties, Jenkins resumed his interest in military-style drumming – and Liverpool Corporation's Tryweryn Reservoir Bill passing through Parliament. Deposited as a Private Member's Bill in

December 1956, the Tryweryn Bill received its crucial Second Reading on 3 July 1957. It was passed by 166 votes to 117. The Third and Final Reading in the Commons on 31 July 1957 was a formality. The Bill was passed with a majority of 96. Crucially, not *one* of Wales' 36 MPs voted in favour of it. While 24 Welsh MPs voted in opposition, the rest either abstained, or just stayed away. This failure to support the Bill presumably reflected the views of the Welsh electorate – no single issue in post-war Welsh history had attracted such consternation across the political, denominational and generational divide. Yet John Jenkins declared adamantly, 'It was not the issue of providing water to Liverpool per se that angered me, but rather the way it was undertaken.' Widely regarded as unjust and wrong, what stuck most in the craw of Welsh nationalists, and John Jenkins among them, was that feasible alternatives which did *not* involve the eradication of a Welsh-speaking community were proposed. But for reasons of what was suspected to be cost, these proposals were rejected in favour of drowning Cwm Tryweryn. It was wholly apparent to the nationalists of Wales – and others besides – that without adequate parliamentary protection, Wales' cultural interests, if not to say political interests, were extremely vulnerable. As he watched these events unfold, Jenkins began to formulate the view that the flooding of Welsh valleys to provide English conurbations with water – and all other attempts to demean and belittle the Welsh nation – must never be allowed to happen again.

Nevertheless, with work to construct the reservoir still to begin, there existed a belief that the drowning of Cwm Tryweryn might yet be prevented through political channels. Asked to quantify his position with regards to politics and how the political machine operated in this period, Jenkins remarked tellingly:

'Well, at this stage, I was still uninformed. I still had respect for people in authority, such as MPs and people like that. But around the time that the Tryweryn Bill went through, I began to realise what they were up to. What they were made of. It was then that I began to change my mind. Prior to this – and maybe even for a while *after* – I still thought that an MP was a person of probity and discretion and knowledge and all the rest of it. I mean, coming from south Wales, I had respect for people like Aneurin Bevan. I admired Bevan for what he had done to establish the National Health Service in Britain, for example. But I began to think it strange that none of these people ever mentioned where they came from. Take Nye

Bevan, for instance: I used to like him until I heard a story which I was assured was true. The story was that when he was coming down from London for a weekend in his constituency in Ebbw Vale – and "coming down" is the operative term – he would be driven to Aust in a bloody great Rolls Royce, while dressed to the nines. Now before they built the Severn Bridge, you caught the ferry boat to go across the Bristol Channel in Aust. But having travelled to Aust in this Bentley, or whatever it was, all dressed up, on arriving on the Welsh side of the channel, there would be an old battered Morris 1000 waiting for him. Having also changed into his old working clothes, with the white muffler and all the usual performance, he would then drive in this old car into his constituency at Ebbw Vale and people would say: "Oh, look! Old Nye hasn't changed a bit!" They tried to keep the lid on this. I mean, not many people knew. But some did, because he had to change into a different car and into different clothes – whatever direction he was going in. Bevan was like so many of them: to further their political careers, they dropped their principles. They have to drop the baggage – and the baggage they are carrying is their south Wales background. As soon as they drop that south Wales background, they can carry straight on, then. And that's what they do. I've seen it happen with Welsh politicians every time.'

If factors surrounding the proposed flooding of Cwm Tryweryn served to further convince John Jenkins that the world of politics was not all that it seemed, events on the world stage at this point also impacted on his political flowering. In 1955, the brave protest by Rosa Parks when she refused to give up her seat for a white man and move to those seats at the back reserved for 'colored' members of the Alabama community registered with John. So too, did the socialist revolution in Cuba in 1959, as headed by Fidel Castro, although Jenkins 'always had this feeling that such revolutionary personalities needed to speak and act in accordance to *truly* prove themselves.' In Castro's case, Jenkins added, 'He *did* prove himself, ensuring that the people of Cuba received one of the finest medical services in the world.' In *that* regard, Fidel Castro had maintained his principles and delivered on his promises, despite 'turning nasty in his old age, becoming something of a dictator and locking up those people who opposed him'. Asked for his thoughts regarding the American Civil Rights Movement during the 1950s and 1960s, John remarked tersely, 'Is there such a thing as American Civil Rights? Good God, civil rights in America is the ability to do as you bloody well like, as long as you have enough money. This is civil rights, isn't it? It's led by the power of the dollar more than anything else.' Had any of the key personalities within the movement for racial equality in the US impressed him? On considering his response, Jenkins declared that Reverend Dr Martin Luther King did inspire respect for adhering to the policy and principle of non-violence, despite appalling provocation.

But one way or another, the single most dominant issue of the 1950s was the escalating ideological enmity between the United States of America and the Union of Soviet Socialist Republics. Now referred to as the world's 'superpowers', the two ideological opponents waged their Cold War on every possible front. At the forefront of the ideological divide was the nuclear arms race. By the end of the decade, both the USA and the USSR had stockpiled nuclear armaments to the point that either side had the capability to annihilate the other – and indeed the planet – many times over. Those who supported this proliferation argued that the 'nuclear deterrent' was necessary to prevent nuclear weapons from ever being used again in conflict as they had been by the US against Japan in 1945. But such a stand-off dictated an uneasy peace. In line with many around the globe, John began to believe that much of the blame for this high-stakes game of nuclear chess had been fuelled by a centralist political policy of imperious land-grabbing throughout the preceding century. The British Empire, Jenkins believed, had 'much to be ashamed of'. As the Campaign for Nuclear Disarmament gathered support in Britain, in April 1958 the first of several marches from London to the UK's Atomic Weapons Research Establishment in Aldermaston in Berkshire attracted considerable support.[41] Asked for his thoughts concerning the Aldermaston march, and those who opposed Britain's nuclear programme, John declared:

'Well, I was aware of the marches to Aldermaston, of course. I mean, you have got to be aware of the big picture before you start involving yourself in small areas. Before you do that, it's first necessary to be aware and to understand the global picture and the possible effects that this might bring to bear on you and those around you. So, of course I was sympathetic to those people marching to Aldermaston and what CND was trying to achieve.'

Yet if one event confirmed Britain's diminishing role on the stage of world political influence, it was the Suez Crisis.[42] The drama began on 26 July

1956, when Britain's Conservative Prime Minister, Anthony Eden, while attending a state dinner, was handed written notice that the President of Egypt, Gamal Abdul Nasser, had nationalised the Suez Canal. Outraged at the perceived threat to Britain's overseas commercial interests, a covert plot was hatched involving the UK, French and Israeli governments, sanctioning military action to safeguard the canal. On 29 October 1956, the Israeli army attacked Egyptian canal defences and invaded the Egyptian Sinai. As already agreed with Israel, Britain and France then issued a joint ultimatum for Israel and Egypt to cease fire and withdraw from the canal area, which was ignored. On 5 November, Britain and France landed paratroopers along the Suez Canal. The Egyptian forces were defeated, but not before the Egyptian military blocked the canal to all shipping. It later became clear that the Israeli invasion and the subsequent Anglo-French attack had been planned beforehand by the three countries. Despite Israel, France and the UK having attained several of their military objectives, the Canal was now useless as a means of transporting cargo in the region.

The international outcry was immediate, with the UN, the US and the USSR fiercely critical of the British, French and Israeli's use of a military option. Fearing an escalation in an already troubled region and mindful of Egypt's close links with the Soviet Union, the US President, Dwight D Eisenhower, pressed the United Nations to intervene. Having warned the UK Government not to invade, Eisenhower now threatened considerable damage to the British financial system by selling the US Government's pound sterling bonds. Forced to withdraw her military presence from Suez, Britain's imperialist aspirations had been exposed. In the eyes of the world, Anthony Eden seemed both naive and deluded as the leader of a government and nation whose political and military clout was peripheral and largely inconsequential. Most historians conclude that the crisis 'signified the end of Great Britain's role as one of the world's major powers.'[43] Asked if the Suez incident demonstrated to him that Britain had lost its status at the table of global politics, Jenkins replied:

'Well, this was obvious before Suez anyway. But the Suez Crisis made it blatantly obvious. You could ignore the other things: they were pinpricks. But you couldn't ignore this. Suez brought it right out in the public forum. The message was loud and clear: "Britain as a world power is out". There were some people of course who chose not to believe it. There are some people who *still* don't believe it, but it's clear to anybody with anything between their ears. The most expensive chair in the world is a seat on the Security Council. To have a seat on the Security Council – and to be a so-called "Permanent Member" – you must have considerable defences, which includes nuclear bombs. And for that bloody seat on the Security Council, the UK Government pays millions every year to maintain the Army, the Navy, the Air Force and its nuclear arsenal – and despite the enormous cost, they consider it worth having. Because in their eyes, if they lose that seat on the Council, they have lost everything.

It's simply a matter of prestige. This seat on the Security Council is the last relic which the UK Government has linking it to its imperial past. And once that goes, the UK will become as insignificant as say, Lithuania, or some other such power. So, the UK Government insists on maintaining this seat. And why? What advantages are provided by having a presence on the Council? Well, supposedly, it gives the UK a voice in international affairs. You are still seen as some sort of an international power. But in reality, you have no power. In fact, the UK's presence on the Security Council is just an empty bloody sham. That's all it is.'

## The Queen declares Prince Charles the Prince of Wales; John marries Thelma Bridgman, moves to Cyprus and learns a thing or two

Nonetheless, with Britain's status as a colonial power in name only blatantly revealed by the Suez debacle, John Jenkins re-entered the British Army as a non-commissioned officer in the Dental Corps on 8 July 1958. He was soon posted to Cyprus. It was not solely a diminishing regard for British prestige and an increasing awareness of Welsh nationalism that were impacting upon John Jenkins at this juncture, as two events occurred which proved to have a seismic impact on his life. To close the Empire Games in Cardiff on 26 July, it was announced in a message recorded by the Queen, who was absent due to illness, that her eldest son Charles would henceforth be Prince of Wales and that he would be invested as such in a ceremony at Caernarfon 'at some point in the future'. If John Jenkins, having resumed his British Army career two weeks earlier, reacted with 'indignation' at the unexpected news, the schoolboy Prince later claimed to feel 'embarrassment and horror' as he watched the announcement on television in the headmaster's sitting room at Cheam Preparatory School in Berkshire.

The other episode which proved significant in John's life occurred on 18 October 1958, when, during a period on leave and following a courtship lasting some 18 months, he and Thelma Bridgman married at St Matthias' Church in Treharris, in the County Borough of Merthyr Tydfil. John was aged 25 and Thelma 19. John's best man was his brother, Keith. On being handed a copy of their marriage licence in 2017, John was asked if it brought back memories. 'It does, yeah,' he replied doubtfully. 'Not good ones, though.' Encouraged to throw light on the day's events, John continued:

'Well, it was reasonable enough. We came out of the church, and went straight down to the pub. There we had the usual refreshments. Both families mixed well. There were no arguments or anything like that. I never held anything against them. In fact, I had quite a good relationship with Thelma's parents.'

Had Minerva felt that Thelma was good enough for her much-loved eldest son? John chuckled, before declaring:

'Well, my mother's thoughts were that she wasn't good enough for me, of course! Naturally! I was the first born and therefore no girl would ever measure up. But on the other hand, if I had picked this girl, then there couldn't be much wrong with her! So in the end my mother gave in. She was alright... My mother was OK, yeah. She and Thelma got along reasonably well. Besides, my mother would never interfere with a decision I made like that.'

Having heard the speeches and received the toast as the happy couple, John and Thelma Jenkins left their wedding reception and headed next door to the railway station. From there they caught the train to Cardiff, from where they travelled again by train to London. On arriving at Waterloo Station, John and Thelma caught another train to Austria, where they spent 'a rather nice' fortnight on honeymoon. Asked to develop the point, John added with a glint in his eye, 'Well, that's not quite the full picture,' continuing with a chuckle that owing to the over-enthusiasm of his amorous attentions, poor Thelma had put her back out on the third day, resulting in her being rendered 'bed-ridden and prescribed rest by a local doctor'. Moreover, 'spent out' by the time they left Austria, John and Thelma 'arrived back home absolutely bloody starving'. Shortly after returning to Britain, having recovered from the 'ordeal' of their honeymoon, the couple left for Cyprus, where John was now posted.[44] Was it more fun going back into the Army a second time as a married man? 'Oh yes,' replied Jenkins, 'it was more fun, at least to begin with... Our married quarters were nice... The work I did in the Dental Centre was the same, of course, but the weather made for a relaxing time.' The experience, however, proved not to be entirely one of sun, sea and smiles, as owing to the EOKA uprising, John Jenkins' Cyprus adventure proved to be as fascinating as it was enlightening.

The British occupation of Cyprus began in 1878. Whether as a genuine attempt at redress or due to logistical and financial expediency following a long and costly war, in 1947 Britain's newly elected Labour government declared a plan to move towards greater self-government for all Britain's crown colonies. On 1 April 1955, believing that only by violent means would the island be rid of British rule, the formidable Georgios Grivas, a Cypriot who until his retirement from it in 1946 had been a high-ranking officer in the Greek Army, founded the National Organisation of Cypriot Fighters (*Ethniki Organosis Kyprion Agoniston* – EOKA). Within hours, the insurgency by EOKA against an intransigent UK Government resolute that 'Cyprus shall never have self-determination'[45] had begun. On 20 August 1955, Greece submitted a petition to the UN, requesting the application of the principle of self-determination to the people of Cyprus. By October 1955 the security situation had deteriorated, and Archbishop Makarios III, the head and chief spokesman of the Greek Orthodox Church in Cyprus and de facto leader of the Greek-Cypriot community, had become closely identified with the insurgency. On 10 January 1956, the British Government ordered a battalion of 1,600 paratroopers to Cyprus to deal with the growing number of guerrilla attacks on British military and police bases.[46] The arrival of the British troops only served to intensify EOKA's campaign. It reached a peak following the arrest and deportation of Archbishop Makarios to the Seychelles on 9 March. In response to this exiling, EOKA launched a series of guerrilla attacks that soon soaked up a large number of British troops in counter-insurgency operations. Makarios was released from exile after a year, although he was forbidden to return to Cyprus. He went instead to Athens, where he was rapturously received.

Asked to reveal what life was like as a member of the British forces during the EOKA campaign, John Jenkins discussed the subject at length.

'We lived in Famagusta but I worked in Dhekelia, which is twenty miles away. I didn't have a car, so to get to work I used public transport, which was forbidden. But every morning I'd wait in a little café, and in there would be all these Cypriots. And as soon as they realised, after a week or two, that I wasn't going to harm anybody, or shout or scream, and I was just coming in and having a cup of lemon juice or whatever, then the bus driver would be sitting there, and he was a nice chap. He was friendly and all the rest of it. So what he used to do was take me up to work, drop me off and then come and wait outside for me when my shift was finished.

Anyway, one day, I was coming out from work and this Army person saw me and he said, "Where are you going?" So I said, "I'm getting the bus to go home." He said, "You can't do that! You can't get on that that bus, it's full of Cypriots." I said, "Well, what's wrong with that?" "Oh," he said, "it's against regulations – and it's not the done thing." I said, "Well, it's the only way I can get home tonight, so tough." But they soon put a bloody stop to it. They didn't like it at all. "Oh, you mustn't fraternise with the natives!"'

Despite receiving a non-official warning from the British authorities, John refused to distance himself from his Cypriot friends. 'I wanted to make my *own* mind up about these things,' he later clarified:

'They were just ordinary Cypriots that I knew. I mean, that bus driver, who would wait for me after to work to take me home – well, I got to know him; just by chatting and passing the time of day, either in the café or as we travelled on the bus. And then one day he said, "How do you get on with your neighbours?" "Oh, not too bad," I said. "We don't bother with each other much." "Oh," he said, "righto." And later that day, he came down with his wife and family, carrying this bloody huge cake; with all these wedding bells and Christ knows what on it. It was a present from the local Cypriots. I thought it was wonderful.

So over the coming weeks they would visit. They taught me one or two expressions in Greek and a song or two, and I would sing them and really enjoy learning about Greek-Cypriot culture. And what happened? The neighbours complained, didn't they? The neighbours, of course, were all service people, and they didn't like all these Cypriots coming around to my place. And I thought, "God almighty. No wonder we lost the bloody colonies. With attitudes like that, how can we hold onto anything? These people are lovely, friendly; and not at all like the demons pushed by the newspapers." And yet these British servicemen, despite being an occupying force in Cyprus, didn't want to know.'

Did this attitude reflect a stubborn single-mindedness on his part? 'All I wanted,' John replied in a tone of firm exasperation, 'was to make my own mind up about this. And to achieve that,' he continued:

'I needed – and wanted to have – *both* sides of the argument. And I was *getting* both sides of the argument, but nobody else was. Not that my Greek-Cypriot friends gave me any information about how EOKA was carrying out its activities. We never discussed whether they were sympathetic to EOKA or not. We never discussed that. Well, we couldn't. To do so would have involved us over-stepping the bounds of our friendship, as it were. On both sides – from their point of view and from mine.'

It wasn't long before John Jenkins saw a facet of the British Army which left him feeling distinctly uneasy.

'There was this chap I knew. He was in the Air Force. He was a nice chap, and having got married, he'd managed get for himself a nice little bungalow in the middle of this village. Well, one day, he was sitting on his veranda, drinking his usual beverage, and these troops came running in with bayonets and all the rest of it. It was suspected that there was somebody in the house who the British thought was nasty. And they'd come to winkle him out. On speaking to this RAF chap, they said, "What the hell are you doing here?" He said, "I live here." "WHAT?" They went bloody mad – and they forced him to move, didn't they?'

But if the raid on the home of the RAF serviceman surprised John, the attitude and the actions of the British Army as the EOKA campaign intensified shocked and appalled him.

'As a member of the British Forces, I am ashamed to say that I was soon astonished at the behaviour of the British troops. Where a short time before, a soldier found drunk in a Cypriot village would have woken up in a bed, having been helped up and looked after; due to the attitude and strong-arm tactics of the British Army, all that changed very quickly.'

Asked to throw light on what led to the breakdown in relations between the Cypriots and the occupying British Forces, John declared thoughtfully:

> 'When searching for a believed suspect, soldiers would enter a village, roughly treat the villagers, damage their homes – and to get a reaction from the men, even touch their wives' breasts. It was appalling: pure thuggery and totally counter-productive.'[47]

It might not have been immediately apparent, but the lesson that John learned – of the importance of winning over the hearts and minds of those whose support was required to either further or suppress an insurgency against the state – would remain with him. Nevertheless, as the situation in Cyprus worsened, a political settlement was sought to bring the conflict to an end. If many hoped, with the discussions underway, that finally the bloodshed would end, Jenkins was soon reminded of the entrenched approach to repressing outbreaks of insurrection within the colonies still prevalent within sections of the British military:

> 'There was always this lurking thought that if the military men had had their way, there would have been an absolute bloodbath on the island. I remember some general or other saying, as the political dialogue began to reach an agreement, "If we could have just a fortnight free of the political interference, we could sort these bastards out." Well, if *that's* the sort of attitude you are going into a political conference with, you're not going to get very far – and they didn't.'

Despite the entrenched attitudes of some within the British military, the process of reaching a political accord involved compromise. The population of Cyprus was 78% Greek. Rather than wanting independence, many of the Greek Cypriots aspired to *enosis* (union) with Greece. The Greek Government supported this aspiration, but it was flatly opposed by Turkey, who espoused the cause of the other 22% of the island's population, the Turkish Cypriots. Finally, in 1958, the Greek Cypriots accepted that Turkey would never agree to *enosis* with Greece, and settled instead for independence under a power-sharing deal that gave the presidency to Archbishop Makarios. The British agreed to leave Cyprus, if they could retain bases at Dhekelia and Akrotiri.

On 1 March 1959, Archbishop Makarios returned from exile to an unprecedented reception in Nicosia, with almost two thirds of the adult Greek Cypriot population there to welcome him back to Cyprus. Presidential elections were held on 13 December 1959. Makarios received two thirds of the vote, defeating his rival, the lawyer Ioannis (aka John) Clerides. In his victory, Archbishop Makarios became the political leader of the whole of Cyprus, as well as the leader of the Greek-Cypriot community.[48] Finally, on 16 August 1960, the island of Cyprus became an independent republic after 82 years of British rule.

Still in Cyprus when Archbishop Makarios returned from exile, John Jenkins was impressed and somewhat entertained as the events unfolded.

'Well, the amusing thing was, when the EOKA campaign ended and the insurgency had been successful, Makarios promised to bring the EOKA army down from the mountains. This he did. But here's the *important* thing. The British authorities and the world's media had been led to believe that thousands were involved in all this. OK, perhaps thousands *had* been involved in the EOKA campaign in some guise or another, but Makarios brought down these EOKA activists from the mountains in a bus! A bus! The actual activists themselves could all be put in a single bus! And I realised then how many troops it had taken to control these people in that bus. And *that* was a lesson I learned very quickly: it doesn't take a lot of people to upset a lot more people! I realised then that you don't need *that* many for an insurgency to be successful. What you need are a few dedicated and committed souls. You don't need hordes of people. I don't even believe that those people who came down with Makarios in the bus were actively involved in the violence per se. It included the organisers, and those involved in training the activists. These people, if you like, were the soul of EOKA. And they did a damn good job, I must say. Just by being in Cyprus at this time, I learnt a great deal.'

John Jenkins also learnt another valuable and wholly unsavoury lesson in Cyprus: that all is fair in love and war, and that the authorities will apparently stop at nothing to see their political will enforced:

'What isn't well known is that the political compromise which was reached in Cyprus was far from simple. You see, Archbishop Makarios, as the head of the Greek Orthodox Church, was a Christian. And he opposed the idea of power-sharing with the Turks, who were, of course, Muslims. And so Archbishop Makarios would not sign the agreement which allowed the island to be handed over by the British. Now, as far as the British were concerned, he *had* to sign this agreement, but he refused to. And so what did the British authorities do about it? They hired a villa and they said: "Look, we've hired a villa for you, where you can hold a party, just to unwind and relax. So we'll leave you to it... and we'll see you in a few days." And so, as far as he was aware, they left him. But this party that Makarios and some followers gave included a number of small boys. And it also included, although Makarios didn't know it, a member of the British Special Branch. And this Special Branch officer secretly took photos of Makarios in a sexually compromising situation with these young boys. The next day this SB officer went to Makarios and said, "These photos are not public yet, and if you sign the document, they never will be." They had all the evidence they needed to blackmail him. So Makarios signed. So there you are: that is British diplomacy at its very best! Was it a good idea to blackmail him? Because having blackmailed him and got him to sign that agreement, it brought peace to the island. So, was that a good thing or a bad thing? It's one of these moral issues that you can discuss, forever and ever, and never get an answer.'[49]

But surely, the moral issue and ethical question hinged on the fact that Makarios, the Christian Leader of the Greek Orthodox Church, should *not* have been sexually interfering with young boys in *any* event?

'But if he hadn't been, there would *never* have been an agreement signed, and there would have been more people getting killed left, right and centre. And it wasn't their business anyway. The British should have left him alone. But there you are. They knew what would discredit him in the eyes of his followers – and he had many followers.'

If the allegedly shameful actions of the British authorities ensured the conflict in Cyprus was brought to an end – by whatever means, fair or foul – what further political lessons did John learn by being in Cyprus during the time of EOKA's campaign for self-determination?

'Being in Cyprus definitely impacted on me. You see, when I was in Cyprus, it was towards the end of the campaign by EOKA. But it hadn't reached the end at the time – it was still ongoing. So I was able to see for myself what happens when a colony decides to free itself, and what the result is and what the attitude is, and so on. It proved to be very interesting. I learned a lot. Particularly as I had Cypriot friends as well. They weren't members of any subversive organisation as such. But they could give me another attitude; another approach from the static Army one. The Army perspective, I'm afraid, is always based on the application of force to a great degree. I mean, I can remember being in the sergeants' mess when some industrial dispute broke out concerning the miners. And as we were watching the news which was addressing this item, this sergeant major starts ranting: "Ah, they want the 1st Battalion Parachute Regiment down there, with their bayonets fixed. That would get the buggers to work." And I thought, "Well, what sort of people think things like this? This is a fascist idea: drive them to work with a bloody bayonet." Of course, they're not *all* like that in the Army. But that type of attitude is somewhat prevalent, I would say. Yeah, definitely. But it would be in all authoritarian regimes everywhere, I think... They automatically have to back up their own approach – which is basically that *everything* is enforceable.'

Had this realisation chimed with a better understanding of developments on the global political stage? 'Yes,' Jenkins confirmed; adding:

'I was increasingly, by now, interested in world events. Well, I was interested because I was in an army, wasn't I? And I was interested in what was happening because this was the time when all these places which had been subject to British rule were getting their freedom. India was free. British rule in Kenya was being challenged, due to the Mau Mau Uprising, and in 1963 Kenya finally won its independence, despite the brutality of the British. With the Labour Government from 1964 keen to cut defence spending wherever possible, there was talk of withdrawing from all commitments 'east of Suez', And so, in 1967, British troops left the port city of Aden, which had been seen as strategically important. So by the mid-1960s, Britain had granted independence to all but a few far-flung remnants of the British Empire. All these countries which had been ruled by Britain were all becoming free. And despite the pressures, they were all making out to some degree. But the important thing was that none of them *ever* wanted to come back. None of them asked if they could be controlled by Britain again. None of them!'[50]

Did all of this contribute to him developing a greater sympathy with Welsh political nationalism? Again, Jenkins confirmed this to be the case.

'At this point, I was beginning to think more about Wales' position within the Union. I was also reading more, and beginning to *understand* more. And to get more than one point of view. That is the important thing: to get more than one point of view. Both points of view are valid. But some points of view are more valid than others.'

Nonetheless, if John's milieu continued to mould his political ideals, he was in for a surprise if he believed that the volatile situation in Cyprus had ended once independence was granted. One evening, as the 'usual scuffles' which predated the peace agreement continued between the erstwhile occupiers and the local population, Jenkins by chance bumped into a couple of Greek-Cypriot lads as he walked alone to the private accommodation he shared with Thelma in Famagusta. Following a brief verbal exchange, Jenkins ascertained that they were EOKA supporters. 'They didn't beat me up too badly,' John chuckled.

'It wasn't too bad – and I understood the reasons for it. I was a member of the occupying force as far as they were concerned. I mean, that was it. What I thought about things and the way I had to dress to earn a living was another story. These young lads wouldn't know about my thoughts, my friendships, any more than the police there would. Neither these two EOKA lads, nor the police, were aware of my sympathies for what EOKA had achieved.'

But owing to the cordial relations Jenkins enjoyed with 'several individuals' in the Greek-Cypriot community, had he ever suspected that he might be the subject of monitoring by either Army intelligence, or the British intelligence services? 'No,' John replied trenchantly. 'I mean, the thought of any member of the Army, particularly a lowly member such as I was, being involved in any way shape or form with politics, would *never* have occurred to them.'

## Anger over Tryweryn continues, the census figures are published and John is posted to Germany

If John Jenkins re-joined the British Army in 1958 believing that the flooding of Cwm Tryweryn might be prevented, little in the coming months gave him cause for hope. His efforts to gauge the political picture in Wales indicated that all further constitutional attempts to prevent Cwm Tryweryn being submerged had failed. In response, Gwynfor Evans, the President of Plaid Cymru and a lifelong pacifist – in what some suspected was a cynical attempt to appease the younger, more radical members of the party – appointed Emrys Roberts, the party's junior Organising Secretary, to consider methods and preparations for a campaign of 'direct action' over the Tryweryn issue. On hearing of this development during visits home in 1959, John maintained the belief that all was *perhaps* not lost.

Yet despite Roberts' appointment, within weeks, Gwynfor Evans had a change of heart. With the Plaid Cymru leader's fourteen-year leadership beginning to flounder, at a meeting of a Plaid Cymru sub-committee – and without consulting the wider party – it was decided to make a U-turn and reject support for a law-breaking campaign. If that was not bad enough as far as Jenkins and others increasingly inclined to a campaign of direct action over the Tryweryn issue were concerned, the party continued to surreptitiously maintain that suggestions concerning passive protest *would* be considered. The more militant-minded party members began to smell a rat.

Did Gwynfor Evans fit Jenkins' description of a politician blessed with the chameleonic ability to change his allegiances and his principles and to rid himself of embarrassing 'baggage' to further his and his party's electoral appeal? By way of reply, John was robust. While Jenkins harboured some respect for Gwynfor Evans for having remained true to his cultural roots, it was nonetheless Evans whom John believed was most responsible for having failed to galvanise the necessary effective opposition required to prevent Cwm Tryweryn being drowned. It was Evans, Jenkins maintained, who had most to answer for, having led Welsh opposition 'into battle with one arm tied behind our back'.

The 1961 census figures compounded Jenkins' fears that the cultural identity of Wales faced a grievous threat, and also that no effective opposition existed to counter it. The figures revealed to John 'a terrible story' that the Welsh-speaking heartlands 'were being diluted' as a consequence of two striking factors: that 1) native Welsh-speakers were leaving due to a lack of employment opportunities, while 2) the area's picturesque landscape and 'safe' environment were also attracting inward migration from areas of England, predominately by those who were retired and so relatively affluent. The result, Jenkins later declared, was both a threat to the linguistic homogeneity of a Welsh-speaking region, and a change in an area's traditional electoral voting pattern. Yet if the census figures proved a source of rancour for John, why did he feel *so* badly let down by Gwynfor Evans and the Plaid Cymru hierarchy over the Cwm Tryweryn situation? By way of response, Jenkins retorted:

'Well, Plaid Cymru was aiming to show, yet again, what a bad show it all was and how Plaid [Cymru] occupied the moral high ground. They did this by doing two things. 1) In November 1956, they paraded in the streets of Liverpool singing hymns. I don't quite know who this was supposed to impress, but it didn't impress the authorities of Liverpool! 2) Because the party leadership could sense the growing anger among the Young Turks in the party, and were increasingly fearful that these Young Turks were determined that something was going to be done, Gwynfor Evans took evasive action by installing Emrys Roberts as the organiser in Cardiff. They put him in an office and said, "Right. Emrys is going to organise the activities surrounding the opposition to Tryweryn." So most people, certainly most of the *young* people, sat back and thought, "Oh, good. Emrys knows how to organise things. Emrys is well known; he's polite and very well respected. He's *just* the person to orchestrate the necessary protest." But unfortunately – and Emrys and I have spoken about this – Emrys discovered soon enough that he was constrained by party politics; that he was unable, in fact, to do anything! Every proposal put forward was rejected for one reason or another. But by doing nothing, he fulfilled the reason for which he was put there in the first place: to *appear* to be doing something, while in fact, doing nothing at all! And what happened? By the time people realised that nothing was going to be done, it was too bloody late. The work to ready the valley for flooding was underway and progressing.'

Has Jenkins forgiven Gwynfor Evans for the position he took over the Tryweryn issue? 'No, I haven't,' John replied resolutely.

'But it isn't for me to forgive him. It's the people of Tryweryn who have to forgive him, because it was due to his attitude that they lost their homes. If Gwynfor Evans had given them the leadership they were entitled to, it would never have happened. I knew damn well that they were seething in south Wales over it, because I was in contact with some people in south Wales who were determined to act over the valley's flooding. It really would *not* have taken much to get hundreds up there. These people could have easily have prevented the work from continuing. And how? Simply by the occupants refusing to leave their homes, and through others preventing the work from being done. But of course, we were told that Emrys was organising it all and that people should submit their protest proposals to him. But the point about Tryweryn is that when the dust had settled and Gwynfor was left alone with his pacifist principles, everybody else was gone, because their houses were demolished. And that is something that you cannot forgive.'

John was clearly preoccupied with events back home in Wales at this point. But in relation to his own immediate domestic situation, how had life been affected by being in Cyprus during this period, and how had Thelma taken to being an Army wife?

'Well, I have happy memories of being in Cyprus. My eldest son, Vaughan, was born there, in Dhekelia, on 7 October 1959. But to be truthful, it was also quite a sad situation, because normally when you had kids, you had Granny around. Both Thelma and me were from the South Wales Valleys, and we were used to having your father and uncles and all the rest of it to turn to. Of course, when we had Vaughan in Cyprus, there was no one there to help us. No one to turn to for advice. We didn't have any family whatsoever. So Thelma and I had to sort of work together and make up for it. And it was a bit of a job. With me out at work every day, she did get a bit lonely. It did put our relationship under quite a bit of strain.'

Deciding that a change of scenery might help matters, and with the number of British military personnel on Cyprus being scaled back, in the summer of 1962 – following a short holiday visiting family in Wales – John Jenkins was posted back to Germany. Whereas in Cyprus fraternising with the Cypriots had been frowned upon, John quickly learned that the British Army took an altogether lighter view of such interaction with regards to the Germans. 'It was,' he declared ruefully, 'a different kettle of fish altogether.' Jenkins discerned that the matter hinged on one thing: 'pure racism'. The English, he reasoned, 'like the Germans, are Anglo-Saxons, aren't they? We are talking about cousins here.'

It was not the only realisation about the British Army that John experienced on moving to Germany. Sergeant John Jenkins quickly established that despite the Army's recent experience in Cyprus, its tried and tested approach would continue. 'The British Army,' began Jenkins, 'really is the last stronghold of violence and prejudice.' He continued:

'And I can understand the need for it in one sense, because we are talking about discipline. We are talking about people dying, and all that. Therefore, there *must* be discipline. But the sort of discipline the British Army was talking about was bloody ridiculous. I mean, one of the things I had to learn to do on becoming a sergeant was to be able to march people round the square. To fall them in and all that bloody nonsense. And on being taught this, I can remember being out on parade, and before it began, the Sergeant Major apologising. "I am sorry about this, lads," he said. "I know it's the atomic age and all the rest of it. But as far as the Army is concerned, we are still marching in squares to repel the cavalry. And that is what we have got to learn now in the next two weeks." I thought then, "God preserve us!" You know – to have the Sergeant Major apologising because we were expected to keep to the procedures of two hundred years ago, which is what it was. But there you are… The Army was very, *very* slow to change.'

Could it be put down solely to intransigence? What other factors might be considered problematic in the British Army's approach to doing things? 'Well, they are all too busy guarding their backsides. That was the trouble with them,' he reasoned; adding:

'All this business about "efficiency" – they're just protecting their own interests! That was *really* the motivating force. They could be called upon tomorrow to go and do this and that – and they would, without a second thought. But the lengths that senior sergeant majors go to to try and become officers is unbelievable. But there you are. I mean, I understand ambition. But I've also seen people stamped all over; and how some have suffered because they've got in the way of a person's ambition. God, these people would sell their own grandmother! I mean there are some excellent people in the Army. They do a good job, and so on. But God Almighty, it doesn't half attract some idiots. But I've seen this attitude in a number of walks of life, and I can't stand it. In my experience, very few people are on the level. Those that are, I've got time for. But there's another lot, and these people will do *anything* to further their career, never mind what it takes. I haven't any time at all for those people.'

With the Cold War at its height and the threat of nuclear attack ever-present, was Jenkins provided with training and a plan of action outlining how the families would be provided for should matters escalate and war break out? 'Well, I was stationed some 120 miles south of Hamburg in Bielefeld, which at one time was an SS training camp,' he replied.

> 'There, we were told of plans that were afoot. If the Russians did invade, the Army would go here and there and all this transport would be laid on for them. And somebody got up and said, "Oh, what about the families?" "Oh, there will be transport laid on for them," this chap replied. But he said it in such a manner, that I thought "Ah, I bet there won't be. There won't be bloody transport provided for ordinary servicemen, and for women and kids. It's men with guns who'll need this transport." So I went back home and devised a bloody escape plan. If war did break out, if Russia did invade, I was going to rush out, go to a pre-arranged spot, seize pre-arranged transport – which was a jeep – get Thelma and the boys, get the provisions aboard and we'd be off. We'd get out on our own. The plan was we'd go down through Europe. I wasn't going to bloody hang around and rely on this lot! I thought, "To hell with them." They wouldn't have cared less about the women and kids.'

Was this escape plan something that he and Thelma discussed? 'Yes, it was,' Jenkins affirmed. 'By this time, Thelma was almost as skeptical about these people and what they amounted to as I was. She understood the snobbery of it all.' Nevertheless, despite the couple's mounting reservations concerning life in an Army marriage, Thelma and John did have something to celebrate: on 5 October 1963, their second son, Rhodri, was born.

Back in Wales, the ever-widening gulf between the constitutional and non-constitutional wings of Plaid Cymru still threatened to split the party. At the annual conference in August 1962, the two opposing factions – on one side, the *Gwynforiaid*; and on the other, the self-styled activists – competed for ascendancy. Following another tempestuous debate, a compromise was reached. No one, it was agreed, 'was to take action in the name of Plaid Cymru, but members were free to undertake specific action when it was a matter of conscience or conviction.'[51]

## Welsh militant protest at the Tryweryn reservoir site and the Clywedog Reservoir Bill is passed in Parliament

It was not long before action was taken. Shortly after 10 p.m. on 22 September 1962, Police Constables Williams and Jones, having 'received reports of loiterers on the Tryweryn site', found David Barnard Walters, a 22-year-old colliery worker from Bargoed and David Glyn Pritchard, a 25-year-old electrical planning engineer from New Tredegar, 'in possession of certain tools'. Following an inspection of the site, it was discovered that a thousand gallons of oil, stored in an electrical transformer, had been released. The two men were then taken to Bala police station for questioning. There, the following afternoon, each finally admitted that their real motive for visiting the construction site had been 'to put the [site's] electricity supply out of action'. On being charged jointly under the 1882 Electric Lighting Act, Pritchard and Walters contacted Elystan Morgan, the Wrexham solicitor and member of the Plaid Cymru party executive, to act as their legal representative. Significantly, in an era when the perception – particulary within the English-based media – was that Plaid Cymru was comprised of Welsh-speakers from the cultural heartlands of west and north-west Wales, both Pritchard and Walters were from the socialist and predominantly English-speaking industrial valleys of south-east Wales, neither was a Welsh-speaker and Pritchard, to the added surprise of some, was even a member of the Plaid Cymru executive.

In Bala Shire Hall Assizes on 3 October, each man pleaded guilty to the charges against him. In defending Pritchard and Walters, Elystan Morgan[52] informed the court that the two accused were men of an 'idealistic frame of mind, and deeply concerned, if not obsessed,' with issues of principle. Their action, Morgan added, was 'conceived from a sense of duty' and undertaken in response to the overwhelming consensus of Welsh opinion against Liverpool's 'acquisition' of Cwm Tryweryn. It was a view endorsed by Gwynfor Evans, who remarked to waiting journalists that it should be the English authorities in the dock facing charges rather than the two accused. Pritchard and Walters – the first men to be apprehended for striking a blow in the name of Welsh nationalist protest since the opening of the Claerwen Dam ten years before – were each fined £50, ordered to pay £26 costs and given three months in which to pay; although, in the event, the fines were paid by well-wishers when Walters and Pritchard emerged from court. Nevertheless, just two days after Pritchard and Walters were fined and despite the controversy surrounding the flooding of Cwm Tryweryn – which was now a landscape transformed owing to the wheels of heavy machinery – it was announced that the River Severn Resources Committee intended to flood Cwm Clywedog in Montgomeryshire. On Christmas Eve 1963, and coinciding with an increase in security at the Tryweryn reservoir construction site, media reports announced that the offices of Birmingham Corporation had received a warning letter purporting to be from *Meibion Glyndŵr* (Sons of Glyndŵr). Birmingham Corporation received the letter because the authority had emerged as the likely leading sponsor of a Bill to flood Cwm Clywedog.

Two months later, on 10 February 1963, during near blizzard conditions and having decided to operate under the name *Mudiad Amddiffyn Cymru* (the Movement to Defend Wales) 22-year-old student Emyr Llywelyn Jones, 27-year-old café owner Owain Williams and 19-year-old former RAF military policeman John Albert Jones attacked the electrical transformer at the Tryweryn reservoir construction site with explosives. A week later, Emyr Llywelyn Jones was arrested and later sentenced to a year's imprisonment. The manner of his arrest has been the subject of discussion ever since; with it claimed that Emyr Llywelyn Jones' dropping of a handkerchief with the incriminating letter 'E' embroidered in a corner near the scene of the Tryweryn protest, along with other incriminating behaviour, provided investigating officers with all the evidence required to lead them to Jones, a renowned Welsh-language activist. Speculation that the widely-respected Emyr Llywelyn Jones wished to emulate his hero, Saunders Lewis, in receiving a prison term in the name of Welsh nationalist protest has only added to the intrigue surrounding his arrest and conviction. Whatever the truth, Emyr Llywelyn Jones' two accomplices, Owain Williams and John Albert Jones, having undertaken a further protest involving explosives on the day of his sentencing, were also soon arrested. Williams received a year's custodial sentence and John Albert Jones was placed on probation for a year. Unknown at the time, the three Tryweryn saboteurs had been trained in the use of explosives by David Pritchard.

With the three Tryweryn saboteurs behind bars, opposition to the proposed Bill to flood Cwm Clywedog gathered momentum. Yet again, Plaid Cymru was at pains to prove its effectiveness as a political force. But with the nationalist party of Wales hoping that sticking to constitutional practice would see it prevent Cwm Clywedog from being submerged, the party faced criticism from sections of the media, which claimed that Plaid Cymru was riven over support for the adoption of 'direct action' to oppose such issues. Even within the party ranks, John Jenkins declared, 'People were saying, "Oh, there's no need for all this nonsense. We can prevent Clywedog being drowned through the ballot box. Or through the courts, or whatever."' So, Jenkins added pointedly, 'The party decided to test this out and act along strictly constitutional lines.' With three farms – totalling 615 acres – facing submersion, in early April 1963 the Clywedog sub-committee devised a new policy. With subscriptions raised by party members, it announced its decision to take out a 25-year lease on 2.6 acres of land at the heart of the threatened valley. Over the following weeks and months, the land was divided into 75 units which were then sublet between groups of people, with donations of varying amounts from sympathisers. This involved some 200 people from Wales, and others from as far afield as Australia, Canada, Iceland, Germany and the United States, who were hostile to the scheme. One of the participants in the scheme was Sergeant John Barnard Jenkins of the British Army Dental Corps. The action was based on a stipulation in land law which stated that any person in possession of land, or property on land (inhabited or not), which was desired by a Corporation, had to be allowed to voice his or her opinion for or against a takeover at a public enquiry, irrespective of the owner's place of residence. This, however, was not the only protection it was hoped the law might afford. It was also claimed that leaseholders had a legal guardianship of the land, and as such, trespassers could be prevented from gaining access. A legal opportunity was thus provided to prevent surveyors gaining access. To counter this, an amendment to the law was issued, stating that it would no longer be necessary to call witnesses and interested parties to the enquiry. The decision caused outrage in the nationalist community. On 31 July 1963, thirty days after Owain Williams was imprisoned, the Clywedog Reservoir Bill was passed by Parliament. When later outlining his thoughts, having followed the granting of parliamentary approval while stationed in Germany, John exclaimed:

'They simply changed the law, which had been in place to offer a landowner protection and the opportunity to voice their concerns on such a takeover. This was the final thing which convinced me that constitutionally speaking, you can't win against people who own all judicial eventualities. These people make the law and if you interfere with it, however unjust that law may be, you are breaking the law. Yet they can amend it in their favour as they wish. So while they can simply circumvent or change a law to suit their political objective, how can you conduct a fight, and campaign against them legally? You can't, because they own the whole of the legal system.

We tried it their way. We tried to use the law correctly to oppose the measure and the UK authorities simply moved the goalposts. So that was a little lesson to me: that those who control the levers of power and the law can change it whenever they wish. In which case, there's no point in attacking them legally: there must be other ways of doing it. These are the people, after all, who formed an empire. And nice people don't form empires; and they certainly don't maintain empires. But these people had, so we were not dealing with "nice people". It was obvious to me that we lived on their "goodwill", and that is *not* a good place to be. But it proved a bit of a job to explain that to the leaders of Plaid Cymru, who kept on about the need to try and shame them in order to hold the moral high ground. I realised that obtaining the moral high ground meant *nothing* when opposing those in authority. Power is *all* that counts to these people.'

Asked for his opinion with regards the protest undertaken by David Pritchard and David Walters, John Jenkins remarked that although it was 'well intentioned, it ultimately achieved very little.' As for the militant strike undertaken by Emyr Llywelyn Jones, Owain Williams and John Albert Jones, if there were some who sympathised with their symbolic, moral and restrained stand, John Jenkins was not one of them.

'If it achieved anything, it confirmed the belief that the Welsh people are quite useless and impractical, and that they are dreamers and idealists who are unable to apply any sort of sanctions. There was this strange feeling that they had to be seen as martyrs or whatever, like Saunders Lewis had been over Penyberth in the 1930s. And to do this, they had to occupy the high ground. Therefore, you had a bunch of people who were prepared to do things, but having done so, who then wanted to go and give themselves up – as if this made any difference to the authorities! It put them on the high ground, yes, but that's all it did. It didn't do anything about what was happening to the land in the meantime. Nor did it make any difference to what the people of the doomed valley were experiencing in the meantime.

It did nothing at all about that. And there were others who believed that if they could demonstrate to the public what was really happening, then the authorities would be shamed into stopping this activity. Again, this was a total fallacy. It simply wasn't true. The authorities didn't care who knew what. They weren't bothered. If they were bothered, they wouldn't have flooded Tryweryn and the other Welsh valleys in the first place. OK, in defence of these people who undertook protest over Tryweryn: it did give a lead to people and it also gave some people the idea that *something* was being done. But had these people not been very badly let down by Plaid Cymru, their protests would not have been necessary in the first place.'

Whether the arrival of another addition to the Jenkins family prompted John to further re-evaluate his cultural heritage; or whether it was because of the precarious position of the world in view of the nuclear situation; or indeed, if John's subconscious thoughts increasingly turning to Wales was born of an escalating resolve to defend his homeland – whatever the reason or reasons, in the spring of 1964 Jenkins wrote to the War Office and requested a transfer either to Wales, or within close proximity of it. His reason for doing so, he explained, was that he wished his son Vaughan to receive his school education through the medium of Welsh. To its credit, John later conceded, 'because the Army believes in people looking after their kids and doing what you can for their future,' his request for a transfer was accepted and Jenkins soon received notice that he would, at a date to be determined, be posted to Saighton Camp near Chester. John claims that the transfer request put paid to any further promotion in the Army.

'Because once something like that goes in it's clear that your heart is not in the right place! Your cultural allegiance is not perhaps as it should be. It demonstrates that you are not a British Empire person, and it also suggests you feel a certain disdain for the jingoism associated with it. So the price I paid was further progress and promotion within the Army. That was the price to pay and I paid it, and I didn't give a damn.'

Thelma was happy to return to Wales and fully supported her husband's decision concerning their son Vaughan receiving a Welsh-language education. In July 1964, Thelma, Vaughan and Rhodri relocated to south Wales, to live with her parents. It would still be some nine months before John's tour of duty in Germany ended. The decision to leave before John ensured that Vaughan attended Ysgol Gynradd Gymraeg Pont Siôn Norton in Pontypridd from the beginning of the autumn term in September 1964 – his first year of schooling. It coincided with the river at the Tryweryn reservoir construction site first being let into the dam on 1 September. Remaining in Germany, Jenkins moved out of married quarters and lived in the barracks.

John spent the summer of 1964 continuing to attend to his Dental Centre duties at Bielefeld. By this point, however, having held the rank of sergeant for some time, Jenkins' responsibilities within the Dental Corps had 'increased quite significantly'. John explained:

'Along with keeping a stock of supplies and equipment at Bielefeld, as part of an inspection team which worked independently, I would visit Dental Centres in the other British Army camps throughout West Germany. This was to ensure that all the British Army camps were receiving the right equipment and sending back the wrong equipment. You can imagine what the Army is like about paperwork! So I was tasked with making sure all the paperwork was checked properly and that it corresponded, basically because these dental supplies involved the distribution of money, and the price of things. Therefore, it was important that these checks were done properly. But another important aspect of my role was to ensure that the standard of dental treatment that service personnel were receiving was 'across the board'. This was achieved by monitoring treatment feedback sheets and complaints forms, etc. I had quite a lot of freedom, really; and being alone and out and about so much enabled me to combine these visits to the other Army camps with also visiting places of interest, such as the Nazi concentration camp, Bergen-Belsen.'

As well as driving alone through the appealing German countryside, John was also travelling back and forth via car and ferry from Germany to the UK, via Boulogne. Also, as a result of a scheme whereby the families of Army personnel stationed in Germany could receive extended visits from relatives, Tom and Minerva stayed with John 'for a few weeks'. It was the couple's first and only trip abroad. One day, John took his ageing parents for a sightseeing trip around northern Germany. As the Welsh touring party traversed their way through the open country, Tom marvelled at 'the villas and sizeable dwellings' dotted spaciously amid the surrounding hillsides. Alone with his thoughts for some moments, Tom finally turned to John and asked, "But where do the poor people live?" To Tom's considerable surprise, John replied, "That *is* where the poor people live." Asked to take up the story, Jenkins continued:

'Well, he nearly fell through the bloody floor. "What?" "Yes," I assured him. "If you come out here every morning at about 6 o'clock, you see them going to work." He couldn't believe it, because as far as my father was concerned, "workers live here and people with money live there". But then, as a proud working man, he couldn't understand how narrow the social gap was between employers and employees in Germany when compared to Britain either. In Germany, both mixed quite happily together. You see, it's quite normal for a German employer to give a little party for his employees at the local pub; for them all to sit and have a meal together. And it got me thinking about how that could never happen in Britain, because the gap between the classes is too large. In Germany, the poor man is quite at home in the smartest hotel. The Germans I spoke to couldn't understand why there's so much bloody trouble in Britain around ideas of social structure and hierarchy. Their attitude seemed entirely different.'

But if John's sociological horizons were broadening still further, one visit home in October 1964 would change John Jenkins' life forever, and see him embark on a journey which placed him – at least in the eyes of some – among the great revolutionary political figures of the twentieth century.

## CHAPTER 3

# If you want the revolution to be successful, you must bide your time

## Jenkins is invited for a chat

In early October 1964, during a period on leave from the Army, John and the Jenkins family spent a week with some of Thelma's relations at their home in Quakers Yard. The visit coincided with the school half-term holiday and the period immediately preceding the UK General Election, which was held on 15 October. Canvassing alongside and on behalf of Dr Phil Williams, the Plaid Cymru candidate in the Caerphilly constituency, was David Walters, who in September 1962 had been arrested with David Pritchard and later fined for releasing oil from an electrical transformer at the Tryweryn reservoir construction site. Nonetheless, with the 1964 General Election just days away, Dr Williams informed David Walters that he wanted to visit an address in Quakers Yard where there was 'a fella interested in helping in the elections and the Plaid.'[53] Asked to provide his account of what next transpired, Walters continued:

> 'So I went with Phil; not particularly to meet John, but because Phil was going to meet John. And that was the first time that I met John Jenkins. I remember me and his wife, Thelma, talking about John's car, because he had a German car that he'd brought back with him. I think it was an open top. A lovely car, as I remember, which you couldn't get over here. Anyway, Phil and John were chatting about the election and how John felt the Plaid Cymru campaign was going – that sort of thing. Then, over the

election period, Phil and me met him once or twice again, because he was back home for a few weeks. We didn't meet him deliberately, it just sort of happened. Well, again we listened to John talking about the election, and how he felt the Plaid Cymru campaign was being run – but also, how he felt about the *general* picture in Wales. I remember listening to the way he spoke and being struck by how well he expressed himself.

Well, I don't know how Dave Pritchard got to know John, but the South Wales Valleys, where we're all from, is a small, close-knit community so he may well have known *of* him. But anyway, having told Dave about meeting John and what we'd discussed, Dave said to me a day or so later, "What do you think?" "I don't know much about him," I said, "but he seems a genuine, level-headed guy." I knew, of course, having discussed the fact that he was home on leave, about John's military experience, and so I said, "Look, Dave, he has military service. He'd be the ideal person that we're looking for, with his military background." I suppose I was thinking about his training and the information he might have. And Dave said, "OK. We'll have a go at him." They were the exact words he used, "We'll have a go at him." Meaning, "let's see what he's like."

So Dave Pritchard got in touch with his MAC contacts in the north and explained that we intended to speak to this chap, John Jenkins. Not that Dave needed their approval exactly, but he wanted to put them in the picture. He wanted them to know that he and I were going to invite John to meet and discuss his thoughts as to the direction an organisation in Wales which was opposed to the way the country was being treated should take. Having done so, I then spoke to John, and I said: "Look, there's a fella who wants to meet you: Dave Pritchard." And of course, John already knew about Dave Pritchard. He knew his name from our protest at Tryweryn and he said, "Oh alright." It was then agreed that Dave, John and me would meet in the Cable Hotel in Bargoed, and so I gave him a date and time.'

Prompted to reveal the evening's events, David Walters continued:

'Well, on meeting at the hotel – I think it was a week or so later – we went into this little back room there and we started to talk to him. By asking him questions, we were trying to get inside his psyche; we were trying to get inside his mind. To see how it worked, you know? Because in that period of time, you didn't know who was being sent to who – because it was after the attacks at Tryweryn. Anyway, we were at the Cable for an hour or two, something like that. It was a long time, but we went through a lot with him. And we weren't just interested in his replies to our questions. We were looking at him a little bit deeper than that. We were trying, you know, to suss him out, as it were. But he seemed to be genuine… trustworthy. I say *seemed*, because we didn't *really* know. But it turned out that he was. He was – and is – a genuine guy. And he did have that leadership quality. You could see it immediately. But *as* importantly, he struck us as being cautious and sensible, and so we also knew that he would not be standing out in the crowd at any time. He'd blend into the background. Even today, you never hear John give a speech, or give a talk anywhere. He would never have it; and he still doesn't do it. He won't go on the platform and speak.'

Asked what fuelled the decision to 'interview' John and what he and Pritchard hoped Jenkins might provide, by way of a response, Walters added:

'I think it [the political situation in Wales] was getting a little restless at that time. We were just fed up that nobody was doing anything, you know. It was a case of – well, like it is today [2019]. It's become a talking shop. Back then, nobody wanted to do anything. Everybody was up in arms, but nobody would actually *do* something physical. And we could all see that – and it was a frustration.'

With Walters and Pritchard increasingly convinced, prior to meeting Jenkins, that the man they needed should not be on the police radar and that he should be reserved, focussed and resourceful, did John Barnard Jenkins strike the two of them as being possessed of the necessary attributes and abilities to take a campaign of Welsh resistance forward? Replying in the affirmative, Walters continued:

'We listened intently to what he felt was needed and what he believed should be done. And the impression we had was that he was quite prepared to do it. I can't recall if the term "militant direction" was ever used. I can't remember the words used, exactly. But I know I never heard him say the word "explosives". It was more on the lines of "direct action". "I would like to take more of a direct-action approach." I'm not saying that those were the exact words he used, but what came across was that John was prepared to do *anything* that he could. John, like me and Dave – and others, of course – was angered and frustrated by Tryweryn. By this point we'd looked into John's background. We knew where he came from, which was Penybryn; and we even knew about his neighbours. In point of fact, one of his neighbours is my neighbour now, so it gives you an idea of how relationships in this area all interlock to some degree. I mean, we didn't ask the neighbours if John was trustworthy. And we didn't tell John that we were looking into his background – only I assume he knew. No. We just took it on our own backs to find out what sort of character he had.

John is a very quiet sort of fella. If you had a group of people together and they were saying, "Right. We're going to do this and we're going to do that," well, John would be the guy in the background who would actually *do* it. And not only do it, but he'd do it quietly. There is none of this being chopsy about it. And that is one thing we were looking for, because if you are going in these places to undertake these protests, you *have* to be understated about it. But anyway, having made these discreet checks into his background, and having heard John state what he felt was needed to address the situation, we arrived at what we believed was an understanding of his character. And so Dave Pritchard said to me a day or two later, "Yeah. He's the ideal fella. He's the sort of guy we need." It was then decided that Dave would approach John and ask him to not only join MAC, but to orchestrate a campaign of effective protest. But again, I'm not sure how this was worded exactly.'

Did Jenkins' military background feature in the evening's discussions, and if so, did what Jenkins disclosed prove useful? 'Yes, it was discussed,' Walters confirmed.

'Well, we were sounding him out, as it were. We discussed his service in Cyprus and Germany. Regarding Cyprus, we got a few stories, but I can't throw light on what was said. You see, we were trying to establish if he was the right person... because of his military background. That's what we were looking at: his military background and what information he could come up with. You see, because of our sources in the British military, John included, MAC was aware about the heat-seekers. These heat-sensing devices with cameras attached, in helicopters. We knew about that before the bloody Russians knew about it. John said, "Oh, they've got these heat-seekers on the aircraft now and in the helicopters. With them you can see footprints on the floor." The Americans may have had this information, but the Russians didn't know the British military had it. So we knew these things were possible. This knowledge didn't mean much to me and Dave, exactly, but were you a far more militant sort of person at this point, then you would have known to be careful where you tread. You would have used the brooks, the streams, the boggy ground, because that wouldn't leave a heat print. That sort of thing. Using the drier ground, the easiest ground to cover, wouldn't have paid off, because with a heat-sensing device on a helicopter, your footprints would be easily detectable. That sort of information was very helpful. But it never came to that. As a piece of intelligence, it wasn't really required, anyway. But it *was* handy to know.'

Nonetheless, the suggestion that Jenkins imparted knowledge of the heat-seeking devices during the interview with Walters and Pritchard is contested by John Jenkins:

'Yes, I was aware that the British military had helicopters equipped with heat-seeking devices, and that these were able to monitor people covering distance on land by foot. But we never discussed that at all. We never discussed any practicalities. Nothing was said as to how the new campaign would be run and what was needed. That was left to us in the new MAC to decide and develop.'

But if the finer details of what was discussed in Bargoed are lost in the fog of the intervening 55 years, hadn't Jenkins' position within the British military – despite a readiness to support the Plaid Cymru election campaign and his alleged willingness to divulge sensitive information concerning British military capability – ensured a *certain* degree of caution was required? 'We didn't see John's military background as a threat or a potential leak to us. Not at all,' Walters replied resoundingly.

'What struck us was that here was an intelligent guy who could command respect and show leadership, you know? Not a "bull at a gate" character, but someone who knew *exactly* what he was doing; and who was very strong-willed and determined. And, at the end of the day, had a love of this country. That came across very clearly, and that is a very important element. You have to *love* your country. It is country before the rest.'

The matter of John Jenkins' recruitment into the shadowy ranks of *Mudiad Amddiffyn Cymru* has puzzled John ever since.

'I don't know why they recruited me. This is what I would like to find out. It has baffled me over the years. There are certain questions which I have, and one of them is: "Why did they pick *me*?" There were other people, *lots* of other people, who were foaming at the mouth over Tryweryn and the proposed reservoir at Clywedog. These people were chomping at the bit and all the rest of it. They would have been delighted to take this campaign forward. But no: they picked me. I would like to know why Dai Walters and Dave Pritch regarded me as the person they were looking for. They knew certain things about me: that I was in the Army and that I was from the same area. I mean, the South Wales Valleys is a small community and everyone knows everybody else. And so – it is a long time ago, but as far as I can remember, me and Dave Pritch had been friends for years, sort of. On and off. You know what I mean? Not to go out with socially and have a drink with. But still friends. We knew each other, and I found that a lot of the things that I thought, they thought, so I was seen as a friend. Even though the uniform and being in the Army would, you might think, put them off. But there again, I never used to wear the uniform anyway. But it's important to have an understanding of how Wales, and certainly south industrial Wales, ticked at the time – because everybody knew everybody else, albeit vaguely.'

Having explained how the social fabric of the area was interwoven, Jenkins then threw light on how he came to the attention of Dr Phil Williams and how all such public displays of political allegiance ended when he was approached by David Pritchard and asked to join MAC.

'You see, at this stage, I was still publicly espousing sympathy for Welsh nationalism. And so my name would soon have filtered back to Phil Williams, the prospective MP candidate for Caerphilly, who I knew vaguely anyway because he lived in Bargoed. I may well have mentioned to a third party that I would like to speak to him to discuss the Plaid Cymru election strategy. But once approached and asked to orchestrate the MAC counter-offensive – as soon as I was involved, I stopped espousing anything, because that was part of the MAC strategy. And it was a strategy which I *totally* agreed with, of course. You espouse nothing, because if you espouse anything, you are on the radar straight away.'

But did Jenkins ever suspect that he was on the police radar anyway, by virtue of the fact that in October 1964 he was a friend, or known associate, of Pritchard and Walters, who were known to the police due to the protest they had undertaken two years previously over the Tryweryn issue? 'No,' John replied candidly.

'Because while the police may possibly have known of our very loose friendship – although I doubt it – the police didn't take their protest, when they released oil from the transformer, seriously. You see, when you look at it, they hadn't done a professional job of it. It was obviously the work of amateurs. So the police wouldn't have been too bothered by that. It's when the explosions become less amateur and much more professional – *that* is when the police and the authorities start getting *really* interested. It's at that point they *really* start worrying. It was only when the MAC protest became professional and it became obvious that this was an effective campaign of militancy that the police began to take an active interest in a person's friends and associates. But by that time, by the time the MAC campaign was *truly* underway, I had broken off all contact with Dave Pritchard and Dai Walters, and so the police didn't have the necessary information to tie us together. But, having said that, in 1964, although Pritchard and Walters wanted to step up the militant response, they couldn't do it because they *were* under police observation. Albeit in a general sense. So they realised that what they wanted to do, and what they were *trying* to do, was to pass the torch onto someone else. And having met me and chatted to me, they decided that I was the person to carry the torch forward.'

But how had he managed to impress upon Pritchard and Walters that they had found the man they were looking for? That he was the person required to take the MAC protest in a more direct, or aggressive, direction?

'In the two or so hours that this interview lasted – it was disguised as a chat, but it was really an interview – I outlined my general philosophy. It was quite intense. After all, it was an important matter. But I wasn't asked to go into details, and they didn't provide any. Because obviously I wasn't at this point "part of the clan", as it were. So they weren't going to say anything which I could repeat at a later date and which would reflect badly on the organisation. So it was a *general* sort of chat about philosophy and all the rest of it. And having outlined my rationale, they obviously felt – having decided on the strength of their own enquiries that I was "safe" and trustworthy – that I was innocuous enough to be able to take it forward. I suppose, in part, this answers my question as to why they chose me. I must have fitted the bill, in some way or other. But nevertheless, Pritch and Dai – and others at the vanguard of MAC – also knew that at that *particular* time, something had to be done shortly; because if it wasn't, then the whole thing was going down the sink. Wales had suffered the ignominy of Tryweryn, which for me – and many other people – is what finally turned the tide and made me realise how politically impotent we were. The flooding of Clywedog was all but inevitable, with work at the site underway, and we knew that at some stage the authorities were planning to hold the Investiture. We knew, when the Queen said at the Empire Games in '58 that because Wales is such a lovely place her son would one day come and be "the new conqueror", that it would happen. And as time went on, the authorities made it fairly clear. Not immediately, perhaps, but as time went on, they were ramming it down our throats at every possible opportunity. And so the need for a militant response was imminent. Something *had* to be done.'

So how did he propose that *Mudiad Amddiffyn Cymru* should respond to these perceived injustices to Wales?

'All I knew, from my own personal point of view, is that MAC hadn't been going in *any* direction. If anything, MAC was going downhill. Because there was nothing. If the group *did* have an objective and a strategy as to how the campaign should be reconvened, I wasn't sure it had the means of undertaking it, anyway! Nonetheless, a few days after meeting Pritch and Dai Walters in the hotel in Bargoed, Dave Pritchard contacted me, we met, and I agreed to join MAC. It was further agreed that I would take over – and *how* I was going to take it [MAC] forward would be up to me. And so I returned to Germany and began to consider what would be needed to successfully undertake a campaign of militant activism. I obviously ruled out military engagement. Such a thing would have been well beyond what we could manage. But I began to think of some mechanism by which sanctions could be applied; and how the authorities could be made aware of the Welsh people's feelings. I knew by then, I think, that reasoned argument wouldn't do the trick. So, how could we hurt them and make them listen? But, having said that, it's important to remember that I *still* hoped that it might be avoided. Even as I agreed to join MAC, I still hoped that a campaign of direct action would *not* be necessary and that those in Whitehall would start showing more respect for Wales.'

# The Labour Government establishes the Welsh Office and the post of Secretary of State for Wales – and John prepares to leave Germany with a new perspective on life

It was not only John Jenkins whose life took a dramatic turn at this point. Following their election victory two days earlier, on 17 October 1964 Harold Wilson's newly appointed Labour administration honoured their election pledge and established the office of Secretary of State for Wales.[54] The first incumbent, Llanelli MP James Griffiths, was appointed on 11 November. Things did not, however, go immediately to plan. Although a passionate socialist, as a first-language Welsh-speaker, Griffiths was vocal in his support for Welsh cultural matters, believing that the nation enjoyed a unique, singular identity. Eight days after taking up the post, Griffiths threatened to resign, owing to the position's lack of political clout. In response, Prime Minister Harold Wilson granted the Secretary of State for Wales devolved authority for housing, local government, road transport and some aspects of local planning, and in April 1965 established the Welsh Office.[55]

As Secretary of State for Wales, Griffiths got a seat in the cabinet and an administrative office in Cardiff, at a time when John Jenkins and like-minded individuals were increasingly believing that only a measured but effective militant response would enable Wales to rid itself of the unjust political shackles and constraints imposed by being in the UK political union. What was the impact of Griffiths' appointment to Jenkins' political thinking at this juncture?

'I did have some respect for Jim Griffiths. He was very community-minded *and* well respected, so in that sense, I did have respect for him. However, I also had severe misgivings as to how much Wilson and senior Government officials would allow him to get away with when they appointed him Secretary of State for Wales. And I was right, when you realise how little power and opportunity he was initially given. There is a story that Griffiths himself used to tell, of arriving at what was called the Welsh Office, to find that they'd provided him, in the back somewhere, a small little office which contained just a desk and a pencil! So it was tokenism on the part of the Labour Party. It was never designed to be a fully functioning institution where real political decisions were made. It was purely symbolic.'[56]

Somewhat resigned to an increasing feeling that a militant campaign might be necessary, John Jenkins, MAC's leader-in-utero, remained in Germany and awaited news of his posting to Saighton Camp in Cheshire. If the British Army sergeant and proud Welshman believed that with his request to transfer back to the UK to ensure his son received a Welsh-medium education granted, the Army's approach had softened in its attitude towards the cultural identity of those nations which comprised the British union, 'a politely worded' letter to the British Forces Broadcasting Service in Germany, outlining Jenkins' request to hear more Welsh-related programmes, such as Welsh hymn singing, provided something of an answer. Informed by way of written reply that 'the British Army did not pander to tribalism', John's request was rejected. The 'haughty and patronising' rebuff only served to convince John Jenkins of two things: 1) 'that the so-called British Army was in reality the English Army; and it is *this* that gets rammed down your throat morning, noon and night', and 2) that Wales' place at the table of British cultural, political and historical influence was being ignored.[57]

This feeling of indifference or belligerence towards Wales, whether real or imagined, only intensified when John finally received notice of the date of his transfer to Saighton Camp. Describing his final weeks in Germany as 'difficult', Jenkins added that events leading up to his departure only served to exacerbate his increasing distrust of the authorities. By way of example, John added:

'The Colonel I had when I was leaving Germany was the only colonel that I ever disliked. He *never* came in to work on a Saturday, for instance, although *we* were expected to. And he was always shouting and bawling about regulations – and yet he used his Army staff car to take his wife shopping on Saturday mornings, which we all knew about. So really, all his bawling and shouting about regulations fell by the wayside. If he himself wasn't prepared to subject himself to the regulations, then why should we? But anyway, the day I was leaving was a Saturday and he changed his mind. For once he came in to the office. I'd heard that he intended to come into work that day at such and such a time, so I decided that I wasn't going to be there. Just before his planned arrival, I jumped in my car and drove home. And later that day I was told by a colleague that he was very annoyed by this, apparently, as it meant I had turned my back on him deliberately – which I did. I didn't *want* to say goodbye to him. I didn't like him. So what did he do? He wrote a letter to my next colonel at Saighton Camp, castigating me for my perceived lack of respect. But my colonel at Saighton knew him and took no bloody notice whatsoever. So my idea of authority, *sometimes*, can be jaundiced – not towards *all* people in positions of authority. But sometimes I am aware that my view can be jaundiced. It all boils down to that sense of hypocrisy again, I suppose. And that disdain for hypocrisy, at least in part, only added to my escalating distrust of the authorities and the establishment. *That* was the main thing, I think, that emerged from my Army career. I got to distrust them.'

It is a fascinating point; and asked to sum up *all* the lessons Jenkins feels he learned during his Army career – whether stationed in Britain or abroad – and if he later utilised this education when spearheading the campaign of militancy in the name of Welsh political freedom, John replied that the Army instilled in him 'the usefulness of punctuality, discipline, unity and organisation'. That said, he added thoughtfully, he was certain he had developed these attributes *before* joining the army. Yet regarding one thing Jenkins remained unequivocal: despite the later media postulation, his position within *Mudiad Amddifyn Cymru* and what the group sought to achieve had nothing to do with his military experience. In further response to those who had drawn that parallel, citing the use of explosives, John protested that he had had no experience while in the Army even of guns, let alone explosives; nor for that matter, had he received instruction in sabotage or subversion. The British Army, he added reproachfully, was 'the last place that one would receive that level of expertise'. Requested therefore to outline the most illuminating aspect of his British military career up to the point he returned to the UK, Jenkins paused in silent reflection and declared that 'of all the factors, attitudes and approaches' he was subjected to, it was the campaign of militancy as undertaken by EOKA in Cyprus which made the greatest impact on his intellectual flowering. Expecting to be confronted 'by an army of thousands', the British Army had been humbled by just how few active fighters EOKA had truly comprised. It had impressed him. But most revealingly of all, EOKA made Jenkins 'realise how, if your handful of dedicated men are handled properly, they will win over the hearts and minds of those people who are *not* committed'. Jenkins continued soberly:

'I am always reminded of when I was over there on active service and there was a village which was known to be friendly to the British military. Well, one day, somebody in the village threw a stone at a passing Army patrol. And of course, the next day, the patrol was back, but this time it was supported by three or four other patrols. And they went in and smashed this village to bloody pieces. Well, the result was that a village renowned for being friendly changed overnight into a resting place for aspiring terrorists, because they all hated the British after that. And I could see it clearly: one man throws one stone, which results in the whole bloody Army piling down here; and now all these people in the village are dedicated EOKA people. Ask them to do anything against the British military and they'll do it, because of what the British Army did to them. And that episode served as a *vital* message to me. It told me that one man who knows his onions can create all sorts of nasty situations.'

John Jenkins arrived at another and no less important conclusion. Despite having suffered an ignominious humiliation, Jenkins deduced that the British military and political establishment had failed to learn from the experience of the EOKA insurgency. Their tried and tested policy of overreaction and robust tactics against a perceived inferior opponent would continue.

What, however, of events in Wales? How, while still stationed in Germany, had the protests over the flooding of Cwm Tryweryn affected Jenkins' view as to the way future direct action should be undertaken? Hadn't the morally or ethically sensitive approach, as adopted by those such as the respected Emyr Llywelyn Jones, provided the 'correct' line of attack? 'What I learnt, while watching these events unfold in Germany,' John replied solemnly, 'was that there is always room for that.'

'This Gandhi "pure of heart" approach. But as long as it's not the *main* thrust. If it's the secondary thrust of your approach, to show that "we occupy the moral ground", then yes. That's fine. But you must *always* maintain the opportunity to exercise sanctions, because if you can exercise sanctions effectively, then they [authorities] listen. If you can't, then they won't. This is the political way. In fact, if you simply adhere to this "moral high-ground" method, all it will do is make the authorities laugh. The IRA doesn't make them laugh. The point is: you've got to understand your enemy; and what hurts him and what doesn't hurt him and what hits him and what doesn't hit him.'

## MAC considers a new approach as the group looks towards its new leader

With John Jenkins'outlook on a Welsh militant response largely moulded and affected by those factors experienced and witnessed up to the point of departing from Germany, it is perhaps necessary at this juncture to briefly consider the history of militancy in Wales in the pre-Jenkins period and how the campaign of violent counter-opposition was both financed and developing. Asked to throw light on the picture prior to Jenkins' return to Britain, a former senior member of MAC declared:

'The only thing I know about what was happening prior to John taking control of MAC was that there were links being established between this band of what I would call "Welsh patriots" and the Libyan Government. And these contacts concerned arms deals being done. And what is more, the British Government is *very* lucky. You don't know how near it got to maybe, *maybe* arms being used. Because although there were arms offered, when they went to the Libyan Embassy to see them, they were found to be too outdated. This group of "Welsh patriots" didn't have a name. It was an organisation which had *some* link to MAC, but was not a part of it. Of course, those people are dead and gone now. One of the men involved – who I know is dead, so it makes no difference to him, and his family are living abroad – was a playwright called Bill Mylan. He was well known. He went to Canada after this and worked in a university there. And he wrote a few plays, and was an actor too. He'd done some acting over here at the time – for the BBC, I believe it was. Well, he was developing links with Libya and he was also developing links with another group in Cardiff, which also had arms we could have used. But when these Welsh patriots tried to sound this thing out, they discovered that the arms being stored in Cardiff were pre-bloody Second World War – and they just weren't good enough either.'

And in terms of those people who you feel *would* have been prepared to use these arms had they been available, how many are we talking about? Would a figure of 50 be accurate? 'We are just talking about numbers,' the former Welsh militant responded intently.

'I won't be more specific. We're not talking a huge number. But we *are* talking about a sizeable amount. It would have posed a "threat", put it that way. And I believe that this Welsh campaign would have been undertaken with a bit more intelligence than you have today. The terrorists today are just murderers, as far as I'm concerned. They go out and murder people. That was *never* the aim of this. It was more interested in ruining the economy than killing people. The economy was of more interest to the English state than a thousand, two thousand, three thousand English men and women being killed. The state government didn't care about that. But hurt the economy to the tune of a couple of billion pounds – different kettle of fish altogether. And so economic targets were considered. We were looking at road and rail links, waterways, electricity supply stations, pylons. That sort of thing. Infrastructure.'

But why then was there a perceived need for the weaponry? Surely it was just explosives that were necessary?

'I don't really know why they wanted them, unless they felt it was inevitable. I can imagine why they wanted explosives, because a pylon needs explosives. Also, you need explosives to blow a bridge up. But why the arms? I never understood that. But then again, they didn't follow it through after visiting the Libyan Embassy and going to Cardiff. And that is the whole point. They didn't follow it through. And I don't know why, but this was nothing to do with MAC. This was to do with an in-between organisation which lasted for a few years. They didn't operate under a name. But these are the most shadowy figures altogether. This is *before* John's time. I don't think he was aware of these people, but they were there. This was even before the protests at Tryweryn in 1962 and 1963, but it was *because* of Tryweryn. It was because of Tryweryn that *all* this was happening – and it could have been *very* serious indeed.'

How had the connection with Libya been established? Was a Welsh nationalist sympathetic to a militant agenda working in Libya? 'No,' the former senior MAC official declared.

'We were aware that Libya was sympathetic to our [Welsh nationalist] position. We also knew that Libya had connections with Cuba – and a lot of the other communist countries, all of whom were opposed to Britain and the capitalist system. And so we reasoned that they would be interested in helping us: through providing finance from these countries.

Or through providing *any* other sort of help they could give. That was the idea behind it. I know, because I was one of those who went to the Libyan Embassy in London. I was asked to go, and on returning to provide David Pritchard with a summary of what they were offering. I do remember that the coffee was as thick as treacle. Bloody horrible. Anyway, that's not important. We told them what we wanted; what we were looking for, and they were very sympathetic towards it. But having reported the discussion back to David, they [the Welsh] never followed the offer through. Nothing happened after that. I don't know why. I was just asked to go and report back what was discussed. From what I remember, David Pritchard knew about the Libyans and what they might be prepared to provide. It was he who made all the arrangements with the Libyan Embassy. I don't know why he didn't want to go himself. But I know that I went, and I was struck by the fact they were fully aware of everything that was happening in Wales. They knew about Tryweryn, for example. I mean, even in later years, David Pritchard and others were still talking about looking towards Cuba – and that sort of thing – for support.'

Also interviewed to discuss MAC's connections and useful contacts was David Walters. He stated:

'Dave Pritchard had contacts in Ireland. He used to go back and forth to Ireland, where he met IRA men; whom, on his return, we always referred to as "snowmen". We used "snowmen" more as an inside joke than as a code word. Although it is true that anyone overhearing our discussions would have been in the dark as to who or what we were talking about – and this was deliberate, of course. Anyway, these trips to Ireland taken by Dave were financed by Trefor Morgan, who was a successful south Wales businessman. Trefor made a lot of money in insurance. This was *before* John's involvement with MAC. But I went to ask Trefor if he would be prepared to finance it – these trips that Dave was taking to and from Ireland. And he didn't hesitate. He just handed an amount of money over, which I then gave to Dave, obviously. I don't know the degree of Dave's involvement in MAC after John joined. I know he was involved in MAC *before* John's time – and I know that he was also involved in this other more shadowy group. But he would also go back and forth to Ireland as well. What he discussed there, I'm not exactly sure. I assume they'd discuss strategy and so on, but I couldn't confirm that.'

In view of Pritchard's earlier protest at the Tryweryn reservoir construction site, isn't it likely that he was being followed when undertaking these trips to and from Ireland? 'I've got no idea,' Walters replied earnestly.

'He probably *was* being followed, but he would have taken that precaution. Dave never drove a car, so he went everywhere by public transport, which was a lot easier. It wasn't done deliberately: he just didn't drive. But when you think of it, you've got a *hell of a job* to follow somebody on public transport. It's much more difficult than it is to follow them in a car. If you get on a train, you can change your seat every so often. Also, they don't know where you're getting off. And so if you *do* get off at a certain station, and someone gets off with you, and that same person then boards the same *bus* as you... well, if you're keeping an eye out for such things, it's much more easily noticed.'

As for having useful contacts, Walters threw light on a particularly revealing incident in the period during which Radio Free Wales was broadcasting.[58] Established in the late 1950s in order disseminate information concerning Plaid Cymru and perceived Welsh nationalist grievances, within weeks Radio Free Wales had become the focus of increased police attention. Unknown beyond the small band of confidantes, Alf Williams – one of the 'eighteen or so' involved in the enterprise – acted as the driver; transporting both the radio transmission set and those individuals involved in an operation to the site of the next broadcast. It was also at the home of Alf Williams, near Maesycwmmer, that the transmission set was routinely stored. One morning, with the radio transmission set *in situ*, there came a sudden unexpected knock on the door. Standing before them was 'this young fella' unknown to the occupants. 'The police,' he stated impassively, 'are doing a raid on you tonight.' With that, he left. Following a brief discussion, it was decided that the party would remain in the house, while the radio set was hidden elsewhere. That night, the police raided Alf Williams' home and failed to find the radio transmission set. Asked if the identity of the helpful informant was subsequently discovered, Walters replied:

'Yeah. We found out who he was. He was a young police cadet from Blackwood. So, this was the sort of information that people were prepared to come and share with you. You know – a young police cadet, who must have heard about this planned raid. We didn't know him from bloody

Adam. But he'd taken it upon himself to come down to the house, knock on the door – the same day the police intended to do it – and say, "They're doing a raid on your house tonight." What does that tell you about the degree of support and sympathy out there for what we were doing?'

It is an interesting point, and worthy of further consideration. With John Jenkins entrusted to take up the reins and consider the means by which *Mudiad Amddiffyn Cymru* could orchestrate a militant campaign of 'direct action' in the name of Welsh political nationalism, what lessons might those at the vanguard of MAC's first incarnation have provided the group's new organiser? Contacted to provide an outline of what the group had learned from its campaign experience so far, a former senior official declared that of primary importance was:

### 1. Policy

'We [MAC] had a policy, and our policy was a simple one. You only knew what you had to know. Simple as that. Dai Walters didn't know which people Dave Pritchard was contacting. And Dave didn't know some of the people Dai was contacting, unless it had to be otherwise. If you don't need to know, then you don't know. You reveal nothing to no one. You would not be able to divulge anything anyway, because you only knew what you needed to know. That's the way the system worked. And it proved very effective.'

### 2. Objective

'What you hoped to achieve and why. It needed to be clear to everyone – the media, politicians and activists – what your campaign was in protest about.'

### 3. Suitability

'If undertaking an operation, don't drive anything flash. Don't drive a car which will get you noticed; which will stick in a person's memory. Drive an ordinary car. A car which is a few years old, which will blend into the background. But *far* more importantly, avoid *anyone* who's flash, or who might stand in a public space and preach. Once you're connected with someone like that, then you're marked. Dave Pritchard was a *very* quiet man. Most of the people involved in MAC were quiet people – outside of the organisation, they were reserved. If you met them and had a chat with them, you'd never suspect them. People like Dave Pritchard and John

Jenkins: both quiet men, sober men – in every sense. They were idealists. And as such, they were the *ideal* ones. Those were the people that you *really* needed.'

**4. Intelligence**
'You must know your craft. Even in preparation for the attacks at Tryweryn, both in September 1962 and February 1963, photographs were taken of the construction site. The entire area was reconnoitred. The layout was well known: where the stores were, etc. Even the shift detail which the men worked – we knew.'

**5. Preparation**
'What do they say, "failing to prepare is preparing to fail"? Well, it's true.'

**6.** Finally, 'but perhaps most importantly of all, you must **love your country.**'

It was a six-stratagem approach which, at least at *that* time, chimed perfectly with the man watching closely from the wings of the movement, John Jenkins. Pondering exactly what was required of an effective counter policy, Jenkins would ultimately determine that only the successful and sustained use of explosives would establish a clear objective for the protest. He noted that regrettably, *only* such an approach would ensure the cause was recognisable to all – the Government, the media and the populace.

## John returns to Blighty, receives some disturbing news and is introduced to 'family'

On 4 April 1965, having recently returned to the UK, Sergeant John Jenkins commenced his dental duties at Saighton Camp, near Chester. Two months later, Thelma, Vaughan and Rhodri relocated to Wrexham, where Vaughan was enrolled as a pupil at Ysgol Bodhyfryd. Outlining the responsibilities of his new post, John stated:

'It was very similar to the role I had in Germany, whereby, along with providing hands-on support to the dentist in house, as the senior Non-Commissioned Officer in Western Command, I was also tasked with ensuring that dental treatment was standardised. Again, this involved monitoring how service people responded to the treatment they'd received, via complaints and feedback forms. But I was also responsible for stores and accounting for the Dental Corps throughout the region, and so the post entailed travelling around the various camps within its district, to check on treatment, equipment, supplies and so forth.'

The position provided Jenkins both the 'permission' and the reason to travel throughout Wales. While undertaking his duties, in civilian clothes, there was, John added, 'nothing to stop me calling in on someone to discuss more "delicate" matters.' The freedom to travel around Wales was an aspect of the MAC campaign which Jenkins later discerned to be 'crucial'.

Shortly after taking up his posting, John met David Pritchard. One thing troubled him immediately. Now privy to more sensitive information, Jenkins was informed by Pritchard that efforts had previously been made to obtain arms and explosives from sources which included Libya and regimes throughout the world imbued with a socialist political leaning and/or which were intent on undermining law and order and the political stability of the UK. On learning that the offers had *not* been followed up, ostensibly owing to the poor condition of the antiquated weaponry, Jenkins concedes that 'This is where I fell out with them [MAC], in fact.' One cause of Jenkins' consternation was that this 'romantic idea' of getting guns via such channels placed *Mudiad Amddiffyn Cymru* 'on the same level as the IRA'. Yet the position of MAC and the Welsh militant community within Welsh society was not remotely comparable to the status afforded the IRA, both within Ireland or on the global stage of militant protest. The circumstances and traditions which enveloped the IRA could not be mirrored by MAC. Nonetheless, on reflection, rather than Jenkins actually falling out with Walters and Pritchard over the issue of obtaining arms and explosives via such routes, it was more the case that 'nothing on the subject was ever said'. But the episode proved instrumental in further convincing John that, under his direction, 'the most important battle' *Mudiad Amddiffyn Cymru* would engage in would be one for the hearts and minds of the Welsh people; and *not* one which involved 'people going around with guns'. Jenkins highlighted the widening gulf between the two approaches by adding witheringly:

'Shooting people and all that sort of stuff was all very well, but it would *not* have earned the hearts and minds that I thought a campaign of militant activity should be all about. In other words, I took a *completely* political view of it, rather than the sort of "outlaw against the state" type of approach. You need the support of the public to succeed – and you would not receive that support without a considered "hearts and minds" philosophy underpinning your protest. We didn't argue about it: no words were exchanged or anything. It's just when they touched briefly on things like that – arms deals from Libya – and they went over to see people in Saudi Arabia and God knows where, I didn't attack them, or criticise them. I just let them get on with informing me. I didn't impress anything upon them, because as I began to formulate a strategy, I knew they weren't going to be involved. They were far too well known. Anyone involved in the MAC action needed to be unknown to the authorities. I have no idea who they were in contact with. I wasn't interested. I didn't row [with them] over it, but I may have given them the impression that I did not endorse this romantic, idealist view of things, as taken by some people, such as the Free Wales Army later. It seemed to me that this romanticism might have done wonders for the egos of the people concerned, but it didn't do much for the cause!

All I wanted to know was what was required and available to reconvene the MAC campaign. And crucially, this included what needed to be avoided. You see, I was also aware that once you make contact with people like that – Libya and so on; and for that matter, of course, Dai Walters and Dave Pritch – you are on the radar, without any doubt. And that would then reduce my effectiveness, as I would be on the radar myself and consequently, by association, I could lose the whole damn thing. So I took a different view. I took very much a "hearts and minds" approach and worked on the principle that "whatever you do, you mustn't upset the Welsh people, except through incremental and considered stages". But I only obliquely hinted at my belief in a "hearts and minds" approach at this stage, because I wasn't going to fall out with them straight away. So I let it go at that. I knew damn well that if – or when, as it turned out – I took control of MAC, they [Pritchard and Walters] weren't going to have any input as far as policy or operations were concerned.'

With Jenkins brought up to speed by Dave Pritchard re developments in south-east Wales, it was decided to take matters to the next level. In order to do so, John was introduced by Pritchard to senior MAC officials in north Wales. Asked to throw light on how proceedings unfolded and why the meeting in north Wales was deemed to be necessary, Jenkins declared:

'Having met somewhere en route, me and Pritch drove up to the north of Wales, where we met three gentlemen. Now, all three were people of great integrity who were trusted by everybody; and all of whom I *had* to get to know before I could make a move anywhere in north Wales. This was because I would not have got *anywhere* in north Wales, in terms of establishing contacts and receiving information, had I not first consulted with these people and been approved by them. Only through receiving their endorsement was I assured that they would pass the word on that I was alright and could be trusted. Had I not received this approval, I wouldn't have been able to get bloody anywhere. All three of these gentlemen are still alive and are still living up there. To my knowledge, none of these three men in the north were aware of this more militant stand of getting arms and so on from Libya. But nonetheless, it was vitally important that I was introduced to them. I was told that they had reason to believe, presumably through having done their own research into me and my background, that I was a reliable chap, and so on. For reasons of security, this was the only contact I had with these three in the north.

As for what was discussed: we discussed our various points of view. But the point, as far I was concerned anyway, was that I shouldn't be bound by *any* conditions or regulations. I would take MAC forward the way that I thought was best and most effective. In that sense, I knew that I was going to be operating on my own: devising a strategy *on my own*. I wasn't going to get any help from anybody, as such. And they made it clear that in north Wales at least, there were no more explosives and no more timing devices to be handed over in any case. There wasn't anything. If I wanted explosives and timers, I must use my head to get them, which later I did. But it having been made clear that there wouldn't be any more stuff in any case, I was glad, because how could it have been passed over to me? If it had involved meeting people... well, I couldn't risk that. Anyway, our chat must have gone well, because it was agreed that they would contact the relevant people and tell them to expect me; that I would be contacting them to discuss matters.'

David Walters confirmed John Jenkins' account of events; and admitted to having known 'what was going on' as Jenkins' affiliation to MAC intensified. Having each decided that Jenkins 'was safe', the decision was taken by Walters and Pritchard 'to pass John on to Pritchard's contact in the north,' he affirmed. After which, from Walters' 'own point of view', his involvement ended and 'the curtain came down'. He had known 'hardly anything' about John's subsequent developments within *Mudiad Amddiffyn Cymru*, 'only that MAC was now in John's hands and that the group was operating largely out of north Wales.' As such, Walters declared, 'it was nothing to do with me. In the sense that you didn't want to know anything, because you weren't involved.'

## John Jenkins assesses the strategic capabilities of MAC, most notably its policy towards 'security' – and makes some startling discoveries

Having received the necessary endorsement of senior MAC officials based in north Wales, the path was now clear for John Jenkins to begin the process of establishing his credentials within the wider *Mudiad Amddiffyn Cymru*. It coincided with John deciding that two factors required consideration: 1) that a period of assessment was required to evaluate the group's logistics and capabilities, and 2) on the strength of previous media accounts outlining militant strikes, a review of the group's security measures appeared to be necessary. Both components, Jenkins determined, were essential if MAC was going to take the fight to the British state.

The period of evaluation, Jenkins disclosed, involved him 'going around' and finding out 'who was who and what was what'. But while it was required that the MAC contacts with whom Jenkins intended to meet recognised him, it was equally important, from a security viewpoint, that they remained in the dark as to John Jenkins' identity. John felt that this was appropriate since despite their allegiance to MAC, the possibility always existed that individuals might be subject to surveillance and monitoring by the police and security services. As for how the proposed meeting was arranged, John revealed that prior to his arrival, those he subsequently approached were contacted and made aware that the anonymous figure [Jenkins] who would shortly be visiting them was, 'in the eyes of Dave Pritchard', a 'friend of the family'. They 'didn't know who I was, where I was from, or what I was doing, as such,' Jenkins declared, continuing:

> 'But they knew I was "safe", because I'd been vouched for by people who'd been "there" for many years. That's why we [MAC] got away with it for so long, because it was a family thing. When I say a "family member", I'm not talking about an *actual* family. I'm talking about a relationship. I was

seen as a member of the "family" and so regarded as trustworthy. In other words, we never took on any strangers... You can only operate this way when you are dealing with men of honour. If they're *not* men of honour, then it doesn't work.'

With the period of evaluation underway, several interconnecting factors struck Jenkins immediately. One dawning realisation centred on John's increasing belief that under Pritchard's direction, security and strategy had been both lax and inept. Despite David Pritchard having divulged to John his 'knowledge and contacts'; and Pritchard's personality traits of being sincere, discerning and approachable, while also self-contained and reserved – characteristics which Jenkins both admired and found compelling – by way of contrast, John quickly determined that Pritchard lacked the necessary strategic skills. 'The trouble was – how can I put this?' Jenkins pondered tactfully. 'He wasn't much good at organising things, and that is why whatever people did, they were caught.' Referring to the incident in October 1962 when, during Pritchard's apparent stewardship of MAC, a red box containing 1,200 detonators was discovered buried in a hedge near Nefyn, leading to the arrest and conviction of those involved,[59] Jenkins added:

'I mean, people had no real concept of security. Say they had a box marked 'explosives', for sake of argument, they would throw it over a fence! I mean, how amateur can you get? And we had to convince the authorities that we [MAC] were *not* amateurs. Otherwise they wouldn't take any notice of us. I mean, crates thrown in hedges! This is schoolboy stuff! I should say though, that during this period [of assessment and evaluation] I was dealing with people, quite a number of them, who had all the brains needed, but no common sense whatsoever. None at all. They were extremely intelligent people; and I could never understand that. How it was that these people were *so* intelligent, yet they couldn't understand these basic facts about security and strategy. Yet, they couldn't. I *still* don't know what it was that they couldn't grasp. But there you are.'

As a former mental-health professional, having later qualified and worked as a social worker, did Jenkins consider that there might have existed a psychological, or Freudian, desire to get caught? 'I don't think they knew any better, to tell the truth,' John replied bluntly, adding:

'But it reminds me of the campaign by *Cymdeithas yr Iaith Gymraeg*, who, of course, during the 1960s and beyond, were agitating for equal legal status for the Welsh language. Quite right too. But you had these ministers of religion who would throw all these road signs written solely in English in front of a police station and then hand themselves in to be charged, or whatever. And they did this in order to shame the people that they were trying to shame! How can you shame people who don't know the meaning of the word? And what was the point in doing that anyway? Shame wouldn't gain you any damn thing. *Fear* would. And this is the unfortunate thing. Fear was the only thing they would listen to. I had come to realise, both because of my Army experiences and life generally, that reasoned argument is no good to these people [the authorities]. It *has* to be something more. It has to be something which applies sanctions, which people can feel and people can see. So, we had to frighten them – and I realised early on, as I began to consider how a MAC campaign should be run in terms of policy and strategy, that we would have to frighten them with our efficiency.'

In view of these irritations and hindrances, was there almost a tangible point at which David Pritchard passed the crown on to him? 'Yes, very much so,' Jenkins replied.

'Although Pritch was involved in another explosion at Clywedog in the months following, his handing the reins of MAC to me effectively occurred after we left that meeting in north Wales with the three senior MAC members. Frankly, I think he was happy to rid himself of the responsibility. Had it been left to Pritch, then I don't think that ultimately he would have taken it [the campaign] forward. But whatever the truth, I decided there and then that I wanted no more involvement with the likes of Libya; and if I was going to formalise a strategy in which MAC could undertake an effective protest, then I wanted no more inefficiencies.'

## John finds himself on the horns of a dilemma as 'progress' is made

Having first determined that MAC's security framework lacked stringency, Jenkins next turned his attention to the dormant group's strength and capabilities in terms of materials and personnel. But if John now provides an honest and illuminating assessment concerning the predicament in which he found himself, 'I was really hoping for one of two eventualities,' he conceded, adding:

'1) That the political situation for Wales would improve; and 2) If this proved *not* to be the case and a militant campaign *was* considered necessary, then having organised a strategy in which a militant response could be successful, that I would then hand this information on to someone else and *they* would pick up the mantle and lead this campaign. Because I cannot stress enough that I was hoping to God to find a group, or a person, that would take this forward after my assessment of the situation, which I initially thought would be a relatively straightforward matter anyway. So for something like two years I travelled all around Wales, eyeing up various groups and the activities in which they were involved. And I found, to my surprise and horror, that my intervention in organising a comprehensive strategy was required.'

Asked to explain why, Jenkins continued:

'Well, for instance, I quickly established that many groups were very badly organised. They had no idea about what they wanted to do; or how they were going to do it; or what they were going to do it with! I mean they were well-meaning, in the sense that they *wanted* to do something, but they had no idea, or understanding, as to how to go about it. From my vantage point, they seemed badly led and badly managed. So an effective leadership approach, I recognised immediately, needed to be introduced. Moreover, to establish an effective strategy, I quickly realised that any future campaign could *not* involve existing members of MAC, because most of them were well known to everyone – including the authorities. Therefore, I decided that any future action could *only* be undertaken by someone who wasn't known. And I certainly wasn't known, never having attended any meetings or protests, although I wasn't thinking of my own active involvement at this stage.'

But what other factors, in terms of equipment and personnel, did Jenkins determine were available to him as the period of evaluation continued?

'I did recognise that MAC – as it had existed – possessed *some* of the functions of a decent organisation. But I also believed that it needed a lot of hedges cutting and sorting out, so I spent quite a bit of time doing that.

Finding out who was who and what was what. This total overhaul included assessing how much stuff we had, and how much stuff we needed. In terms of the equipment available, such as explosives and timers, I was shocked by the fact that there was virtually nothing to work with, and this was the situation across the *whole* of Wales. So we needed to take advantage of the few resources which were available and dispense with anything involving materials which weren't. I asked questions such as, "How much gelignite is available, where is it stored and what condition is it in?" And on being told, I realised quite quickly that we would need to have a significant amount of resources to fall back on, because you cannot create an underground movement with just a few explosives. Not just that, but a whole panoply of factors would need to be in place. This would be necessary because a successful organisation, I maintained, *had* to operate in strict secrecy. This, I felt, was not how things had happened in the past; whereby notice of what they intended to do was practically put on the front page of the newspaper!'

Asked how he had taken to his role of chief assessor and strategist, Jenkins replied:

'Well, I'm not comfortable with this "born" or "chosen" to do it idea. But I certainly felt I fitted the role well. A bit better than most people would have done, I think. But that's because if I go into something, I go into it *fully*. I don't play around with something. I'm sincere about it. I *mean* it. And people respond to that. People recognise it and are prepared to work with it. And so, another step taken up the ladder, as it were, was getting known to people. That was vital of course: to be known and trusted. Because you must remember that MAC was not just a north Wales movement, but an all-Wales movement. We were everywhere. So, it was crucial to be known to those people whom you could trust to keep their mouths shut and their eyes open. And whom you knew could – and would – back you up. It all went quite smoothly. Although during this period I had one farcical encounter with the Free Wales Army, when unsuspecting members of the group, believing I was an undercover Special Branch, threatened to tar and feather me! While on another occasion, a man I'd arranged to meet one Sunday morning turned up an hour late. He'd driven from around the corner, so to speak, and I was on time having driven from Wrexham. Well, that was the end of that, as far as I was concerned!'

So what emerged in relation to how such a reconvened movement might work in terms of an individual's involvement and co-operation?

'Through a discerning attitude and approach, I was able to judge how many people were involved – and, crucially, the extent of each person's association and alliance. Although a degree of overlap existed, I soon established that the movement was composed of two distinct groups. Each, acting in support of the other, was to prove essential to the success of the campaign. The first group consisted of those prepared to undertake militant action in the field. The second group, of near equal importance to the first, comprised the 'sleepers'. This latter group not only proved a source of much needed revenue for the movement, they also provided safe-houses and welfare for operatives in the form of food and shelter, often for several days. The term 'sleeper', or 'sleeping partner', also included people who provided us with invaluable local knowledge: an essential component when an action was undertaken in an area unfamiliar to those involved. I cannot overstate the importance of the role played by the 'sleepers'. By this point, many months into this assessment period, I'd established myself by doing things – and little by little, a picture had begun to emerge. I'd acquired a reputation for being effective; for being a doer. And once word got around, it was surprising how quickly people fell in and provided *further* information. By not just going around preaching and drinking with people, but instead through adopting a pragmatic approach, I was able to determine the *true* picture of the situation; both in terms of the available resources, and in knowing that a network was in place *across* Wales where we would be safe. And only at this point could I say, "Right – we *might* be in business".'

## The recruitment of 'front-line' activists into MAC: some fifteen in total, as Jenkins endorses six while considering another six 'unsuitable'

Yet despite the impressive manner in which Jenkins established the ways and means whereby a successful Welsh militant campaign might be exercised, a series of essential factors still needed to be addressed. Of crucial importance was how recruitment into the elusive ranks of *Mudiad Amddiffyn Cymru* might be safely established: both in terms of a potential recruit's suitability for involvement in a militant offensive *and* the type of system in which all recruits would be deployed. As the names of potential MAC recruits began to filter back to John, he devised a strategy to determine an individual's capability. It was to prove a precarious, if highly effective, induction policy. John explained:

'I was in touch with different people, some of whom were above reproach and members of perfectly reasonable organisations, such as Plaid Cymru. But these individuals, although not speaking on behalf of the party, would say, "Oh, so and so is a good lad, you know. He's really raring to go. He could do with doing something." Now other people within MAC were also receiving such information, and so the word would filter back, because Wales is a small place, [and] a lot of people talk.'

Nevertheless, that said, John added pointedly:

'I know there is an old story about a secret in Wales being something known to only three million people; but in this case, they are wrong. Word would get back to us and we would then keep an eye on this person over many weeks. You see, having decided that all former members of MAC were a security threat due to the fact they would almost certainly be monitored, during this *initial* evaluation period of a potential recruit we'd be researching his background and observing his behaviour with two main things in mind: 1) Did he have *all* the resources, including emotional and intellectual, to be able to deal with this sort of thing? And 2) Was he known? Had he gone to any protests or meetings or marches, or whatever? Because if he *had* attended protests and marches and so on, he would obviously be known to Special Branch. They would have taken his photograph, and therefore he would be of no use to us. As we used to say, "If he's known, we don't want to know." Because we knew that following any action, these were the people who'd receive a knock on the door from the police at 2 a.m. But if he *was* deemed suitable, having cleared these two hurdles, he would then be approached by me, and again over many weeks, he would, shall we say, be "interrogated".'

What form did this 'interrogation' of potential recruits take? 'Well,' Jenkins replied:

'It's important to remember that this individual had been subject to many months of close monitoring long before he came to my attention. He had, by the time he came to my notice, been watched and vetted for an extended period at a local level – by someone who knew him. He had no idea of this himself, of course. But by the time he was recommended to me as someone who might *possibly* be what we were looking for, I knew where he would be – or most likely be – on any given day of the week. We knew his routine. For instance, he had a quiet pint in the Red Lion on a Monday evening; he played darts in the Legion on a Wednesday night; he stayed in on a Thursday night, etc. And so I would just "happen" to be in the pub, and I'd strike up a conversation with him. I also knew, or strongly suspected through the information I'd received, how he felt about Wales and the position it faced. So, I would play the Aunt Sally – the devil's advocate – to get a reaction.

I'd come in as a fully "paid-up Brit" and give him all the usual arguments about the joys of "Queen and country" and the Royal Family and "God bless ole England", and all these lovely things. And I would watch – very carefully – his response. And then I would build on that quietly over time. Because I would just "drop by" and strike up a conversation with him on a number of occasions – over a period of many weeks. Sometimes months – well, as long as it took. Due to other commitments, I might not see an individual on consecutive weeks. But I *had* to test him. To see how he reacted. I had to be satisfied that this person was the sort of person we were looking for. So, I'd go back, time and again, until I was sure. And I had to be that thorough, because I had to be *certain* in my own mind. And if it took months to decide, then so be it. Because I knew that the safety and the lives of other people were on the line too: the wives and the children. They were dependent on this individual I was interviewing, so I couldn't afford to make a mistake. I knew that the safety of this person and of the organisation itself depended upon a proper summing up. And if the summing up wasn't done properly and the bloke was admitted, and he was *not* "healthy", then both things – MAC and this individual themselves – could come crashing down. And do you know, no one ever said: "Oh, not you again!" or anything like that. Nobody ever questioned me, or wanted to know what I was doing there. You would have thought they would, because theoretically, of course, I could have been a policeman. Being in the military, my hair was rather unfashionably short, for instance. But no. And this again – as with the information that I was receiving from across Wales in relation to names, equipment and materials available – made me wonder what it was about me that people trusted; that allowed people to instinctively confide in me.'

Nonetheless, did these encounters always run smoothly? 'Not always,' Jenkins smiled.

'As you can imagine, these "chats" did get a bit heated once or twice! Not so much from my direction, as I just calmly said my piece. But sometimes people were unable to express their full feelings as they were too emotional. One gentleman I met called Arthur, who lived in Conwy, I think, was *really* upset by what was happening all over Wales. And as we chatted about the nation's political and cultural situation, he turned to me with tears streaming down his face and said how he could wholly identify with Llywelyn's court poet, Gruffudd ab yr Ynad Coch; who, following the death of Llywelyn in 1282, wrote one of the greatest Welsh poems, his elegy, *Marwnad Llywelyn ap Gruffudd*. In which, in his intense grief, he asks, "Why, O God, does the sea not cover the land? Why are we left to linger?" Well, poor Arthur saw the parallel between his life and what was happening in Wales in the 1960s, and how Gruffudd ab yr Ynad Coch felt after Llywelyn was butchered by the Norman-English in the thirteenth century. Arthur also felt anguished that the culture, the language, the customs, the very identity of Wales faced annihilation, through Wales being politically mishandled. I should add that Arthur did not go on to join MAC. But he was certainly not alone in feeling the situation as strongly as that. And as a representative of MAC, I was offering these men an alternative – to counter this feeling that you had to just give in. And this reaction [of Arthur's] registered positively with me, because I *had* to know what underpinned their political philosophy. If their motives were based purely on emotion – "We're going to drive them into the sea" – I didn't want to know. Rather, I wanted them to express an idealism which burned much deeper than that; something with a bit more feeling; more analytical. Did they understand Wales' predicament politically? Because it's what's in there [head] that counts, not what's in there [heart] – because nobody with any sense would do anything like this [join MAC]. Having said that, it's both: it's head and heart. But you have *got* to be doing it for a concept, not just because of emotion.'

So how did matters progress to the next level, where an individual was asked to join the elusory *Mudiad Amddiffyn Cymru*?

'Well, after many weeks of contact with this chap, and with their idealism having been expressed in a manner which I considered to be positive, I'd be listening out for a statement which, if professed in the right way, summed up our position and spoke in favour of what we were contemplating. You know, without saying so, they would have to admit support for a militant response; something along the lines of "Something's got to be done", or "I wish there was a way that I, or we [Wales], could strike back". You see, *that*, I suppose, was the key phrase. If they said that, or words to that effect – especially, of course, having passed the other suitability criteria concerning their emotional and intellectual mindset and their not being "known" – I'd think, "Right. He's got what we're looking for." And so I'd say something like, "It's possible that I could manage to put you in touch with one or two people who think like you do." And they'd respond, "Yeah, I'd like that." You know, sort of, "Please do." And interestingly, they said "yes" in exactly the way that I wanted to hear it. Soberly. In a quiet, matter-of-fact sort of way. It would develop like that. Not one person said "no". Not a single person turned round to me and said, "Oh no. I could never subject my wife to that sort of thing." Now, what does that tell you? And that was a tribute to our selection procedure. But I had known them for some time by then and I was familiar with their attitude and their approach. So, it wasn't as if I was putting this suggestion [that I would act as an intermediary] to someone completely new. They were fully aware, I think, by this stage, where the conversation was leading.'

Did Jenkins consider an operative working alone to be the best way forward? 'No,' he replied emphatically, adding:

'I had long since realised that a cell structure would work best; and so, as part of my recruitment procedure, I would only approach the person that I believed possessed the attributes to be a cell leader. Also, at this point, with security uppermost in my mind, I would say, "The only person who will ever approach you – for instance, on a Monday evening in the Red Lion – will be me, and I will possibly be accompanied by another trusted member... If anyone approaches you and I am *not* with this person, then it's the police." Because at this point, while I still hoped to hand it over to someone else, I realised that in the future I'd need to make the necessary introductions between the recruit and MAC's new leader. And so I was keeping the door open, as it were, by suggesting I might return accompanied. But until such time, I was determined to provide these recruits the reassurance they needed in terms of their not being detected.'

Prompted to reveal his thoughts regarding the recruitment policy into MAC that he introduced, Jenkins declared pensively:

'It *was* a long-winded way of going about things. But it was *safe*. It was secure. And as events transpired, with me taking over the leadership, it was an induction strategy that I used with all those who joined MAC. It was the same sort of thing. And this recruitment policy continued throughout the campaign. It was in place before our first protest in September 1967 and it was still working right up to the time I was arrested in November 1969. Because – and this is something else which isn't known – recruitment into MAC looked set to continue into the 1970s. And I say that because of the positive feedback we were receiving via a number of people who *wanted* to join us. Even in the weeks before I was arrested, I'd begun the process of considering a few of those whose names had been recommended to me.'

Not all potential recruits made it through the induction process, however, as Jenkins further revealed:

'Some people stood up reasonably well to the reports that were coming in, but when I went personally to check – which I did with every single one, to get up close to them, or perhaps even to talk to them – I decided on the strength of what they presented to me, or what I overheard, that they weren't suitable. As for why – well, perhaps they weren't interested enough. Or perhaps they were the sort whom I suspected would not be prepared to accept discipline. And of course, I recognised that discipline was an important requirement for security reasons. You see, some people might present, in some respects, very well, but the trouble was, they were very fond of talking to people; they liked to propagandise. And, of course, one of the things that a member of MAC could *not* do was go around propagandising, because that would reveal what he thought and believed. And what you *don't* want is someone who attracts attention. Only if it seemed *more* suspicious if he suddenly stopped voicing his support for Welsh nationalism was he allowed to continue. Ordinarily, what he had to do was either keep his mouth shut, or deny everything: "Oh no, I don't believe in all that rubbish" – stuff like that. So, if it became clear that this was a person, good though he was, who wasn't totally security cleared because the moment he's had a couple of pints, or when he was feeling happy or whatever, he may say something which people can then jump on – because there were always those people around listening, either undercover police or others waiting to hear suspicious remarks to report back to the authorities – then I wouldn't bother. And to this day, he would not know that he was once examined as a potential MAC recruit. And so, through either chatting to them or monitoring their behaviour, I was able to determine whether they were worth taking up or not – and some were not. As for how many I decided were *not* suitable, I can't give a definite figure because there was no documentation. We knew better than to do that, because of the security aspect. So, it's a matter of memory now – but I would say about five or six. And I considered that each was unsuitable for us at various stages of the recruitment process.'

Did the process of returning to an area of Wales to inform a recruit that he had 'passed' the surreptitious induction strategy always go to plan?

'Well, one person I can think of did stand up to the scrutiny – and he passed every stage of the assessment process. And of course, I knew his routine, but when I went down to recruit him, to "bring him into the fold", I learned that he was away. Well, he wouldn't have known I was coming down… I wouldn't have told him to expect me on such-and-such a date. And I *never* wrote to anybody to tell them I'd be visiting and when, because that would have been a lack of security, wouldn't it? That's what made communication so damn difficult, but so effective. Well, it was the only way to do things. If I'd written letters to people stating, "The committee has asked me to call", well, how long would I have been on the loose? Not bloody long! So, this man had no reason *not* to go away that weekend. But that meant that he missed his chance of being in MAC. I suppose it might seem a bit unfair – if he was suitable and willing. But he was a happily married man anyway, so it might not have worked out. Because married men with kids had more to lose, so when push came to shove they might be less inclined. Besides, he went on to greater things. You could say that he eventually became a member of the Welsh establishment. But I'm saying no more. But even today he doesn't know he was under scrutiny.'

## John assembles the MAC cell structure

Encouraged to disclose more about the concept of the cell system and the importance of the cell leader, John revealed that he had been an avid reader of Irish history. He was aware that illegal underground movements were often undermined through being infiltrated by non-sympathetic pretenders, by peripheral informers, and through genuine members imparting information concerning names and contacts under pressure in a police interview. To combat the problem, John Jenkins devised the two- or three-man cell structure. Asked to elaborate as to how such a cell within MAC operated, Jenkins declared:

> 'Well, in the event of a person having passed their recruitment into MAC, I would say to them, "It would be nice if you had a friend who could support you in this venture... There should really be at least two, possibly three, so you can support each other. Someone who feels the same way as you do politically; a person you've known a long time and whom you trust implicitly." And so the cell leader would recruit his own cell, which comprised members who were all known to one another. And I have to say, it worked extremely well. And there you had another cell, and this cell would be completely independent of all other cells. A member of one cell wouldn't know where the other cells were, or who they comprised, or anything. And *crucially*, and I say this because I *did* go on to lead MAC, only the lead member of each cell was known to me. But to maximise the security of the movement still further, my identity remained unknown even to the cell leader – until I was later arrested, of course. And again, I have to say that the strategy worked.'

How did he come to consider that such a cell structure might prove effective? 'Because I realised that such a cell system would be *very* difficult to penetrate,' Jenkins replied, continuing:

> 'I mean, the point is: if the authorities found one cell, they could interrogate the leader all they liked. They could subject him to all sorts of inducements and problems. But he couldn't tell them anything – and he was the cell leader. He couldn't tell them who I was. He could describe me, but then I'm such a non-descript sort of fella, that wouldn't mean anything. So that's all he could do: describe the looks of me. He couldn't say where I was from, who I was, or provide them with my name. You see, he didn't know anything about me. I would just be passing through on my way somewhere. Effectively, he knew nothing. And he couldn't contact me, because there was no contact from his direction to me. I would *always* contact him. And so, having considered the need for security and stringency, I realised that this was the safest, indeed the *only*

feasible way that recruitment into the organisation could work. It had to be run on autocratic lines: a democratic system was too dangerous. In the end, though, the strength of the cell system was its weakness, in that with no one else in MAC possessed of the wherewithal to assemble and distribute the devices, my arrest ensured the MAC campaign ended… [But] I understand that so impressed were they by our cell structure, the Provisional IRA later adopted it.'

So how many were actively involved in the MAC campaign? 'I would say somewhere around fifteen,' Jenkins replied. 'There were no women in the cells. So, yes, about fifteen men: a figure in that region. With me having personally recruited about six.'

## The cell leaders are trained

How did the cell leaders recruited into MAC receive training in the assembling of explosive devices? 'In the same way that Dave Pritchard received training in how to assemble a device – and he gave the training to me, then I gave it to the cell leaders,' John responded earnestly.

> 'We'd discuss it quietly in the pub car park, or we might walk to a secluded place on their patch, where I'd explain it all to them. I'd demonstrate if necessary – well, as far as possible. But then the MAC boys didn't really have to know anything. All they had to know was how to put a few component parts together and place it. That's all they needed to know – how to prime it *in situ*. Because as it later transpired, of course, I assembled and delivered the devices to the cell leaders myself. And so, unlike me, they didn't have to know the ins and outs of it all. One feature we devised involved a way of testing it, so that a light would come on when the circuit was completed – and that was it really. Some picked it up very quickly and one demonstration was enough, but there were some who needed more training than others. You see, these recruits had to be blessed with a natural logic and intelligence. We were not airy fairy, "up in the sky"-type people. But it is true that several, for whatever reason, required perhaps a few lessons. Obviously, I couldn't be everywhere – not even I could be in two places at once. I tried hard, but it couldn't be done. And so three or four people were brought in to train those MAC recruits who needed the greater tuition, which, because of other commitments, I couldn't provide.'[60]

Did the decision to introduce trainers into the strategy cause John unease? 'Well, yes – it did,' he replied candidly, adding:

'Because I realised that in doing so, the scene changed from one of total security to one which was *not* so secure. Not so much because there now existed a potential breach of security, in that people had been brought in to train, but more because I didn't want anybody else to have any influence over these recruits. What I mean is, they were now under the direction of people – although brought into MAC as trainers – who potentially still had their own axe to grind, and as such may not be governed by the same principles and strategies which I felt were needed. This was why I began to appreciate the need for *total* control, because I did not want these devices, or this campaign, to be about revenge. The explosions had to achieve a political objective – and not be used simply for revenge purposes. But I was forced to accept that we had to do this [bring in trainers] and while it did militate against total security, it had to be done. None of these recruits were sent to Ireland to be trained. They were all trained in Wales, by people from Wales who knew what they were doing. But if the recruit felt he wanted or needed more training and I knew that I was prevented from helping him – due to work, perhaps – I'd say, "OK. Stick to your normal routine and I'll arrange for someone to contact you regarding the training side of things", or "stick to your routine and I'll arrange for someone to run through with you what to do." I would then contact the trainer and together we'd return, to say the Red Lion one Monday evening, and I'd introduce them. Well, so to speak. No names were exchanged. Having done so, the trainer and the recruit would then make the necessary arrangements to meet for a training exercise. And again, I have to say, the process worked… Along with information concerning the number of MAC recruits and potential candidates, etc, this is the first time I've spoken about the training aspect, because it involves people still around, you see. But that's how it happened.'

It is clear from discussions with John Jenkins and other informed observers that MAC did not comprise disenfranchised, detached and embittered youth. On the contrary, those prepared to undertake active protest action did so following a period of deliberation during which all the emotional factors regarding their willing participation were considered. Nonetheless, despite the safety procedures introduced – employing a timing mechanism *and* ensuring that the circuit could be tested by inserting a small bulb into the contact point which shone if correctly connected *before* the device was primed with two detonators – was the process of setting a MAC explosive device a safe one? Having paused in reflection, John replied sombrely:

'All those that I personally recruited received full training, so they had a good understanding of what they were doing. But even if they followed the correct and normal routine, the possibility of being killed was about 98% I would say... You see, the point is that I knew we wouldn't have all these big searchlights to operate by when we were in action. As I anticipated, when we operated, we did so with these little handheld torches; and even then, it was on-off, on-off.'

Having calculated that the risk of being killed while undertaking militant protest action in the name of *Mudiad Amddiffyn Cymru* stood at a dismal 98%, a figure compounded by the fact that in order to reduce the threat of deduction only the minimal use of a finger torch could be employed in the final stages of assembling an explosive device, how did Jenkins regard his situation as MAC's chief strategist at this juncture? 'I didn't like it,' he responded gravely.

'Because I realised that whoever handed a device over – me, as it transpired – would be saying goodnight to some people and possibly goodbye to others, because nobody knew if they were going to come back in one piece from these "adventures". But that was the set-up. That was the way it had to be. And I explained it to them as starkly as that. "There is," I said, "no way that anybody can retire, or resign, or whatever. Right?" And they accepted it. Because I knew that the person who ultimately led MAC would have to accept it too. And so, after this protracted assessment, recruitment and induction process, which lasted initially between mid-1965 and mid-1967, I was finally able to say, "Continue with your routine and we'll be in touch with you" – because I maintained contact periodically – "and you will receive your orders in due course."'

Having therefore established an organisation capable of providing an effective opposition, in which direction did Jenkins feel the future lay in terms of his *own* involvement? 'Well,' he replied soberly:

'In formulating an effective strategy through establishing the importance of a "hearts and minds" approach, putting these small active unit teams together and having established the extent of our resources – and "resources" in every sense of the word – I *didn't* want to be the one to take it forward. I didn't want the burden of it. Perhaps more honestly, I was increasingly torn between thinking: "Look, just get on with it. Be the leader – take over", and feeling that to do so was the *last* thing I wanted. Because it would be the wreckage of *everything* from my point of view: including my career, my marriage and my family life. Also, I realised that if I did take this on, I wouldn't stop, as my type of personality doesn't allow for things to be undertaken in half measures. And so the outcome, I knew, would either be death or imprisonment – which I also pointed out to the recruits. And there are not many who subscribe to that! But that is the only reasonable way I could look at it. So I was trying to get somebody else that I could put this burden onto. But I also realised another stark fact: despite the progress made, I knew that it would be some time before this rejuvenated MAC would be ready to strike a blow in the name of Welsh political freedom.'

During the period in which John travelled throughout Wales assessing the logistical strengths and weaknesses of MAC, he returned to stay briefly with his parents in Penybryn. Although not a regular frequenter of pubs prior to joining the Army, Jenkins decided to revisit one of his former haunts for a convivial pint or two. To what extent the area – and presumably the wider industrial region – had altered soon became strikingly, if amusingly, clear. The pub in question, John recounted, was in Bargoed and renowned as 'a straw on the floor and greyhound under the table type of pub; a rough old cider-drinking place.' Feeling 'happy to be home' after years away in the Army, John reasoned a catch-up with the old characters in the reassuring, if insalubrious, surroundings of the pub would ensure his reconnection with the area of his happy childhood and adolescence. Recalling the pub's less-than-exacting dress code, John decided that dressing the part might serve him well. Donning 'rough old clothes', Jenkins walked in, only to discover the place 'had become bloody gentrified'. A quick scan around the refurbished and unfamiliar room revealed a clientele entirely bedecked in 'collars, ties and suits'. As all eyes turned to the spectacle coming through the door, a collective, if inaudible, sense of 'Christ, Almighty! What the hell have we here?' greeted a startled Jenkins. 'I saw the joke,' John chuckled disarmingly in describing the incident. 'But nobody else did. Things had certainly changed a bit while I was away!'

## The opening of Llyn Celyn and the arrival on the stage of the Free Wales Army

The extent to which Wales had changed in recent years became all too apparent at the official opening of Llyn Celyn. It wasn't only MAC which emerged out of the anger surrounding Tryweryn; so too did the Free Wales Army. Led by the charismatic, swaggering and sharply media-astute Cayo Evans, the group made its first public appearance at the opening of Llyn Celyn on 21 October 1965.[61] If the attending Liverpool dignitaries intended the event to showcase the city's municipal splendour, they were to be sorely disappointed. The scheduled 45-minute ceremony was hurriedly concluded in just three minutes amid a chorus of boos, catcalls and some badly aimed stones, thrown by protestors. As the stones landed around the Liverpool bigwigs seated on the decorated platform, they simply stared back in the direction of the assembled and hostile throng, bearing facial expressions which ranged from bemusement and concern, to notable and increasing anger. The cutting of the microphone lead, which resulted in the opening declaration going unheard, ensured the occasion descended into farce. It is widely believed that the protest was *partly* inspired by the attendance of a minimally uniformed Cayo Evans and two other similarly attired members of the Free Wales Army.

As for the Plaid Cymru President, Gwynfor Evans – having initially appealed for calm – was captured by a television news crew turning his back and sheepishly drifting away. Much has been made of Gwynfor Evans' apparent haste to distance himself from the protest as it tumbled into chaos, including criticism from John Jenkins, who felt it was 'another opportunity missed' [to demonstrate nationalist leadership]. But speaking in 2015, former Plaid Cymru activist Gwynn Bowyer appeared to throw light on the party leader's actions. 'I've always felt that I was perhaps responsible for that,' remarked Bowyer.

'Gwynfor and I were chatting about the forthcoming opening of Llyn Celyn and I implored him, in the event of trouble breaking out – which I think we all expected – just to leave. Just to turn his back and quickly walk away. I knew that if he didn't, then the media would focus their attention on *him* and his response to the trouble, rather than the demonstration itself. I still feel that despite the image of Gwynfor appearing to turn and hurry away, that the advice I gave him was correct. I still believe that it was the right thing to do. Both in terms of Gwynfor's standing as party leader and because the protest then became the main focus of the media attention.'

John Jenkins did not attend the opening ceremony of Llyn Celyn. It coincided with the period Jenkins spent establishing MAC's capabilities, and to that end, he was in north Wales visiting a MAC associate. In addition, from a security point of view, it was 'essential' that he stay away and keep his head down. To attend the ceremony would almost certainly result in an attendee's presence being noted by police, John reasoned, and their future appearance on the security radar of law enforcement agencies guaranteed. This was not confined to the opening of Llyn Celyn, but any such mass-meeting, procession, demonstration or march. Consequently, from a 'tactical and security point of view', John 'was not going to be seen at anything'. It was not a policy solely restricted to Jenkins himself. As John considered the security strategy to be adopted by prospective members of MAC, he further disclosed that 'all our people were implored not to attend any protest event, as there should be no incriminating reason why they should be photographed – and fair play to them,' Jenkins added, 'they stuck to it.' If being seen and photographed was curtailed, so too were recruits 'advised not to submit letters to the papers, or to immediately refrain from doing so if they ever had'. In view of this security approach, former or suspected members of MAC connected to earlier protest actions, Jenkins declared resolutely, 'were no good to me'.

Nonetheless, if potential MAC recruits were advised to stay away, someone who did attend the opening ceremony of Llyn Celyn was the wife of Jenkins' host, who arrived back enthused by what she had witnessed. On discussing the protest, it quickly became apparent to John that at the opening of Llyn Celyn, 'the nature of the activities in Wales had *very* much changed'. As Jenkins listened transfixed, his hostess relayed how she and many other attendees had been galvanised by both this 'spirit of resurgence' and how the people, through 'the enthusiasm shown', were able to 'disrupt the whole proceedings'. It was at *this* point, Jenkins declared, 'having begun to think about the Investiture, that I thought: *that's* the answer. I realised then,' he added, 'that the disruptive actions of the Free Wales Army at the opening of Llyn Celyn – which was one of only two actions the FWA *ever* undertook that were a complete success – were also totally spontaneous.

Nothing was planned. Its disruption of the event just happened.' But John continued:

'The FWA and the other protestors were up against the might of the Liverpool councillors, whereas what we were thinking of was the might of the state, and what it [the state] could throw at us. So, while I had learned an invaluable lesson as to the adoption of disruptive tactics, I also knew that we [MAC] had to chart a *course of action* which showed signs of success, and that this ongoing campaign could *only* succeed if planned properly. Because we all knew, of course, that the Investiture was coming. And what was the object of the exercise? It was to change the nature of the activity in Caernarfon and the way it [our campaign] would affect the rest of Wales – and the UK, if it comes to that.'

## MAC targets the Clywedog Reservoir construction site; Gwynfor wins Carmarthen and Jenkins changes his mind

On Sunday, 6 March 1966, *Mudiad Amddiffyn Cymru* attacked machinery at the Clywedog Reservoir construction site with explosives. Although a peripheral member of MAC at the time of the Clywedog explosion and 'not directly involved', John Jenkins was aware that the 'protest was being planned and prepared for'. The Clywedog protest, he later disclosed, was undertaken by Trefor Beasley, Alf Williams and David Pritchard. It was the last militant action that Pritchard undertook as a member of MAC.[62] From this point on, Jenkins added gravely, 'Pritch was almost certainly being monitored by the police.' In 2018, an anonymous former MAC associate confirmed that he had instructed David Pritchard in how to use explosives; and explained how the group had avoided detection when transporting and storing explosive devices to be used in impending protest strikes:

'I was a collier and I had the knowledge about explosives that David needed. I helped him by showing him how best to use it; what to do. And the safety aspect of it, you know. For instance, I showed him how it had to be compacted. You see, the explosive material might be pliable and not necessarily in sticks and wrapped in paper. So you needed to follow a safety procedure whereby you don't compact it with an iron bar, you use a piece of wood; because with wood there are obviously no sparks – this sort of thing. I also showed him how you affix the charge, or the wire, so that when you pushed it in, it didn't catch and break and snap. You had to make sure it went in smoothly and compact it behind [with explosives]. But I also I showed him how to maximise the effects of the explosion: how the device would have to be put into a certain position in order for it to "blow" in a certain direction.

It was also important that the devices were transported and stored appropriately, in order to be collected, when needed, for an operation. So the containers that were used to transport the devices were made out of wood or fabric – absolutely no metal parts at all – because if the authorities came along looking for these things with a detector, they would find them. Any metal piece would be picked up by a detector, but if it's fabric and wood, the detector just goes straight over it. They wouldn't know it was there. I made quite a few boxes for them, and these containers were bound together using only glue as a cohesive, with the fabric really tight-fitting. To make them absolutely waterproof, they were then covered in a coat of tar, which was applied using a paintbrush. These containers would then be buried and hidden until they were needed. But this campaign didn't set out to hurt anybody. It was intended to say, "We've had enough."'

Although John was not directly involved in the protest strike at Clywedog, was Thelma aware that her husband was undertaking a period of assessment into MAC, with the possibility that it would result in him spearheading a renewed campaign of militant activism? 'No,' Jenkins responded resolutely. 'Thelma had no idea that I was assessing the logistical strengths of MAC. She knew I was into politics *in a way*, because I'd accepted Plaid Cymru's offer to buy that plot of land at the Clywedog site.'

Had he tried to discuss his frustration as to the political and constitutional situation with her? 'She would *not* have understood,' Jenkins replied wearily.

'She wouldn't have got it. While we were happy enough in some respects, at least initially, we weren't a couple who instinctively understood how the other thought and ticked. Besides, can you imagine a woman trying to get into this bloody mind? There are, I suppose, some people who consider me an intelligent man, but it is the sort of stuff that the average wife and mother would not want to know about. I should have realised that. But at *this* point in my association with MAC, Thelma was happily in the dark.'

Yet it wasn't only the sands beneath Thelma's feet which were shifting owing to developments in her husband's life. Things were changing not only in John's marriage, but in the nation as a whole. The establishment of the Welsh Office and the creation of the cabinet post of Secretary of State for Wales had appeased certain nationalist opinion that the political interests and fortunes of Wales were finally being afforded adequate and differential consideration. But if John Jenkins harboured 'some respect for Jim Griffiths' for never putting a foot wrong and 'always trying to put a foot right' during his tenure as the first Secretary of State for Wales, the '*big* breakthrough' in Welsh politics came, as far as Jenkins was concerned, with the Carmarthen by-election victory of Plaid Cymru president Gwynfor Evans on 14 July 1966:

> 'That was the first time that I... well... I laugh now when I think about it, but that I actually broke down and cried over a purely political thing. When I heard the news next morning on the television, it just blew me away completely. I was thrilled.'

Importantly, Jenkins also believed that with Evans able to voice nationalist concerns in Westminster, his planned militant protest was now 'unnecessary'. Yet despite Jenkins' optimism, it was not a feeling set to last. As time went on, John came to realise that 'as with the creation of the Welsh Office, this again was tokenism.' Not on Gwynor Evans' part, Jenkins was quick to profess. The Plaid president, he felt sure, 'was genuine enough in his desire for political change for Wales.' However, in weighing up Gwynfor Evans' new-found position within the UK political framework, it appeared to John Jenkins that having been elected, Evans was being 'tolerated' by the establishment 'to do his bit of creeping and crawling about'. Gwynfor Evans, Jenkins opined, was being indulged; and while 'allowed to undertake all the routine things that other MPs do', any political endeavours by Evans to reap *real* political harvest would soon be curtailed. The Plaid Cymru MP, Jenkins felt assured, was never going to be allowed to influence or interfere, in any way, shape or form, 'with significant matters of state.' What could one man – a 'lone voice' – hope to achieve in *any* event? 'From what I gather,' Jenkins continued:

> 'Gwynfor Evans was also attending all these receptions: both prior to and after arriving in London. Furthermore, when he got there, they [the press]

135

were all waiting for him. And I could see even *then*, the vanity of it; the hopelessness of it all. His election to Parliament didn't count. Had more Plaid Cymru MPs been elected, it might have counted for something. That *might* have made a difference. But one man didn't count. They [the political establishment] weren't prepared to concede *anything* of consequence. What is more, every time Evans tried to speak in Parliament, he was scorned and shouted down and ridiculed.'

## Aberfan

With John Jenkins feeling increasingly disillusioned with constitutional political practice, in mid-October 1966, he visited his parents in Penybryn. Jenkins' visit was made during a period of annual leave from work and coincided with a period of heavy rainfall. [63] Both when travelling to his parents' home a few days earlier, and when returning to Wrexham during the afternoon of 20 October, he drove through Aberfan. The following morning at 10.30 a.m., as John sat at home in Wrexham enjoying the last day of his holiday, a BBC television news summary interrupted its scheduled programming. It announced that some 70 minutes earlier a spoil tip of coal waste, rock and slurry had thundered down a hillside onto the village of Aberfan.[64] Early indications, it was sombrely declared, suggested that having engulfed Pantglas Junior School, casualties were expected.[65] Among the 144 killed were 116 schoolchildren, all under the age of 11.[66] That night in Wrexham, watching the grey, grim images from Aberfan, John Jenkins said he was 'inconsolable'. Coinciding with the period of assessment which John was undertaking into MAC, to what degree did the Aberfan disaster impact upon his psychological position at this juncture? 'Oh, I think it was the turning point,' Jenkins replied pensively:

'It was my mother's home village for a start, you see, so therefore I felt a great affinity with it. I felt the disaster very deeply. I'd passed through it [Aberfan] the day before on my way back to Wrexham, having gone down to see my mother, and the next day it collapsed. I found it extremely distressing. I've always felt that it symbolised the oppression of Wales, and how badly Wales has been treated by England.'

During an interview with police following his arrest in 1969, Jenkins stated, 'I felt that Aberfan was the ultimate expression of English disinterest in

Wales. I am a socialist and I care about people. If I had to sum up my beliefs in one line, I would ask you the question, "Who is to stand up for the little man?".[67] Encouraged to revisit his comments for this book, John replied trenchantly:

> 'Well, it's true. It couldn't have happened anywhere else but there – in the south Wales industrial region. It wouldn't have been allowed to happen in Kent, or Surrey, or anywhere like that. There were *many* reasons why I felt angry. But there was the added blow of the delightful Princess Margaret then sending a trainload of toys. Who for? There were no kids left.'

As for Lord Snowdon, Princess Margaret's husband, visiting the village later that dreadful Friday evening – having as a Welshman decided to do so voluntarily to provide emotional and 'hands on' support to the grieving families – Jenkins was nonplussed, believing, perhaps unfairly, that Snowdon's actions were fuelled by reasons of self-promotion. John Jenkins was not alone in his immediate circle in being 'fundamentally affected' by the Aberfan disaster. His mother, Minerva, was also 'terribly upset'. Although Minerva's childhood family home on Cottrell Street was not affected, her bewildered despair, in common with many others, soon turned to anger. An especial reason for the bitterness stemmed from the National Coal Board's decision to contravene official procedure and partly base the tip on ground from which water springs emerged – a fact which the NCB denied in the aftermath of the disaster. Just days after the heart-rending events in Aberfan, Lord Robens, Chairman of the National Coal Board, loftily declared to a TV reporter: 'It was impossible to know that there was a spring in the heart of the tip which was turning the centre of the mountain into sludge.'[68] Similarly, during an interview with the *Sunday Times*, Robens was quoted as saying: 'The Aberfan disaster has produced a new hazard in mining about which we knew nothing before.'[69]

Yet despite the National Coal Board's slippery insistence that it knew nothing of the existence of the springs, their presence on the hillside was common knowledge in the area. Philip Brown, a 61-year-old disabled ex-miner and Aberfan resident proclaimed, 'It was not a hidden spring. The National Coal Board must have known about it, because everyone in the village did.'[70] If further proof were needed, the springs over which coal waste had been tipped were marked on an Ordnance Survey map of 1919 and a Geographical Survey map of 1959 – copies of which were angrily provided by parents during the subsequent inquiry. Furious about Lord Robens and the NCB's intransigent denial of knowledge of the springs' existence was Minerva Barnard, who, inflamed with indignation, informed John that as a child growing up in Aberfan, 'at least three times every year the springs would overrun'; resulting in her 'splashing about and walking around up to her ankles in water'.

The official inquiry into the Aberfan disaster was chaired by Lord Justice Edmund Davies. The tribunal, having held an initial public meeting on 2 November 1966, took evidence in public for 76 days, heard testimony from 136 witnesses and concluded its hearings on 28 April 1967. During the proceedings' often tense and impassioned testimony, Lord Robens was forced to acknowledge that his 'unforeseeable' argument was untenable. This was owing to the revelation that a tip slide of comparative magnitude had occurred a little way down the valley in 1939, while the Aberfan tips themselves had slid in 1944 and 1963. In addition, on 4 February 1909 at Pentre in the Rhondda – although the details were not submitted to the inquiry – a colliery spoil heap collapsed, resulting in 'moving rubbish being flung onwards with the speed of an avalanche'. Four houses were buried, while a fifth was 'severed in twain', killing a young boy.[71] Tip slides were neither, therefore, unknown *nor* unforeseeable.

If it seemed that a crack in the official account had been observed, S O Davies, Aberfan's Labour MP, announced when giving evidence to the tribunal that he had long held concerns that the tip 'might not only slide, but in sliding might reach the village.' He had, however, been disinclined to raise the matter, owing to a 'more than a shrewd suspicion that [had he done so] the colliery would be closed.'[72] It was a line of argument which appeared to implicate Davies as being negligent and partly responsible, in that his failure to highlight his concerns prior to the tragic events unfolding rendered him legally culpable. Yet, S O Davies' apparent admission was rejected by the tribunal. It did so by recording that 'We doubt that he [Davies] fully understood the grave implication of what he was saying.'[73] Both S O Davies' testimony and the tribunal's concession were later greeted with disdainful incredulity by John Jenkins. Had Davies raised the matter, Jenkins countered angrily, job losses *may* have occurred, but 'the kids would have been alive, though, wouldn't they?'[74]

Finally, after months of acrimony, the official report into the Aberfan disaster was published on 3 August 1967. It placed the blame for the catastrophe squarely at the door of the National Coal Board. The organisation's chairman, Lord Robens,[75] was criticised for not providing clarity as to the NCB's knowledge of the presence of water springs on the hillside. But if some observers felt a degree of justice had been exacted, for John Jenkins and many besides, the sense of outrage was compounded still further when the National Coal Board was neither fined nor any of its employees subsequently prosecuted.

The controversy rumbled on. Contrary to the intractable NCB's claims, it was widely believed that the appalling tragedy had occurred not as an Act of God, but because of the greed and negligence of man. It was a sentiment shared around the world. Within months, £1.75 million had been donated to the appeal fund. But such was the furious contention the distribution of the money provoked, the issue was scathingly referred to as 'The Second Disaster'. Although the money, as John Jenkins angrily protested, 'had been sent for the kids', £150,000 was taken from the disaster fund to pay for the removal of the remaining waste tips in Aberfan. In August 1997, Ron Davies, the newly-appointed Secretary of State for Wales, repaid the £150,000 taken from the disaster fund. Despite the fact that the interest accrued since 1966 was not added, nor indeed was inflation taken into account, it was hoped that after 30 years, a highly disreputable page in the history of both the Labour Party and the UK had finally been turned.

But if the way in which the monies were raised to clear the tips seemed distasteful, the approach taken by the NCB to compensating grieving families took insensitivity to an unprecedented and shocking level. For one father, who was typical of many, the torment was further heightened by the fact that those he now sought justice from were what he termed his 'own people: a Labour Government, a Labour Council and a Labour-nationalised Coal Board.'[76] Despite the Disaster Fund Management Committee's protestation that it was financially constrained by precedent, the insensitivity of the National Coal Board's insurance department was later revealed. Memoranda from 1967 not only urged the chairman of the NCB, Lord Robens, to resist any increased demand, it also considered £500 to be 'a good offer'. Moreover, it monstrously claimed that 'a hard core' of bereaved parents were 'trying to capitalise'.[77]

At a further meeting of the Aberfan Parents and Residents Association, a petition was launched demanding that each bereaved family receive £5,000.[78] On learning of the situation, it is claimed that Cayo Evans, the self-styled leader of the FWA, issued an ultimatum stating that unless the money was released to the families within a week, explosives would be used to demolish Methyr Tydfil Town Hall and 'all the councillors inside it'.[79] It is unknown if Cayo Evans' statement cut any ice with the authorities, but the fact remains that within a week of militant action being allegedly threatened, following a four-hour meeting of the fund's management committee, it was announced that each grieving family would receive £5,000. It was, John Jenkins asserts, along with members of the FWA disrupting the official opening of Llyn Celyn, the Free Wales Army's 'finest achievement'. Yet, lacking both the technical ability and the necessary materials, 'the FWA couldn't have followed through with their threat to blow up Merthyr Town Hall and all the rest of it,' stated Jenkins. 'They would have had to come to us [MAC] to make good their threat... Not that they [FWA] knew who we were... Who were they going to contact?'

One aspect of the Aberfan tragedy which has attracted comment is the decision by the Queen not to visit the distraught village until 30 October – nine days after the catastrophe struck. Reaction to the Queen's regretted choice to stay away has ranged from incredulity, consternation and hostility to an acceptance of the Royal position that the Queen feared her presence might distract from the rescue/recovery operation, and provoke an inappropriate media frenzy. But occurring just six months after the militant protest by MAC at the Clywedog Reservoir construction site, might the fear of public discord or the threat of physical assault – either by way of a militant reprisal by MAC, or an attack undertaken by a traumatised member of the local or wider community – have been responsible for the Queen's decision? 'Well, no,' John Jenkins declared candidly.

'Certainly not in relation to MAC. There was no threat then. In those days MAC didn't exist, as such. I have no idea what she thought... All I know is that they [the Royal Family] only do things that they consider to be 'good strategy'. They never do anything spontaneously... They never do.'

Pausing for a moment, as if reliving the horrific events, Jenkins added scornfully, if somewhat unreasonably: 'I don't think it would have affected her. She just didn't care. Why should she bother?'[80]

Whatever the truth surrounding the most shameful and tragic period in recent Welsh history, the Aberfan disaster stiffened John Jenkins' resolve to undertake militant activism in the name of Welsh political freedom. Dissatisfied with democratic politics – most notably as a result of the perceived injustices of Tryweryn, Clywedog and Aberfan – Jenkins also cancelled his membership of Plaid Cymru. The party's ineffectual and cultural 'Primrose League' atmosphere, he decided, didn't suit him.[81] In the weeks following the Aberfan disaster, John Jenkins received technical instruction in the assembling of an explosive device from David Pritchard. In response to how intensive his training in such matters proved to be, Jenkins replied:

'David Pritchard explained [it] to me, as it had been shown to him. Namely, how to make the bomb: how to put it all together – and prime it. But part of it, I have to confess, was innate, I'm afraid. Had it not been, I wouldn't have caught on. What I'm saying is, it wasn't the case that I required intensive training in the use of explosives. A lot of it came naturally to me. Yet again, though, it dawned on me that I seemed to have been made, as it were, for the position that I found myself in.'

Nonetheless, Jenkins maintains that he still hoped that such an ability would not be required, but that he had expressed a desire to be taught how to assemble an explosive device 'in order to be ready' should such knowledge ever need to be exercised. Asked if the events surrounding the appalling Aberfan story proved pivotal to the rebirth of *Mudiad Amddiffyn Cymru*, Jenkins struggled to contain his emotion. Finally, he declared:

'The intensity of the anger was almost palpable among the people I was meeting throughout the country. It wasn't just the disaster, was it? I mean, what words can adequately describe that? But it was the manner in which the *whole thing* was subsequently handled: the NCB's denials, the fact that money from the disaster fund was used to pay for the removal of the tips, and the compensation issue. It was *dreadful*; and the people that I knew were absolutely furious. *Very* angry. So yes. It was a combination of various factors: the disaster of course; the fact that Aberfan was my mother's home village; and the indignity of Tryweryn and Clywedog. But do I think Aberfan was the turning point.'

## The Free Wales Army attempts a militant strike, and John learns a valuable lesson as plans for the Investiture are announced

Despite the apparent success of the FWA in ensuring that grieving families in Aberfan received £5,000 'compensation' for their incalculable loss, John Jenkins had already reached a decision regarding the group's reliability and suitability for a militant campaign. In February 1967, Jenkins was called upon by a MAC associate who had been contacted by the FWA, to assemble an explosive device. Having reconnoitred the site over several weeks, Cayo Evans' group intended to use the explosives package to target the water pipeline from Cwm Elan to Birmingham, at Cefn Penarth near Llandrindod. Having been handed the device via a small chain of contacts, the FWA remained utterly in the dark as to the identity of its manufacturer. Planted at the end of February, it was intended for the device to activate in order to adorn the front pages of the nation's newspapers on St David's Day. But it failed to detonate.

Dennis Coslett, one of the FWA unit involved in laying the charge, later explained how the operation was carried out – and what went wrong. Having removed a manhole cover near the Fron Aqueduct, the device – including 40 taped sticks of gelignite – was laid on a Mini car tyre. On a rope whose other end was tied to a nearby tree, the assemblage was lowered into the water below. Though John Jenkins had regarded the exercise to be generally straightforward, in their haste to set the charge, the group failed to prime it correctly. Having dipped a toe into the icy waters of militant action, Dennis Coslett further disclosed that this was the *only* time that the Free Wales Army attempted to carry out a militant strike in the name of Welsh Independence. 'They made a mess of it,' John declared disparagingly, before adding:

'I was asked early on [in the campaign] to provide a primed bomb for "our friends" who "want to attack a pipeline". Initially, I was unaware that it was for use by the FWA. We hadn't at this stage established the rock-hard security foundations which were obvious a little later on. At this point, I was still prepared to talk to other people, and so I put this device together which ended up in the hands of the Free Wales Army. As for where the explosives came from, I'm not sure. I didn't make too many enquiries about that. But I do know they didn't come from one place – they came from a quarry here and a quarry there. Anyway, it was the only one that I assembled for the FWA, and they made a mess of it, of course. It was meant to be an easy operation. It [the device] was handed to them on a plate – any fool could have planted it. But they didn't prime it properly. There were a few simple tests to follow, which I had been shown some six months earlier. They were simple really, even for me, and I was ignorant on these matters. But even I found the procedure to prime it simple.

But despite our frustrations, I did learn a valuable lesson. I said then to myself, and anybody else that would listen, "If I do decide to take this campaign forward," – and it was looking increasingly likely – "there will never be another occasion when I just hand a bomb over. From now on, the bombs will only go to certain people, to do certain things." This, I decided, was my policy – or at least a component in the *overall* policy which was becoming clearer in my mind. I decided after this fiasco that I had to hold the movement in a tight grip. Only on my say-so would the resources be used, and they would only be handed to people who knew what they were talking about – only to those people who could be trusted to know what they were doing. And this is the way we carried on after that. It was the only way I could ensure discipline – and what's more, it worked. As far as MAC was concerned, there was no more of the "wild man" antics.'

As John was formulating a code by which he could maintain control over a proposed militant offensive, his talent for inspiring people to confide in him – which he had first become aware of during his childhood and adolescence – had also proved extremely useful in establishing the strengths of the dormant MAC, as former active and peripheral members imparted knowledge of weaponry and intelligence during the two-year period he spent assessing the group. But it was during this period, as Jenkins contemplated the battle ahead, that his ability to be the trusted recipient of private information was recognised within his professional arena also. One afternoon, a high-ranking officer in the Dental Corps to which John belonged took him to one side and started explaining how 'bereft' he felt, because he and his wife were childless. This was despite, John's superior sadly informed him, his wife and him having tried for a family for several years. If, as when Jenkins had presented a shoulder to cry on for his grieving neighbour some twenty years before, John again felt somewhat honoured to be trusted with a subject so intimate in nature, he also thought it 'strange'. It was, after all, Jenkins reasoned, 'unheard of for a senior officer to speak to a common old sergeant about matters so delicate'. John felt that his early and tentative assessment of being in possession of 'some sort of a gift' had been confirmed. As for what the gift provided, Jenkins concluded that while he could convey genuine empathy and offer advice, he was crucially *also* able to inspire loyalty and trust. Nonetheless, as the events of the MAC campaign unfolded, Jenkins realised that 'it was a gift' which, in due course, he would find 'useful, if harrowing'.

On 17 May 1967, to the delight of the Labour Government and Cledwyn Hughes, the incumbent Secretary of State for Wales, it was announced that Charles Windsor was to be invested Prince of Wales at Caernarfon Castle on 1 July 1969. If British unionists celebrated the news, more cynical observers suspected that politically opportune motives were at play. They were not perhaps far wrong. The Labour Party in Wales was still reeling from Gwynfor Evans' victory in the Carmarthen by-election in July 1966, and from the disaster at Aberfan three months later, in which the party – and the wider Labour Movement – was seen as culpable. Across Wales, as indeed across the UK, there was increasing unease over Harold Wilson's economic policy. All these issues culminated in a belief within the Labour Government that it needed to pull something special out of the hat; and a royal investiture, a potent symbol of statehood, fitted the bill. On learning of the news, John Jenkins determined that in announcing the ceremony, the British state had thrown down the gauntlet. Asked to crystallise his thoughts at this juncture, Jenkins was typically candid:

> 'I was angry: frustrated by what I could see happening around me. But even at this stage, I was still thinking I didn't want to be put in this position. I was a married man; more importantly, a father of two young boys and to all intents and purposes a respected... establishment figure. But when news of the Investiture broke, a militant response, I think, became inevitable.'

## John returns to Cyprus – and makes a life-changing decision

In the early summer of 1967, John returned to Cyprus with the Gloucestershire Regiment. The visit resulted from the Army discovering that the servicemen who were mounting guard at military installations on Cyprus were due to leave for Germany and that, consequently, a three-week period needed to be covered. Assigned to 'change guard for the three weeks' were the Glosters, who were based at Saighton Camp, where John too was stationed. Having discussed the forthcoming assignment with Jenkins, members of the Glosters 'kindly recommended to the military authorities' that John accompany them. Jenkins maintained 'a great affinity with the Greek people' and, privately at least, still harboured sympathy for the aspirations and achievements of EOKA. Within days of arriving in Cyprus, John 'looked up a lot of his old friends' from when he had been stationed on the island some ten years previously. If Jenkins was pleased to catch up with people, he was amazed 'to see how many of them now had photographs on their walls showing them proudly wearing the uniform of EOKA'. As a result of the trip being more of a holiday than there being an expectation that John would be consigned to dental duties, he was afforded plenty of time to wander the beaches and ponder his situation – most notably with regard to his increasing belief that a militant response from MAC was now unavoidable.

Nonetheless, the extent to which Jenkins was able to enjoy the freedom and sunshine of Cyprus was comically revealed one evening when he returned to the barracks in Akrotiri and went to inform his superior officer that he was back. Attired in his 'usual jeans and T-shirt', Jenkins walked over to the officers' mess, where he was greeted politely by the desk sergeant. Having asked to 'speak to Captain So-and-So', John observed the desk sergeant pick up the phone and put a call through to a neighbouring room. After a period of momentary silence, the call was answered. Following the briefest of formalities, the desk sergeant asked that John's commanding officer be informed that 'a Turkish taxi driver is out here who wants to speak to him.' Struggling to contain his amusement as the officer replaced the handset, Jenkins asked, 'Have you met many Turkish taxi drivers with blue eyes?' 'Oh,' came the desk sergeant's surprised, if impassive, reply.

Asked to consider the importance of the excursion to Cyprus in the early summer of 1967, Jenkins replied pensively:

'You know what it's like when things are getting on top of you... it was a good break, you know? I had been considering for months how a militant campaign could be run successfully, and the trip provided an opportunity to take a step back and weigh up what I now realised I had to do.'

Along with the restful and calming conditions of Cyprus, it is hard not to consider the extent to which observing the photographs of his old friends proudly adorned in the guerrilla uniform of EOKA may also have impacted on Jenkins' frame of mind. But whether or not the EOKA photographs proved an influential factor in John's decision process, a sobering realisation dawned for Jenkins: what he wanted in orchestrating a campaign of militant protest in the name of Welsh resistance was 'sole responsibility'. Encouraged to reveal what he believed adopting such a strategy might involve, Jenkins professed calmly: 'I knew it was going to be tough. But I also figured I would do it my way, or no way.' Had there been a point, even at this juncture, where walking away had crossed his mind? 'No,' John replied phlegmatically.

> 'I mean, God knows, I had asked the question "Why me?" I cursed myself in bloody heaps for admitting in the end, "If I don't do it, nobody will do it." You see, I couldn't find anybody, or any other group, who could take it on. I found several possible groups who showed potential. But I quickly determined that it would take a long, long time before they were ready to undertake something like this: a militant campaign. So, in the end, I had to sit down and properly consider the matter. And the decision facing me was, "Either I do it, or nobody will do it – and this will just rumble on and on, like everything else has done over the years: the resentments, the frustrations, the humiliations." And *that*, I decided, was not tolerable.'

Had he, nevertheless, arrived at a lesser opinion of Welsh patriots, and indeed, not questioned – if these perceived injustices were felt so acutely – why no equipped and functioning organisation existed to meet and combat such encroachments? 'Oh, I knew what was the matter with them,' Jenkins countered:

> 'They had been subjected to eight hundred years of the most careful and efficient browbeating in the world. Without actually being beaten on the head with a bloody cudgel. Unlike the Irish people, the Welsh had not suffered at the hands of the English – at least not as greatly. The conquest of Wales was much more insidious. The Welsh had been seduced, rather than raped. And yet I was looking at a nation which, in spite of eight hundred years of this, could still produce a group of people – not a huge number, but a significant amount – who were prepared to do something

about it; who were willing to say "Unless we make a stand now, our nation and what we hold dear will be lost forever." So that was my choice: either do nothing, or lead this counter-offensive. And it amounted to there being *no* choice really. Look, I would have loved to find somebody else to get on with it, and I would have backed them up – because I saw myself involved in *some* capacity or other – but the burden of spearheading this would have rested with them. But I couldn't find anybody. I looked hard enough, but I couldn't find anyone. And so, finally, at this point, I decided to embark on the course of action to be taken. That was it. The decision had been made. I never considered for a moment turning round and going back after that. There were too many people involved; too many people relying on me, anyway. I couldn't turn back.'

Having spent some two years assessing the logistical and strategic efficacies of *Mudiad Amddiffyn Cymru*, by the summer of 1967 John Jenkins was confident that he had at his disposal an oiled and primed network of cells throughout Wales, ready to take the fight to the British state. The malaise and resignation which in recent years had permeated the Welsh militant community had ended. If the British state had thrown down the gauntlet in announcing its intention to hold the Royal Investiture, John Jenkins had picked it up. The time had come to relaunch a militant response to the injustices suffered by the Welsh nation. Jenkins' decision to orchestrate a campaign of militant activism in the name of Welsh opposition would see the use of explosives as a means of protest taken to an unprecedented level in Welsh political history. The first wave of militancy, which John Jenkins spearheaded as the Director-General of the reconstructed MAC, would primarily be undertaken to protest the flooding of Welsh valleys to provide English conurbations with water. But as all eyes turned to the impending Investiture of Charles Windsor as Prince of Wales, matters were about to escalate, despite the efforts of the security forces to apprehend those responsible. Unbeknown to the nation's law-enforcement agencies, their militant Welsh nemesis was operating under their noses, concealed to some significant extent within the unsuspecting world of the British Army.

# CHAPTER 4

# Heavy is the head
# that wears the crown

## John meets Frederick Ernie Alders

In conjunction with his dental duties – and his more covert obligations – John had for some months been acting as a sergeant instructor to the Corps of Drums of a Territorial battalion of the Royal Welch Fusiliers. It was a leisure pursuit from which Jenkins derived much enjoyment. In the summer of 1967, John met Frederick Ernest Alders. In the preceding weeks, Alders, a television aerial-rigger from Rhosllanerchrugog, had joined the band of the TA battalion as a trainee flautist. It coincided with Jenkins putting the final touches to his plan to use explosives to attack his first target: the pipeline at Llanrhaeadr-ym-Mochnant which carried water from the reservoir at Lake Vyrnwy to Liverpool.

Asked why the 19-year-old Frederick Ernest Alders, known as Ernie, had come to his attention, Jenkins replied:

'I noticed during practice evenings and excursions, as I kept my ears open, that he was often involved in arguments with other bandsmen about the very things that I and others like me were so opposed to. Things like Tryweryn, Aberfan and the decline of the Welsh language and all the rest of it. By this point, of course, I was involved in the process of recruiting people into MAC, and so this marked him out straight away in my mind as a potential candidate.

I was also able to make enquiries into his background, and quite quickly I knew enough about him from the information I received from this close contact to realise that he was just the sort of chap we needed; particularly as he knew everybody and was well known. Well, not well known in the sense that he had a prominent profile. But well known in the sense that he was a member of Wrexham society. Put it this way: he knew who was who, what was what, and where was where – and so he was very handy.'

How had Ernie Alders impressed on Jenkins that he possessed the necessary emotional qualities required to join the swelling ranks of MAC? 'Well,' Jenkins replied:

'Through my recruitment strategy, I'd become quite skilled in recognising the attributes which I felt were necessary. So eventually, having monitored his behaviour and attitude over many weeks, I engaged him in conversation – again, as a means of finding out what he thought about Wales and the situation it faced. I played my devil's advocate routine with him. I'd respond with snidey remarks and watch his attitude – observe his reaction. And I must say that Ernie more than met the criteria that I was looking for. It was obvious that his views were deeply held, and he would attack me back. He was passionate, angry; but crucially, he was also to-the-point and constrained.

When I eventually revealed what I was *really* all about, Ernie was very happy, believing he now belonged to an organisation able to hit back effectively. We shared a bond, but it was only because of MAC. He struck me as an intelligent and able young man; and as I thought then, trustworthy – but it's come out since that he was telling his girlfriend, and later fiancée, Ann Woodgate, everything. Some people feel the need to unburden themselves, I suppose. He must have felt that she was safe. But at this point, of course, I had no idea that he was telling her so much.'

If Alders' indiscretion was yet to be realised, any uncertainty Jenkins felt as to the need for MAC to relaunch a militant campaign had been dispelled. In addition, in the period between arriving back in the UK from Germany in April 1965 and the late summer of 1967, Jenkins had 'developed an organisation which was now armed, trained and willing. All that remained,' John added reflectively, was the need to point the MAC activists 'in the right direction and let them get on with it.'

## Llanrhaeadr-ym-Mochnant

On 30 September 1967, John Jenkins and Ernie Alders carried out their first militant attack in the name of *Mudiad Amddiffyn Cymru*. The explosion, which signalled the rebirth of MAC's militant offensive, successfully breached the pipeline at Llanrhaeadr-ym-Mochnant. Throwing light on how and why the protest was undertaken, Jenkins declared: 'I had reconnoitred the site over many weeks – mainly alone – pretending to be sightseeing. After careful consideration, I decided that the pipeline should be targeted.' Asked to reveal what factors had been considered, John explained:

'I wanted a target which had a political meaning. Something that we felt legitimised our objective and established what we were trying to achieve. The political objective of a particular target needed to be clear to everyone. You want to avoid ambiguity. I mean, when you blow up a water pipeline carrying water to Liverpool, the message is loud and clear. People across Wales would know exactly what you were doing and why: namely, that water was being piped free to Liverpool from Wales, as a result of a populated valley in Wales having been demolished to provide the water. And throughout Wales, people realised this. The action was therefore self-explanatory. But, as I've said, I was also mindful of the need to win the "hearts and minds" of Welsh people. So, while the protest had to be considered and effective, it also needed to be restrained.'

How had the explosive device been assembled? 'I was given all the necessary equipment by Dave Pritchard,' Jenkins revealed, before continuing:

'In the days before the explosion at Llanrhaeadr, me and Pritch met in Rhayader. There he handed to me the explosive material – the nitroglycerine: about 14.5 lbs. It was inside a bucket, because these few sticks of geli' had melted. It had the consistency of thick custard, more or less. It could be manipulated to be used, but it was very dangerous. But it was *just* pliable and consistent enough to hold two detonators. We always used two in case one failed. The point is that you can't test a detonator. It goes off, or it doesn't go off; and if it does go off, it can't be used again. So, there was enough gelignite in this bucket to cause one explosion, but I knew that we'd have to use it quickly and so I decided that the pipeline at Llanrhaeadr would be targeted. But along with this gelignite, Pritch gave me a Venner time switch, so I could set the time of the blast (2 a.m.)

and about 500 detonators – which, regarding the detonators, was enough for the whole campaign, as it turned out. And this was the keys to the Kingdom! 14.5 lbs of very dangerous gelignite, 500 detonators and one Venner time mechanism! To be fair, it was all the equipment that Pritch and Dai Walters had – I had nothing else from them. For one thing, Pritch and Walters had nothing left to give me, and I didn't want any direction or input from them anyway. All I wanted to do was to get out in the field and to lose touch with them both, because, as I say, to some degree, they were on the radar – especially after the explosion at Clywedog. And so the last time I was in contact with Dai Walters was when we met in that hotel in Bargoed in October 1964. As for Dave Pritch, the last time we met was, as I say, in Rhayader just before the blast at Llanrhaeadr – right at the very start of the [reconvened] MAC campaign. You see, it must be pointed out that once they gave me this original cargo of detonators and one load of explosives and one timing device, it was made quite clear that we [the new MAC] were on our own – entirely on our own. I also believed that if this action at Llanrhaeadr was successful, they would realise they could leave me alone, anyway. They would know that I was effective. But at this point, just before the attack took place, I was more concerned with security. And so I let it be known that there was to be no more communication between the new MAC and the old – and this, of course, included Pritchard and Walters. There's been a lot of nonsense spoken about the MAC campaign over the years, such as this business of me having run back and forth to chat to Dave Pritchard about targets and strategies and so on. It's rubbish. It's just unfounded speculation. Once we started, that was it: all contact between us ended. No letters, no meetings, no phone calls: nothing. And that goes for anybody else who was "known". For security reasons, it was out of the question.'

What was the mood in the car as Jenkins and Alders made their way from Wrexham to carry out the operation? Was there a lot of excited chatter as to what lay ahead? 'No, there was not a lot said between us, really,' John replied, adding:

'This was our first job. If we bungled it, we'd be dead. All we had to work with, to provide light, was a small pencil torch. It wasn't much of a night, anyway. It was raining, if I remember correctly. So I knew that we'd be operating in adverse conditions, with inadequate lighting equipment, in a situation with which we were not familiar. As a result, we were not singing and laughing all the way down there! It went off alright, though – no problems. The device activated at 2 a.m., as I'd anticipated, having set the timer. And in the days following we weren't arrested. So in that sense, I was satisfied.'

But had *other* factors existed which determined that protest action at Llanrhaeadr would be undertaken? 'Yes,' Jenkins confirmed, before elaborating:

'An important reason why the pipeline at Llanrhaeadr was chosen was because we had a friend in the village who was able to inform us about certain things. For instance, there was a cottage which directly overlooked the area to be targeted, and living in this cottage was a family. But our friend was able to provide information as to when this person and his family were going on holiday. Having done so, we knew when it would be feasible to attack the pipeline – which is what we did. I wanted this information for two reasons. 1) From a security point of view: because obviously I didn't want to run the risk of us being seen; and 2) From a safety point of view: as I knew we'd be slightly less rushed, and that any damage to the house would be minimal and so none of the occupants risked injury. As it happened, I think one or two windows in the house were smashed, or they cracked or something. But there was no one at home, and this was a crucial factor in why the attack was carried out. Because we could have blown more pipes up, but that would have caused a lot more water to flow and it may well have damaged the village itself. And because of our "hearts and minds" philosophy, we didn't want that to happen. We didn't want to affect people adversely. The people of Wales had suffered enough. So we just did enough for one pipe. This local information, as provided by our friendly contact in the village, proved to be absolutely invaluable. And not for the last time would inside information prove crucial as the campaign developed.'[82]

Having knowingly 'stepped outside the law for the first time', how did he respond, both physically and emotionally, to the protest at Llanrhaeadr-ym-Mochnant? 'Well,' John replied intently:

'From a physical perspective, I discovered that if explosives permeate the skin, it results in a ferocious headache – even the merest physical contact. I also felt very nervous. The thought of handling explosives made me feel physically unwell. But despite the obvious dangers, I knew it was necessary, and it had to be done. Having said that, contrary to what most people think, when this happened there wasn't a fanfare of trumpets and glimpses of angels and all the rest of it. I felt a real sense of sadness. All my life, I'd been a respectable and reasonable member of society, a law-abiding citizen, in a respectable position. I had always held the law of this country in the highest regard. And suddenly, all that was all gone. I was now, although only a tiny number of people knew it, an outlaw. And I knew that I'd never look at life in the same way ever again.

Here I was, no longer a believer in British democracy – the so-called mother of *all* democracies. As far as Wales was concerned, it didn't exist. As a nation, Wales no longer knew what democracy was. And as a result, it had come to this. To think that in a so-called democracy you have to resort to things like this in order to get justice. I felt very downhearted about it. The situation worried me. The mood in the car as we drove back was heavy, certainly not light-hearted. I'd even say it was almost sad. But I should also add that despite these feelings, having undertaken this protest, it did feel as if my whole life had been in preparation for it; and this feeling only intensified as the campaign developed.'

The explosion which breached the water pipeline at Llanrhaeadr-ym-Mochnant was not a college rag stunt undertaken with the impetuosity of youth. Nor was it an act of sabotage carried out by culturally and politically astute students, who earnestly believed in the justice of their actions. Neither, as events unfolded, did it prove to be the protest of a starry-eyed idealist. Rather, the explosion at Llanrhaeadr-ym-Mochnant, which Britons learned of through the morning's news bulletins, was an effective expression of militant activism, chiefly undertaken by a man aged in his mid-thirties who was born in Wales and a serving member of Her Majesty's Forces. But if some shared John and Alders' quiet satisfaction that the operation had been carried out successfully, others took an altogether dimmer view. As politicians across the political divide condemned the attack, the explosion also received comprehensive – and critical – press and television news attention. The *Western Mail* denounced the protest as 'a deplorable disservice to Wales', while the *Liverpool Daily Post* tersely declared that as the rain fell from the heavens it was surely 'more God's than Taffy's'.[83]

*'Circumstances rule men; men do not rule circumstances'*
*'Force has no place where there is need of skill'*
*– Herodotus*

Nonetheless, irrespective of the widespread condemnation of the attack from both political and media circles, 'Llanrhaeadr,' John revealed, 'was one target on a growing list.' Because, despite his reservations, Jenkins did not want the attack at Llanrhaeadr-ym-Mochnant to be a 'one-off'. Prompted to explain his and MAC's position at this juncture, Jenkins continued:

> 'In the days following the explosion, my resolve stiffened still further. I became more determined that this campaign should last; that Llanrhaeadr should *not* be seen as a flash in the pan. It was therefore obvious that MAC could not operate as a militant group without using explosives. Moreover, the reaction within the media signalled to me that only the *use* of explosives would ensure significant media attention. I accept that some people will respond by saying that there are *no* circumstances in which you can excuse violence; that the use of explosives to further a political cause is *not* a legitimate approach. And I wish I could say "You're right", but sadly, I know this simply isn't true. In fact, I will say this: using explosives is a very effective *illegitimate* way of going about it, because nothing captures the headlines like a bomb. Not even the English media could ignore it! It also struck me that up until then, all Welsh protest groups before us had been all but ignored by the mainstream media.
>
> I further suspected that Government interference had resulted in editorial hostility – both in terms of broadcast and print journalism – in enforcing a deliberate policy of starving such groups of the oxygen of publicity. And I say this because years before the Investiture, the Editor of the *Western Mail* – David Cole, I think his name was – announced quite publicly that he was not prepared for 'his' paper to publish any dissidence or any criticism of either the Investiture, or the Royal Party and others involved in it. He was not, he stated, prepared to allow that – and he *stuck* to this directive in the build-up to the ceremony. Well, in a democratic country, what can you do when the Editor of a newspaper announces that he is *not* going to print anything against such a thing? To be fair, Cole probably didn't anticipate a bombing campaign, which is very difficult for the media to ignore. His outburst was more in relation to anticipated abusive letters, I suspect. Yet, even so. But I also knew, of course, that the Investiture of Charles Windsor as the so-called Prince of Wales was on

the horizon; and I was determined that what the FWA had achieved at the opening of Llyn Celyn, we – the new MAC – would achieve at Caernarfon. And we would achieve it by changing the nature of activities surrounding the ceremony through our actions, both in the build-up to the Investiture and on the day itself. So we were developing a list of objectives which we intended to target with the use of explosives.

But I was increasingly aware that we had to be flexible – that each action depended on the situation at the time. Obviously, you don't have targets and stick rigidly to them. Things can happen in the meantime which affect whether an attack goes ahead or not. For instance, in the wider sense, what is the developing political picture? Furthermore, what is happening at a local level? And with this in mind, I soon realised that the exact timing of an attack would have to rest with the cell leader.'

If a campaign of militant activism undertaken by MAC needed to be calculated and effective, what constituted a viable 'target'? 'I intended that MAC would attack interests of the British state,' Jenkins replied, adding:

'So our target list comprised: tax offices, water pipelines, government buildings and infrastructure. But I also decided in the days after Llanrhaeadr – primarily because of the media and public's fulsome reaction to it – to consider other factors. Namely, that each target would continue to be politically driven and self-explanatory, because we'd be unable to release a press statement which outlined why we'd attacked a specific target. But also, I now accepted and appreciated the fact that *only* a campaign of militancy would heighten the political awareness of the Welsh public. While furthermore, I decided that as far as was possible, there would always exist *two* reasons why a target was chosen – which, for the most part, we managed. And so after the attack at Llanrhaeadr, this two-pronged approach set the pattern for the next two years. But in the immediate term, I devised a policy which I believed would ensure MAC's notoriety within the media – both national and international – and establish beyond doubt the group's *raison d'être*. Namely: that every time a member of the Royal Family or those involved in the planning of the Investiture stepped into Wales, there would be an explosion. I believed that this would lead to an inevitable overreaction from the authorities, which as a result, would lead to increased support for the MAC campaign from the so-called "ordinary" people of Wales. And as it turned out, I didn't have long to wait to test my theory.'

## The Temple of Peace is attacked

At 4.04 a.m. on 17 November, two months after the explosion at Llanrhaeadr-ym-Mochnant, a 15 lb device exploded at the entrance to the Temple of Peace in Cardiff. The device had been delivered by John a fortnight or so earlier to the cell leader of a MAC unit based in the city. John had assembled it from explosives stolen from a quarry some months before – in a theft not involving Jenkins – and a Venner time switch, more recently purchased by a MAC associate from the retailer Woolworth's in north Wales. It was to be the last time that Jenkins 'received any equipment or materials from anyone else'. Being interviewed for this book, it was a clarification Jenkins wanted established 'once and for all':

> 'There has been a lot of speculation over the years that we [MAC] were receiving supplies of explosives and materials from various sources. Well, it's not true. I immediately recognised that until we were in control of our *own* supply of explosives, all attempts to purchase any were a potential security threat. And so I began to consider how we could get our hands on an adequate amount to see us through.'

In the weeks prior to the attack, it was announced that the Temple of Peace had been chosen as the venue for the inaugural conference of the Investiture Organising Committee. To coincide with this meeting, *Cymdeithas yr Iaith Gymraeg* (the Welsh Language Society) held a demonstration to protest the Investiture. As a result of the explosion hours before, the police – protestors allege – were very heavy-handed. To his credit, John Jenkins correctly anticipated what would transpire. Requested to throw light on his mindset at this point, Jenkins replied:

> 'As soon as I learned that this meeting was going to be addressed by Lord Snowdon and all the Lord Lieutenants and all the hangers-on who were concerned with this appalling state of affairs, *and* that *Cymdeithas* planned to hold a sit-down demonstration outside the building, my mind was made up that we *had* to attack it.[84] The meeting was really throwing salt in the wound and we knew it. *Cymdeithas* had never actually come across the state before, not really. All their previous actions of removing road signs written solely in English, or painting over them, had merely resulted in them being mildly chastised before the courts, and that was the end of it. But that is *not* to witness the power of the state. These people,

well intentioned though they were, *had* to be shown what the state was *really* like with the gloves off.

So when the Temple of Peace was blown up, the police were extremely angry, because they were getting extreme pressure from their political masters. And so they came out and laid about the *Cymdeithas* people, as we knew they would. The language the police used was appalling, apparently, and what they did to the people demonstrating was appalling also. And I think it's fair to say that when the police stormed in on them, for the first time, I think, *Cymdeithas* accepted what they were *really* up against and how the state reacted when angered. So it satisfied two requirements: it showed the authorities that however well-guarded a place was, you could get there and successfully target it without anybody being hurt; *and* we were able to introduce members of *Cymdeithas* to the power of the state with its gloves off. *And* importantly, many of their respected and horrified parents, who were bystanders and witnessed this. So in those two ways, we succeeded; and nobody was hurt. Well, nobody except the *Cymdeithas* boys! So it was a deliberate attempt on our part to politicise the situation, and it worked.'

Jenkins respected the Free Wales Army for the way the group had undermined the opening of Llyn Celyn and, through allegedly threatening militant action, ensured that grieving families received £5,000 in compensation following the disaster at Aberfan. But if Jenkins had decided that the FWA lacked the necessary strategic capabilities to feature in his plans following the group's failure to target the pipeline near Llandrindod, he felt his judgment was confirmed when the group greeted the explosions at Llanrhaeadr-ym-Mochnant and the Temple of Peace with statements implying its own involvement. These coincided with a series of newspaper articles in which the movement's well-oiled publicity machine churned out additional spurious claims. Dogs with primed magnetic explosives strapped to their backs, declared Dennis Coslett, the group's irrepressible spokesman, had been trained to destroy an approaching tank by affixing themselves to it.[85] Furthermore, the group now comprised '7,000 men, ready to fight to the death to win home rule'.[86] As for the FWA's ever-expanding armoury, it now reputedly included a '3.5" rocket launcher',[87] as well as 'four heavy machine guns' delivered by trawler and landed near Aberaeron – possibly one of a number of 'secluded places' where those who had broken the oath of allegiance to the movement had apparently been summarily executed.[88]

If such claims were designed to attract the attention of the UK authorities, it did not end there. Writing in April 1968 in *Y Ffrynt*, regarded as the mouthpiece of the more militant-minded Welsh nationalist, FWA leader Cayo Evans attacked renowned pacifist and former MAC member Emyr Llywelyn Jones, following his arrest at the Temple of Peace demonstration. 'How ironic that the first victim of the English-inspired gestapo should be Jones,' declared Evans scornfully. 'A pick handle [brandished by Jones] would have made those heroes of the crown hesitate.'

Whatever the thoughts of Cayo Evans, with the reconvened MAC offensive under Jenkins' direction having intensified, it was not only Britain's security network in the dark as to who might be responsible for the upsurge in violence. To John's surprise, members of *Cymdeithas yr Iaith Gymraeg* also refused to countenance the fact 'that this was a *new* organisation'. Prompted to share his thoughts, having been informed of the speculation within *Cymdeithas*, Jenkins remarked wearily:

'When we started our operations, its members kept harking back to "the good old days", claiming that "this could have only have been organised by so and so". I'm not sure who exactly – Emyr Llywelyn Jones, perhaps, but he'd renounced the use of violence years before. But whoever they thought was responsible, it was not the case. As I've said: there was no communication whatever between the old members of MAC and the new members of MAC. Any communication would have been in breach of security and *that* I was not prepared to tolerate.'

Nevertheless, despite Jenkins' insistence that members of *Cymdeithas yr Iaith Gymraeg* were *not* involved in the reconvened MAC protest, at least initially the impending Investiture heralded a high-level campaign by Special Branch and the police against the Welsh nationalist movement. This included the police actively gathering information on members of constitutional Plaid Cymru and *Cymdeithas yr Iaith Gymraeg*. To this end, the Superintendent at Holyhead sent the following 'Confidential' instruction to all police stations in Anglesey:

'In connection with the proposed Investiture of the Prince of Wales at Caernarfon in 1969, the activities of the members of the following societies are being watched: the Welsh Language Society and the Welsh Nationalist Party. Please submit to this office full details of all persons presently known to be connected with any of these societies or being sympathisers therewith. Details should include, if possible, full name and address, date and place of birth and particulars of any vehicles they own or use... Details of movements or activities in connection with these societies should also be reported... It is emphasised that this subject must be treated as **VERY CONFIDENTIAL**.'[89]

Later shown a copy of the 'confidential' memorandum and asked to respond, Jenkins was disparaging. 'They were wasting their time,' he remarked, continuing:

'The authorities wanted to prove that it [militant protest] was all about the Free Wales Army and *Cymdeithas yr Iaith*: organisations that they could quite easily deal with. What they *couldn't* deal with was the secrecy with which we were surrounded, and the fact that they simply didn't know who we were, where we were, or what we were going to target next.'

## Penisa'r Waun – and a meeting in Loggerheads

On 5 January 1968, MAC re-emerged from behind its cloak of subterfuge and with 4lb of explosives attacked the Snowdonia Country Club at Penisa'r Waun. It had recently been opened by a businessman from Manchester and the attack was targeted, John Jenkins revealed, to highlight the perceived 'cultural rape' of Wales, and to ensure that the 'culture vultures' could see that MAC was 'on their side as well'. Asked to develop the point, a vexed Jenkins declared:

'We did not approve of incomers purporting to be getting away from it all, while in fact bringing it all with them. These people wanted to build a nightclub in the middle of a little Welsh village, for God's sake – up in the foothills of Snowdonia. But the decision to target the club was taken in response to local opposition to the scheme, which was based on the local infrastructure being inadequate and the concern that such a venue would only attract further incomers and additional migrants to the area'.

Nonetheless, Rona Rowlands, a villager from Penisa'r Waun and prospective employee at the venue, claimed that some of those who had expressed support for the scheme in the area were Plaid Cymru members.[90]

Involving a small quantity of explosives, this was a 'symbolic' protest, John confirmed. Moreover, any temptation to use more gelignite in the operation had been curtailed owing to the proximity of the club to the owner's house. So, Jenkins added indignantly, 'We couldn't make the device any bigger.'

John Jenkins maintains that the MAC unit involved in the attack at Penisa'r Waun comprised English-speakers Alwyn Jones and George Taylor, but it is a suggestion fiercely contested by the Taylor family, who insist that their father was not affiliated to MAC. Whatever the truth, the two men were killed in Abergele some eighteen months later when apparently laying an explosive device on the eve of the Investiture. Nonetheless, arrested in connection with the explosion was Owain Williams, who in the summer of 1963 had been imprisoned for twelve months for his part in the two Tryweryn protest actions involving explosives. Despite the police being convinced of his involvement in the attack at Penisa'r Waun, Williams was inexplicably granted bail when he appeared before magistrates in Caernarfon on 29 February.

The following evening, 1 March, Owain Williams met John Jenkins at Loggerheads, near Wrexham. The meeting occurred between two performances given by Jenkins' military band to celebrate Saint David's Day, so John Jenkins was dressed in full ornamental regalia. Little did each man realise the significance of the meeting to the eventual detection and arrest of Jenkins and Alders some twenty months later. It proved an emotional, eventful and far-reaching period for both Owain Williams and Ernie Alders. While Williams absconded to the Republic of Ireland the day after meeting Jenkins at Loggerheads, in January 1968, Ernie Alders and Ann Woodgate had got engaged.[91]

## A theft occurs at Hafod Quarry – and the timing of attacks

Having 'plenty of detonators', Jenkins now set about acquiring the necessary explosives to further the MAC protest. On 23 January, with the alarm security system disengaged by an employee regarded as 'friendly, trusted and an established sympathiser', Jenkins and Alders raided the explosives magazine at Hafod Quarry near Wrexham. This one raid provided 'some quarter of a ton' of materials, and as it transpired, this proved 'enough to last right through the campaign'. Jenkins had determined in the preceding months that during the campaign only a cell structure would ensure that a team could operate effectively with minimum fear of infiltration. But how and why were specific targets chosen? Responding in his customary staccato, linear manner of speech, Jenkins replied:

'Knowing the cell leader's routine, I would enter the pub that I knew he'd be in. I'd let him see me, then I'd walk out. He would then follow me a short while later. In a quiet area of the pub car park, I'd hand him the device in a hold-all and give him my instructions for what I wanted targeted. For example, a tax office, or the venue where a meeting concerning the Investiture was to be held. I'd then leave, and he'd get on with it. One thing I did leave to the cell leader, though, was the *exact* date of when an operation would take place. I'd offer a suggestion, of course. I'd mention several possibilities, and how nice it would be if we could blow this up, or blow that up, on such and such a date. Because, wanting the greatest media coverage, I'd want an explosion to coincide, as closely as possible, with when an event or a meeting was being held. But it was *local* information, as known to the cell leaders, which ultimately decided when an explosion occurred. They might be aware of a big Territorial Army gathering scheduled in the town, and as a result, a lot more movement and people in the area than was normally the case – information which was unknown to me. How would I know? I don't read the local papers. I don't know what the hell is going on there; only roughly, and the broad picture. These people would know the *small* picture and with that you can have a successful conclusion. So the precise timing of an attack was left to the discretion of the cell leader.'

## Llanishen Tax Office

In the early hours of Sunday, 24 March, a 10 lb bomb exploded at an office of the Inland Revenue in Llanishen, Cardiff. The blast was heard half a mile away at Llanishen police station, from where officers arrived within minutes to find debris and documents strewn across the area. The constituency MP, Ted Rowlands, was outraged. This, he remarked, was 'Cardiff, not Chicago'.[92] But if Ted Rowlands condemned the attack, his censure was not shared by members of the public, John Jenkins insists. 'When we targeted tax offices, which we did on several occasions, the public neither condoned nor condemned it.' Jenkins added:

'In fact, as I travelled throughout the country undertaking my work duties, I became aware that the public didn't really mind. Politicians and the press may have taken a disdainful view, but the public wasn't outraged and screaming in the streets. Those members of the public whom I overheard while out and about were delighted, in many respects. So again, this convinced me of the need to do things which the public could understand the reasons for, and attacking a tax office was an easily observable reason. You see, people were angry because this was a period of increasingly high taxation under the Labour Government. But at this point, we had no communication with the public at all. So we couldn't do anything other than make each action self-explanatory, which I think we did. And the result was that as the campaign progressed, we won their hearts and minds, in some respects.'

John Jenkins and Ernie Alders had delivered the device to the cell leader of the Cardiff MAC unit the previous weekend. They coincided doing so with staying with John's parents in Penybryn. But her son's visit and subsequent news of the device's activation did not register with the ever-astute Minerva, John declared. At least, not in the sense that he and his mother discussed the matter during telephone calls in the days following. Nonetheless, used for the first time in the attack at the Llanishen tax office was one of 'eight or nine' timing devices recently assembled by Jenkins and Alders. They had been fashioned with the aid of specialist drilling equipment at the dental dentre at Saighton Camp. The decision to create their own timers was taken after Jenkins received news that the sale of Venner time switches from outlets such as Woolworths was being monitored by sales assistants and inconspicuous members of Special Branch. How was an effective timing system produced?

'It was achieved by removing the second hand from an alarm clock and threading wires through holes drilled in the clock face. An explosion could then be effected when the hour hand made contact with the detonator wire. We also continued the practice of enabling a MAC operative to test whether the circuit was functional prior to connecting the charge. This "fail-safe device" operated by way of first inserting a small light bulb rather than a detonator. If the circuit was operational, the light would activate when a switch on the device was pressed. Assured in this way that the connection was there, the explosives could then be plugged in. The whole lot was then put in a shoebox, as it fitted nicely in there. I knew the importance of us getting it right; that a timing device which *we* had put together was effective. We had to show them [the authorities] that we were capable and willing to get on with things; and that we had the ability to undertake things properly. The alternative was failure: and I knew damn well that failure on our part would *never* frighten them.'

## MAC holds a press conference and the UK security community responds to the Welsh 'problem'

By May 1968, the recommenced militant activities of *Mudiad Amddiffyn Cymru* had been ongoing for some eight months. Yet, despite the protest's apparent success, John Jenkins believed MAC's campaign was 'going off the boil' and 'beginning to falter'. Understanding the importance of mass communication, Jenkins decided that MAC needed to engage the media in order to get a message of the group's intent to the authorities. Jenkins explained:

'The problem was, it [MAC's militant protest] wasn't quite as "hard-edged" as it had been. The public was getting used to the explosions. It was almost a regular thing. But more importantly, Special Branch didn't seem convinced that this campaign needed to be taken seriously, so I knew we *had* to get through to them. We had to convince them [the UK authorities] that we *were* serious and that we meant business. Especially, of course, with the Investiture looming on the horizon. And to achieve this, I realised that we had to present a tangible, recognisable threat to the Royal Family. This, I knew, they would *definitely* respond to. And they did.'

Having initially considered sending notification of the threat MAC posed to the Royal Party using letters cut from newspapers, John dismissed the idea as impractical, believing it would take too long. Besides, Jenkins added: 'I wanted to create the right impression – which I felt could only be achieved face-to-face. Not that I wanted our identities revealed.'

Consequently, on 2 May 1968, MAC held a hastily arranged news conference with journalists Ian Skidmore, Harold Pendlebury and Emyr Jones. The meeting, held in darkened surroundings, was illuminated solely by the 'small pen torches' that were provided to the journalists in order for them to take notes. To authenticate their identity as the 'real deal', the incognito John Jenkins first disclosed details of the timing device used in the

Llanishen tax office explosion some five weeks earlier. Jenkins was aware that the description of the 'small, cream-coloured plastic alarm clock' was known *only* to investigating officers; who had not revealed its charred but discernible details to the media. Having done so, the official police record of the quantity of explosives removed from the magazine at Hafod Quarry on 23 January – which 'greatly exceeded' the amount reported in the press – was *also* emphasised by MAC's elusive and enigmatic spokesman. Having done so, the anonymous Jenkins turned his attention to the Investiture. It was the intention of MAC, he sombrely declared, to see 'the bloody fiasco' cancelled. Furthermore, should it indeed go ahead, someone within the movement's 'lunatic fringe', inspired by 'patriotic ideals', might do a 'Lee Oswald' – referring to the tragic events in Dallas in November 1963 when President Kennedy was assassinated. It was time, it was chillingly announced, that the Queen began to consider more responsibly 'her duties as a mother'. As for the decision to send Prince Charles to Aberystwyth University to prepare for the ceremony – as announced six months earlier – it was 'the final insult... a mockery... and a nonsense.'[93] The English Prince was coming to Wales not 'as its friend', but rather 'as a political overlord into his inheritance by right of conquest.'[94]

Encouraged to throw light on what he hoped the meeting might achieve, Jenkins declared:

'It was designed to encourage the belief that if the Investiture went ahead, the safety of the Prince could not be guaranteed. This threat lacked substance, because any attack on the Prince and Royal Party would have been hugely counter-productive in political terms. But nonetheless, I wanted it understood that MAC had the means and was willing and able to do so. And I knew damn well that this message – via these three journalists and more importantly their editors – would be in the hands of Special Branch within hours. Not that the story ever appeared in the press. It was suppressed: and I knew then that we'd won. Our message – which included the threat we posed to the Royals – had got through. The plan worked perfectly. Too bloody well, in fact. From that day onwards, hordes of undercover police officers and intelligence agents flooded over [from England]. They couldn't get here quick enough.'

Another important feature of the meeting with the three 'hard-bitten and respected' journalists – and a point which John Jenkins desperately wanted to get across to the authorities – was the claim that MAC was allegedly receiving 'titbits of useful information' from sympathetic police officers based in Wales. Prompted to outline both the extent and the nature of this information *and* how it came to the attention of MAC and its operational director, John stated:

'We had friends in the Welsh police service – junior-ranked officers who, while not actually doing anything in terms of being *actively* involved, nonetheless imparted information which they presumably thought might prove useful and necessary to us. These officers, two or three in number, never had any contact with me directly. But they – in a very loose way – would socialise with known militant sympathisers and "let slip", over a pint or two, certain "secret information"; for instance, as to the security surrounding a building, or where a certain dignitary might be and when. And then this information would be passed up the chain to me.'

Asked why he believed these officers felt inclined to undertake such an alleged course of action, Jenkins replied:

'It may well be that they were sitting on the fence, in that whoever won in the end, they helped. I don't know. I don't know why they felt the need to help us. I just thought they were well-meaning people who could see what was happening and wanted to do something about it. But I do know that after I revealed to the journalists that we had these "friendly" contacts in the Welsh police, it created paranoia within the police service. They were all busy watching, suspecting and keeping tabs on each other after that. Which is what I wanted, of course. So this also worked like a dream.'

Yet, speaking in the summer of 2018, John Jenkins made perhaps an even *more* startling revelation:

'What isn't known, though, is that we [MAC] were receiving unofficial information from within the Welsh Office too. Not that this was mentioned during the interview with the journalists, but we were being fed certain movement or diary information concerning senior officials – and George Thomas among them – via a contact employed there. Whether this individual was aware of what he was saying and its importance to us, I don't know, but in any event, this contact was providing the information to Dafydd y Dug, who then passed it on to me.[95] Along with Trefor Beasley and Harri Webb,[96] Dafydd was what you might call an "advisor", and he and I would meet and discuss policy and one thing and another. But along with our "friendly" police contacts, this individual in the Welsh Office must have known that this information would be fed back to me. Of course they bloody knew. They *must* have. If this Welsh Office employee and these police officers were discussing matters of security with someone who is a known sympathiser and definitely on their radar, and so in their eyes a little doubtful, a person with a "dubious reputation", they know *damn well* where that information is going! And do you know, without this inside information and intelligence, we could *not* have operated. Without it, the campaign would have proved a failed effort. To make sure all ends and all possibilities are covered, you *have* to have someone on the inside.'

But it was not just helpful contacts within the police service in Wales and the Welsh Office that MAC was cultivating during this period. Jenkins had also developed a relationship with the IRA. Did this relationship extend to regular meetings? 'No, no,' Jenkins replied resolutely, adding:

'I met them when I went over there during my assessment period, and again when they came over here [to Wales] during the same time. So we'd met each other, but that was the sum of it. They certainly knew who we [MAC] were. But once we started operating, direct contact all but ended. You see, I was aware that they might be subject to surveillance, and so it was just too dangerous. Nonetheless, such was our position in their eyes that had I gone across to Ireland, I could have gone straight to them and I would have been alright with regards supplies and equipment.'

Were these senior members of the IRA aware of his British Army status? 'Yeah,' Jenkins replied frankly. 'They couldn't understand it to start off with. Nobody else could either. But they settled down to it. The point was,' John added slowly, 'a lot of them were in the British Army as well!' With regards to exchanging information, Jenkins continued:

'There was nothing they could tell me and there was a lot I could tell them, funnily enough – and I'm not boasting here, but their security was bloody awful. So I distanced myself and MAC from them. I quickly realised that the more contacts I made outside MAC and the more information I got out of these contacts, the more difficult it would be to maintain tight security whereby nobody knew anything. So it was decided that they'd just let me know what they were up to – so that I wouldn't stumble across one of their plans by accident. You see, if I didn't know that they were going to do a certain target, I might look at it and think: "Oh, that's a nice little target – we [MAC] will have a go at that." Knowing what they were intending to hit, I'd make sure that we kept away and didn't interfere. But I didn't pass *any* information to them about what *we* were intending to target, because I wanted to maintain security, and security was our God.'

Jenkins' allegation to the three journalists that MAC was receiving information from 'friendly' contacts within the Welsh police requires further examination. Because, remarkably, the biggest problem facing the security services in apprehending the bombers appears to have been a reluctance within the police service in Wales – as was probably typical of police forces across the UK – to share information and knowledge. This appears to have been born of a certain degree of professional jealousy, and a belief that officers within other Welsh forces were possibly sympathetic to the nationalist cause and therefore providing the militants with inside information. An assumption which, Jenkins maintains, was *not* without foundation.

However, with the Investiture a little over a year away – and possibly in response to the statement given by MAC to the journalists on 2 May – the situation could not continue. Three weeks later, on 31 May, the Welsh Chief Constables, Special Branch and the heads of CID and the Regional Crime Squads held a summit in Cardiff to discuss the escalating militancy in Wales. Believing it had little alternative in order to ensure its own instrumental presence in Wales, the Home Office asked Frank Williamson, HM Inspector of Constabulary (Crime), to report back directly to the Home Secretary. Williamson was instructed to consider the options and propose a course of action. With the situation causing increasing concern, on 7 June, following another top-level review of the investigation by MI5 and Special Branch operatives in London, Home Secretary James Callaghan was advised by a senior civil servant to stamp his authority on the recalcitrant Welsh police forces, even if it touched 'on a number of delicate relationships' and aroused 'the susceptibilities of some Welsh chief constables', it was surely time to take the matter in hand. A response was not long in coming. On 16 July, at a further meeting in Cardiff attended by many of the UK's senior security officials, the decision was taken to establish a special unit. Tellingly, it was further decided that the unit's operational headquarters would be in Shrewsbury, just over the border in England. The 'Shrewsbury

Unit' would be led by officers from the Metropolitan Police experienced in counter-terrorism and be accountable to Whitehall's 'man in Wales', Frank Williamson. The unit's remit was to act as a central base where information and intelligence regarding known militant sympathisers could be collated and cross-referenced. More specifically, the Shrewsbury Unit, headed by Jock Wilson of the Metropolitan Police, was established to ensure both the success of the Investiture and the protection of the Royal Party.

## The Welsh Office and Lake Vyrnwy are attacked

During the early hours of 25 May, an explosion rocked the main administrative block of the Welsh Office in Cathays Park in Cardiff. As a result of the blast, nearly 200 panes of glass in the building were shattered, doors were blown off and filing cabinets were heaved across rooms. The damage was estimated at over £5,000. The building targeted housed the Secretary of State for Wales' office, and the blast came in response to George Thomas' confident assertion, as declared to the media on being appointed to the post seven weeks earlier,[97] that 'the period of violence had ended.' The day after the explosion, while attending a meeting in Llandudno, George Thomas launched an excoriating attack on Plaid Cymru. He accused the party through its promotion of a nationalist agenda – and, by association, fostering the militant campaign – of having created a monster it could not control.[98] Asked in 2017 to respond, Jenkins declared:

'Well, George Thomas was perfectly correct, of course. If Plaid Cymru had done its job, there would have been no need for us. So, in that respect, indirectly, he was right. Plaid was specifically established to protect us [Wales] – and it failed to. And therefore we had to take action to protect ourselves. It's that simple... Plaid didn't create the monster, as such. The monster was created by the party's inaction – because they weren't doing something that needed to be done, and needed to be done urgently to save the honour of Wales.'

Encouraged to outline the importance of George Thomas to the unfolding events, Jenkins was unequivocal. Paradoxically:

'Thomas and his blatant anti-Welsh attitude was our best recruiting agent. God rest him, he was a pious, sanctimonious sod – whose antipathy to

Wales became increasingly irrational and absurd. So much so that we wanted him to *remain* as Welsh Secretary, the same way the Allies wanted to keep Hitler – because he was destructive.'[99]

George Thomas might have had *more* reason to castigate the entire Welsh nationalist movement had MAC successfully attacked the newly constructed – and glass-fronted – Shire Hall in Mold. Having read in the local press that the building was to be officially opened by Princess Margaret on 29 May,[100] Jenkins immediately recognised that successfully targeting the building – as close to the official unveiling ceremony as possible – would reap MAC a considerable propaganda victory. This assumption was further enhanced when Jenkins received notice that Princess Margaret would be accompanied by George Thomas. But despite the intentions of MAC's Director-General, it was not to be. John later outlined what went wrong.

'The plan was that on the same night the Welsh Office was going to be blown, we would *also* target this brand-new suite of crown offices in Mold. Had our plan succeeded, it would have been lovely! But unfortunately, our communication got a little bit confused and the Welsh Office was hit four nights earlier than I intended. It would have been a major coup for us, what with George Thomas coming up from Cardiff to ably assist the lovely Princess Margaret to officially open the building. Yeah, it would have been declared open, with all the windows missing! The whole of the front would have been demolished. In reality, they would have cancelled the event, of course. But this mix-up buggered us, because from then on they were watching for us, and so we had to abort our plan. The result though, was that procedures changed after this.

It meant that I now became personally involved in delivering messages and stuff to people. We didn't have the luxury of being able to deploy "trusted couriers". Nothing like that. The potential threat to our security didn't allow for it. So in order to be sure that the MAC activists knew *exactly* what was being asked and expected of them, I decided to undertake all such journeys myself. It was a nonsensical situation and system, but I realised there was no other way. I *had* to be certain that these individuals who would be undertaking further protests were instructed correctly, so that they had the right idea and not the wrong one. I still left the exact date of an attack to the cell leader, because of his superior local knowledge. But I was far more stringent in stating

169

what I wanted targeting and when! It was quite onerous. But in the event of needing to deliver a message or a device, the most I was away was one night. Well, I wouldn't be away *all* night – I'd come back at say, 4 a.m. But it was quite shattering, as it might involve driving from Wrexham to Cardiff or Caernarfon and back again – returning to Wrexham at say 4 or 5, to be up, ready and back in work for 8; and this might be repeated over two or three consecutive nights. So, tiring – yes. But it was necessary in the interests of security. And up until the end [of the campaign], security was solid. Also, I wanted to create the idea that MAC was operating *throughout* Wales, so it had to be done. The alternative was to be idle. But this would only have led to events catching up with us. And had events caught up with us simply because of idleness or apathy, then it would have been deserved. So no corners were cut and nothing [in promoting an effective strategy] was spared. But it was very wearing.'

John Jenkins refused to be downhearted after the missed opportunity in Mold. Remaining steadfast in his determination to broadly coincide the royal visit with two explosions, on 27 May MAC was responsible for an explosion which damaged the base of a stone and concrete support carrying an emergency water pipeline from Lake Vyrnwy to Liverpool.

## 'Language is the chief characteristic of nationhood' – Éamon de Valera.
## 'A house divided against itself cannot stand' – Abraham Lincoln

One aspect of the MAC campaign which has attracted comment and speculation is the degree to which the movement was comprised of Welsh- and English-speakers. Encouraged to finally provide clarity in relation to the issue, John declared:

'I don't think we ever went as far as to analyse the respective numbers of Welsh-speakers and non-Welsh-speakers. What *was* recognised was the fact that we were *all* keen to do what we were doing, and that we were all prepared to sacrifice and to get on with it. But for some reason which escapes me, there did seem to be more of a spirit of active rebellion in the south than in the north. In the north there seemed to be more of a "bend with the wind and we can come back afterwards" type of approach. They didn't like being "occupied" and they were sort of surly and grumbly about it all, yet they didn't actually get down to doing anything positive about it. Whereas in the south, they tended to be more militant in their approach and less tolerant towards things. Because of the influence of the unions, I suppose. And so, I think it would be true to say that *initially*, there were more English-speakers than Welsh-speakers. Later on it changed, during the Investiture period, but initially that would be true to say.'

Having throughout his life remained a passionate advocate of the Welsh language, did Jenkins feel a degree of frustration with the supportive attitude of *some* Welsh-speakers towards the Investiture – particularly in the months prior to the ceremony? 'Yes, I did,' he replied sombrely:

'What used to annoy me most was a person praising the Investiture in Welsh. So does that mean he's a "proper" Welshman, just because he's using Welsh? No! It's what he is *saying* in Welsh that counts – and it's what someone is saying in English that counts as well. It's the content, not the language the sentiments are expressed in. So at no time did I see being Welsh as purely down to a person's ability to speak the Welsh language. I thought that it was divided into two lots of people: one lot of whom were lucky enough to speak their ancestral language, and the others who were unlucky by fault of birth not to. But that was the *only* difference.'

## MAC attacks again, and Prince Charles arrives for his first royal tour of Wales as the nation's political map is changed – but is MAC a component in Plaid Cymru's by-election successes?

On 27 June, MAC successfully targeted the Liverpool Corporation aqueduct at the Chester-Warrington railway crossing. Despite being 'guarded 24 hours a day', the explosion caused an apparently 'unbreachable' pipeline to shatter. The attack only served to heighten the authorities' concern. The situation was not improved the following day when Prince Charles, while leaving another conference in Cardiff to plan the Investiture, approached the crowd of protestors and asked one wielding a placard inscribed 'Remember Llywelyn' who Llywelyn was.[101] For all the Prince's charm and his public relations successes in the months before the ceremony, his ignorance of the last native Prince of Wales did demonstrate a certain lack of understanding of Welsh culture. It should be noted that this occurred before Charles' 1969 summer term at UCW Aberystwyth, where the Prince learnt about the nation's history and cultural identity. But even so, it left many in Wales wondering, in the summer of 1968, why the so-called Prince of Wales lacked both an understanding of the issues involved and why within *certain* circles in Wales there was hostility to the ceremony.[102]

On 18 July 1968, Dr Phil Williams – for whom John had canvassed during the October 1964 General Election campaign – came within 1,875 votes of winning the Caerphilly by-election for Plaid Cymru. Dr Williams received 14,274 votes, increasing Plaid Cymru's share from 11.1% at the March 1966 General Election to an impressive 40.4%. Coincidentally, the Caerphilly seat was won for Labour in July 1968 by John's former school English teacher, Fred Evans. Nonetheless, Dr Williams' comparative success in Caerphilly followed the significant increase in Plaid Cymru's vote within the Rhondda West constituency. At the General Election in 1966, Henry Victor Davies polled 2,172 votes, or 8.7% of votes cast. Just a year later, at the by-election held on 9 March, Davies polled 10,067 votes and increased the party's standing to 39.9%.[103] Even a 'deeply shocked' George Thomas was apparently impressed by Plaid's apparent breakthrough in these predominately socialist and English-speaking areas. Following the Rhondda West by-election, Thomas approached Gwynfor Evans in the Houses of Parliament and excitedly declared that the vote had changed his mind on devolution for Wales. 'The message is loud and clear,' Thomas remarked. The Labour Government would *have* to re-evaluate its policy on the matter and 'think again'.[104] It is safe to assume, however, that MAC's subsequent bombing campaign did nothing to enhance George Thomas' enthusiasm for political self-government for Wales; if indeed, the Cardiff West MP came to see MAC's militant campaign as providing the impetus and opportunity to further his own political ambitions.

Whatever the truth, the Carmarthen, Rhondda West and Caerphilly election results provided 'clear correlation' to John Jenkins that MAC's militant offensive was impacting favourably on Plaid Cymru's fortunes at the ballot box. But it is an assessment roundly challenged by a former psychiatrist and Plaid Cymru supporter who, while wishing to remain anonymous, declared in 2016 that MAC's 1960s bombing campaign had left him fearing the explosions would 'alienate politically the *very* people Plaid Cymru needed to attract: the 'blue collar' workers of Wales.'[105] Asked to respond, John Jenkins dismissed the claim as 'absolute rubbish'. The extent of Plaid's electoral growth in these working class, non-affluent regions spoke for itself, Jenkins believed. Moreover, he felt that for a psychiatrist, professing to understand the human mind, such utterances revealed an ignorance and inability to appreciate a person's intrinsic response when able to 'see and feel – and not just think'. It was an aspect of the human condition which, he maintains, MAC was strategically and deliberately intent on both exploiting and capitalising upon, as the Welsh public's generally-approving reaction to the MAC protest at that point had surely amply demonstrated? Furthermore, Jenkins continued, while perhaps irksome, it was understandable that the UK-centric political parties refused to draw a parallel between the MAC campaign and Plaid Cymru's electoral advance. But the refusal of *Plaid* to acknowledge MAC's contribution left Jenkins convinced that the nationalist party of Wales 'knew *nothing* of what politics and power was all about'.

John Jenkins may have a point. But if Gwynfor Evans and the Plaid Cymru leadership privately recognised the 'MAC factor' in the party's successes around this time, they also felt that any display of public endorsement would invariably result in electoral suicide for the party – particularly when matters escalated, with horrific repercussions. Others, however, were far more vocal in their opinion that MAC should stand by its convictions and either 'put up or shut up'. To this end, as the period of hostilities intensified, *Mudiad Amddiffyn Cymru* was urged to put forward candidates to stand in elections. It was a suggestion disregarded by Jenkins as 'not feasible'. Prompted to illuminate the point, Jenkins added:

'We couldn't do that. Our whole regime was based on deception. Well, deception and security. To maximise our position and be most effective, they [authorities] had to believe that we were in a position to kill and that we *intended* to kill. If we were unsuccessful in providing that impression, they would disregard us and not respond hard enough, or quickly enough. MAC *had* to be run on the lines of a military battle, based on politics. And so, it [the MAC campaign] was all about politics and deception – and it worked. While others in Wales had thrown in the towel and said that protesting would be futile, we didn't see it like that. We had a job to do and we knew what was needed, so we got on with it.'

But it was not only those ready to condemn the activities of MAC who wanted radicals to 'come in from the cold' and embrace constitutional political practice. The Free Wales Army attempted a 'love-in' with Gwynfor by suggesting that Plaid Cymru and the FWA collaborate to further the Welsh nationalist message. Not surprisingly, it was a proposal met with stony silence by Gwynfor Evans and the party leadership. Yet whatever John Jenkins' misgivings as to the feasibility of MAC contesting council and parliamentary elections, the group's operational director had reason to be cheerful in the summer of 1968. A poll published in August claimed that 44% of those approached considered the Investiture 'a waste of money'. In the 18–34 age group, the figure was 53%. Another poll in 1969, four months before the ceremony, declared that 76% of the Welsh public supported it. On closer inspection, however, the figure dropped to 60% for those surveyed who were under the age of 45.[106] The poll published in August 1968 occurred during a break in the MAC campaign. Asked to throw light on why the group ceased its militant offensive, John declared:

'We didn't want it [the protest] to be too intense. We had to remain true to our philosophy that each target was politically symbolic and not just an explosion for the sake of an explosion. We didn't want to lose the Welsh public by being over-active and predictable – which I think we were in fear of becoming during the early months of the campaign. But it's also true to say that we were not *always* able to attack when we wanted to. There were quite a few targets we would have loved to hit. For instance, we received news that Prince Charles would be visiting Wales imminently to inspect a steelworks or something, I forget now, and as much as we wanted to blow up the gates to the plant by way of providing a "warm welcome", the logistics of doing so proved just *not* possible. One reason being, of course, that any sudden move on our part, i.e. in relation to these gates, would have meant an instant loss or reduction in our security. It would have meant us overstretching our activities and our facilities, simply to be seen as having made an attempt at something. And I was not prepared to do it. We weren't built to operate like that. So there existed a number of factors [for the cessation in attacks]. But I do think remaining true to our political objective was crucial.'

## MAC denies responsibility for the explosion at RAF Pembrey, but ends 1968 on a high

In September 1968, an explosion occurred at RAF Pembrey in Carmarthenshire. Used in the attack was gunpowder. 42-year-old Warrant Officer William Hougham received life-changing injuries to his hands and face when he attempted to move the device, which was placed in a shoe box and left on a table in a ground-floor radio room. Suspicion for the attack fell on the Free Wales Army – which denied responsibility.

The Pembrey explosion remains an enigma, for which no-one has been convicted. But while rumour and speculation has since abounded as to who was responsible, John Jenkins has remained adamant that the bombing was 'nothing to do with MAC'.[107] Little wonder therefore, that as a consequence of the explosion at Pembrey, Jenkins became concerned that a less scrupulous rogue element was also in the field. Jenkins' fears proved well-founded, as further explosions, not attributed to MAC, were set to occur.[108] These explosions – and the attacks which MAC *was* responsible for – were accompanied by a raft of bomb hoaxes throughout Wales.[109] All culminated to make matters worse for the Welsh police, who were already the focus of criticism and ridicule for their failure to apprehend those culpable for the wave of bomb attacks.[110] Nonetheless, MAC was determined to remind the Welsh police and the UK security authorities that it had not gone away. On 2 December, a mid-Wales cell of *Mudiad Amddiffyn Cymru* ended 1968 by attacking the water pipeline running from Cwm Elan to Birmingham at West Hagley, near Stourbridge.

## 1969 dawns – the calm before the storm

London may still have been swinging at the start of 1969, but a day in the life at the Jenkins' family home in residential Wrexham was largely one of rigid familiarity. Asked to outline a typical day, Jenkins replied:

> 'Well, when I wasn't involved in MAC, which wasn't all the time at *this* point, I was undertaking my dental duties with work and living an orthodox life as a husband and father. As for more leisurely pursuits, I was still involved with the Royal Welch Fusiliers TA band. In fact, the TA was running down and eventually they disbanded us, although the band was in fact recruiting. There was a waiting list of people *wanting* to

join. So the whole lot of us, as one group, walked across the barracks and joined the cadets. We then carried on the band, exactly as we had before, except that we were now in the cadets of the Royal Welch Fusiliers...

I had for some time been in charge of the band. And, if I say so myself, I had really whipped them into shape. They looked and sounded *much* tighter. It didn't come without effort and commitment though. So we'd have a practice session one or two evenings a week, and then, of course, there were the concerts and performances. And being involved in MAC, I had to play the part to its fulfilment, which included, if necessary, playing 'God Save the Queen' in a crowded legion hall – which we did on several occasions in the months leading up to the Investiture. And that was alright: I didn't mind. That was my cover and it worked... But I'd also enrolled at the Wrexham Technical College, where I was studying at evening class for an 'A' Level in English Language and 'O' Level History. They were always my strongest subjects in school and I believed then – as now – that without a sense of history, nobody knows where they are. I had one eye on the future at this point, you see, and I was thinking of becoming a teacher.'

What of John's relationship with Thelma at this juncture?

'We didn't have a great deal in common, frankly. I mean to discuss politics with her would have been a bit of a job; she was too busy putting her eyelashes on and all the other folderols that women like her have. You see, Thelma was much more enamoured by this so-called Sixties thing than I was – this idea that Britain was leading the world culturally. On whatever level, it seemed to make sense to her. I would sometimes return home and find the radio blaring in the kitchen and her singing and dancing to songs in the hit parade. I wasn't enraptured by it at all, I thought it was bloody disgraceful. The whole thing just seemed like floss to me, with no substance to it whatsoever. I mean, Britain's political influence around the world was crumbling to dust, and yet the British mass media was putting forward this "Swinging London" nonsense. It was all money-driven, in my view. This stupid bloody idea which believed that "Because I'm from London and I'm wearing this, you've got to wear this too, otherwise you're inferior." What absolute rubbish! And yet people went along with it. And I'm lost to understand why – except that there was money to be made!'

Had anything struck a chord with Jenkins?

'What chimed much more with me was this general wave of protest throughout much of the western world which *also* characterised this period. I thought "Thank God – somebody is showing some sense." It seemed that people everywhere were feeling by the end of the Sixties that the latest fashions seen on the streets of London were irrelevant. The real thing was that people didn't have enough food; people didn't have enough clothes to wear; there weren't enough schools; there were members of society who didn't have enough of the medication they need. In fact, they didn't have enough of any bloody thing! But I don't want to paint too bleak a picture of our day-to-day life. The boys were there, of course, when I got in from work – they'd be watching TV or playing – generally doing their own thing after school. It was OK, yeah. Mind you, the pressure wasn't too intense at this point.'

One relationship which did not survive long into the New Year was that between Ann Woodgate and Ernie Alders. Woodgate later informed police that during the latter months of their three-year relationship and their twelve-month engagement, she repeatedly implored Alders to end his involvement in the militant campaign and 'wash his hands of the whole thing'. Asked to outline the extent of his association with Ann Woodgate, John declared impassively:

'Not that I encouraged visitors in the general sense, [but] as far as I was concerned, I was the trainer of the band, and band members would call at the house for a cup of tea and things like that. And that's what Ann Woodgate did with Ernie: call with him for a cup of tea to discuss the band and bookings, etc. She struck me as a nice, normal girl, and I struck her as a nice, normal bloke. To be frank, I didn't know anything about him [Ernie] telling her stuff [about the campaign]. I slipped up on lots of occasions, but that was a bad one.'

## John receives two offers, and the curtain falls on the FWA

If the ramifications of Ernie Alders' indiscretion were yet to be realised, others further afield were convinced of MAC's aptitude and professionalism. In 1969, East Germany was a vassal of the Soviet Union. The East German secret service, the Stasi – second only to the KGB in its efficiency and ruthlessness – courted MAC, offering to train its members and equip and finance the group. Having apparently recognised MAC's potential, the

Stasi stipulated that this aid would be received as long as one proviso was met: that MAC members travel to East Germany to receive training and instruction. As with Libya some years before – which was also financed by the Soviet Union – the intention was to undermine the UK. This would be achieved through a campaign of sponsored terrorism, which would increase Britain's internal state tensions, necessitating a significant financial outlay. Dispatched from East Germany to act as the connection between the Stasi and MAC was the then notorious ultra-Marxist German agitator Rudy 'Red' Dutschke. 'He came over here with the intention of "piling us on", as it were,' John declared, when asked to discuss the Stasi proposal. 'But,' Jenkins added ruefully, 'you don't exchange a master in London for one in Berlin or Moscow, so I vetoed the offer.' It was also proposed that MAC 'form some sort of an alliance' with *Unvaniezh Demokratel Breizh* (the Breton Democratic Union), which was led by Paol Keineg – the husband of Judith, who later married former MAC activist David Pritchard. 'I looked at it,' John remarked, 'but from my point of view, it would have provided very little gain, while increasing the security risk to us. There was simply no point or advantage to us from developing the contact. So this proposal I also rejected.'[111]

One group which the East German Stasi and the *Unvaniezh Demokratel Breizh* made *no* contact with was the Free Wales Army. Despite having attracted significant media interest through its own inimitable 'campaign of propaganda', on 26 February 1969 the FWA made the headlines again when senior members of the group and other prominent figures within the anti-Investiture movement were arrested in dawn raids. The two contradictory approaches of MAC and the FWA were glaringly apparent to all but the most ardent FWA supporter. Encouraged to evaluate the FWA and its contribution to the militant objective during this period, Jenkins declared dismissively:

> 'After the fiasco at Crossgates, we had nothing to do with them. Not that I knew even *then* that the device was intended for them. I was just told it was for "friends of ours" who wanted to hit a pipeline. MAC and the FWA were *entirely* different. As a group, MAC was understated. You know: efficient and effective. It reflected both my style of leadership and what we [MAC] saw as the best way to achieve our objective. That is why I could never understand the Free Wales Army and the uproar they were causing everywhere. They were so foolish about it as well. So silly. All they

had was talk, but they had nothing to say. Yet they tried to take credit for this, and credit for that, and the press lapped it up. And there are times when I do feel annoyed, because there has been this grey area of notoriety which unfortunately the wider movement has been dragged into, and it's all to do with the FWA. I mean, I understand the need for notoriety on the one hand, but the notoriety of what we were doing and what the FWA was doing are quite clearly two different things. You see, the Free Wales Army never had a philosophical background, or a way that they could justify themselves from that point of view. They couldn't do it, because it didn't exist. All they were was a talking shop. Their message was loud and clear: "Let's drive them into the sea." I mean, that is hardly facing up to the economic and linguistic backgrounds of the situation. But there you are. That's the way they wanted it.

I did hear that Dennis Coslett claimed to have been taken out of MAC to join the FWA – absolute rubbish. It just sums it up. The modus operandi for most of the FWA was simply to get women into bed. All the group did was leave a trail of broken female hearts along its path. They just dined out on their notoriety. Brilliant! OK. I admired them for what they did at Tryweryn – the way they changed the nature of the activities: very much so. And that is what inspired us to do what we did regarding the Investiture. But that, and their apparent militant threat over Aberfan, are the *only* things I ever admired them for. I mean, *nobody* took them seriously. The fact that not *one* person asked me about them after I was arrested proves that the authorities didn't take them at *all* seriously. They knew that that lot had *nothing* to do with the real [MAC] bombing campaign. They were arrested because the authorities *had* to arrest somebody. They were simply convenient; handy. When some of them – Coslett and Evans especially – received their prison sentences, I thought that Thompson [Justice John Thompson] was unduly harsh. They were a joke. But it [Thompson's judicial judgement] was all political, of course.'[112]

But if they were such a cause for ridicule, even disdain, why were the FWA tolerated? David Walters offered his opinion:

'I think they were seen as a way to divert attention and resources. In that sense, they did everybody else a favour. The police and the security forces seemed to be spending so much time looking after them that they couldn't see what was happening behind the scenes. They seemed to think that they had it all under control through concentrating on "this" [the FWA]. But when you concentrate on "this", you can't see what else is happening behind you. I could be wrong, because I had nothing to do with MAC when John was in charge, but I think that's why they [MAC] let it go.'

Contacted to discuss links between the FWA and MAC, Dennis Coslett, the FWA's main spokesman during its campaign period, replied candidly.

'John Jenkins knew who I was through the press. But I didn't know him. I had no idea who he was, or what he looked like. But I do believe that we acted as a smoke screen for them. Of course we did. There was not "one movement", though. It would have been impossible. I *knew* the name "MAC", and I knew that MAC was responsible for the bombings. But the name MAC was never mentioned. It was not allowed to be mentioned, not even among ourselves. Not even between me and Cayo [Evans]. In all honesty, we didn't know who MAC was. The press had no idea who John was – until the end. That was the way it was at that time; the left hand did not know what the right hand was doing. It had to be that way... We were fighting an Empire, for God's sake. We were giving the press a lot of stories and they loved it. We were just feeding them false information. It was all psychological: all propaganda. And we had them going for four years! And yet, even some in the wider Welsh nationalist movement couldn't see what we were trying to achieve. If we had used other [militant] methods, we would all have been in prison long before that. But we supported the attacks on the pipelines, and on the forestry, which was destroying much of upland Wales... Look, do I sometimes wish that the FWA had undertaken an effective militant strike? Yes. Had we done so, it would have stopped all the backbiting and sneering. We could have looked them in the eye. But I will say this too: John Jenkins could have killed civilians.'

But with the Investiture drawing ever nearer, it was not only the Free Wales Army which was attracting the headlines. A number of other nationalist societies also rose – with varying success – to prominence. These included the Patriotic Front, the Patriots Aid Committee, the Young Patriots League, the Confederation of Welsh Workers, the Llywelyn Society, *Cymdeithas Glyndŵr*, the Owain Glyndŵr Memorial Committee, the Patriotic Press, Patriotic Enterprises, Eagle Publishing, *Cymru ein Gwlad* and the Welsh Monarchy Society. It remains open to speculation as to how far these groups shared the same objectives and the same membership.

The campaign to protest the Investiture intensifies, as John attends a family get-together and receives the news he's been hoping for, plus a visit from the military police

One group determined to protest the Royal Investiture, scheduled to be held in Caernarfon on 1 July, was *Mudiad Amddiffyn Cymru*. In the spring of 1969, as the plans for the ceremony were being polished and finalised, the Jenkins family returned to John and Thelma's home region in south Wales to attend a gathering of Thelma's family. Although he is unable to recall what prompted the occasion, a number of aspects surrounding the event have nonetheless stuck in John's mind. Staying at the home of his brother-in-law, Peter, a serving policeman, had they got along? 'Well, I got along with him in that I *had* to get along with him; he was my brother-in-law,' John remarked, continuing:

'But he was *not* the sort of person that I would choose for a night out. When it came to politics, he was a total bloody fascist. I mean, you get reasonable police and you get unreasonable police. He was very unreasonable. It was a very regrettable attitude, but there you are... I expect he had views on Welsh culture, but we never discussed it. He wasn't one for having an opinion of his own. All he could do was bleat out what he'd read in his papers, which were typical Tory rags like the *Daily Mail* or *Express*. I certainly never discussed the MAC campaign with him. Not in any way – obliquely or otherwise. In fact, I didn't discuss the campaign with anybody – not outside those in MAC, whom I trusted implicitly. But I had to laugh, because on arriving at this family gathering, Thelma's sister was with a black man. He was a lovely chap. But I couldn't help but smile, thinking that here was poor old Peter stuck in a room with his family, and one sister is with a black man, one is married to a gypsy and another is married to a terrorist!

Anyway, far more seriously in terms of the campaign, while we were staying with Peter and his family in Nelson for the weekend, I *had* to see somebody about our response to the Investiture. The only way I could manage this was to leave at about midnight, and I didn't get back until 4 a.m. In the morning, Thelma received some strange looks from Peter! He must have heard me leave, and come back in hours later. It was a breach of security, of course, but there was no way I could get out of it; no way I could *not* have gone. It was just too important. I don't think he made any connection between me and MAC. But I think he may have thought I was having an affair, because he was one of these policemen who don't jump to conclusions unless they are wrong ones. But it *was* at this point that Thelma began to think I was womanising and having an affair.'

Why was it so important that he meet this contact?

'Because at this point we were desperate to receive information, and then from out of the blue we got the news we were hoping for. This was why I *had* to meet this contact – because this vital information had been passed to him. You see, while MAC had front-line activists, and other members who enjoyed "friendly" contacts within the police and the Welsh Office, we *also* had a lot of people who were instructed to simply keep their ears and eyes open and to watch for things. Usually this amounted to us receiving snippets of an overheard conversation in a pub. As useful as this information could be in *perhaps* pointing us towards a certain conclusion, it wasn't enough to break through their [the authorities'] security, which by this time was pretty good.

But one day at the end of March '69, when we were desperate to find out the details of when the Earl Marshal[113] would be visiting Chester for a forthcoming meeting about the Investiture, a member of MAC's "listening squad" was in Chester, and a police car drew up beside him. It drew up because there was a red light, and these two senior police officers, who were on the back seat, were discussing this very thing: the date and the time of his visit. Now, that's all we needed, and there they were, discussing this forthcoming visit with all these details written down in front of them. And so, in the time that it took for the lights to change to green, this member of MAC, who was standing on the kerbside and waiting to cross the road, had all the information we needed. This information was fed back to me. Even today, the police don't know how we managed to get hold of this information, which was never published and known only to a select few, but that's how. They were careful, but they weren't *that* careful, and so we were able to get the information we needed. Their security was, as I say, pretty good. There is no argument about it. But ours was better. And it was better because we could recognise them, and they couldn't recognise us – and *that* gave us the edge.'

Nonetheless, despite the group's obvious commitment to its cause, had Jenkins ever feared that either a front-line activist or someone with any degree of inside knowledge of MAC might approach the authorities and disclose information? Having paused to collect his thoughts, John remarked:

'No. There was what I can only describe as the "ultimate sanction". In the event, it was never used. But it was pointed out to people: "Look, you're one of us now. *Don't* let us down." And without going into it any deeper than that, there would then exist an understanding that if they *did* let us down, nasty things could happen. But, it never, ever occurred, as it happened. So yes, there was a "sanction". But they were working through their love of Wales and their need to be involved at some level in what was happening. And my job, with the Investiture fast approaching, was to orchestrate this group and provide them with the devices they needed.'

Did he find assembling an explosive device a nerve-wracking experience? 'I suppose it was a bit alarming, yeah,' Jenkins replied earnestly, before continuing:

'Not *that* bad, though. I mean, I didn't go around sort of shaking and shivering; I managed it. It *had* to be done. It's not the easiest thing, but it's not *that* difficult either. But I was never happy being around explosives, frankly – whether assembling the device, planting it, or delivering it to someone else. I mean, it was not helped when on one occasion I was driving through mid-Wales with about 60 lb of high explosives underneath my seat and the tyre blew and I crashed across the road. Luckily it was alright, but being well aware that it doesn't take a hell of an impact to set off explosives, it was a bit hair-raising! You see, there are two ways to set them off: one is electrical, and the other is impact! At such moments, it's necessary to be a bit of an actor and retain a façade of normality and composure. I simply changed the tyre, and carried on my way. It was a performance I was called on to exercise when one day the redcaps visited the Dental Centre and said to me, "We're looking for mirrors which look around corners." I said, "Oh yeah?" "Yes," they said. "We were told down at headquarters that you've got them stored up here." I replied, "Yes, that's right. But you can't have them unless you're prepared to sign for them." "Oh yes, we'll sign for them," they said. "What are they for, anyway?" I asked them. "Oh, we can't discuss that. It's very hush-hush," they said. How I kept a straight face, God knows. They couldn't discuss it, but I realised that they wanted these mirrors to see how one of my unexploded bombs was assembled. I didn't make life easier for them, but off they went to do whatever they needed to. I think it was for the device that I'd assembled for the FWA. It was still intact, of course, so they wanted to see how it was put together.'

Did he experience any other unsettling moments as he prepared for the Investiture offensive? Smiling and nodding, John declared:

'Following the raid on the magazine at Hafod Quarry, some of the explosives were placed in three or four underground arms dumps across Wales, but I placed a quantity of the explosives in a storeroom at Saighton Camp. I was one of only two people who had a key to this storeroom. A senior officer did too, but I knew that ordinarily he had no reason to enter this storeroom, so it was perfect from my point of view. Not only was the storage available to me at work as good as anywhere, but the intricate drilling equipment at the Dental Centre was also perfect for assembling the devices. Well, having done so, I'd take the device home and store it in my garage for a maximum of one night and deliver it to the cell leader the following day... But I *was* almost caught once while putting a device together. I was there, in front of the window assembling a bomb, when suddenly I felt the need to look up – and there staring back at me was a bloke who worked in the same building as me, but some distance away. He was involved with security and bookings. For instance, he would make the necessary security checks if the Army booked a venue. Also, he was involved with the checks surrounding an individual who wanted to join the Army – and there he was in the window, looking at me. I knew very well that if I dropped my eyes to what I was doing, he would do the same, so I couldn't. I kept looking at him. I just sort of waved, and he cleared off. That was the closest I *ever* came to being discovered before my arrest.'

## Jenkins lays lingering speculation about MAC to rest

It was not solely the problem concerning a lack of information which needed resolving around this time, as owing to 'a problem with the insurance', John's car – a white Taurus – was 'stuck in a garage in Wrexham'. Needing a car to travel to reconnoitre suggested target sites and to meet contacts, Jenkins had to manage as best he could by using Alders and another chap called John Humphreys – who, unlike Ernie Alders, 'was nothing to do with MAC'. Otherwise, Jenkins added, 'I would never have used him [Alders] so much. I would have used my own car. But he had a car and I had to get about.' With Ernie Alders' role within the organisation appearing to be elevated as a consequence of having access to a vehicle, had this led to Alders enjoying greater influence within MAC? More importantly, had MAC, under Jenkins' direction, operated along democratic lines in terms of discussing strategy and policy and making joint decisions? 'No,' John replied firmly; adding:

'Unfortunately, within an organisation such as ours, with limited objectives and limited resources, we had no choice but to be an autocracy. We couldn't operate along the lines of an army council. Nor could we have a democratic get-together every now and then with tea and biscuits. Being autocratic was the only way. Yes, discussions with MAC members could become impassioned. But ultimately, *I* worked it all out [MAC's strategy]. You see, as much as people might have endeavoured to lessen the burden by making suggestions, I couldn't be swayed from my central policy. And that means that while I could and sometimes *did* listen to people, invariably I couldn't take any notice of them. A more collegiate approach might have worked for a short while. But then the security arrangements would have been such that we wouldn't have lasted five minutes. So unfortunately, it had to be an autocracy; as much as I don't like autocracies. But it worked. And my response to those people who say it wasn't a very democratic way of going about things is: no, it wasn't. But it was an *effective* way of going about things... As for Alders: by this stage, I was beginning to have my doubts as to his suitability. Some people are able to bear pressure better than others, let's put it that way.'

Another question which has attracted considerable conjecture is whether MAC was financed by Trefor Morgan. Asked to clarify, John declared:

'There's been a lot of unfounded speculation about the MAC campaign, and one centres around how we were financed. I'm sure Trefor Morgan could have supported us financially; had he been approached. He was an eminent Welsh Republican who firmly believed in Welsh independence, and the need for a robust response. But it was too much of a risk to approach him. I mean, he was a marked man in the eyes of the police. Why? Because he had so much money and had expressed "good views" as far as we were concerned, so he was in a position where he couldn't do a great deal. He couldn't even stick you a couple of hundred quid, really. So all this talk of him financing us is rubbish. Good God, if you had to rely on money from millionaires, we would have been bloody broke! He was nothing to do with us, for God's sake. It was the donations from sleepers – relatively small in terms of amounts, but quite sizable in number – which financed us. And collectively, these funds came from a financial organiser, who passed them on to me and I distributed them as necessary. As for who received these small payments, it might involve money being passed to those sleepers, who'd put someone up for a few nights – that sort of thing.'

Such unfounded speculation, Jenkins insists, has only served to engulf the motives and strategy which underpinned the MAC campaign in a fog of uncertainty. For instance, John continued:

'I've read that Alders later informed the authorities that on my list of places to be bombed was the pay office at Saighton Camp. No, it was not. It's ridiculous. What would have been the outcome? For one thing, working men would have been denied their wages, even if only for a day or two, and how would that have helped our cause? Also, it would bring attention to the camp. That was the last thing I wanted – especially as I had a box full of explosives tucked away there! Similarly, with Owain Williams. He's a nice chap, Owain – and apart from his rather enjoying the women and self-publicity, he certainly did his bit over Tryweryn. But I was told recently that he's claiming MAC intended to target the Royal Mint at Llantrisant during the campaign. Well, it's not true. And frankly, Owain was *not* in the position to know. Why would we have? Targeting either the wages office at Saighton Camp or the Royal Mint would *not* have been of interest or benefit to us, because we operated along political lines and for political reasons. One objective of our political mindset was that we wanted more employment in Wales; and we could hardly get more employment by blowing up the bloody existing employment areas!'

## Chester Tax Office is attacked by MAC, a 'rogue element' enters the field and John learns another sobering lesson concerning 'the hypocrisy of the British State'

On 10 April 1969, following a three-month lull in its campaign designed, John Jenkins later revealed, 'to give the authorities a false sense of security', MAC attacked the Chester offices of the Inland Revenue. The reason for targeting the site was, as ever, twofold: to strike at a government installation, and to coincide with the visit to Chester of the Duke of Norfolk, who was scheduled to speak at the Army headquarters in the city on the role of the armed services during the Investiture. Yet if John celebrated the news that the device had caused 'considerable damage' to the building, his mood may have been tempered had he known that the Shrewsbury Unit had received information that the group responsible for the bombing campaign consisted of a 'policy director... and six highly trained saboteurs.'[114]

When later discussing the press disclosure that the authorities appeared to be making a breakthrough in their inquiry at this point, John Jenkins reacted with indifference:

'You see, another factor of the campaign which has never been touched on is that we were receiving support from within several urban centres throughout Britain, because the Welsh are scattered all around. And some of them were quite indignant about the fact they'd had to move away from a lovely place like Llanrhaeadr in order to find work. And where there are Welsh, there is nearly always a Welsh club; and within these Welsh clubs in Liverpool, London, Chester, Birmingham and so on, there was support and sympathy for us. And again, the extent of this support for MAC was being fed very quickly back to me.'

Asked how the support for MAC throughout the UK might be utilised when contemplating an attack, Jenkins continued:

'The procedure for a protest followed the same pattern. By the time of an attack, you had already visited the site several times. You'd made yourself aware of the surroundings, and who was about and who should *not* be about, and so forth. There would ordinarily, of course, be a supporter – somebody who really knew the place – living there, and from this person you could pick up a few snippets of vital information: namely, what time the police patrolled the area, that sort of thing. And I wouldn't move unless I had this information. This knowledge would be received and digested, because without such information, you are acting blindly. With it, however, you know where you are, and I *always* had to know where I was. And so, armed with all the information I needed, I attacked the Tax Office in Chester. Was it nerve-wracking? Yes – to a point. But it had to be done.'

The Chester protest, undertaken alone by John Jenkins, was soon followed by explosions and militant activity in Cardiff which have not been attributed to MAC. On 15 April, minor damage was caused by an explosion at Police Headquarters in Cathays Park, Cardiff; on 23 April, an explosive device was discovered in a locker at Cardiff's Queen Street Railway Station; on 29 April, an explosion ripped through the Central Electricity Generating Board offices in the Gabalfa area of the Welsh capital, and on 2 May, less than a month after first being targeted, a parcel bomb was intercepted at the city's Police HQ. Asked to clarify if MAC *was* responsible for these attacks, John was disparaging. 'The basic rule,' he declared, 'was if there wasn't an obvious political reason for an action, then we were *not* responsible. OK, a police station might be considered a suitable target, but from what I gather,' Jenkins added, 'the explosive materials used in Cardiff were entirely different from our stuff; nor was the time mechanism similar to ours, and neither were the devices constructed as expertly.'

But with a lone wolf apparently operating, might there have existed *any* degree of understanding within the British Army regarding MAC's protest and the rise in militancy in Wales, even sympathy from Welsh servicemen? Looking askance, Jenkins exclaimed: 'Good God, no,' adding:

'The attitude was as I expected. All the usual stuff about us [MAC] being "mad", you know. Anything that reflects badly on England, they don't like. As for any feelings of sympathy among Welsh Army personnel, I never bothered to find out. It would have been a gross breach of security on my part to raise the matter with people like that. So I said nothing.'

Yet one event typified what Jenkins determined to be 'the sheer hypocrisy of how the state operates', occurring 'about two months before the investiture'. Prompted to develop the point, Jenkins declared:

'Well, the authorities – supported by the media – were playing holy hell because as far as they were concerned, by undertaking this protest in my anonymous role in MAC, I was preaching violence. And yet, one day, the band visited Nesscliff Army camp near Shrewsbury. It was in the process of being what's called "disbanded", in that it was being turned over to be used for the cadets – like an activities centre. Now by this point, we'd transferred the band from the TA and joined the band which the cadets had. And of course, being Army cadets, these lads were only aged 13 or 14.

So it was arranged that we would visit Nesscliff. As far as I was concerned, the day would include a band practice session, and it would also be a way of getting the boys used to the feel of an Army barracks.

But unknown to me, the authorities had something else planned for them: a part of the afternoon had been assigned to teach them how to assemble bloody booby traps! I had no idea about this. I thought they were being taken off to receive drill instruction, which would have been fair enough. But off they went, and a little while later I could hear all this banging and crashing, so I said, "What's that?" And this chap who worked there replied, "Oh, the Welsh Guards are down here teaching the cadets how to set booby traps for when you leave a town and have to relinquish control." They were being taught how to set booby traps in an urban area. For instance, how to set a booby trap so that when people went to the toilet and pulled the chain the whole bloody place exploded. I was aghast. I couldn't bloody believe it! Teaching kids – young lads – how to kill, or to blow people's arms and legs off. And what sickened me most was that they justified this on the grounds that it was all quite in order, "because it's teaching them how to become soldiers when they get older".

This, as far as they were concerned, was commendable, praiseworthy behaviour, undertaken to support our gallant troops who were engaged in some conflict somewhere to save our lives. And they [the UK authorities] are perfectly entitled to take that view. But they cannot then say, "But only *our* people can do things like this. Anybody else and it's 'violence'; it's disgraceful and it's disgusting." It annoyed me intensely. I thought, "How the hell? These people are condemning me and MAC, and yet they're teaching 13-year-old kids how to kill people!" And I thought, "Here we go again, this same old business about legality and morality."'

With the Investiture just weeks away and the protests regarding the ceremony escalating, what was the impact of John's primary position within MAC on his marriage and relationship with Thelma?

'In the months leading up to the ceremony, she had an increasing idea that I was involved, I think. She must have, because I was out far too often, for one thing. And then, on top of that, of course, there were none of the usual signs to show you're "running around": lipstick marks; the smell of perfume on you or your clothes – all that sort of typical stuff, you know. So I had to placate her, really; and to do this, I told her I was running errands for those involved in the campaign against the Investiture. It seemed to work. Having said that, she soon realised that she couldn't push it, because if she did, I snapped at her and became quite angry. So she shut up and never pressed it. But to begin with, I had to convince her that there wasn't another woman involved. I'm not sure I did, fully. Perhaps I did, because things did calm down a bit; but she did start going out a lot more, socialising. But it was a big job trying to convince her that I was *not* meeting women, because there were women involved in the movement; and they were some of the staunchest supporters. They were very good, fair play. In fact, they were sometimes the more vociferous of the two. No woman – at least, none that I was made aware of – ever backed down from what they were supposed to be doing. No woman was ever involved in planting a device, because I suppose old habits die hard. This was regarded as a "man's job"; while a woman's job was to be supportive and to provide her husband with a nice cup of tea when he's finished. "Come on Dai", you know, all of that – provide a calming, stable and safe home environment.'

Did the apparent détente between him and Thelma last as the campaign increased? 'No, not really,' John answered.

'Once Thelma ascertained what I was really up to, it [the realisation] started to fester. You see, what I was doing meant that I could be taken at any time. And in this event, she would be left with no man bringing money home and no house to live in. Because the house was an Army house, and therefore, were I flung out [of the Army] she would be flung out too – which she was, in due course.'

How did this realisation manifest itself? Had Thelma recognised a change in John's attitude as a date of a target operation approached? For instance, had he become more pensive and touchy? 'Well no,' Jenkins replied, while momentarily chuckling. 'I was always a bit touchy and introspective anyway. I was never a bundle of laughs, as such.' Having paused for some moments, John continued:

'Well, the thing is… I don't quite know how to put this, but it seems that when you become involved in something like this [militant protest] you get some sort of an "aura" around you. I don't know how to explain it any better, but it seems that other people can sense it, whatever it is. You just radiate this state of mind. Probably because you're lost deep in thought about what is going to be targeted tonight, or tomorrow night, or whatever. And not that we ever discussed it, but I think Thelma sensed this "aura" around me. Well, that's the impression I get, anyway. But recognising this change, this remoteness in me, she'd say "For God's sake John; cheer up, you miserable old bugger," and things like that. Which is true enough: I was a miserable old bugger. I had too much to worry about! But if she *did* connect my mood with hearing of an explosion on the news, she never said a word to me about it.'

Such a disclosure offers a fascinating insight into Jenkins' frame of mind and his emotional outlook with the Investiture imminent. Encouraged to elaborate, Jenkins stated:

'Well, even from the outset, after the first explosion at Llanrhaeadr, I felt something died in me. I know it sounds a bit grand, but the point is, there was a time when I could talk an elephant out of a tree, apparently. I was seen as gregarious; and although serious and stolid, also congenial and personable. But all that disappeared the minute I started taking action. It had to. There was no other way it could be done. Having said that, I also knew that the only way this would succeed was if I remained my "usual" self. If I'd gone around bursting with energy and laughing and shouting, people would have immediately recognised the difference in my demeanour. You know, sort of, "Oh, he's different from last week." So there mustn't be any change – you must be consistent: the same as last week, this week and next week. Anything else would appear strange. So it was a terrible pressure – this constant pretence. And as well as I think I managed, I'm sure this change in my personality was noticed – especially at home. For instance, my relationship with Thelma became – I wouldn't say frosty, but more guarded, less relaxed. She sensed this change in me and concluded that I was no longer a family man, as such. I was something else. But what could I do? I couldn't stop and turn my back on it [the campaign], could I? And this feeling only intensified in the weeks building up to the Investiture, so I was going around with this weight on my shoulders. Only if I was alone, away from everybody, would I allow myself to break down. Because it all depended on me. If I was caught, if I made a mistake, if I messed up, everybody [involved] would be messed up. I had to keep my mouth shut. So, I did – and this internalising of pressure leads to tension and inner conflict.'

Does he feel that there has been a long-term effect on his personality? 'Yes,' Jenkins affirmed:

> 'To tell you the truth, I've had a little bit of a job in opening up ever since. People say, "Oh, you talk – you talk well." But I know that I've *never* been the same person. I've been much more guarded ever since. I can no longer be free like I was then – before it all started.'

## MAC targets the Prince of Wales monument at Holyhead; another explosion in Cardiff

If the formidable John Jenkins believed he had instilled a strong mentality and a wilful mindset among those MAC activists that he had recruited, he was in for something of a surprise. Because despite the apparent existence of an *esprit de corps* among MAC members which negated the need for 'sanctions', John later conceded that front-line MAC activists *sometimes* lacked the offensive eagerness that Jenkins demanded and expected. In fact, on one memorable occasion, it was the wife of one MAC member, who through her forthright approach, provided the necessary stimulus required of her husband to undertake militant protest action. Asked to throw light on what transpired and whether he ever felt 'let down' by the attitude of certain recruits, John replied intently:

> 'Well, they didn't let me down as such; nobody ever did that. But I should have backed off from one or two things. I was overloading myself. For one thing, I had to remember too much. And I now recognise the symptoms and the signs which point to the fact that I was overloading myself... Things were becoming too personal.'

In what sense?

> 'I was expecting people to be perfect, and I realised that the whole method of my induction strategy was based on them being perfect. And they're not perfect. Nobody's perfect, but I was acting on the assumption that they were. You see, it was crucial that those actively involved in MAC were clear what the objective was. It wasn't about valleys being flooded and pipelines per se. It was that one nation is able to trample on another. And those I recruited into MAC were politically savvy enough to know the

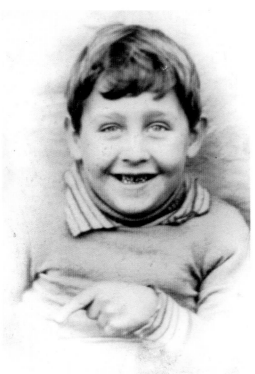

John 'aged 3 or 4', taken when the Jenkins family lived in John Street, Treharris.

John in 1947, smiling happily in the junior cadets' band uniform. 'My childhood was very happy. Some people have suggested that it wasn't, and that is why I did what I did with MAC. But it simply isn't true. The only thing we didn't have was money – and to a child that isn't important at all.'

January 1951. 'Having joined the Army a few weeks before, I was back home on weekend leave from Aldershot.'

Tom and Minerva, *c.*1951. John: 'It was probably taken on a chapel day trip to somewhere like Barry Island. That was the only time they left the village.'

John just after arriving in Austria, December 1952.

John (right) with a colleague in their Dental Centre scrubs, outside the British military hospital in Klagenfurt, Austria in 1954.

'Nan' in the last pub she and her husband managed in Ponthyr (Caerleon) in 1954. John: 'I always referred to her as Nan. She was in fact my aunty, and like her sister – my mother – she was a formidable woman. But also kind.'

Minerva, c.1955.

John marching the dental troops 'for fun', outside the Dental Centre at Bulford Camp, Salisbury Plain, just before leaving the Army in November 1955.

York, summer 1957. After an overnight exercise, John and colleagues in the TA enjoy some leisure time.

John and Thelma's wedding day, 18 October 1958.

Minerva and Keith, *c.*1958.

Thelma and Vaughan on the beach in Cyprus, summer 1962.

Sergeant Jenkins enjoys a social drink with Royal Army Dental Corps colleagues in Cyprus, 1959.

John with Rhodri in early April, 1965.

Tom and Minerva with granddaughter Siân in their garden in Penybryn, *c.*1962.

John and Vaughan, Germany, *c.*1963.

Sergeant John Jenkins of the Royal Army Dental Corps in March 1965, just weeks before leaving Germany to return to the UK.

John and Minerva, early April 1965.

Cayo Evans, leader of the FWA, and Eirwyn Pontsian at the Tryweryn protest in 1965.

(Geoff Charles, with permission from National Library of Wales.)

Commander Dennis Coslett of the Free Wales Army.

(Raymond Daniel)

'God keep the Prince… in England'
(a play on the Welsh word *cadw* meaning both 'save' and 'keep').

(Elwyn Ioan)

George Thomas ridiculed.

(Elwyn Ioan)

Students outside the Old College, Aberystwyth in March 1969, after a hunger strike protesting Prince Charles' acceptance by the University of Aberystwyth. From left to right: Nia Griffith, Manon Rhys, Sioned Bebb, Siân Wyn and Lowri Morgan – John's future partner.

(Ron Davies)

John Jenkins: 'Every mother in the land would have hated us' [had MAC attempted to physically harm Prince Charles].

(Raymond Daniel)

Dave Pritchard and Dai Walters being greeted by Gwynfor Evans after their court case, as their solicitor Elystan Morgan looks on.

Prince Charles being greeted at Pantycelyn hall of residence, where he stayed while studying in Aberystwyth before the Investiture.

John Jenkins (in the front row of the parade, left) on band duties in Wrexham on Remembrance Sunday 1967. It is very likely that one of the flautists behind him is Ernie Alders.

Ernie Alders and John Jenkins wearing the uniform of the Royal Welch Fusiliers, when John was best man for Alders on 18 October 1969.

The aftermath of the Penisa'r Waun bomb, January 1968.

(Wyn Thomas' personal collection)

End of Llandudno Pier, allegedly targeted by MAC during the Investiture period, July 1969.

(Michael Moore)

The water pipes at Llanrhaeadr-ym-Mochnant.

(Wyn Thomas' personal collection)

The scene inside the entrance hall of the Temple of Peace, Cardiff, yesterday after the bomb explosion.

# Bomb 'rebuilt' in hunt for saboteurs
## DAM BLAST LINK ?

Damage caused by the bomb at the Temple of Peace, Cardiff, 1967.

(*The Western Mail*)

1 July 1969: a day of pageantry at Caernarfon Castle, and a day of celebration for many – if not all.

(PA)

Charles pledging fealty to the British Crown as Prince of Wales. Home Secretary and Cardiff South-East MP Jim Callaghan looks on.

(PA)

Detective Chief Inspector Jock Wilson, leader of the Shrewsbury Unit.

The damage after the Abergele bomb. (PA)

Alwyn Jones and George Taylor, who were killed in the explosion at Abergele.

# Freed bomber says he fears exile from Wales

### By CLIVE BETTS

BOMBER JOHN Jenkins was released from Albany Prison, Isle of Wight, yesterday unrepentant for his actions. "Does a man have to apologise for fighting for his country?"

He said he had had any regrets during his seven years in gaol, over his actions.

His first trip was to Abergele, to the graves of the two men killed by their own bomb on the morning of the investiture in 1969. Mr. Jenkins, now 45, was gaoled at Mold in 1970 for 10 years, concurrent on each of eight explosives charges.

A regular Army sergeant, he had simultaneously been operational director of Mudiad Amddiffyn Cymru (Movement for the Defence of Wales). He had admitted his connection with a series of explosions in Wales and Cheshire between 1966 and 1969. His release was delayed by seven days after all prisoners had lost at least a week's remission following a strike earlier this month.

#### CELL SYSTEM

After crossing to Southampton from the Isle of Wight yesterday, Mr. Jenkins, carrying a green prison-issue hold-all, immediately made for London and a train to Abergele.

He said, "I knew only one of the two men. Both were members of MAC but for obvious security reasons we operated on a cell system and I did not know all members of the movement."

Mr. Jenkins, who was born in Aberfan, will be visiting his parents who live in the Rhymney Valley, before leaving for a holiday in the Middle

John Jenkins at Waterloo Station after his release

John Jenkins after his release in July 1976.

(*The Western Mail*)

(above) Minerva with Beryl Bridgman, sometime in the early 1970s.

(left) Capel Gwladys. John Jenkins: 'The cross that cost the state £7 million.'

(Robat Gruffudd)

John Jenkins in 2007, showing part of the ceremonial uniform which, he maintains, led to his arrest.

(Wyn Thomas)

John studies a copy of his birth certificate for the first time.

(Wyn Thomas)

A piece of the Celtic artwork which John completed and posted to supporters while at HM Prison Albany.

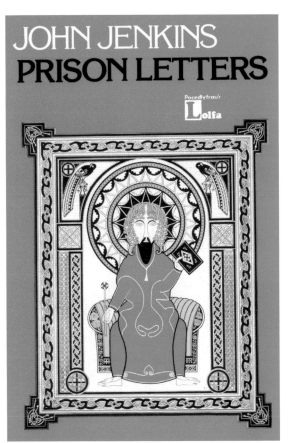

*Prison Letters*, published in 1981 (reprinted in 2019).

John (front row, second from left) with the Cambria Band at the Llangollen International Eisteddfod in 2008.

John Jenkins outside Hope Church in Flintshire, after the Liberation of Hope event in 2009.

difference. It wasn't about simply proving a point; and I certainly wouldn't have asked them to risk their lives just to prove a point.

But I have to admit that on one occasion, I went to a "safe house" – a property being used as a rendezvous point – to meet this chap, hand over the device and suggest a target, only to find that he wasn't as enthusiastic as I would have hoped. In fact, in spite of my efforts to rally him, he was quite lukewarm until his wife appeared on the scene. As I remember, she was waiting some distance away in their car. Anyway, after a passage of some time, she appeared. And she was horrified at her husband's – well, he wasn't exactly backing off, but he wasn't exactly rushing forward either. She knew what he was doing there, and she knew what I was doing there, and she gave him the bollocking of his career for not leaping forward as he should have done. He should be "delighted at the chance to do something for Wales", and all that.

I didn't blame him, actually. He was married with kids. I knew the risks involved as much as he and the others knew the risks involved. You put everything on the line, don't you? Doing things like that. That's it: your whole life – your career, your marriage, your kids, your future – everything is on the line. Once you have overstepped *that* mark, well, then that's it. Anyway, it should be noted that he *did* undertake this action; the protest was a success and everything went according to plan.'

It is a fascinating piece of testimony, which is worthy of further consideration. Because although John appears correct in believing that those who joined MAC did so out of a sense of duty, idealism and a deep love for Wales, it is *also* apparent that operatives undertook protest action out of respect for Jenkins, who led from the front and instilled a resolute mentality and shared purpose. And while Jenkins was not perhaps a black leather-clad 'enforcer', the strength of his personality, along with the strident and fervent influence of others embroiled in MAC's protest, proved instrumental in the campaign's longevity.

Whatever the truth, as the phrase 'Welsh bomb attack' entered the lexicon and psyche of the British nation, on 25 June, a device planted by MAC was discovered at the base of the Prince of Wales monument at Mackenzie Pier in Holyhead. It had failed to detonate. Five days later, on 30 June, a postbox exploded outside the postal sorting office at Victoria Park in Cardiff. Those responsible have not been identified.

## Investiture Day: Abergele, an unusual Royal 21-Gun Salute, Ian Cox and Llandudno Pier

Just before midnight on the eve of the Investiture, one of the four MAC active units armed by John Jenkins to protest the ceremony was planting a device outside the Social Security office in Abergele. The device was accidentally triggered and the two men, Alwyn Jones and George Taylor, were killed instantly. Since the death of her father, George Taylor's daughter Jennie has maintained that her father was not in MAC, but while 'standing some distance back', was trying to talk his friend out of undertaking what she calls 'a foolish act'. Invited to revisit the speculation concerning George Taylor's affiliation to MAC and to clarify unequivocally if Taylor *was* indeed a member of the movement, Jenkins sighed with indignation and retorted: 'Of *course* he was in MAC. Good God – they both were.' Furthermore, George Taylor and Alwyn Jones 'were no strangers to activism', having 'pulled off together one highly successful job at Penisa'r Waun' in January 1968.[115] Asked, therefore, to state categorically the intended target on the eve of the Investiture, Jenkins replied:

> 'I met the cell leader, Alwyn Jones, the weekend before; and on handing him the device, I instructed him to target any government office that was *not* near the train, but which was obviously in the town [Abergele] which the train was running through.'

Because the railway line to Caernarfon passes through Abergele, there has existed in certain quarters the suspicion that Alwyn Jones and George Taylor were in fact on their way to lay the device on the railway tracks in anticipation of the Royal Train passing; but as the two men made their way to the railway line, the device activated prematurely, killing them both. However, it is a claim which has been repeatedly and vehemently denied by John Jenkins as lacking credibility.[116] Jenkins has dismissed the charge, both on the grounds that he did *not* instruct Alwyn Jones to target the railway track, nor had he since their appalling deaths attempted to gain political capital by suggesting that the tracks were indeed their intended target. Information concerning the time the Royal Train was to pass through Abergele *might* have been received had he requested it, Jenkins stated. But he did *not*, as such knowledge was irrelevant to his intentions. It was therefore information neither requested nor received.

Yet contrary to both John Jenkins' belief and a Home Office report which concluded that Alwyn Jones and George Taylor 'were acting in concert in the committing of a criminal offence related to the use of explosives',[117] George Taylor's daughter Jennie maintains that the Taylor family 'strongly refutes' the claim. Having remained convinced of his innocence, George Taylor's family was left floundering for answers. On undertaking their own investigation into the events surrounding the tragic incident, they approached Lord Llandudno, who, on agreeing that the family's findings *did* appear to cast some doubt on the official record, further agreed to champion the family's cause in campaigning for an appeal.

Speaking on BBC Radio Cymru in 2013, Lord Llandudno stated that 'there was already enough evidence to justify an inquiry.'[118] It has provided the Taylor family a glimmer of tentative hope, which albeit temporarily, has pierced the stress and often debilitating grief they have endured since the much-loved husband and father was killed. Nonetheless, despite their endeavours, the official explanation remains unaltered. Contacted in summer 2018, an undeterred Jennie Taylor vowed to do 'whatever it takes to clear my father's name.'[119] The family's commitment to challenging George Taylor's alleged involvement in the MAC campaign, in all its strength, loyalty, dignity and dedication, surely deserves respect. Prompted to outline what he thinks occurred when the two men were killed, John replied:

'I don't know what happened. I don't think anybody does. There have been all sorts of far-fetched ideas, with people saying that "Special Branch or MI5 caught them and blew them up", but I don't believe that. I don't know what is true. I simply think that they made a mistake. That it was an accident – in that when assembling the device, they activated it too early. But I do know one thing: it broke my heart.'[120]

Discussing the character, personality and interests of Alwyn Jones and George Taylor – particularly in relation to Jones being an inveterate letter-writer to local north Wales newspapers, in which he wrote effusively on political Welsh nationalism and Welsh cultural identity; and George Taylor's active participation in Abergele's Investiture celebrations, which included helping to put up Union Jack bunting in anticipation of the forthcoming ceremony – Jenkins intoned soberly:

'It would have seemed suspicious had Alwyn stopped, so he was encouraged to carry on. He tended to get into arguments with people about Wales, and that wasn't a good idea, but it was also felt that the contribution that he had made was positive enough to outweigh the possible problems. The point was, he was already noted for his pro-Welsh attitude in the Abergele area. So had he suddenly stopped this behaviour, it would have aroused comment and suspicion. So too George Taylor – not that I knew George Taylor. But one night – not that George Taylor saw me – shortly after I'd popped into a pub and made eye contact with him, Alwyn followed me out to the car park and told me who his drinking partner, George Taylor, was: that he was a member of his cell. I wasn't aware that George Taylor was involved in Abergele's Investiture celebrations, but as a member of MAC he was entitled to do lots of things to conceal his true identity – as long as it conformed with security. And so he would have been aware, for security reasons, of the need to carry on as normal – as any deviation from his usual behaviour would fuel suspicion.'

Contacted to discuss the matter was a member of the House of Lords, and former leading member of the judiciary. Having requested anonymity, he proclaimed solemnly:

'I did hear through legal sources at the time that on arriving at the Taylor household sometime later,[121] members of the Shrewsbury Unit dropped heavily torn and bloodstained clothing onto the kitchen table and said: "Do you recognise this? Does this look familiar?" If true, then it must have been horrific. But the police had to act quickly. They didn't know if they were dealing with a widespread plot or a conspiracy to attack the Royal Party; and so, from their point of view, they had no time to lose. But it must have been dreadful for the family.'[122]

Asked to outline, from his own perspective, the events surrounding the Abergele explosion, John Jenkins' voice dropped and he declared slowly:

'Two days before the Investiture, Thelma helped me to pack a case with a few things, because as part of the medical unit I was going to be on duty there. I was given a lift by a fellow serviceman and the day after arriving, we were told that all military personnel were ordered to remain on site, owing to the possibility of trouble in Caernarfon. Well, the evening before the ceremony passed quietly enough, really. But the following morning, my tent flap was rudely opened and an officer put his head in and said, "Well, we got two of the bastards last night," and then he went. Now, of course, I didn't have a radio with me, so I went down to the sergeant's mess to find out what was happening. And all they had on was bloody cricket or tennis, or something, so I had to sit there through all that. Because I knew that four groups had been out the night before, but I didn't know which group had been killed, and it was several hours later that I discovered which group it was.'

How did he get through that day? 'With great, great difficulty,' Jenkins replied sombrely; adding:

'It was the most difficult day of my life, because I had to act as if nothing had happened. I had to carry on and laugh and drink with them all, and joke about it and stuff like that…[123] Yeah, it cut me in half. It wasn't until the early evening news that I learned that the explosion was in Abergele. I knew then, of course, who was involved. God knows how I got through that day. I did, but it's the hardest thing I've ever had to do in my life.'

At what point was he able to reveal his true feelings?

'Not until I got back home, the day after the Investiture. I had a lift from Caernarfon to Wrexham – it's quite a long way, and all the way back I had to chat about rubbish. And I was bleeding inside. My whole world had collapsed. But I had to hold myself together, because this person I was in the car with knew nothing about this. And I couldn't grieve. You mustn't grieve. You're not allowed to grieve. But I was shattered. Absolutely shattered. When I did get home, I went to find Thelma, and when I found her, I just broke down. It had to come out. If it hadn't, I don't know what I would have done. Even I couldn't take that sort of pressure. It was agony. Anyway, I ended up telling her everything. I told her that it was me that had handed them the device. I kept saying, "I wish I'd been killed. Why couldn't *I* have been killed? I should have been killed – not them." But that's how I felt: very, *very* guilty.'

Was Thelma sympathetic?

'No. She wasn't sympathetic. She didn't understand. I didn't even to try and explain to her why I was involved. She wouldn't have understood.

She took me saying that I should have been killed as a personal insult; a direct threat to the integrity of the family, in that I was prepared to go off and leave the family – which, of course, I was. I am the first to admit that. Through her eyes, I was the father of children. I was an Army sergeant. I was a householder. I was respectable and looked up to, and all sorts of lovely things. And suddenly here he is, having completely broken down. So naturally she thought I was foolish. It was completely out of character for me to do that. She couldn't understand what all the fuss was about. From someone to be looked up to, I was suddenly someone to be pitied, and I suppose the gap was too much for her to cope with. It was, I suppose, an astonishing paradox: a brushed and polished and respectable member of society, and yet I am embroiled in this utterly different world. It made me wonder who the *real* me was. And it's something I've been trying to work out ever since.'

Whatever the truth surrounding the harrowing incident at Abergele, at 14.15 during the afternoon of the Investiture, just before the Royal Party arrived at Caernarfon Castle on their horse-drawn journey, an explosion was heard. It occurred just prior to the traditional Royal 21-gun salute of welcome – and was 'believed by people in the crowd to be the start' of it.[124] The device, planted by MAC activists the previous evening and described by John Jenkins as 'the main one', had been 'planted in the garden of the Chief Constable' [of the Gwynedd Constabulary]. It had been deliberately timed to undermine the prestige of the salute, by adding a twenty-second blast. 'It worked like a dream,' Jenkins later remarked, continuing:

'How they got that bomb in the Chief Constable's garden was a work of art. Information was passed along a chain to me as to the timing of the salute, so we had a good idea what time to detonate it. But the police surveillance in the area was staggering – and yet, of all places, they managed to plant it there!'

But if John Jenkins was impressed by the audacious manner in which the MAC active unit carried out its attack, retired Lieutenant Colonel Mike H L Lewis, former High Sheriff of Powys, who – as a member of the Royal Welch Fusiliers A Company – provided the guard of honour as Prince Charles stepped off the Royal Train in Caernarfon, claims that although the military had been briefed as to the Welsh militant threat, he, along with his colleagues, had not taken the threat terribly seriously. Asked in 2019 to recall his involvement in the day's ceremonial proceedings, Mike Lewis continued:

'Having joined the RWF from Sandhurst in 1967, I was a Lieutenant by the time of the Investiture, and on the day itself, I was second-in-command to Major Geoff Inkin. Those of us involved in presenting the guard of honour were camped for a week or so at Tŷ Croes on Anglesey. Tŷ Croes is about 30 minutes from Caernarfon, and we had to be up at some unearthly hour, 3 a.m. or something, in order to get to Caernarfon to rehearse before anyone was around. On Investiture Day, in typical Army style, we were there and in position hours before it officially started... I remember that sometime in the morning we were briefed as to this militant threat, and we were advised to be aware of people acting suspiciously; and to be mindful of unattended packages and so on. I don't recall us being shown photographs of potential suspects, as we were later in Northern Ireland, but we were certainly instructed to keep an eye out for anyone acting suspiciously, and to report it. The idea being that this information would then be passed immediately onto the police, who would then approach anyone, or anything, within the crowd causing concern, and deal with it. You see, our role as Army servicemen was in support of the police – and *not* the other way around...

I don't remember the name MAC being mentioned during the briefing. I'm sure it would have been, had more intelligence been available. But if MAC stands for the "Movement to Defend Wales", then I suspect it would have been greeted with derision... I have to say that the threat, as discussed during our briefing, was not taken terribly seriously by members of the military. The suggestion that this group posed a physical threat to us would have been facetiously dismissed by the troops. "Ooh, watch out!", you know! And this group didn't go on to achieve anything great. But perhaps this threat, at the time, should have been taken seriously, because there *was* an explosion on the day, of course. I have since read in the official Regimental Records of the Royal Welch Fusiliers that a device exploded just before the Royal 21-Gun Salute. But I don't recall hearing it on the day. Perhaps, being back at Griffiths Crossing [opposite Ferodo brake factory] where we'd presented the guard of honour a little time before, I was too far away to hear it. Nor do I recall the other explosions; for instance, the one that occurred in Abergele. Only some time later did I read about it. But I'm quite sure that this explosion in Abergele the night before the ceremony would have featured in our briefing. And I'm afraid it would have been regarded, to use very unfortunate Army language, as an 'own goal'. That would have been the operational response...

I am quite certain that the militant threat would have been taken seriously at Government level – naturally, as any such threat to the Queen would be. Obviously, bombings are a serious business. In fact, in the RWF Regimental Records, it states that a "security alarm" was received at Vaynol Hall the night before the ceremony.[125] Vaynol Hall is the residence of the Lord Lieutenant of Caernarfonshire: it's some four miles from Caernarfon and it was where the Queen stayed the night before the Investiture. But I have no idea what this "security alarm" amounted to – and it doesn't say any more in the official records.[126] But I do know that as a result of this "security alarm", some 30 or so soldiers from the RWF were then despatched to support the police with regards crowd control. They were, I'm quite sure, in uniform, and were deployed, along with the police, to line the processional route...

As for any sympathy within the RWF for the Welsh militants: there was a rumour that a Welsh-born officer within the regiment, who was an excellent, first-class chap, had in some way or another been active in this group. I mean, we used to joke about it; and he didn't, as I recall, deny it. But he certainly didn't confirm it either. But I'm quite sure it was nothing more than light-hearted military-style rumour and tittle-tattle.[127]

As for my overall thoughts of Investiture Day: well, the drill A Company provided was good; other than the fact that I allowed my sword to briefly tilt slightly forward. This ensured that it was "out of kilter", which is not good at all, but thankfully there are no photographs of it in the official records! I can smile about it now, but it would certainly have been frowned upon. Look, it was a bloody long time ago: '69, and memory fades. But as I think back, I still maintain a *real* sense of pride. I feel honoured to have been a part of this ancient ceremony, and *very* honoured to have been part of the guard of honour for Prince Charles when he got off the train. So yes, the great day itself holds good memories for me.'[128]

Nevertheless, before arriving at Caernarfon Castle, where the Queen invested her eldest son Prince of Wales, the third of the four devices which comprised the MAC protest was meant to explode. It did not. Encouraged to outline what transpired, Jenkins declared:

'Nine days before the Investiture, I took the "goods" in a shoebox to Caernarfon and handed it to the cell leader. He was instructed to place it "where it won't hurt anybody, but will cause symbolic damage". Being familiar with the area, he knew the town far better than me. There has been this conjecture that they deliberately placed it under an oil tank – but that assumes they knew what it was. They probably just saw a tin thing lying there and thought "Ah, that'll make a nice noise when the explosion goes off." It was timed to detonate during the procession to the castle. All it was intended to do was to create a hell of a noise; and what with the horses coming down the road – because as far as I am aware, this garden was on the route to the castle – that would have caused a certain amount of uproar. But it wasn't a big bomb. It was intended as a small, symbolic explosion – a gesture. That's what all of them were. So they put it there – and I don't blame them. I had no subsequent discussion with them about its whereabouts. But it's worth bearing in mind that given the amount of police and supervision there was in those days, the person involved probably had no more than five minutes in which to plant and activate the thing before getting out of there quickly. There were people up and down all the time – especially on the route. Because of the enormous amount of surveillance that was going on, there was increased pressure, which was getting to everyone by then – and mistakes were made.' [129]

Whatever the group's reasoning for planting the device in its location, it proved an abject failure and a massive strategic blunder. Four days after the Investiture, 10-year-old Ian Cox, on holiday from England, was badly injured when he trod on the device and it activated. Asked to respond to the charge that had MAC notified the authorities of the bomb's whereabouts, the tragedy may well have been averted, Jenkins responded quietly:

'I am truly sorry for the injuries that little boy suffered... I heard it on the news. And I'm not making excuses, I was deeply despondent over it. But nobody was meant to get hurt. When it failed to go off, I gave the order to contact the police to tell them where it was. And having done so, we couldn't attempt to retrieve it in case the site was being watched. When I later asked the police why they hadn't acted on this information, they claimed to have been inundated with hoax calls during the Investiture period – I was given a figure of 16,000. As it turned out, the site wasn't under police surveillance. But we didn't *know* that, and so we had to assume that it was.'

Despite Jenkins' candour, it is an explanation which many observers will regard as insufficient and incomprehensible. Such injuries to a 10-year-old boy, it is argued, can never be justified – whatever the political cause. Furthermore, what happened to the unfortunate Ian Cox reflected the fact that the militant campaign of *Mudiad Amddiffyn Cymru* had derailed itself morally and was now spiralling ominously out of control. Outraged and alarmed by the hideous escalation in violence, the police now redoubled their efforts to bring the Welsh extremists to book. Explosions on remote pipelines in the Welsh mountains was one thing; blood on the streets quite another.[130] But the device planted in Caernarfon which regrettably injured Ian Cox was not the only one of the four MAC Investiture devices which failed to detonate. The fourth device, which was placed on the pier in Llandudno, was intended to prevent Prince Charles coming ashore from the Royal Yacht *Britannia* to begin a tour through Wales the day after the ceremony. It allegedly remained *in situ* until Jenkins' arrest some four months later.

*'You can't hate the roots of the tree, and not hate the tree.'*
*Malcolm X.*
*'Violence breeds violence.' Robert Kennedy*

But did MAC *really* pose a credible threat to Prince Charles? 'Look,' Jenkins replied a little impatiently, 'could we have killed him? Yes, we could have killed him. You see,' John continued:

> 'what isn't known is that one of the hardest fights I *ever* had was with our own people. I spent a lot of time in the weeks before the Investiture travelling around in an Army civilian car, reining people in. They were becoming more, well, *savage* as the ceremony approached. They would say, "The answer's simple. There *can't* be an Investiture if we kill him." And I would have to stress, "OK, but what the hell will we achieve politically if we do? Nothing." But it [assassinating Charles] was possible. For one thing, I was in the Army. I was there. I could have carried a rifle and I could have shot him there and then if I'd wanted.'

Jenkins momentarily glared with hawkish eyes, before adding:

'Furthermore, if I'd said "Right, I want a couple of people who are prepared to do something and not come back from it," I know at least two who would have come forward and volunteered. I'm talking about a suicide operation. They both lived in north-west Wales: one in Caernarfon and the other in the Bangor area, and they were *not* in the same MAC cell. But they both lived in places subject to all sorts of obstructions from the police and the military as the Investiture approached, and contrary to the truth, they were reading in the papers that people were "dancing in the streets" in celebration. And they were furious about all this – and frustrated that legitimate protest against it was being ignored. All it would have taken was to put these two in a cell for this operation and to provide explosives to be strapped to their bodies, or for them to place explosives in a bag somewhere along the route and to detonate it as the Royal Party went past on their way to the Castle – which would have led to bystanders being killed. Or they could have taken out of their pocket a pistol with a rapid-fire action, and started firing; theoretically, they could also have been armed with a rifle and positioned at a vantage point overlooking the processional route, and, well, that would have been it...

I'm not saying that these were *specific* suggestions which I vetoed. I'm talking about attitudes and beliefs in MAC which were, however, available to me. And I will say this: if you are determined to kill someone, you will kill him. And there is *nothing* the police or the intelligence service can do to prevent it. The only way is to kill you. But by that time, you may have succeeded in your action. And with these two MAC boys in particular, even if they didn't want to [die], I have *no* doubt they would have been prepared to do it and sacrifice themselves. Because a cause is a cause; and if it's worth fighting for, it's worth dying for. And although people will baulk at the idea of me being seen as a "moderate" and "sober-minded" person, had I not been in *total* control of these individuals in MAC, then God knows what might have happened.'

So did Jenkins consider MAC's Investiture Day protest to be a success? 'As far as I am concerned,' John replied empathetically, 'our protest achieved its objective: which was to change the nature of the activities.'

'And July 1st in Caernarfon was something to behold. I was there and I know what the feeling was like – the atmosphere was electric. And crucially, it was not the great celebration and jamboree which the establishment and organisers claimed it would be – and *that* is the main thing. I know people say, "Oh you failed, you didn't achieve your objective, because the Investiture went on". Yes, it went on. But we never intended to stop it in the first place. That would have taken more of our resources and people than we could spare. But I maintain that had we *wanted* to stop it, we could have stopped it. And while that is true, I have also said *this* all along: the MAC protest surrounding the Investiture was *not* about Charles. It was about Prince Charles as Prince of Wales, and what the title now represented. As far as I am concerned, the Investiture can be summed up in one sentence: we gained a prince and lost a kingdom.'

Asked to develop the point and to sum up what he believed the Investiture exemplified, and who he felt most badly betrayed the Welsh nation during the Investiture period, John declared intently:

'The point is – and the big thing about the Investiture which people seem to forget – we were being invited to celebrate the conquest of our nation... I was sickened by the attitude of some in Wales to the Investiture. I was at the time – and I remain – utterly convinced that the MAC campaign was the *only* thing on this earth which was defending the honour of our country. Plaid Cymru didn't do a damn thing. They were utterly ineffectual in the way they meekly objected to it. But not just them. I just *cannot* understand why Welsh men and women would want to join in the celebrations for the replacement of their slaughtered prince by another prince from another nation. What sort of a people would do that? Or take pride in pointing at a bloody chair they sat on during the ceremony and saying, "I sat there when Prince Charles was being invested." I don't see why it should be considered normal to invite a conquered people to celebrate the fact that they are now conquered, and to celebrate the fact that they're the victims of conquest. I don't see anything to be happy and smiling and jolly about in all of that. Do you see the English celebrating or having big parades on Hastings Day to commemorate their defeat by the Normans in 1066? No – and it's the same sort of thing, really. And yet the Welsh are expected to celebrate their own conquest – and to my astonishment, many of them did! I try to understand such people and I can't. They are beyond the ken. Had Hitler won the war, would these same people be celebrating now? Celebrating the fact that Hitler won? And I think yes. Because that sort of person – these quislings – would, of course. They *would* all be there [behaving] just the same.'

Whether dismissed as part propaganda and part fantasy by some, wasn't support for the Investiture in Wales reflected by the degree to which the *majority* of the Welsh populace celebrated the occasion? 'No, not entirely,' Jenkins responded firmly.

'Because those people who supported it and attended the ceremony were *not* the full story. I know, because in my capacity within Western Command, I was still driving around Wales in the months before the Investiture – and this enabled me to gauge the grass-roots reaction. And a minority, but a *considerable* minority, felt disenchanted and resentful toward the whole bloody thing. And so we were determined to give that disenchantment a voice. I'm not saying that everyone in Wales supported us. But those people in Wales who opposed the Investiture, especially as the ceremony neared, were being *ignored*. Like those across the Welsh demographic who had the temerity to raise an objection and highlight the situation from a Welsh historical perspective. They were either ignored by the media on the grounds that it was dissent which conflicted with their official party line, or they were accused of 'stirring up the past'. The attitude was, "Oh you Welsh, digging up the past again. For God's sake leave it there." And yet, when it suited them to justify their own position, they were saying, "History *is* important. After all, we [Royals] came over with [William] the Conqueror". Well, we [Welsh] were here when the bloody Romans came, mate! So don't give us the old nonsense about that!'

## John returns to Penybryn and hears some disturbing thoughts from Minerva about the events in Abergele

A fortnight after the Investiture, John returned alone to stay with his parents in Penybryn. With his brother Keith a regular visitor, it was the first time that he, John, Minerva and Tom had been together since the ceremony – and the protests. Did John and Keith discuss the matter? 'No, never,' John replied; continuing:

'We never discussed me being in MAC. But I suspect Keith knew I was involved. Because he knew me – and he knew where my sympathies lay. He also knew that I am *not* the sort of person who stands idly by when things like this are going on. So knowing my likely reaction, he'd assume I was involved. But he never said anything, of course.'

Having established that he and Tom 'never chatted about politics', had John and Minerva discussed the recent events? 'No – we were close, but I never discussed politics with her at all, much less MAC or the anti-Investiture actions. That said,' Jenkins added dolefully:

> 'While I was staying there, she mentioned it once. Only once, and she made what I thought was a derogatory and facetious remark about the two lads who got killed. I think she was trying to cheer me up, and thinking that I was for the other side, she said something like, "Oh, those silly boys – what a foolish and stupid thing to do."
>
> Well, this got me very angry and I said to her, "Don't you go saying things like that about people you know nothing about. Right?" And she backed off straight away. She must have realised then that there was some involvement on my part, but she didn't say anything. She didn't come back at me; the matter rested there. And it stayed there – we never said another word about it. But after she said it, I stormed out.'

Still reeling from the ghastly and horrifying events at Abergele; the deplorable injuries suffered by Ian Cox; and no doubt further unsettled by the way he had verbally rounded on Minerva in an uncustomarily heated manner, John retreated to Capel Gwladys. It was here that he could always be assured of rest, peace, inspiration and solace. The latter of which, as John sat quietly and thoughtfully among the tranquil ruins of this chapel, he now required more than ever. Prompted to express his frame of mind at this juncture, Jenkins declared:

> 'Well, if the pressure was bad before the Investiture, it bore down much more heavily after the two men got killed and the little boy got hurt. That's when it started to weigh really, *really* heavily. Because it was my responsibility: nobody else's, mine! And I had no one to talk to. I was having disturbed sleep; I wasn't eating really; and I was more crabbed around the house. I knew enough about mental health to recognise the signs: I was becoming depressed.
>
> I've never suffered with depression, nor have I been prescribed anti-depressants. Not before, not then, nor since. But I'm only human, after all, and the stress I was under was noticed. I'd have people saying to me, "Oh you're looking awful worried and worn, you can see the stress

in your forehead." I'd say, "Yes, I've got a lot of work on," or "I'm worried about the kids."

But what could I say? I mean there were times when I didn't sleep for bloody days because of all the visiting, assessing recruits and delivering and taking possession of things. But while you have to take that into account, you've got to carry it. Because the point is, although you're tired out, the people you're working with don't know why. As far as they're concerned, you've not long been out of bed; when in fact, whether due to preparing for a protest or to anxiety, you haven't slept for two days! So, they can't understand why you're just a little bit tighter than usual.'

In the winter of 2018, John Jenkins was asked to comment on documentation held at the National Library of Wales including a handwritten note from Jenkins in which he asked Alders to take control of MAC in the weeks after the Investiture – an offer which Alders allegedly refused, on the grounds that Jenkins 'operating on a 50% efficiency quotient' was still greatly in excess of his own 'best form'.[131] John replied thoughtfully:

'Yeah, it does ring a bell. But it wouldn't have worked: Alders was too emotional and he lacked the intellectual maturity. Not just that. It takes a certain sort of chap to run something like MAC, when you are so far away from everybody. Your influence and your control has got to reach them, no matter where they are – and they've got to give in to that. Well, Alders wasn't the type to exert that sort of authority. He was a nice chap, but he didn't have the presence. He didn't have the kudos, or the respect of the other MAC boys to take it forward... He was younger than most of them.

To be honest, I was always afraid that Ernie would buckle under the pressure, but particularly as time went on. And that in turn was only adding to the pressure that *I* was feeling. And the last thing I wanted in *that* game was for someone to buckle under the pressure. Not just Alders. I had my doubts about everybody – particularly those who hadn't been tested. And the only way they could be tested was by going out and undertaking an action. So the pressure just seemed to be multiplying, in a number of ways. And I suppose, in trying to increase Alders' responsibility, I was trying to offload some of that pressure. But no, it was a bad idea. But that's how desperate and despondent I was by this point.'

## MAC continues its protest – *'The Welsh... that unconquerable race...' Winston Churchill*

In August 1969, the police investigation 'switched to Wrexham'. It did so after police learned that Alwyn Jones and George Taylor had 'contacts' in the Wrexham area.[132] Unaware of the development in the police inquiry, on 14 August MAC targeted the South Stack Relay Station on Holyhead Mountain. Asked to throw light on the operation, John replied:

> 'We were attempting to destroy it, because the direct communications network between the British mainland and Northern Ireland went straight through South Stack; and with all the troubles in the province escalating, the explosion was sanctioned to show the IRA that we did not appreciate what the British Army was doing in Ulster.'

Three days later, owing to the fact that 'Prince Charles is the Earl of Chester', Ernie Alders was instructed by Jenkins to target a council premises in the city. Whether caution overcame Alders remains unclear. Had the ghastly business in Abergele and the appalling injuries suffered by Ian Cox played on his mind? Perhaps, aged just 21, Ernie Alders had reconsidered his affiliation to MAC owing to his impending wedding. Whatever his reason or reasons, Alders disabled the device. It was discovered at 7 o'clock the following morning, by a hospital porter on his way to work. The device lay unguarded and positioned where Alders presumably placed it some hours before – beneath an anorak on the doorstep of the Council Health Office.

On 18 September, John was interviewed by two detectives at Saighton Camp. Asked if he sympathised with Welsh extremism, John replied empathically, 'Good heavens, no. They are a menace to everyone.' Apparently reassured by Jenkins' response, the officers left.[133] Having no reason to suspect that Alders was also the subject of the police investigation, Jenkins moved the remaining stock of explosives – stored since the theft at Hafod Quarry 'in an ordinary wooden packing case' within the locked cupboard at the Dental Centre – to Alders' home in Rhosllannerchrugog.

Had the visit by the police unsettled him? 'Oh, I knew they were on to me,' John replied; adding:

> 'Apart from them visiting me, certain things were happening in work. I knew then, straight away. I noticed, for instance, that in the last couple

of weeks, the colonel I worked alone with was almost deferential to me. It was very strange for a colonel to behave in such a way towards a sergeant. So I realised *then* that there was something that had changed – our relationship had changed. He was treating me more as an equal than as a subordinate. I think the police visited him at his home and told him who I was and what I was involved in. He'd been instructed to engage me in conversation, because he was very carefully asking my opinion and discussing matters. Nothing specific in relation to the MAC bombings, as that would be too obvious, but we spoke about the general effect of violence being used for a political objective: when it's necessary and when it's not necessary. That sort of thing. I didn't say much by way of response, as it would have seemed odd if I had – owing to the gap in our ranks. But, nonetheless, he was deferential in his approach to me, in that he paid attention to what I was saying, when normally this would *not* have been the case. Well, I don't miss much, and I wasn't going to fall for that. I mean, it was so out of the natural military order that I knew then that something was up.

There were other things, too. I was told that someone had been reported walking around the Dental Centre at night – and ordinarily, there was no reason why this should have happened. They were probably searching in cupboards for the explosives I'd hidden there – before I moved them to Alders' place. And then to cap it all, when I went to a cadets' band meeting, there were people there who shouldn't have been there, and they were saying silly things like, "Oh, we've got a bloke who's looking for a job. He's an ex-explosives expert and we're wondering where we can find a job for him." It was as clear as the nose on your face that something was going on. I think they thought that I'd approach him, or something. It was ridiculous. I've no doubt that my mother's home was being watched and her phone bugged too by this point.'

## Jenkins and Alders are arrested

The circumstances surrounding the arrest of John Jenkins have attracted conjecture. They have also caused a certain degree of rancour between John and Owain Williams ever since. During the evening of 1 March 1968, John and Owain Williams had met, as arranged, in Loggerheads. The meeting occurred between two performances given by Jenkins' military band to celebrate Saint David's Day. Further to Jenkins and Williams discussing the political situation in Wales, Owain informed John of his intention to abscond to the Republic of Ireland the following day, in order to avoid appearing in court on 6 March in relation to the explosion at Penisa'r Waun some two months earlier.

However, John maintains that Williams contravened MAC's established security framework by taking along a girlfriend. Despite her remaining in Williams' car, parked some distance from John and Owain's rendezvous point, she caught sight of Jenkins, dressed in 'highly distinctive ornamental rig', when John stepped out of his car and was caught in the glare of a passing car's headlights. Months later, following the events in Abergele and aware that her former partner Owain Williams was somehow involved in the militant campaign, Owain's female companion approached the authorities and informed investigating officers of the encounter in Loggerheads. Having quickly established that only four people in Wales were wearing that ceremonial uniform that night, the link to John Jenkins proved easy to make for a coterie of detectives desperate for a breakthrough.[134]

Owain Williams, on the other hand, is adamant that the breakthrough in the police inquiry into John Jenkins' activities came as a result of the information provided to officers by Ann Woodgate. Her reasons for doing so remain unclear. But whether fearful for the welfare of her ex-fiancée Ernie Alders, distraught by the increase in militancy, or perhaps motivated by news that Alders was once more engaged, so soon after their own relationship and engagement had ended, Ann Woodgate informed her father of Alders' involvement in the MAC protest. He, in turn, implored her to notify the police.

Whatever the truth surrounding these events, during the morning of Sunday, 2 November 1969, John Jenkins and Ernie Alders were arrested at their respective homes. Prompted to throw light on what transpired when officers arrived, John remarked:

'I was upstairs having a shave at the time; and I wasn't in uniform as has been alleged... Almost immediately after hearing a knock on the door, Thelma called up the stairs, "John, there are some people here to see you." So I came downstairs, and of course as soon as I saw them, although they were in plain clothes and not uniform, I knew. I still played along, though. They were quite formal, but polite, and after exchanging pleasantries, they said, "The thing is, we're here on behalf of the police, because we're investigating a matter concerning money and the cadets." I said "Oh?"

He said, "Yes, there seems to be a mix-up and some discrepancy with the finances. I wonder if you could help us sort it out?" I said, "Yeah, of course," and before I had the chance to ask them in, he said "But not here. Will you go up to the station with us and make a statement so we can get this matter cleared up?" I said "Righto." Although, I knew this business about the finances of the cadets was a load of absolute rubbish…

None of us were wearing uniform and it was an unmarked police car, so there were no curtains twitching, or neighbours out on the street as we left the house. Besides, although Range Road was an 'Army road,' in which the houses were lived in by Army families who worked at the Wrexham Barracks, our house – number 9 – was back a bit from the other houses, so my leaving with these two policemen wasn't noticed. There were probably a lot more police surrounding the area, just in case I decided to make a fight of it, but I knew the game was over. But I did say when I got in the car, "How long is this going to take, then?" and one said, "Oh, about ten minutes." Ten years later, I was released! Other than that, though, nothing was said until we arrived at the police station in Ruabon.'

If the harsh reality of John's predicament had yet to register, added clarity was provided on arriving at Ruabon police station. 'They said to me, just before I was questioned, "You're entitled to a solicitor." Well, I knew that anyway,' John stated, before continuing:

'So I gave them the name of a solicitor in north Wales – and they just adopted this rictus smile, shook their heads and said "No." I was bloody annoyed. They wouldn't contact the solicitor I wanted – I think in case he was a member of the organisation. He wasn't anything to do with us [MAC], but I was aware that his approach was the right sort of approach. He was fair, and believed in seeing two sides of a story. He was an ex-judge, actually. Anyway, I assume they were worried that I would tell him things in the confessional, as it were, which he could then have gone out and seen about. So they wouldn't allow me to have him. Apparently, they never even told him.

I realised right then, and not for the last time, how the authorities twist the rules. Actually, it amuses me, but they keep on about the need for 'rules' and for 'regulations' and how important it is that we all abide by them. Yet they break them all the time.'

## Minerva reacts to John's arrest, Peter Bridgman is pulled over by the police and the Jenkins' family home is searched

How did the indomitable Minerva hear of John's arrest – and how did she react? 'As I recall, Thelma phoned her that evening,' John replied.

'The media weren't outside the police station in Ruabon when we were transferred to Wrexham, but I think she saw it on the news too – that two men had been arrested. But in any case, I wrote to her a few days later, just saying that I'd been arrested in relation to this [bombings] business. I mean, what else could I say? She wasn't too upset; nor when I was sentenced. You see, although she was matriarchal, my mother's love was *not* conditional. It was sort of: whoever's fault it was, she knew that it wasn't my fault! I also told her not to worry. She wouldn't worry too much about me, because she knew I could take care of myself. Having said that, I think she would worry because the police had got me.'

As fate would have it, Thelma's brother Peter and their mother Beryl were on their way by car from Treharris to visit the Jenkins family in Wrexham. Before arriving, the pair were allegedly pulled over by the police. John later explained what next transpired:

'Well, he was on his way up with his mother to visit us and the police caught him halfway up, near Rhayader apparently, and beat the living shite out of him, thinking that he was one of the police officers that I had told the journalists [in May 1968] were "friendly and sympathetic" and telling us things. He was my brother-in-law, so in their eyes, it stood to reason. But it wasn't true, of course. Peter was a typical blue-blooded Tory; an out-and-out fascist, frankly, and the thought that he could be connected in *any way* to MAC was so far out, it's unbelievable. Anyway, the poor devil. He apparently had a hell of a time. No wonder he hates my guts.'

Asked if he could recall the morning of his father's arrest, John's son Rhodri replied:

'I can remember the police coming into the house and searching everywhere. Whether that is that *time*, I don't know. It may have been.

They were OK with us – fine, yeah. But I remember my nan, Beryl [Thelma's mother] going for them, you know. Trying to hit them with a saucepan and screaming at them, "Get out of this house. Get out, we don't want you here." And them saying something like, "We have a job to do, Mrs Bridgman."

Documents stored at the National Library of Wales reveal that 'the search commenced at 10.30 a.m. and was completed by 12.30 p.m.' It was undertaken by four male police officers and one female officer. Moreover, it was noted that Thelma was 'most cooperative', which rendered the search warrant 'unnecessary'. A second visit was paid to Jenkins' home the following day, but this was merely to recover an exhibit: a wooden drum.[135] Had he been alarmed at the thought of the police searching his home? 'No,' Jenkins responded trenchantly; adding:

'Because I knew that there was nothing for them to find. The police expected this to be the typical political raid, where you would routinely find evidence of ideology and motivation. Books telling how to do this and that; papers and documents with lists of names and addresses; and letters. And what did they find? Nothing! I do know that they had a van outside waiting, as they were expecting to get sacks full, and they found not a single incriminating thing. They were very angry about it. They did find at Alders' house, though, the quantity of explosives which I'd removed from the Camp a few weeks earlier.'

## Jenkins and Alders are questioned and remanded into custody

At Ruabon police station, John Jenkins made a statement and was then transferred to the police station in Wrexham. There, for the first time, he saw Ernie Alders. Forbidden to speak or to communicate, at 22.45 on 2 November, having been questioned all day, John Jenkins and Frederick Ernest Alders were jointly charged with breaking and entering the magazine at Hafod Quarry and stealing explosives. The following day at Ruabon Magistrates, they were remanded into custody. Four days later, they appeared before Wrexham Magistrates and were charged with conspiring 'with persons unknown' to cause various explosions in Cheshire and Denbighshire between 1 January 1968 and 2 November 1969.[136] A fortnight later, Jenkins and Alders appeared again before magistrates in Wrexham. They now faced a third charge of 'attempting to cause an explosion at the Health Offices in Chester' some three months earlier. On each occasion, applications for bail were denied. Three days after hearing of Jenkins' arrest, a MAC activist detonated the group's final stores of gelignite. Their activation was timed to coincide with the annual Guy Fawkes celebrations.

Did he experience any degree of physical intimidation from police officers following his arrest? 'Only from one; the rest were too afraid to,' John replied, before stating:

> 'They'd brought this chief inspector down from London, who I'm guessing had a reputation for getting people to talk about things, and he was trying to give me the "old business" in the cells at Ruabon. He grabbed me around the throat, before readjusting his grip and placing his fist at the top of my shirt. I think he was trying to intimidate me, hoping by doing so, that I'd start saying things. I don't know what the hell he thought I was. But I just stared back at him, with this sort of implacable look on my face. I think he realised then that far from me being afraid, he was in an area which was full of people he didn't know, but who knew me – and they might not like him for what he was, and for what he was doing. He seemed to realise the situation, and who I was, and he let me go. I never experienced anything like that again – either from the police, or when I was in prison. I think the authorities left me alone because they didn't know what I could do; what "sanctions" I could take against them if they did anything wrong. So, they didn't *do* anything wrong.'

After spending several weeks at the police station in Wrexham, John Jenkins and Ernie Alders were transferred to Shrewsbury Prison, before being transferred to Risley Remand Centre. It is affectionately referred to by Jenkins and the prison fraternity as 'Grisly Risley.'[137] Finally, they were committed to stand trial in Mold, at Flintshire Assizes. Given that he had refused to assist the police inquiry to *any* degree during the questioning process, did any events strike a notable chord during this period of being questioned and transferred from one facility to another? 'Well, one thing *has* always stuck in my mind,' Jenkins responded thoughtfully, before continuing:

'On the day that I was taken from the police station in Wrexham to the prison in Shrewsbury, we went through Ruabon and right on the corner stood little Vaughan, still with his school bag on his arm. I don't know where he'd been, or what he was doing there. But there he was, standing on this one corner. And I said to the police, "Would it be alright if I stopped for a moment? If I see my son and say..." "Certainly not!" this chap barked from the front. They wouldn't allow it. Well, this particular person wouldn't allow it, so we drove past. I drove past my son. I think he saw me and was waving, but I'm not sure. But I was bloody angry then, because it was only civilised, I thought. But no, they wouldn't have it.

I've wondered ever since why he should have been standing in Ruabon, when he was in school in Wrexham, about 5 miles away. I've never asked him how he got there. Did the police take him? Was it designed to soften me up? Possibly. I don't know. But how could he have known what time I'd be going past? It wasn't even a standard police car, but an ordinary, unmarked police car. Yet there he was – as if waiting for me. I know they [police] tried getting stuff out of the kids and out of Thelma. They couldn't get anything out of them because they knew nothing, but it didn't stop them trying, apparently. And I do know that Vaughan has been bitter and angry about the police ever since, because of the way they treated him. But we've never talked about it directly.'

One afternoon at Risley Remand Centre, as they awaited their trial, John's contemplation was disturbed by Alders shouting from a neighbouring cell window. He had, Alders informed Jenkins, been offered 'a deal', which – should he 'agree and co-operate to some degree' – would ensure he received 'a better sentence'. Should he accept? Implored by Jenkins to do so, it was advice which ultimately ensured that a trial expected to last months was concluded within a fortnight. With the passage of time, does he regret his decision to give Alders the OK? 'Yes,' he replied slowly, before adding:

'When I think about it now, I still feel uncomfortable and annoyed with myself. It wasn't the best thing to have done, was it? It was right that I told him to accept a deal. He was only a young bloke, and he had just got married. But I assumed Alders agreeing to co-operate "to some degree" meant that he would divulge nothing really urgent, nothing truthful. But I failed to make that clear. My consent should have been with the usual proviso that you don't say *too* much. Unfortunately, I didn't say that. I should have considered that I was faced with the old story: once people open their mouths for one thing, then they open it for other things. That's why the police come into your cell or the interview room and offer you a cup of tea or, "Would you like a cigarette?" And "It's a nice day, isn't it?" and all that. Because once you start, that's it: the floodgates are opened and you talk – and I *should* have realised that. I was a bloody idiot.'[138]

Alders' request coincided with John being approached by his defence counsel, Peter Thomas QC, and told it would be in his judicial interest to attend a meeting. Having agreed to do, Jenkins quickly determined that the 'twenty or so sober-looking men dressed in dark suits and ties' were members of the British intelligence and diplomatic community. Moreover, as their line of questioning intensified, it became quite clear to John what the thrust was. Namely, 'who was *really* behind MAC'. Developing the point, Jenkins continued:

'They would *not* accept that this was purely an indigenous matter: raised by us and *for* us – with nobody else involved... When I was in Berlin, had I met members of the East German Communist Party? When I was in Cyprus, had I met members of EOKA? Did I know, or had I ever met, members of the Angry Brigade? Had any other group provided us with training and weaponry? They would *not* accept that MAC was indigenous. There *had* to be a group, or organiser or whatever, advising us, telling us about strategy, and providing us with resources. It wasn't true, of course. But you see, and I found this out later, not only were they desperate to find a link between MAC and another group which provided our direction, they were keen to discover that a *foreign* group had governed us, so that they could then charge me with treason. They wanted it from my own mouth that I was helping a foreign enemy against the British State. That is treason. And this is what they were hoping for – and what they were trying to establish with our court case approaching... It was obvious what they were after. They would have *loved* to see me convicted of treason.'

Nonetheless, so determined were the authorities to unearth the extent of Jenkins' affiliation to other protest groups that John alleges that 'they actually placed someone in Risley', tasked with discovering any information either from an unsuspecting John, or via a Jenkins associate. 'He made the mistake of saying he was from the docks in Liverpool,' an amused Jenkins declared, continuing:

'But unfortunately for him, I knew one or two blokes who were with me in the same area of the remand centre, and they were from the docks in Liverpool. So they'd picked the wrong bloody area to have him come from. They said to me, within minutes, "He's not from the docks in Liverpool. Watch him. What he's saying is a load of bollocks. He's not from anywhere near the place." They knew straight away and they told me.'

## The trial of Jenkins and Alders

On 9 April 1970, at Flintshire Assizes in Mold, the trial of John Jenkins and Ernie Alders began. In opening the case for the prosecution, Tasker Watkins QC described Jenkins as a 'clever, ruthless fanatic.'[139] In response, Jenkins pleaded not guilty to all nineteen charges against him.[140] Fifteen of the charges he faced jointly with Alders. Having pleaded guilty to eight charges, Alders' plea of not guilty to seven more was accepted by the prosecution in exchange for his testimony. The prosecution commenced its case by offering compelling forensic evidence. Significant testimony was then heard from 'key witness' Ann Woodgate. John Jenkins maintains that he and Woodgate were at best formal acquaintances, who had been brought together solely because of Ernie Alders' involvement with the marching band. But from the dock, Ann Woodgate had another tale to tell. Asked to outline the true nature of her relationship with John Jenkins and what she knew of the MAC campaign, Ann Woodgate informed the court that she and Thelma had been threatened with 'sanctions' should they disclose information concerning the MAC protest; that Ernie had revealed much detailed information concerning the attacks at Llanrhaeadr-ym-Mochnant and the theft of explosives from Hafod Quarry; and that far from enjoying a formal and remote connection, that the two couples had occasionally socialised together and that she and Ernie often babysat for John and Thelma while they 'enjoyed a night out'. But the most sensational piece of evidence was Woodgate's assertion that prior to ending her relationship and engagement with Ernie Alders in January 1969, John Jenkins spoke openly of 'stopping the Investiture' by 'drawing Prince Charles away by means of explosions'. These would occur, she proclaimed, 'in different places in Wales and in England', and were intended to make the Government think that it was 'too dangerous to invest the Prince of Wales'. Most damning of all was Woodgate's final assertion that Jenkins had expressed it perhaps necessary for MAC 'to take more drastic steps', affirming that the group would 'maybe have to kill him'.[141] Asked to discuss this crucial piece of testimony in 2018, John Jenkins exclaimed resolutely:

'I did say it, yes. And it was deliberately intentional, done for public consumption. Woodgate wasn't speaking on my behalf as such, because I maintain that she didn't know anything about my connection to MAC. She knew I had certain feelings about things. But then a lot of people did, although it didn't mean that they were involved in anything. But I wanted her to genuinely believe that this was the situation – that this threat was real. Because our whole system rested on the fact that people believed there was a credible threat to the Prince of Wales. It was absolute rubbish, but there you are.'

Had Jenkins, nevertheless, feared that Ann Woodgate would inform the authorities of his outburst – at *any* time prior to the Investiture?

'Well, the thing is, you have to understand what Wrexham was like. It was a place where there existed a natural reluctance on the part of the inhabitants to go to the police with anything. They would *not* want to be seen as collaborating with the authorities. I knew that Ann Woodgate was a Wrexham girl, and so, while I never worried that she would inform the police, I did think that she'd discuss having heard this threat with other members of the Wrexham community – and that in doing so, unintentionally, she would be furthering the cause. In that this threat would then spread and gather momentum and interest; and eventually it would reach the ears of the authorities. But by then, there would be no direct link back to me. Well, even if her overhearing me say this *had* proved incriminating, I was too far gone to worry about things like that anyway.'

Aged just twenty at the time of the Investiture, Prince Charles was a young man. On a human level, the taking of his life was surely unacceptable, irrespective of the Prince's 'political' – indeed, bestowed – role? Invited to establish unequivocally whether there existed a threat to the Prince of Wales, John Jenkins pondered his reply before declaring slowly:

'I do believe the taking of life is something that is taken *far* too lightly these days; and I do feel that killing him would have been a gross breach. That is *not* what we were trying to do. On the other hand – and I will finally admit this – if I'd thought that political capital would come from it, that killing him would prove strategically advantageous, I *was* prepared to sanction such an action. If somebody could have proved to me that this would have enhanced and *furthered* our cause, and brought our aim of an independent Wales much nearer, then I would have acknowledged the fact that there would be something to be said for it. Had it provided the political outcome we desired, then yes, I would have agreed and authorised it. Of course! We were a cause, and we were on course; and we had to further *that* as far as we possibly could. And if that could have been furthered by this, then we would have done it. I would have considered his death regrettable but unavoidable in the circumstances, because it would have helped us on our way.

But as it was, there was no point – none whatsoever! It wouldn't have helped us on our way. In fact, the political fallout of Charles being damaged in any way, shape or form would have held us back by several years. It would have meant us being forever in limbo after that – nobody would have touched us with a barge pole. For one thing, every mother in the land would have hated us... We wanted the people of Wales to feel and to think. We didn't want them to feel nasty towards us. And to launch such an attack on the Royal Party on Investiture day would have been a step too far. We could not afford to lose sight of our main objective: which was to affect the hearts and minds of the Welsh people. Killing Charles, or anyone else, would have turned the people of Wales from supporting us and towards the establishment in its battle *against* us. So there you are.'

Next to give evidence against Jenkins was his former devoted disciple, Ernie Alders. To John's consternation, anger and frustration, Alders 'started displaying emotion and showing a lack of control' as he divulged certain information concerning the MAC protest.[142] Had Alders possessed much knowledge of the MAC campaign? 'Not as such,' Jenkins replied, before continuing:

'But he knew enough. He didn't know all the really important details. And meetings – he didn't come to them. So I would doubt very much if he knew the names of people involved in MAC. But while it wasn't the names of people he could divulge, I was increasingly fearful that he *could* divulge the names of places we'd visited together, which would lead them to the right conclusions. For instance, all he needed to say was: "On one occasion, we went up to such and such a town, and Jenkins went to this particular residential street. I'm not sure which building he entered exactly. But it was approximately two doors up from a particular shop. He was in there for about an hour, before he returned to the car." That is *all* the information the police would want. Armed with this information, they could soon find out who it was in MAC that I had met without Alders having provided names. So I had to shut him up.'

But Alders did not stop there. On being asked to describe his relationship with Jenkins, he declared:

'After Abergele, I expected him to say: "Well, that's enough: two men have died." But when I did meet him, all he wanted to do was to cause more death. He was talking about buying guns and crossbows. I was shocked. I could not say a word and this convinced me that he was mad. I didn't want any more to do with it... But I was frightened, not only for myself and my family, but for every other member of the organisation.'[143]

Under cross-examination from 'the brilliant, fearful and respected' Tasker Watkins, as John refers to him, over the two days that Alders gave evidence, Jenkins recognised that his junior confederate 'was breaking down' and 'beginning to turn Queen's Evidence' against him. Finally, John Jenkins informed his counsel, Peter Thomas QC, that he now proposed to change his plea to guilty and accept all the charges against him.[144] Namely, of causing explosions at Llanrhaeadr-ym-Mochnant, Lake Vyrnwy and at Hapsford in Cheshire; also, to procuring and counselling persons unknown to attack with explosives the Llanishen Tax Office and with supplying the explosive material used, unsuccessfully, to target the Mackenzie Pier in Holyhead. The remaining charges related to the Hafod Quarry break-in and the all-encompassing charge of conspiring to cause explosions between January 1966 and November 1969.

It left many questions concerning the MAC offensive unanswered – most notably, how many more explosions undertaken by MAC John Jenkins was responsible for. Approached to discuss the matter, one former associate of Jenkins' stated that, John now having pleaded guilty to the charges against him, the authorities had 'barely scraped the surface' of Jenkins' involvement in the MAC militant protest. Asked to respond, John conceded to having planted somewhere between 'three and five devices' for which he was not convicted.

Nonetheless, invited to sum up the Defence Counsel's closing testimony, Peter Thomas QC announced that Jenkins' feelings when he committed these offences had been 'activated by the disaster at Aberfan'. On being informed of details surrounding the tragedy by his brother-in-law Peter Bridgman, a member of the police rescue team, Jenkins was said to be 'insensate with grief'.[145] John Jenkins, Peter Thomas continued, 'was not motivated by greed, or by self-interest... but by a deep and intense concern for Wales' and its future. A man of previously untarnished character, in undertaking this course of action Jenkins had risked 'not only his career and his family, but also his liberty for his feelings'. Nevertheless, despite the evidence suggesting that 'many other people' were involved in these crimes, Jenkins had instructed Peter Thomas to inform the court that he did not intend to disclose their identities. To do so, Thomas continued, Jenkins considered 'contemptuous'. Called by Peter Thomas by way of mitigation, Captain Ronald Watson – company commander of 19 Company, RAMC Saighton Camp – informed the court that Jenkins' military character had been assessed as 'exemplary', the 'highest grade possible'. As for a plea in mitigation for Alders, the court was notified that he 'no longer had any interests in the activities in which he was engaged' and had no future intention of even 'joining a Christmas Club'.

Not unexpectedly, when winding up the case for the prosecution, Tasker Watkins QC took an altogether dimmer view of Jenkins' and Alders' actions. They had, Watkins sombrely declared, adopted 'unprecedented violence' in the modern British context, 'in support of a claimed political objective – namely independence for Wales'. Each man belonged to this 'sinister organisation known as *Mudiad Amddiffyn Cymru*', which was an organisation 'wedded to the use of violence', and comprised of members who 'scorn the ordinary peaceful methods of achieving political objectives'. Before handing down his sentences, Judge Thompson declared that Wales would 'not approve or applaud' what Jenkins and Alders had done:

> 'On the contrary, she will condemn the terror you contrived to spread among her people by your wicked deeds. Wales will disclaim and disown such methods of promoting her interests and those who use such methods. She will expect you to be punished for your own misdeeds and to discourage others who might be disposed to imitate you.'

Having described the offences as being 'of the utmost gravity for which the law provided stern punishment', Thompson had nevertheless, 'no desire to pass crushing sentences'; but he did 'have a public duty to perform'. In reaching his verdict, he had correctly taken into account that Jenkins and Alders were men of 'hitherto good character with many good qualities', and that the motive prompting them to commit these crimes 'was not personal gain, but a misguided notion' that they were 'patriotically promoting the interests of Wales'. Justice Thompson then credited each man for confessing their guilt, even if Jenkins had done so only after days of evidence – which was perhaps more an acknowledgement and recognition of the proceedings' 'inevitable conclusion'. But if Alders should be commended for apparently repenting his participation both before and after his arrest, Jenkins did not appear to have relaxed his determination or his resolve. They were both, Thompson continued, 'intelligent' and 'aware' of what they were doing as they undertook their course of action; and as such, 'they both knew what to expect' if apprehended.

To a tense, electrified and silent court room, Justice Thompson then passed down his sentences. John Barnard Jenkins was sentenced to ten years on each of the eight charges and Frederick Ernest Alders to six years on each charge. The sentences were to run concurrently.[146] It is worth noting that had John Jenkins been found guilty of high treason, in whatever capacity, it is conceivable – if unlikely – that Justice Thompson might have returned a statutory verdict of 'death by hanging'.[147] But if some observers believed that Jenkins and Alders received a punishment that was commensurate with the significance of their crimes, then it might come as a surprise to learn that Jenkins alleges that prior to the sentence being passed, he was approached in his cell by his legal counsel, Peter Thomas QC, and asked if he 'would accept ten years'. Having initially joked that 'two years was more agreeable', Jenkins then instructed Thomas to convey to Justice Thompson that he did not think that ten years was overdoing it. 'What could I say?' John asked phlegmatically in 2018:

'They were going to hit me hard. Well, naturally. They were wounded and I was caught. So I had to suffer for it. I would do the same in their position. It was the right thing to do. I mean, I was down and out. I had had a go at them, and I had beaten them at their own game as far as the attitudes of these people were concerned. It was now their turn.'

Did that suggest that the authorities believed there was no one else to arrest: that John Jenkins had been responsible for all the explosions carried out in the name of MAC?

'Well, I'm sure that scenario would have greatly pleased the police, because they could have pinned the lot on me. But along with my fellow servicemen, I was confined to our temporary quarters the night before the Investiture because there had been so much trouble in Caernarfon with fights breaking out between the local lads and the soldiers. And so, to avoid any further animosity and violence, we were banned from going out. And these fights are things that nobody gets told about. According to official accounts of the events, it was sweetness and light and dancing in the streets. Well, it isn't true. And I know this, because having arrived in Caernarfon late on the Sunday afternoon – with the Investiture on the Tuesday – I popped into Caernarfon for a quick walk, just to soak up the atmosphere. As I walked into town, I was verbally abused by a car full of local lads, on account of the British Army uniform I was wearing; which, despite looking suitably nonplussed, I thought was wonderful. But more importantly, the device which very unfortunately injured Ian Cox was planted the *following* night, the night before the ceremony – so that ruled me out. But if I know the police, they probably did think that I got away with it – *and* spread that rumour – simply to save face.'

Had he and Ernie Alders exchanged comments or communicated at all as they stood together in the dock prior to being sentenced? 'No. I didn't even look at him when our sentences were being read out,' Jenkins remarked tersely, continuing:

'They'd promised him five years for his "cooperation", and they gave him six anyway. That's the British State for you! And I haven't seen him since – not since the day we were sentenced. If I were to meet him again, I'd have nothing to say to him. All I can do is condemn him. But then, he may feel the same about me. I did give him permission to arrange this deal, but I didn't give him permission to expose anything, or anybody. He took it a little bit too far.'

On leaving court, Thelma Jenkins was approached by the press. She informed reporters that her husband 'loved Wales' and the Welsh people. Furthermore, she 'thought the world' of John and 'would wait for him.'

He was, she continued, 'a good husband and father' and together, they had enjoyed 'a very happy family life... He was not a violent man', but was rather 'kind and considerate' and 'very good to the boys'. Together, they would go 'walking and swimming'. They would 'miss him'. Asked how she had been treated by the wider community since her husband's arrest, Thelma replied that she 'was not afraid to face people', but that no one had been unkind, or pointed the finger, or failed to approach her. It had though, Thelma conceded, 'been a very anxious time'. Her immediate problem was to preserve her family life, and to this end, she would soon return to live near her parents in south Wales. It was 'hard managing alone', but Thelma was 'quite determined' to face the future and pick up the pieces of her shattered family life.[148]

## Thelma, Vaughan and Rhodri are 'marched out' and John is left to ponder

A few weeks after John was sentenced, Thelma, Vaughan and Rhodri – to use military parlance – were 'marched out' of the house the Jenkins family had shared on Range Road in Wrexham. A close family associate who wished to remain anonymous confirmed that those undertaking the removal of the household items had 'treated the family like dirt', adding:

'From what I've been told, it was uproar the day they came and kicked Thelma, Vaughan and Rhodri out of the house. It was horrible, apparently. These men showed them no sympathy at all. As far as they were concerned, Vaughan and Rhodri were just brats.'[149]

On being told of the contributor's testimony, John bristled with annoyance and stated:

'I was unaware of that. I thought Thelma's mother and father came to help them move out, because for a short while they lived with them in Treharris – before moving to Trelewis. But if the Camp was involved in the removal of our items, it was the civilian arm of the military. They were based at Saighton Camp and would sort out housing and accommodation issues. They'd check the boilers and make repairs, all that sort of stuff. It was an Army house and was furnished basically by the Army – and when I say "basically", you know what "basically" in the Army means. A bedroom was a place with a bed in it. All very functional. The bits and pieces which make it a home, you get yourself.'

But with his conviction and prison sentence received, did Jenkins feel any degree of relief that the campaign of protest was over? 'Yes – I was, I would say, relieved,' John replied, before adding tentatively:

'I mean, all I can say is, there existed an almost subconscious desire to get caught. I can't really describe it, but I was almost complacent by the end. It's impossible for me to express it any better, but there was a definite desire to get caught. It wasn't actually a stated desire: "I want to be caught." It was more a feeling that lay behind everything I did; as if I was thinking, "I hope this will end soon." Because the pressure was quite sublime. You see, I knew I wasn't going to be around forever. I mean, the law of averages dictates that this couldn't go on indefinitely. I had got away with it for several years, and from the point of view of wanting to change the nature of activities regarding the Investiture, we'd achieved our objective.'

What of MAC's longer-term strategy?

'Well, yes; we were looking to continue into the 1970s, and we did have a dozen or so other symbolic targets in mind. But for the most part, we'd only got as far as thinking about them. You see, everything took a long time: formulating strategy, recruiting, training, targeting – every aspect of this campaign. But as St David said, "Do the small things." And if there was a motto in MAC, that would have been it – and *that's* what I practised. Never mind about the big vision, which is all very nice. It's the small things: that's what you get caught out on. Always reduce the intangibles to an absolute minimum, because it's *then* that you have a chance of success. When you leave things and think, "Oh, it'll be alright," that's when things go wrong... So while we were making plans for future targets, we hadn't addressed the minutiae required. For instance, we were aware that the Queen was coming to Wales to open something or other. One more advanced plan, though, was to target Big Ben. And without going into detail as to how this would have been achieved, other than I'll admit it involved a London-based Welshman, our plan to blow out the clock face when the News at Ten started was quite progressed. But as I say regarding my own involvement, I also knew that there had to be a conclusion.'

How did John believe his affiliation to MAC might end? 'I knew I faced either capture or death,' Jenkins replied gravely, adding:

'And were I captured, it's true that there was no one to replace me. People have suggested that in preparation of anything happening to me, I should have prepared a successor. And yes, it would have been nice. It would have been a good response. But I suppose there were two factors to consider. Firstly, nobody knew me – and that's the whole point of why I got away with it for so long. And so I would have had to pick somebody who was equally as unknown. How was I going to do that? Very, very difficult. There wasn't anybody within MAC ready to take it on, and the reason is always the same: domestic matters. And I don't blame people if they put their family first. As for potential candidates *within* MAC: perhaps Trefor Beasley? Well, he did tick a lot of boxes. For a start, nobody knew him. But while that's a good thing, it would also mean that he would have to start the process of leadership all over again. And in order to meet the requirement of having a legitimate reason to travel, he would need to have a job whereby travelling was a part of his normal work system. Which is what I had, but he didn't. How was Trefor Beasley going to travel around Wales with loads of explosives and so on in his car – and nobody was expecting him anywhere? How was he going to do that with his existing job? How could he fit it in? Not to mention the pressures provided by his family.

So, yes: while I can see the advantages of grooming someone internally for the role, it was a complex picture. And some potential or possible names I'm thinking of *outside* MAC were too well known by the authorities. They'd attended marches and protests. So I soon realised that preparing a successor would introduce an extra element into the security situation. It would have made the security less effective, so I felt the most effective way to avoid capture was to take *total* control. But that meant, with my arrest, the campaign ended. But it does say something about the Welsh nation that there *wasn't* a worthy successor that I knew about.'

And what of the possibility of being killed while undertaking protest action? 'Well,' Jenkins replied slowly:

'I mean it's easy enough to make a mistake. The authorities say, "Oh, anyone can put a bomb together." Yes, maybe. But while the weather wasn't *always* bad, if you have to go out on a wet, cold night when it's bloody freezing, and you've only got a little pencil torch, and you've got to go ploughing across fields with dog shit and cow shit and all the usual things, and everything is very wet and windy... and knowing that despite your cold fingers, one slip-up, one mistake, and that's it: you – or both of you – are gone! Well, it's not glamorous. It's no bloody joke. I did it because it *had* to be done. Put it this way: I wouldn't have changed my job with anyone I liked! But my attitude was, "If I don't do it, then somebody else will have to, and why should they do it, if I can't?" The MAC campaign – and all it entailed – affected me all along, but I felt increasingly unable to control or hide my emotions. And so, in a way, when I was arrested, I was almost glad. "Thank God that's over, I haven't got to kill anybody else." So by the end, I was waiting for the knock on the door. And when it came – yeah, I felt almost relieved. That said, when I was arrested, I still had my doubts that people would buckle if approached. These fears proved unfounded, of course, and that's owing to the fact that our recruitment and induction process was so good. The MAC boys recognised the importance of security, and other than one or two having funny ideas about punctuality, I can't fault them. But also, there was still a supply of [MAC] explosives out there and that was causing me anxiety. But that, too, was ultimately dealt with efficiently.'

As the Jenkins family got used to their respective new surroundings, reaction to the campaign of activism orchestrated by John Jenkins was divided. To some, John was not a criminal but a hero – a man who extolled the virtues of courage and sacrifice, having fought to save the soul of Wales. But did Jenkins derive pride from having been MAC's Director-General during the late 1960s when the group undertook militant protest? 'Well, I *have* been called that [Director-General], but it's not a title that *I've* ever used,' John replied with an air of detachment. It is perhaps a candid, indeed, factual evaluation of the position he held in MAC. Nonetheless, it is also a curious and somewhat insufficient, if not disingenuous, response. Because as much as John might want to distance himself from the MAC insurgency, particularly as the dust has settled since the group's campaign of violence ended, it is difficult when assessing the MAC protest to see where *Mudiad Amddiffyn Cymru* ends and John Barnard Jenkins begins. They appear, at least for many spectators, to be completely interwoven. Whatever the truth, a new chapter in John Jenkins' story was about to begin. Yet this too – at least in part – would be no less difficult and no less solitary.

# CHAPTER 5

# 'They got me for anything'

## HM Prison Winson Green; John reproaches the authorities and launches an appeal

On being sentenced to ten years' imprisonment at Mold Crown Court on 20 April 1970, John was transferred to Winson Green Prison in Birmingham. Within hours of arriving, John's cell door was opened and in walked a member of the Church Army. Jenkins later described what occurred as, sitting next to him on the bed in his cell, the Church Army officer declared to John:

> '"They are hard on people here, but the one thing the prison service *cannot* do is stop you coming to church." I said, "Is that right?" "Yes," he said. "It's all laid down in the regulations; they dare not. It's the *one* thing they can't stop you doing." "Well, they stopped me," I said. "Contrary to prison regulations, I wasn't allowed to go to church when I was in Shrewsbury Prison, and I was there for quite a while awaiting trial." "Oh," he said. "I will see about this; and I'll come back and tell you exactly what happened." And guess what? I never saw him again! And I know what will have happened. He will have gone to the Winson Green prison authority and relayed our discussion and they will have said to him, "Well OK, but if you decide to take the matter further, your status as a visiting officer will have to be reviewed." They simply applied pressure to shut him up – and it worked. His job was more important to him than his principles. I can't say I was shocked, though, by what transpired. As was the case with the solicitor that I requested when I was arrested, here too: despite their great noise about the need for rules and regulations, the authorities were behaving exactly as they wanted to.'

Within days of being visited by a member of the Church Army, John received three further visitors. The first was a colonel from the Army Medical Corps, who formally gave John a dishonourable discharge from the British Army. It followed an interview during which the colonel attempted to establish whether Jenkins' membership of the Army had been a contributing factor in his militant activities. 'Of course, it hadn't,' John later countered; adding:

'It was nothing to do with job stress, or anything like it. And he didn't, or couldn't, raise the question of politics with me, because it's against military law for serving members of the military to discuss together politics, religion and sex. Of course, these are the only things people *do* discuss! But under military law, you're not permitted to. But he was a nice chap, who treated me with respect. Frankly, he was very deferential; and I respected him for that, but I couldn't believe it. He all but called me "sir", and I acted as if this was normal. Normal! When a full colonel more or less puts his cloak on the floor for a sergeant to walk on! It's not normal at all! But he did let something slip. In trying to establish my mental health in the weeks and months before I was arrested, he contacted my colonel in the Dental Corps to discuss my attitude and behaviour and so on. Having established that my mental health had not given any cause for alarm, my colonel also told him that the police had questioned him as to where I'd received my training in electronics and explosives, and from where I'd obtained my knowledge about politics and how to set a militant group up. My colonel apparently thought this very amusing, and tried to explain to the police that they were the *last* things the Dental Corps would be trained for, or involved in. To add insult to injury, my colonel then told the police that such areas of military training were very complicated and that the cost of setting up such a covert group within the regular Army, who were adequately trained and equipped to successfully undertake such attacks, would run to many thousands of pounds. And of course, the colonel from the Medical Corps knew all this; he knew how complicated it all was; that it wasn't simply a matter of throwing a bomb at a building. And so, when he arrived to formally discharge me from the Army, he was very deferential.'

Jenkins was next visited by a prison psychologist, who questioned John as to whether he believed he had been followed by the police in the weeks prior to his arrest. Having replied 'yes', John was then informed that such a response provided 'evidence' of his 'instability', and indicated patterns of delusional paranoia. Jenkins later observed soberly,

'It just went to show that some of these questions aimed at normal members of the public who commit a criminal offence certainly didn't cover people like me – because I definitely *was* being followed. I mean, I'd been around too long. I knew all the signs.'

Having been sentenced to serve his prison term as a Category A prisoner, John was asked to throw light on what such a stipulation entailed.

'Well, a Category A prisoner means that you're like a registered parcel. You are subject to solitary confinement and so can't go anywhere on your own. Wherever you go, you must be accompanied by one or two officers. They have got to take you, they've got to deliver you and they've got to bring you back. Somebody has to sign for you all the time. And this is how it happened; this was my fate. I was accompanied by one or two guards for the next five and a half years, until I was eventually taken off Category A. But if that wasn't bad enough, unlike most prisoners sentenced to ten years, parole is denied to anyone on the A list – although that is against regulations, of course. Regulations say that all prisoners should be offered parole after, I think, two-thirds of their sentence. Parole and things like weekend home leave are offered to 'normal' criminals in return for their good behaviour, but they negated that by putting you on the A list. As a Category A, you were punished if you misbehaved, but you were not rewarded if you did behave. So yeah, not very funny, but I got used to it. In fact, I quickly saw it as a blessing. Being in solitary confinement for much of the time meant I had my own cell and I didn't have to mix with the ordinary criminal class of prisoner. Which, considering some of the characters you get in prison, was bloody fine by me! But more seriously, I saw myself as different to them. They were just criminals. I was serving a prison term for a cause – and so my belief and my faith in that cause served to reduce the damaging impact.'

No doubt aware of how many prisoners subjected to Category A regulations suffered the psychological effects of such a measure, a fortnight into his prison term, John was visited by two police officers from Special Branch. Jenkins was assured that his very restrictive Category A status, including solitary confinement, 'would be lifted tomorrow' and his 'life made much easier' if John was prepared to give them just one name from MAC. Having rejected the proposal to identify another MAC activist, Jenkins 'was thrilled', he later admitted; adding:

> 'I thought then, "We've won; they can't get anybody else," despite all the time and money they'd spent on trying. I subsequently discovered that the police didn't have the power to remove me from the A list anyway. It's a prison thing, not a police thing. So I had to do the full time; and it was annoying in a way – because, for instance, one bloke came in after me who'd been sentenced to 15 years; and he was released long before I was. But this is what made me laugh: he wasn't a threat to anybody except other people. I was regarded as a threat to the state, and that puts you in a different kettle of fish.'

It was also at this juncture that John formally challenged the police for not having searched the garden in Caernarfon in which the device that ultimately injured the hapless Ian Cox was planted. Jenkins no doubt further inflamed the passions of the establishment by then maintaining that an explosive device had been secreted by a MAC unit beneath the pier in Llandudno, 'which was set to go off early on Investiture Day'. It was hoped, with Prince Charles having returned to Holyhead after the ceremony to board the Royal Yacht *Britannia*, that the device's activation would prevent Charles from disembarking from *Britannia* at Llandudno Pier as planned the morning *after* the ceremony, to begin a royal progress through Wales. But this device, like the bomb planted in Caernarfon, had failed to detonate.[150] John further alleged that despite MAC following 'the usual rules', whereby 'the police were telephoned and letters sent to newspapers' outlining the bomb's location within hours of it failing to activate, the device had remained undetected for several months and that no publicity was afforded its discovery, or secret removal,

> 'because the police did not want to admit the degree to which Prince Charles, having walked within five feet of it the day after the ceremony, had been exposed to danger; nor did they want everyone to know how close the public had been to it when walking by.'[151]

The police later dismissed Jenkins' claims that a device had been located and extracted from the pier at Llandudno as 'nonsense'; while asserting that all telephone calls to the police relating to bombs had been thoroughly investigated. It is a standpoint police officers continue to maintain.[152]

As was tragically demonstrated with regard to the desperately unfortunate Ian Cox in Caernarfon, the bomb is the most indiscriminate of weapons. Its ability to cause collateral damage is massive. But if John Jenkins is to be believed, the device planted by MAC at Llandudno Pier lay undisturbed and potentially active for many months; until Jenkins reiterated to the authorities the whereabouts of the device *after* his conviction. It should be noted, in view of this disclosure, that such a cavalier approach to the welfare of those who – presumably in their hundreds – passed or frequented this popular tourist attraction sharply contradicts MAC's oft-repeated policy of wanting to avoid injuring anyone, in order to maintain public sympathy with their cause. Where is the evidence of MAC's adherence to such an approach and ethos during its operations in Caernarfon, or at Llandudno Pier?

But whatever the truth surrounding these events, such accusations were hardly likely to endear John to the British judicial establishment, a rather curious strategy given that on 11 May 1970, Jenkins formally lodged an appeal against his ten-year prison term. He cited a number of factors. These included an assertion that during his sentencing speech, Justice Thompson had 'displayed bias towards the establishment in detriment to the impartiality of pure justice'. Moreover, Justice Thompson had demonstrated a 'naivety' in relation to 'Welsh political matters'; while having also been 'misled' in his submission that Jenkins was 'unique'; the 'ruthless fanatic'; and 'the driving force' behind the insurgency. In response, Jenkins asserted that contrary to the testimony provided by Ernie Alders during their trial, he had *not* proved the 'catalyst' which led to Alders embroiling himself in militant activity. Rather, Alders' 'mind was made up to cause explosions before he even met' Jenkins. Furthermore, when Jenkins and Alders convened at Jenkins' home following 'the tragic events at Abergele', far from having 'exerted pressure' and acting as 'a slave-driver', it was Jenkins who had suggested retiring from front-line activity, having offered to hand control of MAC over to Alders. In that moment, Alders had 'the power to halt the campaign and retire' Jenkins. But, Jenkins claimed, Alders had refused, and instead had persuaded Jenkins of their joint need to continue; with each then amicably concluding that as their consciences would not allow them to retire, they would soldier on. This apparent revelation sharply conflicted with Alders' trial testimony, during which he claimed that having met Jenkins after the explosion in Abergele, he deduced him to be 'mad'.

In response to Justice Thompson's 'constantly reiterated phrase' that Jenkins 'chose to take the violent path rather than the peaceful, democratic one', Jenkins asserted that this presupposed that he had a choice, and that he had deliberately turned his back on normal methods, which Jenkins argued was simply not true. To illuminate the point and to highlight Justice Thompson's apparent woeful ignorance of the Welsh political landscape, John continued that 'the Welsh nation – which has one of the oldest cultures in Europe – was dying'. Moreover, 'every method possible to prevent this had been tried – and all had failed; the machine was too powerful to beat, or even argue with. Tryweryn, despite the whole of Wales having united to oppose the scheme, had proved this.' By driving Wales 'into a corner', and 'removing all means of redress', the British 'establishment had made us inevitably revolutionaries'. Jenkins was therefore, he maintained, the 'result of an environment created by the Government'. He was 'the reaction and not the cause'. For having 'become a law-breaker through the purest of motives', he had lost his 'liberty, career, gratuity, pension, family life, good wages – everything'. By comparison, his associate Alders had 'lost only his liberty'; and that 'for only 6 years'. The evidence proved that Alders was 'a very willing accomplice', John claimed. Indeed, there had been times when Alders had 'forced the pace'. If Alders' sentence was considered 'correct', then Jenkins' was 'too heavy in comparison'.

Justice Thompson's assessment that Wales would 'disown' John Jenkins was also met with incredulity. Such an appraisal, John responded, conflicted sharply with the degree of support he had received throughout Wales – and across the nation's demographic – since his arrest and incarceration. This, Jenkins felt, might be owing to the fact that 'constitutional and linguistic concessions to Wales' had been 'most numerous in the period of multiplying bomb incidents', and, perhaps as a consequence of these developments, Wales had 'applauded far more than condemned' Jenkins for what he did. In reaction to Justice Thompson's declaration that Jenkins' deeds were 'wicked,' while they were admittedly illegal, John countered, such a description was beyond the judge's province. Justice Thompson 'may represent the Queen', but he did *not*, Jenkins stated emphatically, represent Jesus Christ. As for Justice Thompson's closing statement, in which he justified the severity of John's sentence as a means 'to discourage those who might be disposed to imitate' him, Jenkins said that he could only assume that he was 'being punished not for what he did, but for what others might do'. In 2018, John was asked if he felt any degree of anger or frustration at the prison sentence of six years that Alders received. It was a suggestion to which Jenkins tersely objected.

Whether true or not, despite the impassioned eloquence of his appeal statement, John's legal challenge to reduce his own prison sentence came to naught.[153] Asked why he believed his appeal was rejected, Jenkins replied:

'It was thrown out, which I knew it would be, because I was accusing the British state and establishment of having acted immorally; while, in total contrast, the MAC campaign was based on morality – and *that*, they couldn't bloody stand.'

## HM Prison Wormwood Scrubs, and John meets new friends

At the end of May 1970, John was transferred to HM Prison Wormwood Scrubs, in north London. Asked to describe a typical day within the prison system of the early 1970s as a Category A prisoner, John declared:

'Well, you were woken by the bell ringing at 7 a.m., and then you'd go down to collect your breakfast. And I say "collect" because you didn't eat with the other prisoners; you took all meals back to your cell and you ate them there. For the first few months I was at Wormwood Scrubs, I spent 23 out of 24 hours in my cell. During this one hour, I would exercise alone in the yard, or I'd go to the library – all the while, being escorted and monitored by the two guards, of course! Eventually, however, some weeks after arriving, I was able to go to work, and work started at 9 a.m. Having worked throughout the morning, it was the same routine then of eating your lunch alone in your cell; and then back to work in the afternoon. After tea, you could spend time in the library if you wanted to. Or, as I was no longer prevented from doing so as I had been at Shrewsbury Prison, I could go to church, or whatever – accompanied, of course, by the obligatory one or two guards. Then, having been "signed for", I was escorted back to my cell for some reading – at least, that's all I did at this stage of my time in prison. The bell would ring again at 9 p.m., by which time the other prisoners had to be back in their cells for lock-up. And the lights were then switched off at 10 p.m.'

Did he have to work alone as a Category A prisoner? 'No,' John replied; adding:

'The prison authority couldn't enforce lone-working because you were working with other inmates in the prison workshop; although the guards were always there. In fact, when I arrived in Wormwood Scrubs, imprisoned there at the same time were a few of the Great Train Robbers; people like Gordon Goody and Ronald 'Buster' Edwards. Actually, I worked next to Buster for about two weeks in the prison workshop. I wasn't much bloody use, never have been at that sort of thing. But we were tasked with unstitching material, and also making minor repairs to furniture which had been brought in from somewhere. Of course, to while away the time, we chatted; and the conversation turned to the Train Robbery. I wasn't too interested, to tell the truth. I mean, the Train Robbery did bugger all for Wales! I was interested in one thing he told me, though; which was that the police were boasting that they'd regained most of the money. Buster said, "Yeah, we put a lot of the money in three large sacks, each of which was full of money. But when the police finally found where these three sacks of money were hidden, they maintained they'd recovered most of the money from the robbery in *two* sacks." Buster concluded that the police must have kept one bag of the money for themselves. "Where else would it have gone?" he asked. Well, who knows. But I must admit, the tales I heard of police corruption, and not just from Buster – well, I couldn't believe it! Because I still had this trust in the police. And yet it was the normal thing, apparently, that the police – or the London police, anyway – could be bought off to drop charges.'

Had he and Buster Edwards discussed the MAC protest?

'No, I never discussed politics, still less the MAC campaign with Buster and his kind. Although we belonged in the same prison category, I had nothing in common with him or the other Train Robbers. See, I was careful not to get myself mixed up with any... the only word I can use is the word they use, "common" criminals. As long as I didn't mix with them, I could claim to be a "political" prisoner. Once I started mixing with them in a more social context, and adopting their ideas and their morals and mores, then I was no different to them – particularly in the eyes of the other prisoners, and more especially, the prison authority. Buster may have had a Welsh surname, but I saw no point [in] trying to explain to him that I belonged to a group called MAC which had opposed the Investiture, because he, and others like him, wouldn't understand how it [the political situation] worked. I mean, he certainly knew who I was in the sense that I was a "political", who had been involved in a bombing campaign. But he wouldn't have understood the intricacies of *why*. So, for a few reasons, I didn't bother to try and explain it all. In fact, I didn't bother with the Train Robbers much. I mean we got on well enough. People like Buster respected my "status", my prison "rank", because I was in the same category as them. So I had to mix with them, because if I mingled with the baby burglars, that would lose me status, and that would lose me power, and I had to have that power in order to maintain respect.'

Prompted to throw light on the prison hierarchy, John stated:

'Well, when I was in prison in the early '70s, you had to be aware of the hierarchy. There was – and still is, I'm sure – a very definite hierarchy in prisons. At the top, they ranked people like me and the IRA. Along with us were the Train Robbers, armed bank robbers and murderers. Beneath that top level were the adult burglars and what have you. Then followed the baby burglars, and beneath them were the sex offenders: the rapists and the child molesters. And depending on where you fitted in, you were afforded a certain status from *all* within the prison. And I mean, even the prison officers recognised these unstated, but applied, rules.'

Nevertheless, on one occasion John found himself in a difficult situation, when this unmentioned hierarchical structure was not observed by a new prison officer from Swansea. It occurred, Jenkins revealed, when he 'walked into the main office to collect mail', and the new arrival, unfamiliar with prison 'protocol', or presumably the identities of the prison's occupants, saw John entering the mail room and 'bawled' at him 'in front of a large number of other inmates'; many of whom were baby burglars. These 'kids', John added, 'were only in for two weeks for minor housebreaking, or for having broken open public telephones to get the pennies out, you know, silly things. Well, this isn't done. So,' Jenkins continued:

'I thought, I'm not going to be bloody humiliated by a screw who should know the rules better. So, the next morning, I was down in front of the [Prison] Governor to complain about him. I explained that I had simply entered this room and there was no necessity for him to shout and scream and behave in that manner. If he'd wanted me to do something, he could have just mentioned it and it would have been done. And of course, I said, "I thought I'd better bring this to your attention, because who knows what happens to people who go around shouting. These things can be so dangerous." He said, "Are you threatening?" "No!" I said. "I am trying to *avoid* problems. But bear in mind, you don't know who my friends are, and I have got many friends" – and the prison authority knew that from the amount of mail I received. "If this were to continue," I said, "well, I might get stressed. And while not thinking clearly, I might inadvertently mention to them, either when they visit me, or in a letter, that an officer here from Swansea has been wearing a big uniform and abusing his power. Well, if people in Swansea were to find out, who knows what they might do? It could get very nasty. Well, I don't want to see people getting hurt, or this officer's family being abused in the streets, or attacked. And so I've come to see you to try and avoid all these problems."

Well, he could hardly rebuke me for wanting to stop problems, so he said: "OK. Leave it to me." The next day, this prison officer approached me and apologised. First time that's been known to happen in prison! But, yeah – fair play. He came up and having apologised for shouting at me, he said that he hadn't realised the way things were; he hadn't got used to the hierarchy and what is done and what is *not* done. He was used to it then, though! It did get the message across – and it wasn't purely for him either. It was a message intended for all the guards, which said: "I have people who support me on the 'outside', so if I'm abused, I have the means to retaliate." After that, I never had any trouble from a prison officer. And it confirmed what I had thought all along: if people know you can apply sanctions, they will treat you differently.'

One person with whom John exchanged correspondence while imprisoned at Wormwood Scrubs was Judith Keineg, who in 1975 married the former MAC activist, David Pritchard. Speaking in 2018, Judith declared:

'John used to write to me and my then husband Paol [Breton cultural activist] and ask for things when he was in prison. It used to bring tears to my eyes. He'd ask for carpet slippers and a radio. So, I'd have a whip round and send them to him. I was a bit surprised actually, in that here was a man imprisoned for his cause, and yet no one had thought to provide him these things – even his wife. Although Thelma was a bit frivolous, and no great intellect.'[154]

Asked how much these gifts had improved the quality of his life whilst behind bars, John replied:

> 'Oh, it made a *big* difference. The radio wasn't allowed to receive the FM frequency, as the prison authority claimed that FM would interfere with the delicate mechanical instruments within the prison. I think this idea has been rejected now in prisons, as it has in hospitals. But anyway, alone in my cell, I was able to listen to the news and lose myself in radio programmes – you know, plays and discussions. Also, I'd listen transfixed to classical and choral music. It was so uplifting. Her children would also paint pictures for me and send them in. It was wonderful. Judith, or Judy as she was known then, is a good woman. I'll always be indebted to her.'

In October 1971, Jenkins lodged an appeal against the length and terms of his imprisonment with the European Commission and Court of Human Rights, based in Strasbourg. Citing much of the same evidence which had formed his rejected appeal in May 1970, this appeal was also unsuccessful. This may perhaps in part have been in response to John's increasing friendship over the preceding months with imprisoned members of the IRA. Encouraged to discuss this relationship, Jenkins replied:

> 'My relationship with the IRA developed because after a few months at Wormwood Scrubs, I was able to spend more time out of my cell – during the evenings, for instance. And on meeting one another we clicked immediately. We *understood* each other. While we never discussed the whereabouts of weaponry, we used to discuss tactics and strategy in the broad sense. I met them first in Wormwood Scrubs. Later we met again, when we were all, although not at the same time, transferred to Albany Prison [on the Isle of Wight]. And it was always the same: we were very respectful of one another. They knew who we [MAC] were, alright. I'm pretty sure they also knew that I devised the three- or four-man cell structure which the IRA then adopted.[155] It did so because these wide-sweeping arrests and police interrogations had resulted in the IRA taking big losses, owing to names being divulged. But those I met in prison were really foot soldiers who carried out orders, not members of the IRA Ruling Council who implemented and adopted such policy changes. But yeah, these IRA lads in prison referred to me as 'the General'.[156]
>
> I mean, we were all Category A, but we still had access to each other – in that, as I say, we could visit each other's cells during the evenings

– and so we could still talk and discuss things. And we spoke as equals. I used to enjoy it, speaking to people like old Joe Cahill [a key figure in the foundation of the Provisional IRA], who was brought in to Albany for a while. He and I had many a decent chat.[157] As I did with another called Gallagher – Willie, I think it was – who, as I recall, was a bomb-maker. In fact, after I was released from prison in July '76, Gallagher was attacked by prison officers and they broke his leg. It was nothing to do with me leaving, as such – they wanted to sort him out anyway. Because there is this attitude, so common in fascists and some uniformed people, that if you break a man, or beat him to death, you've achieved something – that if you attack him he will change his opinion, or his attitude. It doesn't work, of course, but they don't seem to understand that. Anyway, they waited for me to be released first, because had it happened when I was there, I might have informed the press about it when I came out. So they did it after I'd gone. Very clever! But as for other IRA I met, I was particularly close to Micky Gaughan. He was such a bright, affable young man. As a mutual gesture of respect, Micky would come to the St David's Day church service, and I would go to the St Patrick's Day service in the same church. When I later learned that he had died as a result of the injuries he sustained while being force-fed in Parkhurst, after going on hunger strike, I was heartbroken. He was a lovely lad: very proud, highly intelligent – and such a brave young man.'[158]

How did these IRA prisoners regard the political situation in Wales? John replied earnestly:

'Well, when I was in Wormwood Scrubs, I was attacked by a couple of members of Plaid Cymru. They didn't like it because I was writing letters and commentaries which were getting published in *Welsh Nation*, the Plaid Cymru periodical. They were included because my old friend Harri Webb was the Editor; and for as long as he could, before the intelligencer of Plaid – if there is such a thing – told him *never* to mention my name again, he went against party policy and kept inserting articles which included quotes from me and what have you. Although Harri was 'officially' against MAC, he was determined to keep me and MAC in the public eye: both for propaganda purposes, but also to remind the public that there were people imprisoned for nationalist principles. Bless him; we always had a good write-up from Harri. But typically, of course, there were people in Plaid who didn't like this; nor the suggestion that MAC had aided the party vote; and so they attacked me for what they regarded as my sermonising and moralising from prison. And when the IRA boys found out about it, they were absolutely shocked. They couldn't believe it. They said, "Good God. The official Welsh nationalist party criticising a member who's in prison for the cause?" When I replied that it was true, they were like, "No, we can't believe it!" Because of course, and as they told me, this would never happen in Ireland – never. Within nationalist or republican circles there, it would be unheard of.'[159]

Asked how the other prisoners responded to his friendship with imprisoned members of the IRA, and whether being a so-called 'political' ensured a different – if unofficial – regime, John replied:

'Well, those beneath me in terms of prison status wouldn't have raised the matter of my friendship with the IRA. To do so was beyond their rank, as it were. But for those prisoners in the same category as me – people like the Train Robbers – it was a strange situation. Because while all of us on the long-term wing were Category A and so theoretically governed by the same restrictions, the IRA lads and I quickly realised that contrary to regulations, these restrictions were applied far more stringently and harshly to us. We considered ourselves political prisoners, but we were never acknowledged as such. We didn't set out to kill, maim, or rob anyone; all our actions were done for a good, political purpose – and *not* for reasons of personal gain or benefit. But if we raised the matter of us receiving political status, we were told by the officers and the prison authority, "No, no. You're in here for a criminal crime; and we're not going to discuss the matter any further." And of course, the only way they could have changed my mind would have been to argue me round – and none of them could do that.

Yet, despite this differentiation *not* being officially recognised, people who'd robbed banks with a sawn-off shotgun or the Train Robbers were afforded far more opportunity in terms of receiving visitors and being able to send and receive letters. They could send and receive letters weekly, but my quota ensured I could only receive one letter per week, and send one letter every three weeks. On the other hand, though, the Train Robbers *also* recognised that the prison authorities treated us more humanely. You see, we didn't have anything to prove to anybody. People like Buster did. They might have been the "Great Train Robbers", but they still had to prove that they were tough guys through fighting in the cells.

Whereas we didn't. Although, later on, I did surround myself with a couple of 'minders'. But this was more of a precaution than anything – because the prisoners *also* knew how many cards and letters of support I received. So, as with this 'implied threat', which existed towards the family of any prison officer who might take it upon himself to shout and bawl, or worse, the prisoners were aware that such an implied threat extended to their families too.'

Had other factors ensured his 'safety'? 'Well,' he asserted, 'another reason why the prisoners left me alone was because they thought I was "favoured" by the authorities. And it simply wasn't true.' Encouraged to elaborate, Jenkins continued:

'I wasn't favoured by the authorities. It's just that I did what I was supposed to do and the officers did what they were supposed to do. And so, as a result, there was no uproar and rows and shouts and screams going on. For instance, something which was certainly true in relation to me, and I'm sure I speak for *all* the "politicals" – officers soon realised that while we were *in* prison, we weren't *of* prison. We were living there, but our minds were elsewhere. We weren't thinking about being down at the Old Bull and Bush. We didn't focus our intellectual energies on acquiring things like cannabis, and all these distractions, and the prison officers recognised that.

Also, we showed these officers respect and courtesy, and they gave it back. Some would call me Mr Jenkins, for instance. They also knew I wouldn't deliberately set out to upset people; to get them beaten up or whatever – either inmates or guards. Officers knew I wasn't the sort of bloke who would do that because I am not vengeful, as such. So they knew jolly well if they left me alone, I would leave *them* alone. So, yeah, throughout my time in prison, we got on alright. The other prisoners assumed that this was because I was bringing pressure to bear on the officers to lay off me. But I didn't *have* to bring any pressure; they laid off me because they didn't want any trouble either! I was simply playing the system. It's one of those things: you have to play the system. You cannot live in a prison, or be in any environment where people are involved, without playing the system. And there is no way that anybody, no matter who they are, can get away with it. So you have to acknowledge it, deal with it and learn to play it.'

But if John was content in the knowledge that he was 'playing the system', he was in for an awakening, because on New Year's Day 1972, he was 'ghosted' to Albany Prison on the Isle of Wight. Prompted to explain the term and what transpired, Jenkins declared:

> 'To be 'ghosted' means you are literally moved without warning. And that's what happened to me. Quite suddenly, during the afternoon of New Year's Day, my cell door was unlocked and in came a group of officers who said, "Right. Get packed. You're off". Simple as that. The prison authority had been informed of a plan the IRA had of arranging for a helicopter to land in the prison yard during the exercise period to collect me and the IRA boys and spirit us away, back to the Republic.[160] Apparently the Prison Governor had been made aware of this plan by a grass. I must say that in retrospect, I'm glad it didn't happen. It was better that I serve my time and leave properly. But the IRA seemed to have some funny ideas about secrecy, and this inmate should neither have known about it, nor should he have told the Governor. But there we are. I was transferred that afternoon to Albany Prison on the Isle of Wight, where I spent the rest of my prison term.'

## HM Prison Albany; John acquires two 'minders' and a new job

Despite the haste in which he left Wormwood Scrubs, John quickly deduced on arriving at Albany that it was 'a much better place than the drab and deliberately imposing, Victorian-looking Scrubs'. While 'it was still a prison, of course, Albany,' he explained, 'was more modern. It had better facilities; it was a lighter, not so oppressive, and a more spacious environment' in which to be incarcerated.[161]

John had not been at Albany many weeks when one evening, as he perused the books in the prison library, he was approached by fellow inmates Norman Bassett and John Elliot. The two men respectfully engaged Jenkins in general conversation concerning social interests. It was quickly established that the three prisoners shared 'certain interests in common', such as 'radio plays and discussion programmes – particularly of a political, topical, or criminal nature. I was delighted,' John admitted. 'Normally in prison, people are fixated with the bloody football results, or other inconsequential pap. So I was very happy to make their acquaintance.'

Nevertheless, Norman Bassett and John Elliot had another reason for approaching Jenkins: they proposed that forthwith they should act as his 'minders'. 'Being a "top status" prisoner, I was entitled and expected to have "minders". I didn't have any in Wormwood Scrubs, but it had crossed my mind,' John declared, adding:

'Not that I ever experienced any degree of intimidation, but you could never *really* be sure if someone had a surprise in store for you. So there always existed the possibility that you might need to prove yourself. But looking at the size of Norman and John, especially Norman, I thought, "Right, let's see you try and get past these two." I mean, these were tough guys. And after that day, I never moved without them. But they had their own motives too, of course. You see, as long-term prisoners, they knew which way the wind was blowing. They knew that in prison, you can't get anywhere unless you are "known". So the more they maintained my profile, the greater was their own status. And so it was their job to make sure I was "known", and this is what they did by providing a cordon and a buffer around me. They guarded me, and in turn their own status, very jealously. If anyone took "liberties", as it was called – if anybody tried to push in ahead of me, or if I was approached by a "lower rank", or a baby burglar, who might have funny ideas of elevating their own status by attacking or abusing me, they would get the "rough end". And they were all treated the same – although there was no physical contact. Norman and John would just impose themselves through providing a physical presence. You see, even for a baby burglar to be seen trying to talk to me – or Norman and John – would negatively affect my status, so therefore, this buffer was crucial; and Norman was a big, strong bloke. Not just that, though – he was clever too.'

Was the subject of their imprisonment ever discussed? 'Yeah, almost immediately,' Jenkins replied matter-of-factly, before continuing:

'I said to Norman, "Why are you in here, Norman?" "Because I killed my mother," he replied. "Why did you kill your mother, then, Norman?" "Because she burnt the toast," he said.[162] Quite naturally. "Oh well, there we are then," I said. "And what about you, John?" "Oh, I killed my friend with an axe," he said. I can't recall why he killed him. But every time John saw blood after that, he nearly fainted, because it brought back all the memories of killing his friend.'[163]

243

Yet as the months passed and John settled into life at Albany Prison, it was not only minders that he acquired. Having established a reputation for being trustworthy, amenable and intelligent, Jenkins was offered a job by the Prison Governor. The first thing John did was to ensure that his minders, Norman and John, were able to work alongside him. 'We weren't given a job title or a number which related to the job we did, but it was a coveted position, and as the job developed, I was given the responsibility of carrying out a number of functions,' Jenkins later revealed. Prompted to outline what this unspecified position entailed, John continued:

> 'Well, I don't know how it happened really, but after several months, I somehow emerged as the leader and the spokesman for the prisoners; and so I would be invited to attend meetings in this particular office with the Prison Governor and officers, where I would then relay any concerns and suggestions the prisoners had for improving practices and how things might be done. It usually concerned issues such as the food, or what films and TV prisoners could watch, but also how discussion groups might be formed and organised for those – such as me and Norman – who wanted and needed more intellectual outlets. I would then be allowed to work in this particular office, in order to type up the minutes of these meetings.
>
> But I was given the task of typing up the prison officers' internal meeting minutes also. The weekly meetings that officers had with the Governor, during which internal prison policy was decided upon, various resolutions and motions were passed and the production figures in relation to the workshop and the hospital supply figures and targets were discussed. This was in order to determine how well the prison was coping with targets that had been set for us. Was the prison meeting these targets, or was it failing to reach them? If so, why? Was it owing to a shortage of tools and materials? Or was the prison exceeding the targets it had been set? All that sort of data was provided with these figures. Well, this was unheard of – for a prisoner to be given access to this information. But I would be handed this handwritten report by one of the civil servants employed in the prison's Civil Office and asked to type it up until it was no longer a mess of figures and words, but instead a readable report which was easy to understand.'

Had the operation run smoothly? 'Well,' John replied tentatively, before declaring:

'Of course, as soon as the officers got wind of the fact that these private meetings being held between the Governor and his minions were being read and typed up by me, they objected. It was, as far as these officers were concerned, all wrong. What they didn't know was that I had been typing these damn reports up for about six months before they realised! But to strengthen their case against me, the guards then complained that as there was a phone in this office, I had direct access to the 'outside'. Well, it's true: there was a telephone in this office, which by dialling 9 first, or whatever, you could dial out. But it never crossed my mind to do so. Yet, in any event, the officers arranged for a wooden cage to be built in the workshop, which the phone fitted into, and this cage could then be locked by way of a key and padlock, and the key was kept by the on-duty officer in the area. So this denied me access to a phone I'd never thought of using! I should say that it did work out alright, though. When they realised that I wasn't against them and that I was just there to do a job, and do it well, they left me alone...

I really enjoyed it; just being tucked away in this office to work on the reports. In fact, I then devised a system whereby the accounting figures were far more exact and more easily accessible. Off my own bat, I produced a long sheet of notated paper, on which we recorded the daily output figures. This provided a far more illuminating position as to our daily target figures, rather than a weekly or fortnightly one. Nobody had thought to do this before and the idea really took off. To the initial consternation of people working in the workshop or the hospital, the overall production people said, "This is a splendid idea, just what we need. This is what we'll do in future." But it worked. By simply referring to these daily recorded output figures, the prison authorities and everyone who worked in the workshop or hospital could immediately see how performance and productivity could be increased. Oh, I got a lot of pats on the back for that! The Prison Governor approved this system and the prisoners could see the fruits of their labour.

I'm not sure all the officers were that supportive. There were some who were angered by the fact that here was a prisoner improving systems, and so on. But I didn't care. Actually, Norman and I then redesigned the workshop so that the tools and equipment could be stored away tidily. It meant that everyone knew where a specific tool was stored and where an item of material could be located. Before that, the guards could spend bloody days searching for the tools and things that the prisoners required! Again, the improvement in terms of productivity which resulted from this simple system was immediately apparent. Even the prison guards, some of whom weren't terribly keen on this idea either, eventually came to see that this was an improvement on the system. Despite their initial suspicions, it wasn't meant to show up their failings, but to show up areas where improvement could be effected without turning the whole world upside down.'

## Ian Brady and other infamous prisoners; John divorces Thelma and goes on hunger strike

Nonetheless, despite the improvement in his life within Albany Prison, the reality of Jenkins' incarceration was routinely and starkly hammered home by way of a grim reminder. 'It was a *hell* of a place,' John remarked, adding slowly, 'Well, you wouldn't believe it.' Encouraged to develop the point, Jenkins continued:

'Along with the fights and the constant tensions, something would happen to bring your situation sharply into focus. For instance, one evening I was escorted to the prison library, and there on the library noticeboard it was chalked up that a book written by, or about, Gilles de Rais, the appalling French paedophile and child killer, had arrived and was awaiting collection by Ian Brady – the Moors Murderer. I never saw Brady – he was not in the prison, as such; he was down in the "dungeons", as they call it. He was placed in solitary confinement and segregated from the rest of us under Rule 43, I think it's known as; whereby an inmate, for his own protection, or the protection of others, can apply to be placed in a Vulnerable Prisoners Unit, away from the main body of the prison. It ensures that he never sees anybody and that the other prisoners have nothing to do with him, otherwise they would kill him.'

Having declared that observing the choice of Brady's reading material had left him 'sickened', John candidly conceded to having felt 'irritated once again by the hypocrisy of it all'. Pausing in momentary silence, Jenkins then continued:

'I'm sure that my annoyance reflects the degree to which I was by now, at least to some extent, conditioned and institutionalised by my situation. But for months, I'd received cards, magazines and letters of support from Breton nationalists; among them Paol and Judith Keineg, the Breton cultural activists, who sent me copies of *Le Peuple Breton* – which was a newspaper that reported on the political situation in Brittany. But on one occasion, *Le Peuple Breton* had a report on me, the MAC campaign and what was happening politically in Wales. The prison authorities, having looked through the pages, saw this article, and informed me that I would no longer be able to receive it. And when I challenged the prison authorities as to why, I was told it was because the political nature of *Le Peuple Breton* corresponded to my offences. I said, "How can you stop a newspaper, for God's sake?" "Because it contains political information," came the reply. Now, this only occurred a week or so before this business of Brady's book. And yet Brady had requested to receive this repugnant book, which was specifically related to Brady's own offences of the torture and murder of children, and he received it through the prison authorities!'

Other notable internees at Albany Prison during the period when John was imprisoned there were Charlie Kray, the older brother of the twins Ronnie and Reggie (the notorious East End gangsters); Robert Welch, another of the Train Robbers; and John Duddy, who was involved in the murder of three policemen in London in 1966. Asked to reveal the degree to which he had contact with these infamous prisoners, John replied bluntly:

'I didn't bother with any of them. People like that don't interest me. The point is, they were *nothing* to do with Wales. They were just scum from London as far as I was concerned. We shared top-rank prisoner status, so it certainly wasn't a case of keeping out of their way, it's just we had no reason to be in contact. In fact, the nearest I came to the Krays was during a brief period when I was in London and working as a social worker for an agency. On arriving at the Social Services team in Islington, I was handed a pile of files, and a file concerning one of the Krays – Reg, I think – was among them. He was a detainee in a prison medical service centre. But I never did visit him, because after a few weeks, I secured a position within the Social Services team in Barking.'

In June 1972, after weeks of John being transported intermittently from Albany Prison to Cardiff Magistrates Court to attend the court proceedings, John and Thelma were divorced. The decision to annul the couple's fourteen years of marriage was taken by him, John maintains. Prompted to explain why, Jenkins added:

'Broadly speaking, Thelma and I divorced on the grounds of irreconcilable differences. It was due to a question of her loyalty – or lack of it.[164] But the marriage ended quite amicably. We were still friends at this point and remained so for some years after. Thelma agreed that I should have custody of the boys and be awarded the legal responsibility for their welfare and education. First time it has ever been known for a Category A prisoner to be granted such a thing. I had grown increasingly concerned, having received information that Thelma was socialising a lot. The point is, when I went to prison, there was an understanding that Thelma would put the boys first, but she didn't. Frankly, I don't think she liked, or wanted, the responsibility of being a parent. I think she felt it cut down on her sense of freedom. So with the divorce granted and these conditions accepted by the court, I was able to take the major decisions in relation to the boys' education and their living arrangements. In the case of their education, by appointing guardians to oversee their progress – and that is what Thelma wanted anyway.'[165]

Nevertheless, if John felt gratified by the decision of the court to award him sole responsibility for Vaughan and Rhodri's education and welfare, it should be acknowledged that much of Thelma's testimony during the divorce proceedings did not reflect Jenkins in a positive light. Thelma claimed that she never really knew John fully; and that even at their closest, she 'always felt a distinct barrier' between them. Furthermore, after ten years of married life, she still felt 'uneasy' in John's presence, as all her female friends were too. There was worse to come. Her mother, Thelma continued, had confessed that John 'was the only man she was afraid of';[166] and that Jenkins 'was the only male in the family never to have been insulted' by Thelma's father. It was also noted by these women, Thelma added, 'that men who normally smoked very little, became chimneys' in Jenkins' company. The conclusion reached by Thelma's family was that John was 'evil and cruel to make men nervous and women uneasy'.[167]

But if John considered that his troubles had turned a corner, having both divorced Thelma and been granted control of Vaughan and Rhodri's education and welfare, he was left disappointed. Between 21 August and 30 September 1972, John went on a 'quite horrific' water-only hunger strike. His decision to do so had been taken in response to John being denied visits by the two appointees, Eileen and Trefor Beasley, whom Jenkins had selected to monitor and relay the educational progress of his son Vaughan.

Asked to outline why he felt such a protest necessary and how matters transpired, John declared:

'I decided to go on a "water-only" hunger strike in protest at the failure of the prison authorities – and the Home Office – to apply their own rules and regulations. I was a Category A prisoner, imprisoned for political reasons and yet denied political status. But compared to the other Category A prisoners, who were there for purely criminal activities, I was severely restricted as to the number of letters and visits I received. So that was frustrating enough. But to then be denied access to Eileen and Trefor Beasley – Eileen was a teacher at Ysgol Rhydfelen, which Vaughan attended, and her husband Trefor was also actively involved in school policy matters – was very frustrating. I *genuinely* wanted to know how Vaughan was getting on in school because I have always been interested in education, as I think it's the answer. So having asked the Beasleys to monitor Vaughan's educational development, I then wrote to them inviting them to visit me to discuss Vaughan. But having agreed to do so, the Beasleys then received notice that their request to visit me had been rejected. They were even visited at home by their local police and discouraged from visiting me – "Don't you know what he's done?" And this contravened the Home Office's own policy, which quite clearly states that every effort will be made to maintain a prisoner's contact with his family and people connected to his family. So I took it up with the prison authorities and asked why they had been prevented from visiting me. I was told it was a "security matter". I do *not* believe the authorities were aware that Trefor was a member of MAC, but still they forbade it on the grounds of "security". So I went on hunger strike, to try and point out the stupidity of a system which guaranteed one thing, but in fact, enforced the opposite.'

Was it physically discomforting? 'Oh, it was painful after the first day,' Jenkins retorted; adding:

'All sorts of funny things started to happen. I lost all my physical strength and so I couldn't walk anywhere, and I began to suffer nightmares... But there we are, I managed. But nothing was ever granted. The authorities wouldn't give me an inch. I got nothing. Nothing whatsoever. The Beasleys were allowed to visit me to discuss Vaughan about once every six months; whereas other Category A prisoners received similar such visits every day of the bloody week! I was determined to see the hunger strike through to the end if necessary, but I received a letter from a group called something like the Preservation of the Rights of Prisoners, urging me to come off it as they feared more chaos, uproar and social unrest if I continued. So, after deliberating for a few days, I ended it.'

But Jenkins' decision to cease fasting was not the end of the matter. On 23 October 1972, during a BBC Radio Wales discussion regarding John's hunger strike, Tom Ellis, the Wrexham Labour MP, defended Jenkins' stand. It was a position sharply contested by another contributor to the discussion, Viscount Colville, who – a listening Jenkins believed – clearly laid his integrity open to question when he accused John of 'exaggerating' both the duration of his hunger strike and its effects on his physical health.[168] An angry rebuke was not long in coming. On the grounds that Jenkins had been on hunger strike for 40 days and not two months as Colville stated, and that in the process John had lost 1.5 stone from his prior recorded weight of 12 stone, letters were immediately despatched to Viscount Colville demanding a retraction, and to the Home Office requesting the right, in the event of Colville's retraction not being received, to sue him 'for defamation of character.'[169] Both requests, like John's earlier attempts to appeal against the severity of his prison sentence, were dismissed. Although with regard to Jenkins' appeal to the European Commission and Court of Human Rights, Strasbourg had 'expressed disquiet concerning the political censorship of newspapers and periodicals' posted to Jenkins, and was 'calling for an explanation from the British state'.[170] By February 1974, posted copies of Le Peuple Breton were still being retained by the prison authorities. Believing the matter to be hopeless, John wrote to Judith Keineg, asking her to stop buying the paper and posting it to him. It would, Jenkins explained, save her money and him frustration. With John no longer receiving copies of Le Peuple Breton, the issue ended there.[171]

## John is transferred to HM Prison Bristol, develops some interests and retains his faith

In December 1972, John was transferred to HM Prison Bristol for one month, to receive accumulated visits. Along with visits from Vaughan and Rhodri, John was also visited by Minerva. 'She came alone,' he revealed, 'because my father was a worried sort of chap – and being inside a prison would have unsettled him, so he stayed at home. It was the first and only time my mother visited me,' Jenkins recalled, adding by way of mitigation:

'Well, until then, I was too far away. I mean, my mother was now rather elderly and quite a big lady – to expect her to travel to Birmingham, for God's sake, or worse still to Wormwood Scrubs... She couldn't walk! I was amazed she made it, because when she got there she couldn't bloody breathe. But while my mother didn't visit me again, she wrote a letter to me every week when I was in prison – as she had before I was sentenced. In fact, after I was released from prison, we continued to write weekly to each other throughout her life. After I was released, we carried on our earlier practice of speaking on the phone once a week too. It was a good way to keep in contact. But going back to prison visits: I'm sure that the distance was deliberate, to ensure that family and friends visited me as infrequently as possible. I wasn't disappointed by the lack of people who visited me throughout my prison term; you see, the rigmarole which surrounded receiving a visitor – the forms which needed to be filled in, their end and mine, outlining their relationship with me and why the visit was being arranged – also acted as a deterrent for people. The government and the prison authorities don't care. They only care about the public reaction. And the public didn't seem to worry too much about what was happening [regarding inmates being imprisoned far from home] so why should the establishment worry?'

What had been his mother's emotional reaction on seeing her eldest son behind bars? 'Well, in the visiting room at Bristol Prison, you weren't behind bars, as such,' John related.

'Although, as was strictly enforced with all my prison visits, no physical contact was allowed. You weren't allowed to kiss, or hold hands – even touching someone affectionally on the shoulder was prohibited. But no, Mum was alright; she was quite stoic about it. As far as she was concerned, if I had done it [the MAC offensive], then it needed to be done and so it was quite right for me to have done it. We didn't discuss anything specific – certainly nothing to do with the campaign. It was just general chit-chat about life.'

Did any member of the Bridgman family *ever* visit him? 'Good God no, I didn't want to see Thelma, or her family,' Jenkins exclaimed; adding thoughtfully:

> 'But a father and son who I knew from our days in the [TA military] band in Wrexham came to see me in Bristol. Being affiliated to the Army, it was against regulations for them to visit me, but they risked it. As with Mum, we didn't discuss anything specific. It was just general chit-chat – and the memories we shared of being in the band.'

Whether it was owing to the emotional elevation of having received higher number of visitors when at Bristol Prison, in response to the psychological turmoil of the previous months or fuelled by a sense of resignation, on being transferred back to Albany Prison in January 1973, John decided a change of attitude and approach to his incarceration was required. It coincided with Jenkins having received a Christmas gift from a supporter in Wales. Prompted to outline his thoughts as to his change of perspective, John declared:

> 'Well, another lady I have great respect for is Sara Erskine, or Sara Thomas as she later became. She's dead now, God rest her. But Sara was another correspondent; and as a result of her sending a Celtic Art booklet to me over Christmas 1972, I developed a great interest in Celtic art – which I thought was lovely: so complicated and yet so perfect. In fact, it was at this point that I began to see prison as an opportunity rather than as a punishment, in that I could get something from it. And the prison authorities didn't mind; they actually encouraged interest in art and education. So, henceforth, I would use the time to my advantage – and I did. In fact, I ultimately received a reward for my artwork, because what I was doing was trying to incorporate Celtic traditional art into modern requirements. So I began to produce Christmas cards and birthday cards and eventually a poster that said "The Lord is My Shepherd", and so on. Because of my job in the prison office, I was able to get my hands on paper of various thicknesses, and so I hand-made about 100 of these Celtic-design cards. And I was also able to fold the thinner A4 paper into envelopes, and over a period of *many* months, post them out to people. Well, over time, this resulted in me receiving a lot of cards and letters from supporters, not least among them Saunders Lewis, the noted author and playwright, and even ministers of religion. But most of the letters

I received were from old ladies! It was a political thing, and a biblical thing – where they wrote to me to say how right I was according to the laws of God; and how they were praying for me every night! They weren't trying to steer me away from it at all. It was very nice, yeah. But I also realised that I could concentrate on communication. I was writing letters to people – many of which were later published.[172] And as the months passed, I decided to concentrate on education.'

What other interests helped John pass the time? 'I joined the prison choir,' John replied, chuckling. 'In fact,' he continued:

'I encouraged many of the other prisoners to join too – and they enjoyed it. The pianist was particularly overjoyed, because she'd never had so many prisoners interested in the choir, or music, before. So much so that we put on a creditable Christmas concert, which included the choir singing "Gaudete", a popular Latin carol which was a Christmas hit that year [for Steeleye Span]. That took the choir a bit of teaching! But during the concert, I also sang "Emmanuel" as a duet with the Deputy Prison Manager. So yeah, the concert helped lift the mood in the prison a bit, because the atmosphere was always subdued around Christmas. It would begin when cards started arriving. The prisoners became quiet, with their situation weighing on them as they remembered happier Christmases. Also, since being sentenced, many had experienced family developments: deaths and so on... I mean, the food wasn't too bad, and the officers – while maintaining this line between themselves and the prisoners – did their best to try and liven things up a bit. But prison is a grim place. It's built to look grim and designed to reinforce the fact that you're stuck there. So I always noticed how glum the prisoners were over Christmas...

I also tried to learn Welsh at Albany. But I only managed to learn a little. I'm not much good at languages. I had books sent to me by supporters – Cyril Hodges and Watcyn Owen. Cyril sent me Welsh learners' books, and Watcyn sent letters written partly in Welsh and I'd send a letter partly written in Welsh back to him. But the authorities made this difficult, by sending them off to be "deciphered". And this would take months! Whereas a letter written to a prisoner in German, or a number of other languages – they'd get them the same day. And again, I realised that this rule – whereby letters not written in English needed to be translated and deciphered – was being applied far more strictly to me, because of my name, than it was to other prisoners.'[173]

Did he maintain his faith during the period of his imprisonment? 'Oh, after being initially prevented from attending church when at Shrewsbury Prison, I attended church regularly in all the *other* prisons I was in,' John replied. 'You see, even though I'd very rarely attended a Christian service before I was imprisoned, I *always* retained my faith. So, in that sense, it was not a case of re-engaging with it when I was sent to prison. Although,' John added, 'I always declined to receive communion.' Asked to explain why, Jenkins continued pensively:

> 'Well, my decision not to receive it did cause some comment; because everybody else received communion, but I didn't. After some weeks, I was asked to explain why "such a good-living person" as myself never went up for it. And I said, "Well, the reason is, I may in the future be called on to do things in the name of Welsh freedom which other people might consider to be in conflict with the receiving of the bread and wine. And so I don't want to take the communion, in the knowledge that I may have to break its vow later on." So I never did.'

## John receives a disturbing visit from his son Rhodri – and begins an Open University degree course

In 2018, during a discussion with John's younger son, Rhodri, he was asked to discuss the experience of visiting his father while he was in prison, and the extent to which these prison visits had impacted upon him. Rhodri responded:

> 'I remember going down with my mother and my first stepfather to visit my father when he was imprisoned on the Isle of Wight. Of course, being Category A, it wasn't a nice affair at all. When you arrived, you'd be checked in to see if your name was on the visiting order, and as you lined up, there would be screws patrolling with dogs. Then you'd enter this room and my father would be sat behind this thick, bulletproof pane of glass. So you couldn't touch him – well, not during the earlier time when he was imprisoned at Albany; and you had to talk over a phone. You had a phone in your room, on this side of the glass, and he had a phone in his room, on the other side of the glass. I'm sure we went every year. We'd stay on the island for a few days, you know. The distance didn't help, but I think there may have been other reasons why we didn't visit him

more often. But anyway, this one occasion sticks in my memory, and I remember it because my grandmother – Thelma's mother – in the days before we visited my father, had been shouting at me in the house about how my father had "murdered that little boy"; you know, referring to that poor lad who got damaged in Caernarfon. Well, I heard it, and I must have been mulling it over. Because, of course, I was about the same age as the boy; and so when I went in, I sat and talked to my father and I asked him "Is it true?" And he went off in a rage, and shouted to Thelma, "You are to stop your mother talking to them, right?" And after that, because he'd forbidden it, Thelma's family *never* spoke about what my father did again – not that I can *ever* recall it being mentioned anyway.'

If visits to his father were restricted to 'a couple of times over a few days every summer', was there any other contact between them? 'Well, I'd receive, as I think so too did my brother, the occasional card and letter.' Rhodri then added:

'But also – it didn't happen *that* often, but I sort of got used to hearing a knock on the front door on a Saturday morning and on being called by my mother, finding a man I didn't know standing there, who said, "I've been sent by your father to take you out for the day." I didn't mind. I got to have a burger at the Wimpy! And on one occasion, with another man, I think we went to a zoo, but I can't be certain.'

In September 1973, John began an Open University degree course in Social Sciences. So too did his 'minder', Norman Bassett. The two were the only candidates, out of a starting figure of 37 across the UK prison service, to successfully pass the course. It was no small achievement, as their degree course was followed over three years, rather than the officially approved four years. Had the prison officers supported Jenkins' efforts to complete his artwork and degree studies? 'To be fair,' John replied, 'usually the officers were quite helpful.' He went on to add:

'I had by now immersed myself in my art projects and my degree essays, and I couldn't have people putting the lights off halfway through my work, so after the official lights-out time of 10 p.m., they would keep the lights on in my cell so that I could continue working. You see, because each cell had an internal phone, I'd pick up the receiver and ask the on-duty officer, sat at the front desk of the wing, if he could leave the light on. And when I'd finished, I'd ask, "Can you turn it off now, please?', and most often they were fine about it. I know there are people who say that *all* prison guards are rotten, but I would say that the majority of officers were reasonable people. Not bad people at all – the sort of person I would chat to on the outside. But it is also true to say that *some* prison officers enjoyed their power and flaunted it. You see, there were some officers who pinned these small swastikas under the lapels of their prison jackets. They couldn't wear them openly, of course, so, they would pin them there and then flash them at one another. It was a way of establishing if a colleague was "one of us".

Encouraged to outline the importance of his Open University degree course to his emotional and intellectual well-being, John declared:

'It provided a definitive objective to be worked towards; and I revelled in the challenge of meeting such an academic standard. Mind you, I knew damn well that everything I wrote was being handed to Special Branch; and so I wrote one essay on "organisations"' to do with MAC: why it came into existence, what it intended to achieve and how it undertook its campaign – all in sociological terms. It was written purely to wrong-foot Special Branch. Everything I wrote was designed to confuse them. For instance, knowing these essays went straight to Special Branch, I wrote that MAC was financed by a wealthy backer. It was a red herring – done in the hope they would waste a lot of time and money trying to locate him. In another essay, I wrote that in 1968, MAC was intent on assassinating the head of Special Branch. Again, there was no truth to it at all. MAC never intended to harm anyone.'

How Special Branch reacted when reading Jenkins' essay is unknown, but John's tutor W G Hannam was impressed, awarding Jenkins a B for his essay entitled 'Formal Structure and Informal Political Processes'. The paper, Hannam stated by way of feedback, was 'well-written; an extremely interesting piece of original analysis' and the product, he should imagine, of 'someone with first-hand experience'. Moreover, Hannam continued, 'I don't know what your present standing with MAC is – but clearly you have been involved in the organisation, which is considered subversive by the establishment.'[174]

## Vaughan is summoned to see his father, and Albany Prison has a fire

If John found solace and a sense of intellectual escape from the confines of his imprisonment through his educational and social interests, the pressures of trying to raise a family, he insists, were never far from his mind. News in the spring of 1974 that his eldest son had 'gone off the rails' resulted in Jenkins arranging to have Vaughan brought to see him by his social worker, Margaret Roberts, and her husband, Emrys, the Plaid Cymru activist. During their subsequent encounter, in which John learned of the events surrounding Vaughan having broken into a local shop with much older boys, John 'tried to put him right, in my limited fashion'. What Vaughan needed above all, Jenkins wrote to Judith Keinig, was 'a firm hand to control him, wielded by one he respects – and that is exactly what he does not get.'[175]

Nevertheless, if John was struggling to maintain control over his son Vaughan, one episode graphically illustrates the degree to which *some* prison officers regarded their position not as a vehicle to promote ideas of reform and rehabilitation, but rather as a means of exercising abject and cynical control over the lives of those they considered to be under their authority. Encouraged to recount what occurred, John replied sombrely:

'There was a prisoner who – having been called up one day to see the Governor – was told that he was being transferred to, I think, Wandsworth Prison; which had a hellish reputation as a place where they were very nasty indeed with prisoners. He was told he was going there and this got him really upset, and as far as I can recall, it wasn't even *true* that he was going there. They told him this just to wind him up; and they wound him up so much, that using his own cell key – because we all had a key to our own cell, although our cell keys couldn't unlock the doors to leave the wing, of course – he locked himself in his cell and wouldn't let the officers in. And he kept shouting that he was going to set fire to his cell unless something was done about this transfer. But they just ignored him, so he set fire to his cell and they couldn't open the door. So one of the officers went down to the front office to get the master key, but the fire was raging, and on arriving back, they discovered it was the wrong key – so they had to go back down again and get the correct key, and, of course, by this time he was dead. And their argument was that the regulations stated that they

257

had to keep the other key in a separate area for security reasons – and that was it, he was dead. Well, I never heard him, luckily, because I was on the other side of the prison, but he was screaming, apparently. But from our wing, we could smell him. We could smell him burning. It brought home, in dramatic and awful fashion, the extent to which the prisoners were subjugated and at the mercy of these people. They were in total control of our lives. Just awful.'

That said, although the prisoners were angry about it and the atmosphere in Albany was both tense and subdued for a day or two, the prison soon returned to normal. You see, a prisoner being burnt in his cell was not unusual. So nobody was going to pay too much attention, sadly – not for long anyway. It wasn't like that.'

## John's Category A status is lifted, he and the IRA smell a rat, John receives two job offers and is released from Albany Prison

From being sentenced in April 1970 until May 1975, John was imprisoned under Category A status. Considerable credit is due to the Welsh Political Prisoners Defence Committee and the then MP for Meirionnydd, Dafydd Ellis-Thomas, whose representations to the Home Office were significant in the campaign to have Jenkins' Category A classification removed. Asked to outline what changes to his day-to-day existence this brought about, John responded wryly:

'Officially I then became a Category B prisoner, but in reality it made little difference. The same restrictions were more or less applied. For instance, I was now eligible for parole, but it was never granted. Although, despite being unofficially ineligible for parole, I did receive a third off my sentence owing to good behaviour – something awarded to all prisoners if they behave, irrespective of parole. However, despite now being Category B, I continued to receive the same number of letters – about one per week, less than other Category Bs – and the palaver which surrounded a visit remained. The only real difference to being taken off Category A was that I was no longer accompanied everywhere by one or two prison officers.'

The removal of John from Category A status coincided with him developing an enduring interest in socialism, while also maintaining a fierce affiliation with the doctrine of political nationalism. Although, as John pointed out, discussions regarding *any* political ideology with a prison officer were pointless, owing to the fact that a prison officer 'automatically assumes his knowledge is superior' to an inmate's. For example, John continued, 'If an imprisoned professor of sociology discussed sociology with a prison officer, even if the officer was studying sociology at a rudimentary level, the prison officer would *always* assume his argument was correct and the professor was wrong, because he was a prison officer and the professor was a prisoner.' Yet if discussions with prison officers were consequently inhibited, in this period John struck up further conversational friendships with imprisoned members of the IRA. Asked if the group's unparalleled campaign of violence – which included the appalling explosions in pubs in Guildford in October 1974 and in Woolwich and Birmingham a month later, and the Balcombe Street siege in December 1975 – had provoked a reaction within the prison, John replied, 'Well, if there was a reaction, it was not something that I ever noticed.' Prompted to develop the point, Jenkins added, 'For whatever reason, presumably because to do so might prove inflammatory, everyone – officers and inmates – kept quiet.' John added reflectively:

'But I think it's more likely because prison life is so insular. Nothing was ever said about *anything* happening on the outside, really... It didn't stop me and the IRA chatting about policy and strategy, though. No wonder we referred to Albany as the "University of the Revolution" – although this was in mock reference to the general discussions regarding criminality which took place there, rather than our own discussions... We'd still afford one another the prison etiquette of knocking on someone's cell door before being invited in. I mean, that's the prison way. But these discussions, held during the evening before lock-up, were always respectful, friendly and reasonably open. While we shared common points of interest, when it came to actual, real practicalities such as targets, and the location of equipment – well, obviously these were issues of tight internal security. Not that the prison authorities didn't try and infiltrate our discussions. We were joined once or twice by this loudmouth called Graham Ennis, from – well, apparently – southern Ireland. And he comes into the cell one evening and starts explaining to me and the IRA boys how we should make bombs, and how the IRA should go about their business. We automatically distrusted him. Christ almighty, he was so obviously a grass. We just laughed at him and he left… Eventually, most of these IRA prisoners were sent 'home' to serve their sentences in Northern Ireland, and a lot of them had never been *near* Northern Ireland – some were from London, for example. So, I went to see the Governor and said, "I want to go back to Northern Ireland." He said "You've never been there." I said, "Well, neither have half these buggers been there." "Oh," he said, "it's nothing to do with me – I just do as I'm told; and that's what you've got to do: do as you're told". That was the end of the matter, but I was hoping for a prison transfer to Northern Ireland just to be among kindred spirits.'

In the weeks before his release from Albany Prison, Jenkins entered into written correspondence with 'a former political acquaintance' by the name of Parry. 'The day you are released,' Parry informed John, 'you should come straight to Tehran, as there is a job waiting for you.' The position, John revealed, involved acting as 'Parry's assistant manager in heading up the computer section of the Shah of Iran's government.' Despite 'never having seen a computer', as John remarked wryly, 'it was a very attractive offer'. Notwithstanding the prison authority's obligation 'to assist soon-to-be-released prisoners to obtain employment' and the Shah's pro-Western allegiance, it would seem that all efforts by Jenkins to receive the required inoculations, his passport and air ticket were hindered by the Home Office, intent on preventing John from taking up the position. Jenkins explained:

'The plan was that I would leave Albany in the morning, head to London and then fly to Tehran in the afternoon. But every time I went to check that the vaccine for leprosy, or whatever, had arrived, it had always been delayed; while typically, other prisoners being released and going on holiday would receive their inoculations within days. After weeks, I complained, of course: "Are you telling me after three weeks that this phial still hasn't arrived?" "Yes," they'd reply. But it wasn't just that – there was always some reason why I couldn't book the flight; they blocked clothes I wanted; and I'm sure they stopped my passport from arriving; and when I asked why there was such a delay, they explained it was "because of all the trouble with the railway controllers", as rail travel at this time was severely affected by strikes and hold-ups. They tried to claim that my passport was "probably in transit on a train somewhere". It was just deliberate bureaucratic obstruction, although they were too clever to admit it was being done deliberately. But this hindrance went on for weeks. And in the end, the idea just fizzled out. God knows why the UK authorities objected to this idea. Perhaps they wondered what me and the Shah were going to cook up together!'

It was not, however, the only offer that Jenkins had at this juncture. He received another in the days before his release from Albany Prison, when he claims to have been approached by an officer from MI5. With Jenkins' liberty imminent, his visitor enigmatically declared how nice it would be if John cooperated and helped them with their enquiries. 'Well, I knew what *that* meant,' Jenkins commented, 'and I immediately recognised the signs.' Prompted to elaborate, he added ruefully:

'There was something about his deportment, you know; the way he conducted himself, and the manner in which he spoke, which led me to deduce that irrespective of the police uniform he was wearing, he was in fact an agent of the British intelligence service.'

Whatever his true identity, John politely and firmly declined the mysterious visitor's proposal. Asked to describe his emotional mindset in the days prior to his release date from Albany Prison, John remarked:

'Well, there was none of this "I'm going straight down the pub" nonsense... In one sense, it was a feeling of "Oh well, here we go again!" Not so much in terms of protest, more in anticipation of life on the outside. You see, unlike long-term prisoners coming up for release, both then and today, who are slowly reintroduced to the outside world with supervised day and weekend releases, I received nothing whatsoever like that. I wasn't even given a chat about what to expect. I was just released! Actually, I asked if I could stay on for a couple of weeks to finish my degree coursework, because after nearly three years, I'd established a good learning pattern and didn't want to break it. Besides, all the books, etc. I needed were there. But anyway, they were having none of that! Although I did stay on for one extra week, as it happens, owing to having lost a week's remission for good behaviour for having signed a document circulated by the prisoners. It was in protest at the way an inmate was being treated; and a demand for an increase in prisoners' rights: daily access to a shower, improved visiting rights, that sort of thing. I had tried to distance myself from internal prison politics, because it didn't mean a bloody thing as far as I was concerned. It didn't prevent my activities within the art world, or my activities in the educational world, and so therefore it was of no interest to me. But to some prisoners, it meant *everything* to them and they could get really upset over such things.

But I must say that as the day to leave approached, it dawned on me that I'd made the best of what I could, and I like that. The fact that I'd used my time inside productively; that it hadn't got me down; that I'd utilised my intelligence and my "status" to exert enough pressure to live a reasonable life in prison – which I did. Well, it wouldn't be reasonable to people on the outside, but it was reasonable to *me* in the situation I was in. The evening before I was released, I was visited by the friends I'd made – among them Norman, John and the IRA boys – all of whom wished me well. As for the IRA, it was the last time I *ever* had any contact with them.'

## John begins a new life and is faced with some changes

John Jenkins emerged from Albany Prison shortly after 9 a.m. on Thursday, 15 July 1976. He was carrying a green prison-issue holdall and in his pocket was 'a small allowance' with which 'to buy cigarettes and a meal or two'. Having briefly surveyed his surroundings, John made his way to the ferry terminal and crossed to Southampton. From there, Jenkins caught the train to London, where he was interviewed by members of the media at Paddington Station. Asked by reporters if he harboured any regret for his actions involving *Mudiad Amddiffyn Cymru*, Jenkins was unrepentant, declaring trenchantly, 'Does a man have to apologise for fighting for his country?' With a train ticket booked while in prison, Jenkins caught the train to Holyhead. It was intended to mislead Special Branch officers, who John believed, if not 'probably on the train', would be waiting at the Welsh seaport to monitor his overnight ferry departure to Dublin. A 'couple of train stations' before reaching Anglesey, however, Jenkins 'nipped off smartly' and made his way, as previously arranged, to the home of one of his prison correspondents, Watcyn Owen. 'It was a reward really, more than anything else; a thank you to Watcyn,' John later explained.

'He'd been so good in writing to me for years, and was very anxious to "get me home". So when he offered to put me up for a few nights, I gratefully accepted. But it wasn't for long, as I had the boys and my parents to see.'

Having enjoyed the 'warm hospitality' provided by his host, his wife Edwina and the couple's daughter, Eira, John left the Owen household after the weekend and made his way to Penybryn and the home of his parents, Tom and Minerva. John stayed there for the next six months. At no time was the MAC campaign ever mentioned, either by Tom or Minerva, or by any member of their extended family. During this period, Jenkins 'spent a good deal of time renewing old acquaintances' and received social security payments by way of income. The decision to visit lots of people ensured that 'monitoring police officers would fill dozens of bloody big notebooks' keeping track of John's movements and 'waste time' ascertaining the identities of the 'many, many people' he was meeting. More productively, perhaps, Jenkins also submitted the final essay required to complete his degree course. Some weeks later, John received a letter from the Open University informing him that he had passed the course, and was being awarded a degree in Social Sciences – although he decided not to attend the official graduation ceremony. John disclosed that it did not take long at all to readjust when released from prison. For instance, the once familiar sounds and ritual of the nightly lock-up was soon a memory. Yet while readjusting to life on the outside, what changes did John encounter in the British way of life?

'Well, the coinage defeated me, for a start. You don't handle money in prison, of course, and so I was unfamiliar with the changes brought about by decimalisation. When I went in, the only "new coins" were the 5p and 10p, which were introduced in spring 1968, and the 50p, which was introduced just before I was arrested. So I was faced with all these new coins and values. It was a bit of a job.[176] The punk thing was going on, too, when I came out. But I was stationed in Berlin with the Army just after the war, remember, and the attitudes depicted in the film *Cabaret*, which would be regarded as fairly forward even now, were quite common in Berlin when I was there. In the post-war period, Berlin still prided itself as being a "go-ahead" place, where the populace was not generally given to official structures, and fashion was expressed on an individual basis. So punk rockers with green hair weren't going to shock me!

But more importantly, there seemed to be a general fed-up-ness with the government of the day when I was released. More misery from the "man in the street" was being expressed than I had noticed earlier; and yet, at the same time, overall living conditions seemed to have improved. I found this rather difficult to put together. For instance, the streets were full of cars – which was a sight new to me – and yet the people who *owned* the cars were moaning and groaning and being condemnatory of the Government. I also felt that there had occurred, during the time I was imprisoned, a great loss with regard to a sense of community. Whereas community spirit was once viewed as something important and to be proud of, it now seemed that people didn't want to be disturbed by political tensions because they were too busy watching *Coronation Street*. In other words, they were becoming lost in a proxy life, as their own lives passed them by. People no longer wanted to think. The populace lacked interest in the authorities and what the authorities were trying to do; and yet these people, having turned their back on society and the influences of political society, were terribly interested in what the Sex Pistols had for breakfast! And I found this paradox and shift in attitude very strange.'

## Owain Williams provides John a plot of land, John begins a relationship with Lowri Morgan, and returns to employment

Despite any lingering tensions surrounding the circumstances of Jenkins' arrest, one of those from the Welsh nationalist community with whom John was reacquainted at this juncture was Owain Williams. Before Jenkins' release from prison, Williams offered John 'a small plot of land' on which 'to build a bungalow'. It was located on the farm land Williams owned near Pwllheli. John explained that he 'did not pay money' for this patch of land, 'it was a gift' from Williams. Although, Jenkins added, having previously spearheaded the MAC campaign, he considered that he bought the plot through his actions. In order to meet the cost of the bungalow's construction, a fund was established by a committee. The committee comprised a number of prominent Welsh figures, among them the author Dr Kate Roberts; the Anglican priest and poet R S Thomas; and Jac L Williams and J Gwyn Griffiths, professors at the University of Wales. Another contributor was the Wrexham Labour MP, Tom Ellis, who, having donated £5 to the fund, was 'attacked violently' for doing so by the *Western Mail*. Unrepentant, Ellis justified his generosity on the grounds that it 'behoves us all to jump in and offer a helping hand to anybody coming out of prison.'[177] Yet not all appear to have shared Ellis' charitable reasoning. After 12 months, only a nominal figure of some £1,000 had been raised to finance the project's completion. 'Although the monies raised were very nice' and appreciated by Jenkins, 'it was nowhere *near* enough in practical terms', he intoned. The situation exemplified to John the disparity between how those who undertake protest action in the cause of Irish Republicanism are supported in Ireland, and how former militant activists in Wales were provided for. Encouraged to continue, Jenkins added:

'When IRA men went into battle, everybody in the immediate and wider Republican community knew about it. Committees existed and these ensured that functioning organisations such as the Prisoners' Aid structure were behind the prisoners; that they were looked after, and things such as bills were taken care of. This meant that these people could actually go out and do things with a clear conscience really; their families were not going to have to suffer for it financially. Well, in Wales, there was nothing. An IRA-type structure to support prisoners just didn't exist in Wales.'

Asked what happened regarding the proposed bungalow, John replied:

'There was a big row in papers like *The Express*, because having been contacted by Owain for reasons of self-publicity, he told them he had given me land to build a house; and they retaliated by claiming the leader of MAC was being rewarded for his exploits... But in the end, the idea just fizzled out. I waited, fully intent on moving up there and having this bungalow built. But of course, eventually, as the time passed, my life moved on. I also became uncomfortable that it might be seen that in Wales former militants live together in a sort of commune. I felt that the idea might attract criticism and even ridicule, in that it might lend the movement the appearance of being rather homespun. If you look at Ireland, Republicans live *across* the island, of course... But I still own the deeds to this patch of land. I might be interested in selling it one day. When Owain sold his farm land to a neighbouring farmer recently, he wasn't able to sell this strip, as it legally belongs to me.'

One example of how John's life moved on as he waited to receive the necessary funds to complete the bungalow's construction was his flowering relationship with Lowri Morgan. Her mother had been the headmistress of an independent Welsh-medium boarding school, and her father, Trefor Morgan – who financed the school project – was the successful businessman and eminent Welsh republican. Explaining how their friendship blossomed, John stated that he 'first met Lowri when she came down to Albany' to see him with Welsh-language activist Neil ap Siencyn. Jenkins added:

'Lowri became a regular visitor; and when I was released, I met her again at the home of Siân Wyn, Neil's ex-wife. We bonded because of an exchange of views, which included a belief in a militant response to the political injustices which Wales faced. You see, while Lowri was at Aberystwyth University in the early 70s, she lived at Pantycelyn, the hall of residence occupied by the Welsh-speakers. She belonged to *Cymdeithas yr Iaith Gymraeg*, and was one of those students who campaigned to see Welsh granted greater legal status; she lay down on the road in London to stop the traffic, all that sort of stuff. So she had done a bit of time as well. So it was natural, I suppose, that we were drawn to one another. As we got to know each other, we saw ourselves as two old lags together. She was also an attractive lady. Anyway, shortly afterwards, we got together.'

In February 1977, John moved in to live with Lowri at her home in Trelewis. In September 1977, John was appointed Community Organiser at the South Wales Anti-Poverty Action Centre (SWAPAC) in Merthyr Tydfil. 'It was a political body,' John explained, 'which aimed to support people in Merthyr living in poverty.' During a period of escalating economic uncertainty, had the local authorities welcomed the support provided by SWAPAC? Jenkins refuted the suggestion:

'I was struck by the number of community councillors who didn't want social work interference, and this was because, as representatives of the community, they regarded *themselves* as providing the essential link between the community and the authorities. But it soon became obvious to us at SWAPAC that the knowledge these community councillors possessed was limited to a few local issues, like street cleaning. They weren't able, or equipped, to deal with the more complex demands of society.'

The help provided by SWAPAC to those requiring support within the community took many forms, Jenkins added – for instance, food vouchers were issued. But it was legal assistance which Jenkins found particularly gratifying. John continued:

'You see, one of my roles was to act as an advocate for people at DHSS [Department of Health and Social Security] tribunals. People would put in for something to which they were entitled – say a house, or financial assistance – but they would be turned down. And so we would call a tribunal and I would go there and represent them; and quite a few times, even when it seemed that the odds were stacked against us, we won the case. This got up the nose of the local authorities and it soon came to the attention of the police, who I'm sure resented it. I mean, it might seem strange now, because attitudes within the police appear to have moved on so much. But I'm quite sure that SWAPAC, at any rate, was regarded in certain police circles as just a group of left-wing trouble-makers; and of promoting left-wing propaganda, even of being anti-authoritarian. Yes, I would think so – we would have been seen as "getting above ourselves". But what could they do about it? We had on our staff team, among other people, a lawyer. So the police would think twice before busting into SWAPAC and throwing things about.'

In February 1978, Lowri and John moved to live in a house which Lowri bought on Conway Road in the Canton area of Cardiff. Ten months later, while on the way 'as arranged to collect Lowri from a pub following an evening socialising with friends', Jenkins was arrested for 'importuning a male to engage in sexual activity'. John admits that 'it was not the first time' that he had engaged in such consensual sexual practices with men after his release from prison, but that 'nothing had happened' before he was sentenced in April 1970. Asked to throw light on the incident, and how the matter was subsequently addressed before the court, John replied:

'It occurred in a toilet at the city end of Cathedral Road. Special Branch were very clever and set it all up. It was about 9.30 p.m. when I entered the toilet, and there was a man already there. We got on with what I would describe as a minor sexual encounter, and then he left. Moments later, a Special Branch man came rushing in and I was arrested. Obviously, this fella was part of it. But when it came to court, despite finding me guilty, the Judge refused to fine me.[178] Contrary to usual procedure, although I lost the case, neither did he state that I should pay costs – which indicates that he was not satisfied with the verdict. He could see it was a put-up job, and that there were lots of holes in the case for the prosecution. But his decision to only impose a conditional discharge caused some controversy among the police and those opposed to me, because the rules of the game said that having been found guilty, the Judge should have fined me.'[179]

Prompted to reveal how Lowri reacted to the incident, Jenkins was circumspect. 'She didn't sit in judgment in any way at all,' he replied incredulously, continuing:

'I don't mean to say that she knew better than to, but I think she thought I was just expressing myself sexually and she loved me for who I was. But to the frustration of the *Western Mail*, who I'm sure would love to have emblazoned the story across its front page, there was a printers' strike during the days following the court hearing and so the story was never published.'[180]

## John is turned down by Swansea University, and Operation *Tân*

In October 1979, John applied to follow a one-year Social and Community Work course in the Department of Social Policy and Social Work at University College of Wales, Swansea. Having submitted the admission form, Jenkins waited to be called for an interview in relation to being awarded a place on the course. On 13 December 1979, *Meibion Glyndŵr* undertook the first attack in their arson campaign. The following day, John was interviewed by BBC Wales for the Corporation's Welsh-language news magazine programme, *Heddiw*. The interview with Jenkins, during which he restated the call for Welsh political independence and innocuously attempted to outline *Meibion Glyndŵr's* objective, was never broadcast, owing – John believes – 'to both political interference and police intervention'.[181]

In February 1980, Jenkins was invited to attend an interview at Swansea University. On receiving a favourable response from the panel of interviewing course tutors, having outlined the experience gained through his employment at SWAPAC, John also volunteered information concerning his involvement in the MAC campaign and his subsequent imprisonment. Assured that 'that was then and this is now', John awaited confirmation that his application to attend the course had been accepted. Five weeks later, having not received any correspondence confirming the offer, John contacted Swansea University and was informed that his application had been rejected. When asked why, Jenkins was tentatively told by a member of the Registry Department, 'Well, you know.' The following morning, John received a letter from the Registry informing him that his application to attend the course had not been accepted. No official reason for the decision was provided. Jenkins later remarked,

'The funny thing is, I discovered that Hilary Creek, of the notorious Angry Brigade, was already on the course that I applied for; as was a former Chief Technician in the RAF Signals Unit who'd been discovered broadcasting to the Russians and sending them all sorts of secret documents. He was paroled from prison on the condition he attended this same university course at Swansea.[182] So Swansea took these two, but they wouldn't touch me with a barge pole! I later learned that having been accepted onto the course by the interviewing course tutors, their decision was vetoed by a committee headed by the Principal, Professor Robert Steele; who apparently convened this meeting of the committee to discuss my application, during which he mentioned a suspicion that I was involved in the *Meibion Glyndŵr* arson campaign – which wasn't true.'

Despite the efforts of sympathetic members of staff, Members of Parliament and trade union figures to champion John's cause, his application to attend the course at Swansea University ended there. Yet, despite his insistence that he was not involved in the *Meibion Glyndŵr* arson campaign, during an interview broadcast by the BBC's news magazine programme *Nationwide* on 12 March 1980, a baleful Jenkins outlined the aims and determination of those undertaking the holiday-home arson protest. If this was not incriminating enough, a written statement concerning the arson campaign previously handed, by a person unknown, to a BBC journalist was signed *Mudiad Amddiffyn Cymru*, which he was informed was 'one of the two main groups' responsible. Although the ramifications of the *Nationwide* interview were yet to be realised, it would return to haunt John Jenkins.

Nonetheless, at 6 a.m. on Palm Sunday, 30 March 1980, sweeping arrests were made across Wales during what became known as Operation *Tân* [Fire]: the search for the *Meibion Glyndŵr* arsonists. Among those detained, perhaps unsurprisingly, was John Jenkins. Also arrested were Welsh-language and political activists Neil ap Siencyn, Emyr Llywelyn Jones, Gethin ap Gruffydd, publisher Robat Gruffudd, Huw Lawrence (a lecturer in English at Carmarthen College of Further Education), 50-year-old forestry worker Eurig ap Gwilym, and many others. [183]

The manner in which the arrests were carried out, resulting in several children being left unattended when their parents were taken in for questioning, became the focus of sharp criticism from those interned and the media. The hostility was aggravated owing to the fact that the whereabouts of those arrested was withheld from family, friends and even legal advisors. In response, the police issued a statement declaring that 'to allow the sort of access being demanded would inhibit investigations and impede the course of justice'... The decision [to withhold information] had not been 'taken lightly', but at the 'highest level'. It was an explanation given short shrift by solicitor Michael Jones, who responded that 'people cannot be allowed to disappear off the face of the earth when they are, in fact, in the hands of the people responsible for law and order.'[184] Encouraged to outline his experience of these events, John replied:

'They arrested me at home and took me to the police station in Rumney, where they held me for, I think, five days. I protested, of course – as did, I'm quite sure, the others who were arrested – which the following morning I was told by police numbered 150 throughout Wales! But they said to me, "It's alright for you activists to shout and bawl the odds about this, but wait until we've finished our operation and *then* see who does the shouting." And how many were convicted out of that 150? One! And that was *very* dubious. He was a forester, so of course he had a shed, in which he kept a can of petrol, along with bits and pieces you need to light a fire when you are getting rid of the slack and the scrub in the forest – which is what his job was. And they got him for that![185]

I mean, they treated me well enough; they weren't nasty people. But they had to release me in the end because I worked for SWAPAC, and we had a lawyer on our committee, and he wasn't going to see me lurking about in a police station when there was work to be done in the office. So I contacted Thelma, with whom I was still on friendly terms at this point, and she contacted him, and he came along and got me out. The following morning, I attended a hearing and was formally cleared. But asked to explain their actions in court, the police said, "Well, of course these people have a very good intelligence system. They knew we were coming, and *that's* why we couldn't find anything." So in other words, if the police found something we were guilty, and if they *didn't* find anything, we were *still* guilty – only they couldn't prove it. That's the sort of people you were up against.

And where was the fuss kicked up about the way this was handled by all these democratic councillors throughout democratic areas of Wales? Where was the screaming and shouting then? It was notable by its absence. It's terrible that this sort of thing was allowed to go on. I was lucky: I only lost a week's work. But other people, who were also held for a similar period, lost their jobs over it.'

Asked if he harboured any degree of sympathy for the police and the position in which they found themselves, John replied:

'I do appreciate the amount of political pressure placed on the police in those days. Every day there was an article criticising them for their failure to apprehend the *Meibion Glyndŵr* arsonists. And although I wasn't treated badly, I was still aware that the police had a reputation for using force at this time. The ends justified the means, if it meant they got their man. You see, MAC and these other groups did give the police a savage clout on the bloody jaw because of the way they were doing things – and they deserved it. But they've improved. The police today are a different bunch to what they were then. They just seem better trained; more intelligent somehow. And it's good, because the police need to realise that they want friends among the public, and not for the public to view the police as the enemy. But there again, who am I to tell the police what to do?'

Despite his protestations regarding the way in which police undertook their investigation, had Jenkins known the identity of those responsible for the arson protest? 'Well, I wasn't *unaware* of names,' John replied enticingly. 'But, despite what the police have claimed, and probably continue to maintain, *I* certainly wasn't involved in the arson campaign,' he insisted. Did he believe the campaign of burning holiday homes was fruitful? 'Oh, it was *very* effective,' Jenkins retorted, adding:

'It pressed the same buttons that we [MAC] were trying to press – and the general public understood. There wasn't a big scream of uproar when they came out and burnt down over two hundred cottages. You would have thought there would have been. There was a scream in the *Western Mail* of course, but nobody echoed it. And why? Because the Welsh people understood *why* it was happening; and that nothing else would stop these buggers moving in. So it was a success, because it was "understood".

What of the school of thought which suggested the action was ultimately the destruction of Welsh property by Welsh people? Did Jenkins concur with such an appraisal? 'But this *wasn't* Welsh property being attacked,' he asserted. '*That's* why it was destroyed.' He continued:

'You had a cottage which had been lived in by Welsh people for two hundred years, and then the people living there would die. But the young people in the area couldn't afford to buy the cottage, because local prices had been inflated by outsiders buying up similar properties; and so only an outsider could buy it. As a result, no longer could this be seen as "Welsh" property.'

## Cardiff University and John is arrested again

In September 1981, after 'four happy years acquiring the necessary community work experience', John left his post at SWAPAC, and having successfully passed the interview process, enrolled as a mature student at University College of Wales, Cardiff, to study for a Diploma in Sociology and Humanities at the School of Social Work. The degree course was 'very intense', John explained, partly because 'It was a three-year course, condensed into two.' The pressure was intensified, however, owing to the fact that the course was evaluated through continuous assessment, with essays as well as final exams counting towards their final grade – which was a pass or fail – and by way of their being appraised while undertaking field work at hostels across the region which provided support to various client groups. As if this workload were not heavy enough, 'among only a few students on the course', John was further 'selected to do a certificate in Social Work – the qualification required to become a social worker'. Did he enjoy the experience provided by the course? 'Oh, I had a great life. I was a kept man,' Jenkins chuckled, adding:

'I was able to concentrate on my degree in Sociology and Humanities and the Certificate in Social Work, but it was *very* hard work. But yeah, I thoroughly enjoyed it. I was also elected to represent the students throughout the School [of Social Work] to attend the Court of Governors, which is basically the ruling body of the university. The meetings of the Court of Governors were held four times a year, and when the representatives from each School within the university were elected – and so became a member of the Governors – they were officially welcomed by the Chancellor of the University, who at that time was Prince Charles; and who I also understood took his role as Chancellor *very* seriously. But when I came to be welcomed, rather than Charles in the Chancellor's chair, sitting there instead was some Lord or other, I forget now. The Prince was "indisposed", apparently. I took it as a compliment. But there were several people on the Court of Governors quite sympathetic to the idea of MAC, and when the newly elected representatives were welcomed as a body, there was one person cheering and clapping. It was unheard of in an august area like that – but it made me smile.'

But if John's life appeared to be on an upward trajectory, the storm clouds were once again gathering. On 19 March 1980, the first of the thirteen bombings or attempted bombings that were later to feature in the so-called Explosives Trial in November 1983, occurred. Sites across Wales and in Birmingham, Stratford-upon-Avon and London were targeted with incendiary devices of varying sophistication. They included: Conservative Party premises; an Army recruitment office; the home in Crickhowell of the Welsh Secretary of State, Nicholas Edwards; and the offices of nationalised industries considered to have caused economic suffering in Wales. Asked how Lowri reacted as these events unfolded, John replied:

'She and her circle of friends, some of whom she had known at university, were open supporters. I mean, if there was one of these dreadful explosions, they would all start cheering in the pub. But every time an office or whatever was blown up, the police would automatically come to our house the next morning and say, "Would you come with us to assist us with questioning?" To which I'd say, "No, I'm not going to come down and help you." And they'd respond, "Right. You're under arrest," and they'd take me away for a day or two for questioning. They got me for anything. Well, the course I was on was highly concentrated – even missing an hour could be important. It became very frustrating.'

The *Nationwide* piece broadcast on 12 March 1980, for which Jenkins had been interviewed in relation to the arson protest, also contained an interview with Robert Griffiths, national secretary of the Welsh Socialist Republican Movement (WSRM), of which Jenkins was a member. Consequently, the police were firmly convinced that leading figures in the WSRM were implicated in the arson campaign and also in the bombings. When another group, the Workers' Army of the Welsh Republic (WAWR) emerged in October 1982, claiming responsibility for many attacks, the police considered that the personnel in WAWR and the WSRM were inextricably linked – so much so that the same people were involved in the upsurge of Welsh militant activity. It is little wonder, therefore, particularly in view of MAC's apparent participation in the arson protest, that John

Jenkins was deemed a principal target in the police investigation. Into this already inflammatory situation entered Dafydd Ladd.

On 30 June 1982, just one week into a 'very informative field-work' placement at Dyfrig House, a home for recovering alcoholics in Cardiff, John was arrested again. Taken to Rumney Police Station, he was held 'illegally' – Jenkins maintains – 'for the next five days.' It was later alleged at the so-called Explosives Trial that on 12 May 1982, John provided Dafydd Ladd with the address of a 'safe' house in Cardiff. Asked how he knew Dafydd Ladd and to throw light on how he became embroiled in the saga, John replied:

> 'We met because he was imprisoned at Albany when I was there. We got on OK. We chatted to some extent during the exercise period, but we stood on different political platforms. Ladd was involved with the Angry Brigade, which was not a national body like MAC but a class-based body, which is a different thing altogether from what I believed in. I mean, the Angry Brigade's idea of action was to scratch the side of a Rolls Royce! It certainly wasn't mine. And Dafydd Ladd was wanted by the police, because he was considered to be involved in this renewed bombing campaign – which, broadly-speaking, was more a strike at economic targets rather than to further the Welsh nationalist cause per se. Finally, however, after a period on the run, Ladd was arrested on 7 June in London and brought to Wales for questioning. Two weeks later I was arrested.'

Asked how the police interviews developed, Jenkins responded:

> 'The police were trying to establish a link between me and these recent arson and bomb attacks *and* between me and Dafydd Ladd. Furthermore, the police remained adamant that I was at the forefront of a political movement which originated in some foreign land, or that I'd received – and continued to receive – technical instruction from the IRA. I denied it, of course, because neither scenario was true, but they said to me, "So, when do you have a chat [with the IRA]?" I said, "We only spoke when I was in prison. Look, *you* put me in prison, *you* put me among these people, so naturally I was going to talk to them." And they just stared back at me, astounded. "Talking to the IRA?" I said, "Yes, why not? They were in prison the same as I was, for the same reasons. But I was *never* aided and abetted by a foreign political power, and there has been *no* contact between me and members of the IRA since I was released from Albany."

But they just refused to listen. "Oh, we know all about it," they said. "Well, if you know all about it," I said, "you know more than I do." But they'd keep on: "No, no, we can't accept that." It was ludicrous.

What didn't help, though, was that despite my university workload, I'd also been busy putting together a republican marching band – which proved successful and did exactly what it said on the tin: it was a band which marched to military music during parades. But the police thought it was the same sort of thing as in Wrexham, with people in the band working with me. Yet it was nothing of the sort. But the police then said, "Have you been approached by people and asked to undertake further militant action?" And I answered honestly, "Yes, I have. But I've ignored them. I am not incognito anymore – you know who I am! Besides, these people who have approached me and suggested that I get involved in such things were unknown to me. They could have been Special Branch, for all I know!"

So how was the matter of his arrest resolved?

'Well because my university studies were so concentrated, I was desperate to get back. Moreover, I knew that because of my being arrested so much, they [the university authorities] were just waiting for an excuse to chuck me off the course. They couldn't, because my work was excellent, but this would have really done it. And so as the days went by, I was becoming increasingly anxious. So in the end, as it became clear that the police were not going to release me, I said to my solicitor, "Look, I *have* to get back to university – can you give me some indication of what I can tell them that will get me out of here, but will not have a long-term detrimental effect on me?" And he said, "Yes, just tell the police that you gave Ladd an address to go to. That will get them off your back and you'll be out of here in no time; and there'll be no ill effect on you at all." And so I told the police that I gave Ladd an address to go to, on the advice of my lawyer. But despite what I told the police – and what's been written since – it wasn't true. There had been *no* contact between me and Dafydd Ladd since we were both imprisoned at Albany. *None* whatsoever. But in the short-term, although I was bailed to return, at least it got me out of there.

The police then returned me home from Rumney nick and I went straight back to the university. But I'd made up my mind that enough was enough. I thought, "to hell with this". You see, thankfully, when I returned to Dyfrig House the following day, the owner was sympathetic

275

and said to me, "Luckily I got to know *you* before I knew who you were. If I'd known about your past first, you wouldn't have been allowed inside the place." He then said, by way of advice, "Make sure, wherever you go [to work], that they get to know *you* before they learn of your past. You won't get anywhere if they don't get to know *you* first." I'm pretty sure the police had already contacted other managers too.[186] So I thought, "Right, I need to distance myself; I'm sick of these people poking their noses in. I can continue my studies through submitting essays as I have been doing, and I can apply to work at an appropriate location in order to receive the required practical experience." And this is what I did. Within days of being released, I applied for a post as a trainee social worker with Westminster City Council. And a few weeks later, having got the job, I moved to London.'

How did Lowri respond to these developments? 'Although we decided to continue our relationship, she understood my reasons for leaving,' John reflected, adding:

'When I was arrested, Lowri was *also* taken in for questioning – and they held her for twelve and a half hours. They questioned her about my alleged involvement in this bombing and arson business. They treated her alright, but like her mother, she hated the police. Anyway, they had nothing on me, so they had to let her go.'

## London – and John returns to prison

John spent the next 17 months working as a social worker in Victoria, an experience he 'thoroughly enjoyed – particularly after both graduating and becoming a qualified social worker in summer 1983', while living alone in a flat behind Victoria station. Having been charged in relation to Dafydd Ladd with 'intending to impede the apprehension or prosecution of someone [alleged by police] to have been in possession of explosive substances for an unlawful object', he was also travelling back and forth to Cardiff between July and November 1982 to attend preliminary hearings at the city's Stipendiary Magistrates Court. Asked how his employer, Westminster Council, reacted to these somewhat regular departures, John revealed that they 'were not bothered,' as they considered the court hearings he attended 'had nothing to do with the high standard of my social work, which was real rough-edge stuff, working with acute schizophrenics who'd been brought in off the streets.' Nevertheless, John added, 'The court case did drag on.' Did it play on his mind? 'Not really,' Jenkins replied blithely. 'I'd be bailed to reattend on a surety of £5,000 – which Lowri stood for – and once I'd returned to London, I'd sort of forget about it until the next court hearing.'[187] It's an interesting reaction, because it appears that in confessing to both providing Dafydd Ladd the address of a safe house to go to *and* in appearing on *Nationwide* speaking favourably about the arson campaign, John had placed himself in an extremely precarious position.

If John came to believe he was a 'bloody fool' in implicating himself – albeit acting on the legal advice of his solicitor – in relation to Dafydd Ladd, what had prompted him to speak in such self-incriminatory terms on *Nationwide*? Might there have existed within John a subconscious, even egotistical attempt to indicate his continuing involvement in an ongoing Welsh militant struggle? Was he fanning the flames of his notoriety and prestige? Or was he trying to convey the seriousness of the situation, while nonetheless adopting a detached, if informed, position? Whatever Jenkins' reasoning, such utterances were never going to endear him to the authorities.[188] On 14 November 1983, to audible gasps of surprise from the public gallery at Cardiff Crown Court, Mr Justice Farquharson sentenced Jenkins to a comparatively harsh term of two years' imprisonment as a Section B offender.[189] Was he surprised by the sentence? 'In one way, perhaps,' John responded, continuing:

'The night before the final court hearing, my solicitor, Steven Hopkins, went to a function during which he met Tasker Watkins, who was a senior presiding judge by this point, and he was assured by Mr Watkins that my sentence would *not* be custodial. So the following morning, Hopkins telephoned me at Lowri's and passed on the message, to allay any fears and worries. So, expecting a fine, I didn't even take a bag of clothes and toiletries with me. But I stood up in the dock and the judge says, "Two years." I didn't fall back. I wasn't surprised, because nothing the British legal establishment does would surprise me. I know it all works hand in glove and that these matters are decided long before anyone stands trial. So I was under no illusions in expecting justice from them. I mean if I had, I'd have been very disappointed. But it was laughable. In Victoria I was doing a *very* useful job, and they throw me in prison and give me two years for that!'

John was immediately taken to HM Prison Cardiff, from which, on 23 December, he was transferred to the 'grim and absolutely freezing' HM Prison Dartmoor. During Jenkins' first period of incarceration, he survived, and indeed prospered, through immersing himself in art and education *and* because of an entrenched belief in the legitimacy of the MAC protest. By contrast, his second period of imprisonment was initially endured beneath a dark and depressing cloud of psychological discontent. Three developments, however, ensured that the ordeal later became 'bearable'. Prompted to outline his position at this juncture, John replied:

'I felt increasingly disconsolate. I mean, as a Section B prisoner, I didn't have any "minders" this time – they weren't needed – and I noticed immediately how much more courteous the officers were. It was "would you mind", rather than "do this", when addressing those under Section B. But still, there was no work for a prisoner like me to do. Then one day, there was a knock on my cell door and in walked the Prison Governor. "As you are no doubt aware," he said, "we have a prison farm where we grow our own food; and the trouble is, no one has looked at the books for about ten years. Seeds and growth materials and so on have been purchased, and produce bought and sold, but we've lost track of the amounts and what's needed. All we have is a mountain of receipts. Would you like a job, sorting it out and bringing it all up to date?" Well, of course, I jumped at the chance! God knows, it took a while, but eventually I got all the farm books and accounts in order. I was then given a job looking after the farm dogs – there were seven or eight of them. There was one who, I suspect, had been ill-treated by one of the officers, because she was very frightened of him – well, and me to start with, but through stroking and fussing her and feeding her and talking to her, after a few weeks she began to trust me. We became firm friends – but the officer didn't like it. And finally, I was given a job as a teacher's aide, because some inmates were slower than others at grasping mathematical ideas and formulas during lessons. I'm hopeless at Maths, but I knew enough to able to walk around the tables and sort out their problems by explaining and simplifying things. All three jobs made my time at Dartmoor much more enjoyable. In fact, when I left, a couple of the inmates were in tears, saying how much they were going to miss having a decent chat with somebody. Also, they were going to miss my help, as they'd receive official letters which they couldn't understand, so I'd "translate" the jargon for them. I was more used to the bureaucracy of life than they were... but such is life, and I was relocated.'

## John is released from prison; Lowri and John's relationship ends and John 'moves on'

In January 1985, John was transferred to HM Prison The Verne, a Category C prison located within the historic Verne Citadel on the Isle of Portland in Dorset. From there, on 15 March, Jenkins was released. He returned to live with Lowri in Cardiff. It soon became apparent, however, that their relationship had run its course. Asked what instigated their decision to part, John declared ponderously:

'It was probably because I'd spent so much time in prison, both before and after meeting Lowri. I wasn't used to talking to people, for a start – not about anything that meant anything to me. Even now I find it difficult to talk about things. But Lowri – as a way, I think, of trying to establish a commitment between us – would want to discuss matters concerning MAC. She saw it as an act or a demonstration of trust on my part. Not names, exactly; just in general terms. It could be that she was just curious about how it seemed so impenetrable. So she'd ask me about it, but I was in no position to discuss MAC. It was policy that I remain silent... She should have realised that my adherence to the cause did not threaten my adherence to her. But it got to the point where the easiest thing [to do] was to walk away. But she's a good girl, Lowri – a lovely, bright and attractive woman. And although we enjoyed a strong relationship, we both realised that it wasn't going to work out. I mean, we'd already drifted apart. While I was in prison, Lowri had other male friends, and that was fine. I encouraged it. So we broke it off... But Lowri then sold the house she'd bought in Canton and offered to give me half the money, just as way of saying goodbye and to help me along. But I declined the offer. I didn't think it was appropriate to accept, but it was such a generous and kind gesture – it just shows what kind of woman she is.'

In June 1985, having applied for the post within weeks of his release from prison, John moved to Brighton; where, with accommodation provided with the position, he was appointed the deputy manager of a social housing project for Brighton Housing Trust, catering for clients with mental health and alcohol issues. In March 1986, John left Brighton after being appointed Officer in Charge of a housing project in London's Waterloo district, which supported clients with various physical disabilities. Living in a flat in Lewisham, John travelled to and from work via the tube. To his surprise,

John was reacquainted – albeit reservedly – with an old prison companion: the former Great Train Robber 'Buster' Edwards. Jenkins later threw light on what unfolded. 'I'd see Buster as I walked to work,' John explained.

'He had a flower stall outside Waterloo train station. He recognised me, in the sense that we acknowledged one another. We'd exchange curt but respectful nods, but nothing was ever said. It was the last bloody thing I wanted, to be in *any* way associated with someone I'd been in prison with. Had we been seen chatting, it would quickly have gone wrong were he implicated in any further criminality. I'm sure neither of us would have wanted any sort of publicity, so we kept it simple. A few years later, I learned that he'd hanged himself. He was alright, Buster.'

## Brent Mind and Barking – and John returns 'home'

John remained in the post at Waterloo for twelve months, leaving in March 1987. It was, he revealed, 'too central, with far too many people roaming around'. It was a situation which left him feeling 'uneasy'. At this juncture, John moved to Cricklewood and worked for 'various agencies'; most notably in Islington, where Jenkins met his former prison 'minders', John Elliot and Norman Bassett. John enjoyed 'quite regular contact' with Bassett, who lived and worked in the borough. In autumn 1987, John was appointed a social worker at Brent Mind. Working once more alongside schizophrenics, it was, John declared, 'much more in my preferred line of work and the sort of place I was looking for'. John remained 'happily in the post' for seven years. Two years into the position, having reasoned that if people found him 'approachable and easy to talk to, it was a gift he could use to help others', Jenkins decided to train as a counsellor. In 1990, John was awarded the last of his three higher education qualifications, when having followed a three-year study programme, he was awarded a Diploma in Counselling and Supervision. It was a qualification achieved alongside his full-time social work commitments. This graduation ceremony Jenkins also didn't attend. Nonetheless, John soon put his skills to good use. 'I had the privilege of building up a counselling service,' he remarked; adding:

'I concluded, after years working in mental health, that the problem schizophrenics faced was there was nobody to talk to, like trained counsellors. When I arrived at Brent Mind, the figure was one coordinator and two counsellors. When I left, it was one coordinator and sixty counsellors. It was the biggest counselling service in London and it never cost the NHS a penny. It was all done by word of mouth. I would approach a counsellor, explain what I was trying to establish, and they would offer their services for free. It was a great success. And within a year of me leaving, they closed it down. Two years later, the results of a public survey revealed that what was needed in the mental health field was counsellors! Oddly enough, some of those receiving counselling were prison officers from Wormwood Scrubs. They'd come in and discuss the pressures they felt. The main one centred on the fact that within prison, they were treated like a god, but at home, they were just "Dad". People were no longer deferential – in fact, sometimes they were the opposite, so there often existed this discrepancy between their expectations and what confronted them in "real" life. The situation required an ability to compartmentalise one's feelings, and to be two different people, depending on the situation. And for some officers, this emotional conflict caused psychological problems.'

In July 1994, 'having decided to seek pastures new', John was appointed as a social worker for Barking and Dagenham Council. Eighteen months into the post, with John's line-manager 'talking about promotion', the head of Social Services received a telephone call from the police. Unable to provide information regarding John's imprisonments, as it was against the law to do so, the police nevertheless tantalisingly declared, 'You have a man working for you: John Jenkins. If only you knew what he was.' When John returned from annual leave the following week, he was asked to attend a meeting with the head of Social Services and members of the Human Resources Department. Jenkins was provided an ultimatum: that he either reveal the details of his past, or leave the council's employment. John refused to discuss the matter. Social Services, he maintained, 'was not an arm of the state', and so it was not 'obligated to do the work of the police'. Having been provided an opportunity to contest the council's ultimatum by Human Resources, Jenkins elected to resign from his post instead. He later reflected with disdain and sadness:

'Even as late as 1996, and against strict Home Office regulations, the police were hounding me this way. Perhaps I should have said that it was to do with MAC. They [council employees] may well have laughed it off. But I thought, "Why should I be expected to discuss my politics with anyone?" The worst thing is, those who spoke to me from the council probably thought it was something to do with kids or something – you know.'

It is a feature of the employment process today – notably when a prospective employee applies for a position involving children or vulnerable adults – for the employer to check the criminal record of the applicant through the Disclosure and Barring Service (DBS). Had such a vetting procedure been in place when John was taken on by Barking and Dagenham Council, details of his criminal past would, unquestionably, have been provided. Nonetheless, John's allegations concerning the police – that they contacted his employer and alluded to historic and unspecified misdemeanours – highlight a questionable, if not disturbing, pattern.

But if John's life had reached an unenviable impasse, the sun soon reappeared from behind the clouds. In 1996, in an attempt to address the city's housing shortage, the Greater London Authority introduced the 'Construction and Regeneration' programme. This stipulated that a tenant would receive a maximum of £16,000 – the amount received being dependant on where in London the rental property was located – if they left the greater London area and relocated to a region outside of the city. The idea was hatched, John revealed, as 'The London authority realised it was cheaper to redevelop property than to build new houses.' At this point, John was renting a property in Cricklewood through a sub-letting agency called Network – and some properties in the company's portfolio were eligible for the 'Construction and Regeneration' scheme. A tenant in another Network property in Cricklewood – which, like John's rented accommodation, was eligible for the programme – was a former social work client of John's called Peter Cridland. Spending increasing time together socially, John and Peter decided to leave their flats in Cricklewood and take advantage of the 'Construction and Regeneration' scheme. In the summer of 1996, while undertaking agency social work throughout north London, John – with the understanding that Peter would move to the property also – began the process of purchasing a house in the Wrexham area.

On 21 October 1996, ten years after her husband Tom had passed away at the home the couple had shared for many years, 94-year-old Minerva Jenkins died at the Hill View Care Home in Aberbargoed.[190] Throughout the six months that Minerva was a resident, receiving palliative support,

John lived in London and was a model of filial loyalty, calling in to see her 'nearly every weekend'. Three days after Minerva passed away, on a dark afternoon with 'the rain beating down', John and Keith laid their much-loved and respected mother to rest at Gelligaer church. It is a short walk from the family's former home in Penybryn.

A month later, in November 1996, John Jenkins and Peter Cridland moved to Johnstown, a suburb south of Wrexham. With houses in the area typically reaching £40,000 at the time, the move to Bryn Avenue was funded through Peter and John having pooled their respective £16,000s from the GLA and John's savings; and because they were offered 'a good deal on the purchase of the property' by the seller, owing to the 'long friendship' she and John had shared.

John had always intended to return to the Wrexham area. It was where, during the 1960s, he experienced 'the most eventful period' of his notable and bustling life. Initially, on moving to Johnstown, John rented out rooms to men who, with his support, were readjusting to life in the wider community after being discharged from mental health facilities. However, some ten years ago, in his mid-70s, John decided to end the practice. Since retiring, having spent years working at the coalface of social care's most demanding issues, John has enjoyed a sedentary lifestyle. He has spent his time writing; listening to the radio; reading books, including biographies of revolutionary figures such as Che Guevara and Ho Chin Min; and participating in the occasional media project – especially around the time of significant anniversaries. For these television appearances, Jenkins has invariably been dressed in his customary black – a symbol of his wilful individuality. Increasingly in recent years, John has attended the funerals of former MAC activists and associates; and the funerals of those who earned his respect through their endeavours to further the Welsh nationalist cause.

On arriving at John's home, a visitor's attention was drawn to the CCTV camera which scanned the front door from its position above. John refused to purchase a computer, from concern that the authorities would 'plant incriminating evidence'. It is not a fear he considered to be unfounded, because on picking up the telephone receiver, he 'quite often heard funny little clicks and noises' on the telephone line. Such 'peculiar sounds', which Jenkins believes 'really shouldn't be there', have led him to deduce that despite his advancing years, he is still 'on the radar' of the state. He adds sardonically, 'They will heave a big sigh of relief when I am finally lowered into the ground.'

In the summer of 2017, after sustaining a broken hip in a fall at his home, John was admitted to hospital. Having largely regained his health, he was transferred to a nursing home, where he resides today. Prior to these developments, John 'rarely stepped inside a place of worship', and yet, as he has throughout his life, John retains his faith, following what he calls 'a Christianity of private contemplation and spiritual reflection'.

# Conclusion

On meeting John Jenkins, he is a pleasant if somewhat daunting figure. He has light blue eyes which pierce deeply, as if probing for clues as to motives and reliability. This cautious approach is maintained until, having eventually gained his confidence, John reveals a kind and considerate personality. Even if some of his utterances can *perhaps* be dismissed as sophistry; if occasionally his reasoning and justification is uncomfortable or peppered with colourful platitudes; even if some answers – particularly during early discussions – appear both rehearsed and rehashed; when John is convinced of your sincerity and you have earned his trust, he is gracious and unassuming and displays an honesty, intelligence and vulnerability which is as impressive as it is endearing.

The authorities were caught blind by John Jenkins; and at the age of 86, John is still persuaded by the justice of his cause. And why, perhaps, should he not be? But while his guilt is undeniable, what factors underpinned his motives in leading *Mudiad Amddiffyn Cymru* in a campaign of unparalleled militant resistance in the name of Welsh political freedom? How significant were the educational, cultural, spiritual, political and sexual influences on Jenkins' behaviour? Because it is only with a full appreciation of these effects that the life of John Jenkins can best be summarised and evaluated.

It is surely time that such an appraisal was attempted, because as MAC has been subject to rather fleeting inclusion within the pages of historical analysis, so too has John Jenkins attracted scant and speculative attention. Little consideration has been given to trying to understand *why* John Jenkins did what he did.

## The significance of John's early years – heredity and environment

If it is agreed that the factors and experiences which shape an adult can be found in their childhood and early adolescence,[191] what can be said of John Barnard Jenkins? Certainly, the significance of 'nature and nurture' on an individual's emotional development is not lost on someone as contemplative as John, who speaking in 2018, stated his belief that:

> 'The people around you – your family, neighbours and peer group – and everything that happens to you in your first 10 to 15 years determines both the course of your life and how you subsequently respond to events.'

Blessed with a prodigious memory, a precocious imagination and seeming older than his years, John's formative period comprised trekking over the hills to visit historical and/or religious sites, reading books about geography and adventure, watching Pathé news at the cinema, attending religious services and listening to Welsh choral music on the radio. Such were the pleasures of a sensitive, inquisitive and intelligent lad in Wales in the 1930s and 1940s. Nonetheless, while all these leisure pursuits were significant, of particular importance is Capel Gwladys. Located on the windswept moor above Gelligaer, Capel Gwladys proved a place of beguiling mystique and sanctuary for John. Crucially, it also provided him – owing to the question of when the site was founded – with the first indication that history is written by the victors and can be manipulated for a political objective.[192] 'Ah, there it is,' John remarked wistfully in 2019, on seeing photographs of Capel Gwladys – before adding sardonically, alluding to the site's importance in influencing his ultimate decision to lead MAC, 'That cross cost the state £7 million!'

## John's relationship with his mother, Minerva

It is clear from discussions with John that he held his mother in strong affection. What is notable is their apparent and shared ability to each be trusted with the concerns of others and to empathise and impart advice. But asked to reflect on the degree to which his mother's character formulated and influenced his *own* thoughts and personality, John was cautious. 'She formulated my approach to things, but not my thoughts themselves,' he asserted. 'She didn't tell me to do this, or to do that. It was her general approach to things that was formidable.' Asked to elaborate, Jenkins continued:

'Well, I think the mother/son relationship is very strong, and it enables your mother to pass on certain aspects of her character which may not always be considered a good thing. What I mean is, you may inherit from your mother a belief in standing up and taking action, even if it is morally the correct thing to do, but it means breaking the law. Because that is what counts in the end: apparently, it is *legality* which is the measure of morality. That's the way it is. That's not the way it *should* be, but that's the way it is. But my mother didn't believe that – and neither do I.'

So, having instilled in John throughout his childhood and formative years a determination to stand and be counted during trying or difficult times in life, did he and his mother enjoy an emotionally intimate relationship in adult life? 'Well, I was certainly closer to my mother than my father,' he explained, continuing:

'But I was more upset when my father died than when my mother died, oddly enough. It wasn't anything to do with harbouring any sense of anger or frustration – in that she hadn't told me any of the details about who my [birth] father was, or the circumstances surrounding it. So I don't really know why I felt greater sadness when my father passed away than when my mother died. I held him in high regard, of course. He was a hard-working, nice man. But one thing happened during his funeral. The house was full of grieving, and I just broke down and started sobbing. I just couldn't take any more – and in that moment I reverted back to being a child. And I went straight to my mother and she enfolded me in her arms and treated me, more or less, as an infant. And it helped. I was ensconced in my mother's arms. I needed her, and she responded. I broke down only because of the grieving for my father. Not because of anything that had happened in MAC... She hadn't seen me cry since I was a boy. But of course, when my mother died, I had no one to turn to. So perhaps that's why I was able to grieve [more openly] when my father died.'

## 'The fanatic is always concealing a secret doubt' – John le Carré

But what of John's illegitimacy? Despite their apparent closeness, John has always denied feeling deceived by his mother's failure to throw light on the identity of his father, or the details surrounding his conception. Nonetheless, was he not tempted to raise the matter when he went to live with his parents following his release from prison in July 1976? After all, with his mother aged 72 and John aged 43, they were both adults. 'No,' Jenkins insisted.

> 'I had always accepted things as they were, so there was no need for me to feel that things were, or had been, hidden from me. Not then, nor at any time. It had never occurred to me as a child either to ask, or that anything was not what it seemed. Because there were never any arguments between my parents over who was what, and so on, and I never had a word from any of my mother's brothers and sisters about her past. And because of that, I accepted things as they were.'

That said, John later conceded:

> 'I do remember there being some tension between my mother and father around the time I was adopted, when I was aged 10. I think there was a spat or two between them over the terms of my adoption... I think she was pushing him a bit too hard. But I do know that she never forgave Hughie, my father's brother. She hated him. I think he tried to talk my father out of it. I think it was brought home to him that I wasn't of his blood. Whatever was said, it upset my mother and she never forgot it. When my father's father died, she refused to allow Hughie to the wake, which – after the funeral service – was held in our house. I remember him lurking around outside, wanting to come in because it was his father's funeral and my mother saying, "No. He is *not* coming in here."'

Does Jenkins, nevertheless, now wish he *had* asked his mother the circumstances surrounding his conception? Following a pause, John stated, 'No. I had no reason to ask her. I was happy the way I was.' But surely discovering that he was illegitimate when aged 10, and indeed, the manner in which he realised the fact, must have impacted on his emotional well-being? In fact, it is surely plausible that such a revelation led to feelings of repressed confusion and frustration, even anger? Finally, in the winter of 2018, John declared:

'Did discovering that I was illegitimate have an impact on me? Well, I may have suppressed this ever since. But OK – it came as a hell of a shock. And so I accept that it must have affected my emotional outlook. And it *might*, psychologically-speaking, be why I joined MAC – because it's important to remember that I didn't invent MAC: it was already there in some shape or other. But maybe I was drawn to join it, at least in part, because I didn't like being treated like a backward peasant, which is how I felt that we [Welsh] were being treated by the authorities; the Labour Party in particular. Perhaps, and I know that I'm sticking my neck out here, but perhaps I was born into the wrong class. I'm told that this does happen, and very often people fight to get out of the class they were born into. They fight to leave it behind. But I didn't want to fight to leave my class behind – I am *rooted* in my history. All I wanted was fair play. That's all. But I don't think I ever got it.'

Might the question of class and the sense of not quite belonging within one's surroundings be in response to his biological background? Having pondered his reply, John eventually declared:

'The identity of my biological father means nothing to me. Was he the wayward son of this wealthy Dodington family? I have no idea. Do I care? Not really. What's a name after all. It wasn't Churchill, I'm sure of that! I think it was Underhill, or Underwood. It certainly wasn't a name that I grew up hearing. Besides, if it was Dodington, they sound like *nouveau riche* from Cardiff. God help us. Or perhaps, as I recall from the address on this adoption letter, he was from Bournemouth. Of all bloody places! Although that doesn't necessarily mean he was English. That said, I don't give a damn what he was, or what he wasn't. He must have been someone with income, if he paid for my upkeep until I was aged 10. But he didn't give a damn what I was like, so why should I give a damn what he was like? But I have no knowledge other than that [the maintenance payments]. I don't remember my mother ever discussing it or taking me to meet him. But my mother was a strong woman and so she may have said [to him], "Just keep paying and bugger off." All I know is: my mother's friends and close siblings stuck by her. And if your friends stick by you, then you're alright.'

But what of the theory that he is likely the product of two intellectually able people? 'I've been told that I'm intelligent,' John replied. 'So, I suppose I might be the result of two bright people. But,' he continued:

'I reject the idea that this is because my biological father, if he *was* from a wealthy background, may have been educated at a public school. That would be to confuse intelligence with someone educated at a public school. Most of them I've come across are bloody idiots! No, it doesn't always work like that: this idea of intelligence being hereditary. Has my upbringing, in all it entailed, impacted on my adult character? Well, possibly. I am both confident and vulnerable. Maybe that's a legacy of what I experienced. But then again, who isn't? So, there you have it: I was born illegitimate. Mind you, they've been calling me a bastard for years. They were quite right there!'

What of Minerva's own upbringing? Might this throw light on the extent to which the relationship with her father deteriorated so dramatically when she became pregnant with John? 'There isn't much for me to go on, really,' John conceded, before stating:

'There was never any mention of him, or my grandmother, when I was growing up... Well, once or twice my mother alluded to the fact that he was a bit of a drunkard – and renowned for it. A noted boozer in Aberfan. Now, that takes a bit of bloody doing! But she didn't criticise or run him down, or anything like that... I remember coming back on the bus to Penybryn some years later, and I struck up a conversation with a rather elderly woman sitting next me. She was a native of Aberfan and when I told her that I was from Aberfan as well, and mentioned my mother and the Barnard family by name, her reception more than indicated that the respectable folk of Aberfan weren't very keen on my family. That ended the conversation. I thought, "Oh, nice." I mean, she was a respectable woman! You can't expect her to consort with people like this, who go out drinking on a Saturday night! Whoever heard of people drinking on a Sunday? Good God! Her response may have been due to his drinking. But of course, in those days, you only had to leave the garden gate open and the whole street was in uproar! So, you know, it didn't take much to get people going back then. I think this woman knew who my mother was, and that she had me out of wedlock. She never said it, but I think she knew. She was disgusted about something! I have no idea if my mother went to either my grandfather's or my grandmother's funeral. I don't remember there being any photographs of family, or their keepsakes, around the house. But there again, my mother wasn't one for photographs of any description... My brother used to keep them all. I don't think my parents' wedding photo was on display. I don't recall it.'

John's testimony provides a fascinating insight into Minerva's mindset. On the strength of such information, it is not unreasonable to speculate that Minerva's inability to forgive and forget when crossed derived from being the daughter of a renowned drinker who later rejected her when she became pregnant with John. But whatever her thoughts on being ostracised by her own parents, Minerva's feelings for John remained untarnished following his arrest and conviction for being involved in the MAC protest. Speaking just weeks before he passed away in May 2017, John's brother Keith revealed how their mother had reacted to John being arrested and sentenced. 'Our mother,' Keith declared proudly, 'stood by John.' He continued:

'My father would have no idea what was going on – not politically, like that. He had no understanding of that sort of thing. But my mother was behind John, yeah. She had no idea that he was involved in MAC at the time. It was only when John was sent to prison that she became aware of it, but it made no difference to how she felt about him.'

So what can be said about John's childhood? Despite all disclosures, John remains unequivocal that his childhood was 'idyllic'. It was, he maintains, not constrained in any negative way. Rather, he was allowed – and indeed encouraged – to roam and explore his literal, cultural, creative and emotional environments. When later discussing the matter, John declared:

'It was my mother, you see, who encouraged me to join the kazoo junior marching band in Penybryn, and it proved a godsend. I was, I suppose, seen as well-liked and approachable in Bargoed Grammar, but none of my friends from primary school went up to the Grammar School. So on getting back home at five o'clock, or whatever it was, I had no friends to go and play with. We no longer had anything much in common. So with my mother's support, I joined the marching band. Playing kazoo to begin with, but eventually learning to play the drums with them.'

John can occasionally appear wistful when discussing the past, especially when recounting the period before he left the family home at Penybryn. Yet from the outset, it appears that John felt cared for and protected. It was within this nurturing, cosseted and invulnerable environment that John derived a love for the Welsh language: hearing it before his much-loved brother Keith was born. But despite John's subsequent admissions concerning the degree to which the discovery that he was illegitimate impacted upon him, there are factors which require consideration when evaluating Jenkins' rigid assessment that his childhood was 'idyllic'. It is important to note that John rationalises this belief as a result of his professional career as a social worker and counsellor *and* having spoken to friends and confidants regarding their own experiences. Consequently, is it not unreasonable to concur with John that his childhood and upbringing was 'happy', and indeed, 'idyllic'? Minerva, it would seem, encouraged her sons' passions and ambitions and supported both John and Keith in all their endeavours. As for the berated and beleaguered Tom, he seems to have been happy with his lot, and why, perhaps, should he not have been? After all, Minerva, through her consistent and steady approach, established a safe and affirming home environment; one in which all inhabitants felt secure and loved and knew where they stood.

## John's spirituality and relationship with the Chapel

As a young man, John readily engaged with Chapel society. But for all the uplifting reassurance provided by being part of an impassioned congregation, the questioning adolescent soon became uneasy about what he discerned to be the 'cherry picking' approach of the established Chapel and Church. Indeed, its 'prescribed guilt' and distorted and hypocritical dissemination of the 'true' Christian message affronted John, leaving him irked and disconsolate. But in view of John's Christian convictions and his later connection to MAC, can any parallel be drawn between the historical Jesus Christ, a radical and revolutionary figure, and Jenkins' subconscious reasoning – particularly in view of accusatory comment that Jenkins is inclined towards a messianic disposition? 'I really don't think that I've ever considered any such link,' John replied, somewhat surprised, before adding thoughtfully:

'Only in one way. And that was the business of Jesus angrily entering the temple and actually physically whipping the money lenders and throwing them out, because the temple was a place of worship. That's the only connection I can make, because I felt that the Government had *also* overstepped the mark; in fact, many times. And having done so, that they should expect to pay the price. But apart from that, I can see very little to compare what I was doing and what the historical Jesus did. No... I was simply following the line of traditionalists who also rebelled against an existing situation... Besides, very little else of what Jesus said made any sort of *political* sense. You know: "love your enemy"; "pray for those who abuse you". That's all very nice and lovely and it sounds wonderful in church. But try it! It's not always practical or realistic.'

The difficulty that John Jenkins has experienced with being expected to extend the hand of Christian friendship to those who he feels have crossed him is certainly something which most – at some time or other – have surely wrestled with. But did Jenkins ever regard the established Welsh Church or Chapel as a potential ally in MAC's struggle to ensure that external pressure influenced central government's policy decisions? 'I *was* trying to create some sort of relationship between ourselves and Christians, and any other organisation which felt the same way we did,' John agreed, adding:

'But it was very difficult, because politics kept coming into it all the time. And so we were attacked, as everybody seemed to be saying: "Well, of course – you use violence, don't you?" Well, I am at a loss to work out what they were trying to say. Because how can you get *anywhere* without any sort of violence? You can't!'

Yet if there are some who believe that John Jenkins is a presuppositional Christian who is intent on learning and appreciating a broad-church outlook on life, there are others who feel, perhaps understandably, that for all John's pronouncements of being deeply imbued with Christian doctrine, his actions departed from Christian principles when orchestrating the audacious MAC offensive. After all, Christianity renounces violence; with Christians expected to 'turn the other cheek' and venerate the sacred life of the individual. Why? Because man is created in God's image. A steadfast acceptance of Christian dogma leaves many observers of the MAC campaign struggling to endorse its militant protest. Because even if it is accepted that MAC never *intended* to harm or kill anyone, injuries and deaths – as suffered one way or another – were perhaps inevitable. Furthermore, while John should be applauded for the manner in which he 'reined in' those MAC activists intent on undertaking more drastic action, both Alders' courtroom testimony highlighting Jenkins' escalating belief in a militant agenda *and* John's subsequent admission that he *would* have sanctioned the assassination of Prince Charles had it provided MAC a strategic advantage in its battle to attain political independence for Wales, present a disturbing truth.

But if Jenkins' reasoning is unpalatable for many spectators, it is nonetheless true that he has retained throughout his life the emotional intensity – and uncertainty – of spiritual faith. There is also an enduring honesty to Jenkins' Christian observance, as demonstrated when he declined to receive the Holy Sacrament in prison, on the grounds that he may be called to act once again in the defence of Wales. And such an evaluation ensures a quandary: is John Jenkins a dark, deviant and sanctimonious egotist, or a deeply spiritual, honourable, decent, if pragmatic man? Whatever the truth, John Jenkins remains convinced of the legitimacy of the campaign of protest which he so effectively led and feels no compulsion to atone for his sins. Yet this begs a final question: what of John's cautious disclosure that along with the coincidences and opportunities both leading up to and during the campaign, there seemed to exist a spiritual dimension to his orchestration of the MAC offensive? Who can know? But however outlandish the claim might seem, John Jenkins' belief that there existed some degree of spiritual guidance or governance *surely* warrants consideration?

## John's political flowering – and Plaid Cymru's 'toothless appeasement'

The younger man, brimming with energy, ideas and passion, is perhaps no more. Additionally, John's tendency to drift into obstinacy has waned somewhat. But aged 86, John Jenkins is as astute, shrewd and informed as a person half his age when discussing life in all its rich colour. Still prone to being irritable and impatient – particularly when misunderstood or misinterpreted – Jenkins nonetheless retains the ability to speak fluently and forcefully, particularly when the subject turns to politics, which still infuses everything for John. In the winter of 2018, John Jenkins was still harrumphing over British society's fixation with celebrity culture and lack of political engagement, although he recognised that the arrival on the UK political stage of Jeremy Corbyn had altered this to some degree.

Nevertheless, if we accept that psychology often underpins protest; if it is agreed that anger and the need to lash out are rooted in suffering, then the question of Jenkins' political flowering cannot be underestimated. According to the probation report compiled immediately prior to his trial in April 1970, John's 'extreme political views' and 'political grievance' appear to have developed in response to the Aberfan disaster. One person in no doubt as to the importance of the horrifying events at Aberfan to John's political mindset was his wife Thelma. Interviewed for the report, Thelma informed the probation service that her husband was 'a gentle person' who was 'particularly upset' by events at Aberfan. His 'political feelings', she disclosed, had 'dated from that time.'[193] Yet, interestingly, neither Thelma nor the pre-sentencing probation report mentions Tryweryn or Clywedog in relation to John's intensifying political awareness.

But if John's testimony that Tryweryn *was* pivotal to his increasing belief in a militant response is accepted, it should also be highlighted that he was not alone in feeling that Wales was under threat and that the nation's unique cultural identity faced extinction. It was an opinion shared by a significant cross section of the Welsh community during the Tryweryn period. Similarly, it must be noted that the Investiture struck many in Wales as being an extravagant charade *and* somewhat laced with imperial overtones. Yet, importantly, this consternation was expressed by members of the Welsh electorate who were both constitutionally and less-constitutionally minded – most of whom neither joined nor supported *Mudiad Amddiffyn Cymru*.

Asked to sum up his feelings as he watched events unfold over Tryweryn and Clywedog, John Jenkins responded resolutely:

'I felt a sense of humiliation, in that those people who should have been representing us were not only failing in their duty to represent us, they were representing the system which was killing us. Although I accept that Gwynfor Evans was a very nice chap – very wily and a brilliant man in many ways – as President of Plaid Cymru he made a big mistake over Tryweryn. The party's response was a big miscalculation and a missed opportunity – it was backward, unresponsive and insensitive. It was utterly spineless and the party's appeasement led to the birth of both the FWA and MAC... You see, for all Gwynfor Evans' undoubted political talents, he is the only nationalist leader that I can think of who never went to prison – and the reason he never went to prison is that he never did anything to go to prison for. And that hardly makes him a nationalist leader. People have said to me, when critical of MAC and its "direct"' style of political protest, "Ah yes, but the pen is mightier than the sword." Well, the pen that *is* mightier than the sword is the one that signs the death warrants and the cheques! And I know one thing: had I not been in the Army and away in Cyprus and Germany, I would have stopped Tryweryn. Plaid Cymru and Gwynfor might have been unable to stop this valley being flooded, but I would have. The vote to flood the valley might have gone through, but I would have stopped the construction work being done to build the reservoir *and* the inhabitants being forced from their homes. And I would have done it through organising a campaign of militancy!'

But if Tryweryn and Clywedog saw the political scales fall from Jenkins' eyes, resulting in him losing faith in democratic politics, it must also be remembered that it was not Plaid Cymru and the party leadership's adherence to constitutional methods that flooded the valleys. Cwm Tryweryn was submerged by Liverpool Corporation, aided and abetted by an English-dominated Parliament. And this despite the fact that not one of Wales' 36 MPs voted in support of the Bill – a voting pattern which presumably reflected the views of the Welsh electorate. So when the vote to flood Cwm Tryweryn is considered in a UK political context, the decision to back the project was entirely justified constitutionally – even if to John Jenkins, and many others besides, the decision was loaded with colonial entitlement. But what seems to have disconcerted Jenkins still further is that the apparent willingness of Plaid Cymru to ultimately concede the issue only served to highlight the subservience of the Welsh people.

Both the British State and the established Chapel and Church in the UK were part of a wider structure and societal system which John took pride in; and which prior to the events surrounding Tryweryn, Clywedog and Aberfan he resolutely believed in and supported. Each was an organisation in which John had invested considerable emotional and intellectual energy. And yet each, Jenkins felt, in its own distinctive but similar way, let him down. Is it any wonder that the increasingly iconoclastic John Jenkins felt ignored, frustrated and impotent?

But what other 'outside' factors affected John's political reasoning? John's repudiation of Empire is significant, as is his estimation that 'nice people don't form empires and they certainly don't maintain empires'. Particularly enlightening, however, is John's endorsement of the EOKA campaign, which he witnessed when stationed with the British Army in Cyprus. Surely integral to Jenkins' view of militancy – and the manner in which it was exercised by *Mudiad Amddiffyn Cymru* – owes much to fact that EOKA's protest was successfully achieved by a modest number of active fighters.

Yet, while Jenkins' rejection of the British Empire is perhaps understandable, even if he concedes that 'good things were done in terms of the infrastructure it introduced in the regions under its control', his vindication and justification of some attitudes and behaviours is more perplexing. John's rejection of the tactics adopted by members of British Intelligence to ensure the signature of Archbishop Makarios to end the conflict in Cyprus, on the grounds that such tactics were 'underhand', is disconcerting. Surely the most reprehensible aspect of this episode is Archbishop Makarios' alleged sexual proclivity for underage boys? As Jenkins has repeatedly voiced disgust at paedophilia, it leaves his clumsy reasoning that 'what Makarios carried out in the privacy of his own home was his business only' very difficult to comprehend. Yet, however unpalatable, it appears that aged 86, John Jenkins is the product of a less enlightened age: one in which the sexual abuse and exploitation of children and the devastating repercussions routinely suffered by the victims was tragically neither fully appreciated nor understood. It can only be hoped that such crass and ignorant sentiments are consigned to the past.

## John's first love and sexual awakenings

Asked if he had suppressed homosexual tendencies prior to his arrest in Cardiff in 1978, John replied tentatively:

'Well, nothing happened before prison. And even while there, nothing particularly. I mean, you can't do much in prison. It's not the sort of place where they encourage that sort of thing. There were one or two feelers put out. But no, nothing that you could put your finger on and say, "That person is trying to make contact." But I was in Bargoed Grammar School when I first became aware that I had what I now believe were homosexual

297

tendencies. I was struck by one lad, and he and I were the best of friends for the whole time I was in Grammar School, which was about three and a half years. His name was Anthony John Eden – which sounds ridiculous, I know, in view of the politician, but there you are. Well, it's only in the past five or six years that I've come to realise I was in love with him. I didn't realise it before... I do remember that he lived alone with his mother. Anyway, throughout school, he stuck to me like a limpet. He wouldn't let me out of his sight. Although there was never anything in it that was what you would call homosexual. Well, I suppose there was one thing. On one occasion, he asked me to go to the cinema in Bargoed with him. And as we sat there in the darkness, about an hour or so after arriving, his hand reached across to mine. Before I had time to realise what was happening, he took my hand and placed it on his private parts. I sat there, thinking, "What the hell is this?" I just moved my hand away and nothing was ever said about it. And that was the only point of homosexual contact I had with him. My first proper homosexual experience came much, much later.

Anyway, several years after this, I bumped into him on a train. We were both travelling back to the Valleys for the weekend. I had in recent months joined the Army, and he had joined the RAF for his National Service. We began to chat about the time we'd spent at Bargoed Grammar School. He said, "Where did you disappear to? One minute you were there, the next you'd gone." I explained that I'd just had enough and wanted to see more of life, hence my blacksmith's apprenticeship. He also castigated me for not joining in the typical school jollifications; saying that I'd always been a bit of an outsider; a free spirit, who, unlike other pupils, had never bothered with, or been impressed by, gaining an Empire Medal – which many school pupils strived to be awarded at the time. I told him that I thought it was all just nonsense. The Empire to an extent, but certainly all the jingoism which surrounded it. Anyway, I got off the train at Ystrad Mynach, and that's the last I saw of him.'

But how important to John's emotional development is the lady that he shared his first sexual experiences with – and the failure of this relationship to be definitely concluded? Significantly, as far as John is concerned, she remains his only true love. While John is not so blinded as to believe that his first love has survived the ravages of time unscathed and unchanged, she remains a doe-eyed, blonde haired and pink cheeked vision in his memory. More pertinently, however, the passage of time has given Jenkins the time to consider whether their relationship might have provided him the necessary distraction when his political stirrings truly began, in that so enamoured does John believe their life together would have been, that there is a possibility he might not have subsequently affiliated himself with MAC and militant protest. It is certainly an interesting thought – and one complicated still further by the relationship's abrupt and ambiguous end. Yet on reflection, John believes that he was always likely to be attracted to taking responsive action in the name of Wales, owing to the other factors in his life and background; for instance, his illegitimacy, upbringing and the protective feelings he developed for Wales and the nation's cultural heritage. But while it is clear that John, by his own admission, has idealised his 'first love' and only 'soulmate', the reasons why require further comment. Did the intense feelings which Jenkins developed for her provide a release for him, in the sense that these burgeoning emotional and sexual affections provided a normalcy, somewhat at odds with those feelings which resulted when John developed an emotional attachment – if not sexually expressed – towards his male school friend?

## Thelma: marriage and divorce

What of Thelma and John's marriage? Might it provide clues for John's behaviour? This was not a harmonious relationship: no meeting of minds, no *coup de foudre*. But while Thelma and John's relationship was not perhaps 'love's young dream,' their destinies were intertwined, and despite their apparent incompatibility – intellectual, spiritual, political and emotional – it appears in the early years of the marriage that Thelma and John were happy. Thelma appears to have enjoyed the prestige and safety provided by being the wife of a respected and 'brushed and polished' sergeant in the British Army. Having been raised in the industrial Welsh Valleys, on marrying John, Thelma was transported to a new world and introduced to a class structure which she would not have experienced had she remained in Treharris. What is more, Thelma revered John – at least in many respects. Invited to comment in 2018 on his parents' union, Rhodri Jenkins responded thoughtfully that prior to his father's arrest, he believed that his mother loved his father. And indeed, Rhodri added reflectively, 'I think my mother still loves him today.' But was their marriage 'enough' for John? Did Jenkins' exacting personality and questioning intellect require 'more'?

When later revisiting the causes of their divorce and the breakdown of their once-cordial relationship, John reiterated that Thelma had 'betrayed the loyalty' in which he put considerable stock. 'She did not,' John remonstrated, 'emerge with any laurels' from the period when their lives were shared. He then continued:

> 'Her idea of loyalty and mine differ quite considerably. My loyalty is *total* loyalty! No compromising. None of this "a bit here and a bit there". And if I don't get total loyalty, then I don't want to know. I am not interested.'

It is a position which John reiterated many times when discussing Thelma and the demise of their marriage. At this point, however, Jenkins paused. After appearing lost in contemplation for some moments, he elaborated on his previous comments and declared pensively:

> 'Perhaps I put too much emphasis on loyalty. Perhaps it was my fault. It is never any one person's fault. There were a few people at fault here. It was partly my fault... Yeah, I admit it. It wasn't easy for her – I can see that now. She'd want to talk about coats and shoes for the kids, and so on, and that was fair enough of course. But I'd be distant, as my mind would be on other things – like our next political act. I think any woman, to be fair, whose husband has a vital interest which is not vital to *her* interests, or the house's interest or the children's interest, is going to be a little bit annoyed. Because his life is outside the garden gate, and no decent woman would tolerate that. And I understand it better now. You see, I've also come to appreciate that while at no time did I expect my wife and sons to sacrifice anything, I did expect them to bear the brunt of *my* sacrifice. I was letting the family down, to all intents and purposes. But there was no other way I could have done it. You can't be two things. You can only be one thing.'[194]

Could it be argued that Jenkins put everything into orchestrating the MAC campaign, in a manner which was over-and-above what he afforded both his Army career and his role as a husband and father?

> 'Well, I have always prided myself on my ability to compartmentalise, and I was able to say, "MAC is here, home is there, work is there", and so on. And that way, I was able to juggle my way reasonably successfully through these things: I rarely let anyone, or anything, impinge on the

other. But I do feel a sense of guilt. You see, I am not accustomed to letting people down. And during the MAC protest I was letting my family down, because in the end, my function is to guard the gates of the family home; as a father especially. That is my basic function. But things have to be sacrificed – and in sacrificing what I felt I had to sacrifice, I let my family down. What else would you call it? I can say, in truth, that I was thinking of the long-term aims of the family, rather than the short-term aims. The short-term aims would be to look after them. The long-term aims would be to ensure that the future was composed of a system in which they could find fruition and they could go as far as they wished.

It may be difficult for some people to understand now, but I wanted to do something my grandchildren would be proud of.[195] I saw the MAC campaign as a way to rid Wales of its political shackles. But in order to achieve that, it involved stepping outside the garden gate. Basically, I put the tribe before the family. But if everybody's loyalty was to their family and *only* to their family, nothing would ever get done. If everyone said, "Oh, I'm going as far as the gate and that's it", what would get done? Nothing! So somehow you have to get over that bloody obstacle of "the family is all" and "the family is everything" and "inside the garden gate is all you need to be worried about – and nothing else". Because once you start thinking like that, they [the establishment] have *won*. I know that if you look at it coldly, then my marriage and my role as a father came second to MAC, and that was the choice I made. The only other choice I had was to give MAC up – and I wasn't going to do that. It was a sacrifice that not many people are prepared to make. The most that the general public will do is stagger down once every five years and vote – and to expect them to risk anything more than that is unrealistic. But it did happen in the 1960s in Wales, because there were enough disenchanted young people to make it possible – that *were* prepared to sacrifice. And these people you could rely on. But I know that isn't typical, and I don't blame them. I understand it. People are people. And you can't blame people for being human. But yes, I regret that I let my family down... but I also feel that all these feelings of guilt are overridden by other feelings of justification. And these feelings override feelings of guilt because the issues involved were *too* important... I did what I could for my family. I couldn't do any more. So there you are, that's how it goes. I can't say any more than that.'

At this juncture, John disclosed information of a sensitive and delicate nature. With disarming honesty, John conceded that 'before, during and after the MAC campaign', Thelma had engaged in sexual relations with other men. When revealing these details, rather than looking disapproving and angry, John seemed somewhat sad and resigned. 'I was always vaguely aware of what was going on,' he declared reflectively, before adding:

> 'There was no love or even attachment involved, I suspect. She never hinted at leaving me and the boys. It amounted to what might be termed "sexual favours". I was in the process... I was thinking about leaving... about leaving her. The only thing that held me back for years was the kids. It's not a pleasant experience when your wife lets you down. But it happens. I had plenty of opportunity myself. More than plenty. With women I worked with and women I didn't work with. But I never strayed once. I was tempted once or twice, but I never strayed.'

Were the men with whom Thelma was involved known to John? 'No, I don't think so,' he replied.

> 'They never came to the house, you see. I didn't want strangers coming around. I discouraged it, in fact. I mean, I didn't want anybody to know where I lived, or who I was. That was the whole basis of the security operation. Nobody was to know anything. That did make communication – for example, between me and cell leaders – extremely difficult. But part of the MAC security strategy was to remain anonymous; and to blend in unnoticed within the community. And, of course, I adhered to this too. Well, especially me. So, no unusual visitors, no late-night parties and no coming-and-goings.'

John and Thelma's marriage was annulled in a reasonably amicable divorce in June 1972.[196] Although, in the legal sense, the details of care and custody in relation to Vaughan and Rhodri were agreed without complication, some of the testimony was not pretty. Despite remaining congenial for many years, in recent years the relationship between Thelma and John has broken down completely and they are no longer in contact. Despite repeated attempts to discuss with Thelma the events considered in this book, she has declined to comment. But an interesting observation was provided by her former employer in Narberth, who, speaking in 2017, revealed that 'some years ago', Thelma informed him that her first husband 'used to be active politically'. Had he detected any embarrassment or shame in her statement? 'No,' he replied, 'I got the impression that she was rather proud of him.' Asked to respond, John remarked:

> 'Well, she may have been. But not to my knowledge. As far as I'm concerned, like any other woman, she saw any external matters of importance as threatening the integrity of the home. She believed that it [John's involvement in MAC] slammed open the garden gate. That it let them all come tumbling in, and that gate was supposed to protect her and the kids. Well, she may well be right. But there again, she can't complain: owing to her behaviour and her affairs, the garden gate wasn't fastened that tightly anyway. And so, broadly speaking, Thelma and I divorced on the grounds of irreconcilable differences. But it was due to a question of loyalty. I have always, for good or ill, attached great importance to a person's loyalty. I've had to, I suspect. It's probably in response to the shocking discovery that I was illegitimate and adopted. And I believed that Thelma acted in a way which destroyed that concept of loyalty between us. I should add though, that her betrayal did not involve in any way divulging details of the MAC campaign; not that she knew a great deal about it anyway.'

## John as a father to Vaughan and Rhodri

What of Jenkins' specific role as a father? Did his involvement in the MAC campaign directly impact negatively on his relationship with Vaughan and Rhodri? 'I have to admit that it did,' John reflected plaintively. He continued:

> 'I mean, I suppose we did have some nice Christmases when the boys were young – not bad. Because it's a kid's time, isn't it? But if I'm honest, I don't think I enjoyed being a young father that much. It didn't come naturally to me. Partly because I'm not good at showing my feelings – I'm not the demonstrative type – but also, because being a father to two young boys is a responsibility. What I mean is: I do tend to take my responsibilities seriously, and anything I do, I have to dedicate myself 100% to it. So, had it not been for MAC, I would have dedicated 100% of my time and commitment to being a better father. As it was, *because* of MAC, I found the responsibility of being a father quite demanding. There were times when I enjoyed the interaction with them, but it depended on what sort of mood I was in and the latest exploit regarding the campaign.
>
> I tried, as I've said, to place my roles in compartments, but you can't do it totally. I mean, you're aware of what's going on outside

the bubble that you're in, so you can't totally enjoy yourself or totally *not* enjoy yourself with all those other things. I mean, they were little boys and so they were quite demanding, but it wasn't too bad. I do regret some of my actions, though. I was trying to watch the news, for instance, and *that* was one of the things that was sacrosanct. I would watch the news, and I expected silence to watch it. Particularly around the time of an announcement. As far as I was concerned, it was vitally important, and I had to hear it. I *had* to know about it. And Vaughan would come rushing in and start banging things about, and I'd be more annoyed than was reasonable because I was watching the news. Anyway, I threw his toy onto the fire. Normally I wouldn't have been so annoyed about it. He was just doing what little kids do, but it meant that the domestic was intruding on the professional, basically, and the two don't mix – not really. You have to keep them apart. And, of course, if I'm watching the news, that's professional. And if he comes rushing in waving toys about, that's not professional – and that means that I'm distracted, and I can't think straight, and I don't like that…

I've tried to make my peace with them, but, how can I? I was never there… well, yes and no. I wasn't away *that* much – one evening and night a week perhaps, and sometimes Saturdays and Sundays. That said, our relationship is reasonable. It's always been reasonable – which is more than can be said for the relationship either of them has with their mother, which is non-existent and has been for years. Both have lived with me at one time or another – Vaughan is staying with me now… Neither Vaughan nor Rhodri knew anything about the campaign of course, other than the fact that I'd get very irritated if they disturbed me when the news was on. That's all they knew of it. I don't think you can be both a family man and a politically active person. It's one or the other – you can't be both. I don't know of anybody who ever had a successful life and joined in to any extent with the other [campaigning]. I don't think it can be done.'

To look firstly at John and Thelma's married life, it seems that John's affiliation to *Mudiad Amddiffyn Cymru* – and the resultant resentment, anxiety and perhaps even jealousy on Thelma's part – had a corrosive effect on their marriage. But it is hard not conclude that their relationship was no love match from the outset. As a way of trying to understand Thelma's extramarital actions, had she suspected, or might John have provided any indication, that he harboured feelings of sexual attraction towards other men? 'No, I don't think she did,' John stated. 'Well, there was no reason why she should.' Nevertheless, while this may be true, it begs the question: did the loss of trust and what might appear to be an acute lack of intellectual compatibility which John experienced with Thelma lead him to later develop and seek out homosexual relationships? One thing does appear to be certain: the Jenkins' family home was not a haven. Furthermore, while John's honest assessment with regards his failings and inability to be a more giving and accessible father and husband must be acknowledged, some may also counter that despite his reasoning, Jenkins – especially with two exuberant sons to care for – had his priorities wrong. But by way of conclusion, it is interesting to note that the probation report compiled for John's trial in April 1970 declared him to be 'obviously held in affection by his wife and children as a good husband and father.'

## Other factors which may explain why Jenkins did what he did

Was John Jenkins perhaps, in some senses, a product of his age and environment? Raised in the 1930s and 1940s, John's emotional development occurred during a period when British society held and promoted values such as heroism, duty, responsibility, loyalty and courage. Added to these broader British ideals, the adolescent John was further influenced by the industrial Welsh society which surrounded him. Today, the upper Rhondda Valley is a place of peace and beauty. The coal mines that once dominated the landscape are long closed, their spoil heaps merged into the surrounding mountains. But John, like others with a connection to the industrial Valleys, has not forgotten the region's heritage and its historical significance. Later recalling both the impact of seeing men he admired and respected injured or crippled through injuries sustained at work, *and* the stoical manner in which they, their wives, their mothers – and indeed, the wider community – responded during such times of tragedy and bereavement, it is 'no wonder,' John later proclaimed, 'that the area became a hotbed of social unrest, which led to political change.' This was an area which believed passionately in fairness; and which historically had proudly confronted inequality and demanded for its workers protection, political recognition and justice through the Socialist and Trade Union movements. Therefore, the notion of *not* standing up and fighting for your beliefs was incomprehensible to John Jenkins. Particularly when, from Jenkins' viewpoint, all constitutional avenues to safeguard Wales' landscape and cultural heritage had been humiliatingly rejected.

Nonetheless, on leaving prison, John worked as a social worker and counsellor. These are vocations which suggest a caring disposition – somewhat at odds with a person driven to use explosives for a political objective. As a reader of history, John understands the importance of chronology in relation to development and progress. As a Social Science graduate, he has a considerable grasp and understanding of how life was lived in the past and the events which influenced it. For instance, Jenkins professes that the British Empire and colonialism was racist in its concept, and pitiless in the way in which it enforced its will. But John also recognises that in the nineteenth century it was Great Britain which led the world in beginning to tackle disease, child labour, brutal sexism, slavery and exploitation.

Yet, for all these suggested prevailing factors, can reasons for John's behaviour and actions be found closer to home? Contacted to reveal her thoughts on John Barnard Jenkins and the MAC campaign, the world-renowned American psychiatrist Dr Dorothy Otnow Lewis, who specialises in possible correlation between adult violence and child clinical behaviour, refused to comment on the specifics of John's case as she has never met John or discussed his childhood with him. Nevertheless, on the strength of her work with neurologist Jonathan Pincus on the neuropsychiatric and family histories of people who have used excessive violence – although not terrorists – Dr Lewis theorised that 'a combination of CNS dysfunction (i.e. autism, bipolar disorder, depression, etc.) and paranoid ideation (suspicion of being persecuted, tormented or treated in an unfair manner by other people) and a history of early family violence and/or ongoing abuse seemed to be a recipe for violence.'[197]

Having denied ever having received support or counselling for depression or psychiatric concerns, John was asked to throw light on how he and his brother Keith were disciplined when children. John remarked that while his father had neither disciplined the two boys in *any* notable way, nor displayed any degree of favouritism, their formidable mother, Minerva, was a 'shouter' whose idea of punishment for particularly mischievous behaviour extended only so far as a 'cursory clip around the ear'. This, John clarified while chuckling, occurred only when their mother was truly annoyed or 'at her wits' end'. Therefore, on the basis of Jenkins' repeated assurances, it would seem not only that the family home environment in which John was raised was indeed loving, nurturing and consistent, but also that the discipline used to mould John and Keith's behaviour was well within the acceptable standards of the time.

What of the letter which John discovered when aged just 10 years old, which outlined his illegitimacy – leading to his adoption by Tom Jenkins? Might the discovery of this letter be a factor in John's later actions in spearheading the MAC bombing campaign? John Jenkins is an intelligent and fiercely articulate man who is quite capable of discussing, with convincing clarity, his support for Welsh nationalism. But was Jenkins' deep emotional attachment to Wales and its threatened cultural identity born of a need to control his own emotional environment? On revisiting the subject of the letter's discovery, John conceded that the 'shock' of reading its content '*must* have had an impact' on his emotional development. Asked for her thoughts on this matter, Dr Lewis suspected that 'something about the way he [John] was regarded and treated by both parents before and after the "discovery" had more to do with his maladaptive behaviors than the piece of paper documenting the circumstances of his conception.' But 'even then,' Lewis continued, 'in a loving household, the child would have been able to discuss his discovery with his parents.'[198]

The highly respected Dr Lewis may well be correct. But it is important to note that the incident occurred during a period when sensitive matters were routinely 'swept under the carpet', and in fact neither John's mother nor his stepfather were ever aware that he had discovered the letter – either through discussion or owing to a significant change in John's behaviour. So on reflection, the matter appears to fall into one of two camps: either John's resolute mother, Minerva, exuded such an air of imposing authority that the subject was prevented from being aired, or John failed to raise the circumstances surrounding his conception at any time throughout his life because, as he emphatically states, his mother's 'happiness was the most important consideration' and he 'would not have wanted to upset her feelings that way'. Yet it is hard not to conclude – particularly in view of John's apparent afterthought that 'she might have taken it as some sort of attack on her' – that the truth can be found somewhere between the two possible scenarios.

## 'Psycho-babble' and other attempts to explain both MAC and John's motives

In recent years, John has become wary of pithy attempts to explain his involvement in the MAC campaign. One particular theorist who wrote to John, offering to write his memoirs, aroused Jenkins' ire by suggesting that he had become involved with MAC for reasons of 'social mobility'. It was a proposal fiercely dismissed by Jenkins as 'absolute bloody rubbish'. Utterly refuting the charge as 'psycho-babble', an irritated John continued:

> 'What do I want social mobility for? My affiliation to MAC, according to this so-called expert, was nothing to do with nationalism. Nothing to do with a love of Wales. No, no, no. I just wanted to "rise in the ranks". I wanted to be the General and all the bloody rest of it. What rubbish! Anybody who has known me for all these years would say that this is absolute bloody codswallop, but that was his attitude. I just ignored the letter. Do you know, I curse the day I was born a Welshman? I curse it because I would not have this sense of duty to protect Wales. If I was the average Englishman, all I would be worried about is where my next pint is coming from, or who I'm going to wake up with tomorrow morning. What a wonderful bloody world it would be, as far as I'm concerned!'

It would seem that Jenkins has good reason to reject as fanciful the claims that he joined MAC for reasons of personal prestige or upwards mobility. Nevertheless, having decided to join the group and prepare it for a further militant offensive, the importance of Jenkins' leadership philosophy, through which he instilled an effective and professional mindset in the movement, cannot be underestimated. This is because under John Jenkins' stewardship, the second iteration of *Mudiad Amddiffyn Cymru* proved adept at withstanding police investigation; and crucially it was not ravaged and undermined by interpersonal conflict. What is more, Jenkins remains adamant that while the ultimate decision regarding the implementation of policy rested firmly with him, the general tone during policy discussions was not one of fawning credulity towards whatever policy Jenkins was adopting, but rather the scene of lively, impassioned and often polarised debate. Yet contrary to this apparent belief in his desire to have control over subordinates, John regards his MAC associates as more akin to a 'band of brothers'. Invited to elaborate, Jenkins continued:

'Oh, good God. The MAC boys made life worth living. I mean if someone says to me, "What did you get out of your MAC days?", *that* was it. The fact that I was able to move among people who had free minds. They weren't bowed down with celebrity and trivia. They could see what needed doing and they had the guts and the knowledge to do it, so they did it. That is what I liked. None of them ever received any money, not even in terms of expenses. Not a penny. Money never changed hands. They involved themselves out of a love for Wales and an anger at what was happening. They were just ordinary members of the Welsh public, prepared to do extraordinary things to protect the Welsh nation. I like being amongst such people. I find it uplifting to talk to people like that, because you are not talking rubbish – which is what most people talk out there.'

Did John nonetheless believe that it took a *certain* egotism to become embroiled in a campaign of violence, particularly one underpinned by such a political objective? 'You tell me,' Jenkins replied, with a wry smile of indignation, before adding thoughtfully:

'You may be right, but I didn't get involved with MAC to advance my personal standing. I might have been held in some regard by those who knew of my identity in MAC, but those were very few in number. I didn't want *anyone* to know who I was. I wanted to remain anonymous. I hoped not to get caught. And had I evaded capture, I would not have the notoriety I have today – which I don't much enjoy. Only in so far as my 'fame', for want of a better word, helps to further the cause.'

Yet it is not only those who are discounted by Jenkins as opinionated dilettantes who have attempted to explain the MAC protest. Prompted by an 'appreciation of male company', on moving to Wrexham in 1996 John embarked on 'a couple of relationships with men', both of which, he later confirmed, 'could be said to be sexually based'. Since the MAC campaign ended, speculation has abounded that the group was bonded and motivated by reasons which included homosexuality. It was a line of inquiry broached by police during their interviews with John following his arrest in November 1969. For whatever reason, the subject of Jenkins' more recent sexual experimentation has led to conjecture that a feature of his affiliation to MAC was sexual repression. Each charge, however – that an aspect of the MAC protest centred on the homosexuality of some of its members; or that Jenkins was himself sexually repressed – is dismissed as 'nonsense' by John. Such unfounded accusations, Jenkins believes, typify the authorities' tendency to clutch at straws when at a loss to understand a protest movement's *raison d'être*. In the case of MAC, Jenkins later protested, 'They had to imply that there was something unsavoury about it, rather than an intellectual and ideological meeting of minds.'

John's refutation is convincing, but the subject of his sexuality appears to cause him unease. This might be generational and a feature of John's cultural background. Nevertheless, in response to assurances that such matters are unimportant, Jenkins remarked in 2017 that 'nobody has a past that they're absolutely proud of', before adding pointedly that while 'we all have skeletons in the cupboard', neither of these same-sex relationships – whether intellectually and emotionally – had meant more, or proved more important to him, than those relationships enjoyed with females. Yet, for all John's abashment, these are not scandalous revelations. Nor for that matter is John's arrest in December 1978 for 'importuning an adult male to engage in sexual activity' heinous, sordid or particularly shocking; just part of the tapestry of a life lived. It is surely time to end the unfounded rumour that homosexuality was a feature of the MAC campaign.

## Comparison between David Pritchard and John Jenkins' leadership – and how each is viewed within Plaid Cymru

As discussed, the first incarnation of MAC operated under David Pritchard. How did Pritchard's approach – and indeed his character – differ from his successor's? Contacted to discuss the matter was David Pritchard's widow, Judith. She declared:

'They [John and Dave] were very different characters. I can't speak for Dave, and I can't ever recall us talking about it, but I *think* Dave thought that John was quite an assertive person, or assured. You know, single-minded… obsessed. A fanatic. A bit extreme, and not cautious enough. Dave was very cautious – and very meticulous about everything he did. For instance, Dave didn't confide in me at all [regarding his campaigning]. He used to say that what I, and others for that matter, didn't know, we wouldn't be able to tell anybody. We married in 1975 and Dave died in 1980. He had been ill for some time and I think he was – well, tired, in a way. If there are rumours that his death is suspicious in that it coincided with the *Meibion*

*Glyndŵr* campaign, that's rubbish. We were living in Brittany then. Dave had been suffering from poor health for some time. You see, Dave was also a worrier and an anxious personality. He would never have wanted to do anything which risked the life, or the safety, of anyone. I'm not saying that John deliberately set out to hurt anybody, but I'm not sure Dave felt that such an approach [of planting timed explosives] was the right way. I suspect it would have left him feeling uneasy. He [Pritchard] was much more balanced in his way of doing things. He believed in symbolic protest – as opposed to John's more "hard-line" attitude.

But Dave was also a realist, who recognised that Plaid Cymru needed a more – for want of a better term – "militant wing" running alongside it, though unlike others in the party, Dave never criticised Gwynfor Evans. I think he held Gwynfor in high regard, actually. I'm sure that Dave is well respected within Plaid too. That's certainly the impression that I've had over the years. I'm not so sure about John. There was some support for John, of course, but I think it [the bombing campaign] divided people as much as it united them, and I think that's what Dave thought too. And that sense of it having caused division is true of people within Plaid and outside it... I mean, I don't know what John was thinking, but if he really thought that the Welsh working man was going to rise up in revolt against the British state... well, he was mad! I also think that Dave was concerned that when John came out of prison [in July 1976], John would want him to be involved in campaigning again, and so I don't think he wanted to get too close to him. I think by that time, Dave was weary anyway. He wasn't in good health, although he still worked and was president of the local allotment society – but I think he felt that he'd done his bit, and he just wanted to be left alone. But I should say that John was very nice when Dave died, and helped to arrange the funeral.'

It is a heartfelt and impassioned summary of her husband's involvement in the MAC campaign. But Judith Pritchard's testimony, perhaps understandably if she is unaware of much detail, fails to appreciate the 'hearts and minds' approach of Jenkins' tenure as MAC's principal strategist. Although in Judith Pritchard's defence, the appalling deaths and injuries do continue to overshadow the MAC protest in the eyes of many observers. But what of Judith Pritchard's thoughts as to the emotional mindset which may have underpinned the more militant wing of Plaid Cymru in that period? She continued:

'In the early Sixties, I spent time at Garth Newydd, Harri Webb's home in Merthyr. It was a meeting place for similar-minded individuals within Plaid Cymru – who perhaps favoured, I suppose, a more militant approach. People like Dave and David Walters, Harri, Meic Stephens [the writer], Tony Lewis [not FWA] and Alf Williams. All these men – and others I met later, like Gareth Miles – were romantics, really. I mean, don't misunderstand me, they all believed strongly in Welsh independence. But on another level, they were idealists and dreamers!'

Judith Pritchard's assessment, that many of those who comprised the more militant wing of Plaid Cymru were possessed of a romantic idealism, requires further examination, because since his arrest in 1969, John Jenkins has been denounced by his detractors. This evisceration of the 'feckless' Jenkins and his 'not-the-Welsh-way' political tactics has found favour with many in Plaid Cymru. Jenkins is derided for being, if not exactly an ideologue, then a fanatic, who shares with an ideologue the ability to justify anything, while ensuring there is clear distance between himself and any culpable blame. But this view of John is not universal – even within Plaid Cymru. Jenkins, his advocates maintain, is an honest, intelligent and courageous man, who far from being duplicitous, has never attempted to absolve himself of the responsibility of his actions. All he has tried to do, his supporters believe, is highlight Wales' political subjugation and the means by which the nation's fortunes might be reversed, through the creation of a credible and effective 'threat'. And all, John steadfastly insists, through a considered and restrained 'hearts and minds' approach.

## Why has John Jenkins been broadly rejected by Welsh society?

Nonetheless, rejection of John Jenkins and the campaign of militant protest by *Mudiad Amddiffyn Cymru* is by no means confined to Plaid Cymru. Because, whatever the mitigating factors surrounding Jenkins' decision to orchestrate a campaign of resistance against what he surmised to be unfair encroachments upon Welsh national life, there are those who believe that he has been generally disowned by mainstream Welsh society.[199] If true, then why is this? Asked for his thoughts on the matter, Jenkins replied trenchantly:

'There is a body of people who are quite determined to forget about the Sixties; who are determined to ignore what really happened. These reputable historians, who say that the MAC campaign went against the general run of things. That it went "against the grain". That it didn't "fit in". Well, of course it didn't bloody fit in! That was the whole object of the exercise. To show that there was an alternative strategy which was not prepared to put up with this. All I can say is that historians like Professor Hywel Teifi Edwards, God rest him, accuse me of "rocking the boat". Well, that is because I – and lots of us – didn't like the way the bloody boat was going! It was heading straight for the damn falls. And so therefore we felt, to wake the Welsh to that fact, that we *had* to shake the boat a little bit. Which we did. And Teifi's answer is to just ignore it. "Oh no, we can't have something that rocks the boat".

Are these people blind, or what? What is the matter with them? Why don't historians report the facts as they find them? How can they regard themselves as reputable historians and yet be governed by politics? Yet you see it happening throughout history, and so-called meritorious historians just accept it. They never accept that they are wrong. Look at old Venerable Bede and British Christianity. On discovering that the British Christian Church was in fact established *before* the Anglo-Saxon invasion, he ignored it. Look at how the English now regard King Arthur as one of their own. According to films and even more "considered" programmes, Arthur was an English King who will return to fight for England during its hour of need! An Englishman? Now if you can make sense of that, you can make sense of anything! Because the historical Arthur was a Briton; a Welsh warlord who fought *against* the invading Saxon English! It is staggering... The English attitude is, "Oh, the Welsh: they're just impractical dreamers." Well, if MAC's actions helped to dispel that rumour, then good: we succeeded in what we were trying to do! Because however much these people try to dismiss it, or ignore it, the MAC campaign was the first organised uprising in Wales since Glyndŵr.'

John Jenkins expresses his supposition that mainstream historians have deliberately airbrushed MAC out of the historical annals in a manner which is typically engaging. But might Jenkins *also* be the strategic victim of the police and intelligence services, which have historically sought to undermine the reputation of an individual considered to pose a political threat within a community; particularly those sympathetic towards a militant struggle, and most notably, those rumoured to be involved in such.

This policy of discrediting usually involves intimating perceived character flaws and weakness, such as a target's perceived racism, sanity, credibility, negative lifestyle choices, popularity and/or sexual orientation; and indeed, the individual's alleged connection – invariably for financial reward – to the intelligence services. When considered necessary, these individuals have also periodically been the focus of state-sponsored Orwellian monitoring, through the aid of phone taps, mail interception and surveillance cameras placed inconspicuously throughout their home and/or vehicle.

But perhaps the way Jenkins has been largely ignored by Welsh society runs deeper. John believes that 800 years of conquest fuelled the MAC campaign – in that there were some in Wales who felt the need to strike back. But so too does Jenkins feel that this prolonged period of subjugation has created a mindset which has led to the subsequent negative reaction to the MAC protest being expressed by general opinion in Wales. If true, then why? It is certainly true that historians in Wales, however acclaimed, have traditionally shied away from subjecting the MAC offensive to careful, considered and nuanced analysis; and fear of being seen to condone the protest has been cited as one reason for this.

It is also true that, historically speaking, John Barnard Jenkins is the product of a country subject to 'divide and rule', and more recently, held in the tight grip of non-conformist religious observance. To examine each phenomenon in greater detail: a society subject to a policy of 'divide and rule' notoriously tends to turn in on itself. It is perhaps unsurprising, when one's political masters foster and encourage mistrust, suspicion and resentment among the populace. Little wonder then that, on invading Wales in the early mediaeval period, the nation's Anglo-Norman conquerors were quick to implement such a policy of 'divide and rule' when attempting to subjugate and govern their new territory.

As for the more recent role of the Church and, more specifically perhaps, the Chapel in Welsh society, for all the positives they provided, each also exercised a significant degree of social control over much of the population, ensuring that any considered attempt to raise one's head above the parapet was beaten down and criticised. However outlandish it might seem to highlight a link between these historical factors and the plight of John Jenkins, it is difficult not to recognise, even in contemporary Welsh society, the prevailing need to squash one considered to have swum against the tide; not to mention a certain disdain for those deemed worthy of the need to be brought down a peg or two. Even if it should also be recognised that a feature of the Welsh character is an acceptance of individuality – certainly if the expression of individuality is considered to be genuine.

Nonetheless, even within 'know your place' Welsh society, might the apparent rejection of John Jenkins by collective Welsh opinion be an altogether simpler matter? Might it be because the 'reasonable man' or woman of the legal definition cannot find it within themselves to advocate such a campaign of indiscriminate and potentially catastrophic violence? It does seem probable, while it must also be noted that despite best efforts to rid Wales of its language, identity and culture, such attempts have been fiercely resisted down the ages. It is therefore difficult to ascribe Jenkins' predicament to any one cause, leading to the implication that John Jenkins has been sidelined by mainstream analysis, owing – in part, at least – to *all* of the reasons outlined above.

## The social, cultural and political impact of the MAC protest

Whatever the truth surrounding why John Jenkins remains a peripheral figure in Welsh history, what was the cultural and political impact of the MAC campaign, both contemporaneously and when viewed through the lens of hindsight?

Firstly, what of its cultural influence? In 1966, Joe Orton's *Loot* – a dark farce that satirises the Roman Catholic Church, social attitudes to death and the integrity of the police – made a non-specific reference to the MAC protest. It occurs when the venal, corrupt and sadistic Police Inspector Truscott, posing as a Metropolitan Water Board official while investigating a bank robbery, walks through the garden with Nurse Fay McMahon. His Metropolitan Water Board subordinates, Truscott informs her, are 'looking for freshly turned earth'. Asked why, the Inspector continues officiously, 'We are investigating possible sabotage to our pipelines; Welsh nationalists have been reported in the area.' Two years later, the BBC police crime drama *Softly Softly* devoted an episode to the pipeline issue, with a storyline featuring an angry, disenfranchised young Welsh idealist caught up in militant protest action, and its impact on his distraught mother.

Also in 1968, when visiting New York to promote The Beatles' company Apple, Paul McCartney and John Lennon were asked by an interviewer to comment on the social, political and cultural changes sweeping the globe. To substantiate his point as to the far-reaching nature of the shift in attitudes, Lennon remarked, 'Even in Wales, they're rioting.' Surely this, at least in part, was a reference to the MAC protest? Invited to respond, John Jenkins later enthused: 'Well, of course it was. He [Lennon] would have been well aware of the bombing campaign. But not just that: I suspect he would have known about the protests concerning the Welsh language and the rise of Welsh nationalism as a political force. That said,' Jenkins added calmly:

> 'I don't like it when there is this blustering attitude of, "The Beatles changed the world." They didn't change my world; and I don't know anybody else's world they changed! Nor for that matter people like David Bowie, who no doubt was a clever, talented chap. But I feel that the death of Micky Gaughan [the IRA prisoner Jenkins befriended] is *much* more significant than the death of David Bowie, because for all Bowie's contribution to art, it hasn't altered people's lives. People should be more relaxed in their appraisal of such figures. They should say, "Bowie's music made a great impact on the music scene and it changed a number of attitudes." But "changed the world" – *really?*'

It is an opinion destined to attract both positive and negative comment, particularly considering the extent to which many lives were altered by IRA and Unionist paramilitary groups during the so-called 'Troubles'.

Nonetheless, speaking in 2009, to mark the thirtieth anniversary re-release of Monty Python's *Life of Brian*, John Cleese stated that the amusing plot-line about the attempt to kidnap Pilate's wife involving incompetent 'terrorist' groups named the People's Front of Judea, the Judean People's Front and the Campaign for Free Galilee – which comprised men with music-hall Welsh accents – was inspired by fellow Python, Terry Jones. On returning to London in the late 1960s from visiting relatives in his native Colwyn Bay, Jones had regaled Cleese and the other Pythons with news that myriad Welsh protest groups, all of which appeared to be similarly titled, had sprung up to protest issues affecting Welsh cultural and political life. Although John Cleese was unable to recall what the Welsh groups were protesting about, surely the timeline suggests it was the Investiture.

All such references have convinced John Jenkins that the true story of the 1960s has been ignored, and that much of the accepted historical analysis requires re-examination. 'It drives me mad,' an exasperated Jenkins declared. 'The 1960s wasn't just about the Mods and Rockers fighting on the beaches of the south coast of England, as some writers and historians would have you believe. And I should know: I lived through it!'

But what of the effect of the MAC campaign on the political landscape of Wales, or indeed, the wider political agenda? By focusing on the electoral pattern of Plaid Cymru through the period when MAC was active, it is noticeable that the party's share of the vote in Wales increased from 61,071 (4.3%) at the 1966 General Election, to 175,016 (11.5%) at the 1970 General Election. Yet closer examination reveals that 1970 was the first time that Plaid Cymru contested each of Wales' 36 electoral seats. It is very possible that this alone explains the party's overall increase in electoral support. As for the broader political picture, it should be noted that since the MAC campaign ended in 1969, while a small number of Welsh valleys have been flooded, no populated valleys in Wales have been submerged – a development which John Jenkins adamantly believes is because the UK authorities are today wary of incurring similar protest again.

Nevertheless, if there is an acceptance that MAC affected its cultural and political milieu, can reference to the group's militant protest be found in analytical studies which address the subject of terrorism – either committed in the UK, or on the international stage? There is no mention of *Mudiad Amddiffyn Cymru* in *The Defence of the Realm: The Authorized History of MI5*, by Christopher Andrew.[200] Nor does it feature in either Michael Burleigh's *Blood & Rage: A Cultural History of Terrorism* or Peter Taylor's *Talking to Terrorists: Face to Face with the Enemy*. Yet more recently, perhaps in response to the so-called 'terrorist phenomenon' attracting media attention and the picture of relative peace in Northern Ireland, British and global terrorism has been the focus of greater academic scrutiny; and as a consequence, MAC's position has been increasingly recognised – if not endorsed. For instance, Welsh militancy is afforded attention in *Does Terrorism Work? A History*, by Professor Richard English[201] and *The Dogs That Didn't Bark: Political Violence and Nationalism in Scotland, Wales and England*, by Dr Nicholas Brooke.[202]

But the question of MAC's political impact and the group's inclusion in the annals of terrorist history requires further examination. What are MAC's militant credentials? Is this a protest movement worthy of serious consideration? Assessing the MAC campaign can feel slightly vertiginous:

there is a sense of peering over the edge of an abyss into a chasm of uncertainty and destructive escalation. Between 1963 and 1969, there were twenty explosions in Wales and England which are thought to have been carried out by Welsh political extremists. The majority were undertaken by units, or individuals, within *Mudiad Amddiffyn Cymru*. One explosion has not been attributed to any group or political cause; and six further devices were intercepted or failed to activate.

In a wider sense, MAC's militant campaign involved to some degree: the *Unvaniezh Demokratel Breizh* (the Breton Democratic Union), the Provisional IRA (whose subsequent adoption of MAC's 3-man cell structure proved crucial to the group's successful paramilitary offensive) and – allegedly – the East German, Libyan, Cuban and Saudi Arabian authorities. Surely therefore, any group or campaign which was that far-reaching cannot be dismissed lightly? So then to the question of whether MAC *really* posed such a threat. On reflection – while the extent of the group's militant protest should be kept in perspective – it would seem that it did. Whatever the truth, it leaves many to thank Providence that matters did not escalate as they may well have done. Therefore, such an assessment, albeit brief, of the social, cultural and political impact of the MAC offensive, surely culminates in the belief that the relevance of this militant protest cannot be ignored.

*'Nationalism is an infantile disease. It is the measles of mankind.' Albert Einstein.*
*'Nationalism, like virtue, has its own reward.' Mahatma Gandhi*

Having considered the emotional and political reasons why John Jenkins may have aligned himself with *Mudiad Amddiffyn Cymru*, and the political and cultural ramifications of the MAC protest, it is necessary at this juncture to briefly consider how the protest action of MAC fits within a theoretical framework. If it is agreed that those who were drawn to undertake militant protest action in the name of MAC did so because of nationalist principles – namely a nationalist sense of duty to protect Wales – how can 'nationalism' best be defined? What, in essence, does 'nationalism' mean? It is, according to broad definition, the devotion or allegiance to the nation by a people of shared characteristics, which is often used to inspire and/or motivate people to undertake patriotic acts. But if this definition appears to be clear, what is the opinion of prominent nationalist historians when evaluating the subject of nationalism?

Much has been said of nationhood being an 'imagined community,' most notably by Benedict Anderson,[203] and of nationalism and identity being a mere construct or projection in that members of even the smallest nations will never meet or even hear of most of their fellow-members. Yet, while there is much to be said for this position, it fails to capture the full power of nationalism. It fails to recognise the raw emotion that 'nationality' can produce. What is it about 'nationalism' which can drive educated, thinking people to do both great and dreadful things?

Ernest Gellner rules that 'nationalism is not the awakening of nations to self-consciousness; it invents nations where they do not exist.'[204] Here too, Gellner appears to suggest that 'nationality' is a falsity; and therefore, 'nationalism' masquerades under false pretences. But what are the reasons that *unite* a people and which therefore fuel nationalism? Does not a shared understanding of commonality, such as language and history, provide a collective vision and purpose when it is considered necessary to protect and safeguard the very reasons which ensure the existence of commonality? Simply stated, is it not commonality which acts as a reason why people of a geographical region who share history, culture and language unite to defend encroachments toward that history, culture and language? This view would appear to have support – at least in part – from Eric Hobsbawm, who asserts that 'there is no more effective way of bonding together the disparate sections of restless peoples than to unite them against outsiders.'[205] History suggests that this is true, but if regarded within a UK political context, Peter Scott maintains that 'Britain is an invented nation, not so much older than the United States.'[206] Which begs the question: does cultural allegiance afford a greater sense of belonging than political allegiance? Certainly, from a nationalist perspective, this would seem to be correct. Yet, to focus on the singular importance of language to nationalist thinking: while it should be noted that early European cultural nationalists such as Johann Herder proposed that language was a pivotal element to an emerging nationalist sentiment,[207] a number of twentieth century scholars such as Ernest Gellner, Eric Hobsbawm and Anthony D Smith accept the importance of language in providing communal cohesion, but also contend that language is one of a number of factors which can foster a nationalist movement.[208] It is a fascinating viewpoint and one which certainly chimes with John Jenkins' assessment that MAC was predominately comprised of English- rather than Welsh-speaking front-line members.

Therefore, to conclude: critics of nationalism argue that it is often unclear what constitutes a 'nation' or whether a nation is a legitimate unit of political rule. At the same time, nationalists are denounced for being insular and rejecting multi-culturalism. By way of response, nationalists hold that the boundaries of a nation and a state should coincide with one another. Thus, nationalism tends to be fuelled by shared commonality, such as a shared history and/or language. Importantly however, more progressive and enlightened attitudes are inclusive and tolerant of dual-identity expression. But what of John Jenkins? While undertaking the MAC protest, was John acting in a classic way according to 'nationalist' theory? It would appear so, as John has always maintained that his actions were founded on the belief that a 'shared historic identity', fuelled by geography, is what unites a disparate people – irrespective of whether they have met or not.

*'Terrorism is the tactic of demanding the impossible, and demanding it at gunpoint.' Christopher Hitchens.*
*'I don't even call it violence when it's in self defense; I call it intelligence.' Malcolm X*

And so, with an understanding of 'nationalism', what of 'militancy' and 'terrorism' – and how do these fit within a nationalist arena? While militancy is defined as the use of confrontational or violent methods in support of a political or social cause, academics disagree on a universal definition of terrorism. Most definitions agree that terrorism is the use of organised political violence by non-state actors in order to create fear, as a means to achieve a political or religious objective. It is essentially a form of 'asymmetric warfare', in that it entails conflict between political actors of unequal strength, through which the weaker party attempts to neutralise its opponent's strength by exploiting the opponent's weaknesses. To take our understanding one step further, it appears that most definitions of terrorism share three key elements: 1) It is political in nature or intent; 2) Perpetrators are non-state actors; and 3) Targets are non-combatants, such as political figures, bureaucrats, or innocent bystanders.[209] Yet, one contemporary terrorism expert, Audrey Kurth Cronin, adds a fourth element: Terror attacks are unconventional and unpredictable.

But are these definitions and theories too rigid, especially when applied to the campaign of *Mudiad Amddiffyn Cymru*? Can it really be said that MAC used 'fear' to further its political ambitions? Although on the face of it this suggestion seems to be broadly inaccurate, John Jenkins concedes that at least one senior MAC official proposed that MAC associates carry out serious sexual assaults on Welsh women while wearing British Army uniforms. The public outcry in Wales, the MAC official reasoned, would ensure an escalation in the violence, leading to an inevitable brutal counter-reaction from the British state. This in turn, it was hoped, would lead to heightened conflict and, ultimately, a negotiated settlement and political independence for Wales. It was further proposed that senior UK political figures be assassinated. This too, it was suggested, would provide the UK authorities with a pretext for unleashing a vicious counter-response, which again MAC could utilise to its advantage as vindication for a campaign of terrorism, culminating in political settlement and Welsh independence. It seems inconceivable that there were members within MAC who were willing to perpetrate outrages of the worst kind against Welsh women, but whatever the veracity of these claims, it is important to note that John Jenkins vetoed all such proposals. Nonetheless, it cannot be ignored that within MAC there existed individuals – whether through desperation or for cynical strategic advancement – who were increasingly prepared to countenance such abhorrent methods to further the group's political objective. Such knowledge leaves many to be thankful that John Jenkins was arrested before escalation in the MAC campaign threatened to result in near catastrophe.

Where does MAC fit within theory in relation to modern terrorism? A useful starting point is Professor David C Rapoport's 'The Four Waves of Modern Terrorism', one of the most widely debated theories in the field of terrorism studies, and considered one of the most influential.[210] Rapoport posited four distinct waves of modern terrorism: the Anarchists, 1880–1920; Anti-colonialism (nationalist), 1920–1960; the Leftists, 1960–1989; and Religious terrorism, (1979–ongoing). Each wave had a precipitating event and each lasted approximately 40 years before receding and fading – with some overlap – as another wave developed in its place. Nonetheless, although credited for having a high degree of explanatory power, criticism has been levelled at Rapoport's 'four-wave theory' for its rather elegant and simplistic rigidity. There is, its critics maintain, too little emphasis on the *degree* of overlap, with Jeffrey Kaplan claiming that in its 'broad-brush' approach, Rapoport's theory fails to recognise the minutiae and the detail and diversity of life and conflict – in that terrorism will vary in different countries based on geo-political factors, rather than because of the time period.[211] Believing Rapoport's four-wave theory to be incomplete, Kaplan also suggests a 'fifth wave', which takes into account the new tribalism and 'localistic' movements which have emerged in Africa in the recent period.[212] On the face of it, MAC, would appear to fit within this fifth wave, in that the group's militant endeavours were undertaken to protect the 'Welsh tribe', irrespective of the nation's regional differences.

Yet to return to David C Rapoport's *The Four Waves of Modern Terrorism* and consider MAC within this context, *Mudiad Amddiffyn Cymru* appears to fit into the Anti-colonialism (nationalist) group in terms of its political nature, but also within the Leftists, 1960–1989 field, as MAC was operational within this timeframe. As for criticism levelled at MAC for a perceived right-wing, neo-fascist dogma, it is a charge roundly dismissed by John Jenkins on the grounds that MAC was not anti-English per se and that MAC activist Alwyn Jones was married to Marie, a black woman from Jamaica, who was pregnant with their child when Alwyn Jones was killed in Abergele on the eve of the Investiture.

## Files relating to MAC still closed

Asked in 2019 to sum up what he feels the MAC campaign achieved, John Jenkins replied pensively: 'Never again will Whitehall take us [Wales] for granted.' Time will tell, but perhaps some credence can be attached to Jenkins' claim – and the associated seriousness of the MAC protest – when files pertaining to the MAC action which are still closed to public access are collated,[213] as well as those files concerning the WAWR protest in which Jenkins became embroiled in the early 1980s.[214] Encouraged to comment on why a number of files relating to MAC should still be subject to closure fifty years after the protest ended, John declared candidly:

'The only thing I can think of is that they still want to keep under wraps the communication and discussions being held internally between the

Government, the top police people, the security services and some of the politicians. For instance, it would be nice to know what is contained in the files about George Thomas, God rest him, because he stood to rise or fall according to the Investiture itself – and he was determined not to fall. So in that sense, it would be interesting to see what was being said and/or contemplated.'

## The emotional legacy of the MAC campaign

But having considered the ongoing legal/archival ramifications of the MAC offensive, what of the more 'emotional' repercussions of the policy of 'direct action' as adopted by John Jenkins when operational director of *Mudiad Amddiffyn Cymru*? John confesses to an outlook which, when inspired, borders on 'tunnel vision.' Despite its advantages in clearly identifying the means by which an objective might be achieved, such a mindset affords little consideration for the ripple effect of actions undertaken. Asked in 2018 to discuss the events under review, John's younger son, Rhodri, declared:

'He let a lot of people down. He wasn't a good father. Nor, in my opinion, a good grandfather. I gave him the opportunity to make amends by being a grandfather, but in all honesty, he made hardly any effort at all, which was very disappointing. Um, 0% interest, shall we say? He'll speak very quickly on the phone to my son, you know? Not much to say. It's the same now, when I phone him at the nursing home. It's like, "Yeah, I'm alright. I've got to go now. Ta-ra". Or he'll tell the staff to tell me it's not convenient, or whatever. As for being a dad when I was young: well, for one thing, he was away such a lot. And when he *was* at home you had to be quiet. When he arrived back from work... Well, you knew he was back. It was "Hush, hush." I remember that. He was very strict. I can remember playing with my toys in the lounge and he must have been trying to watch something – the news perhaps, and he got up and very angrily threw the toy I was playing with on the fire. He used to say it as a threat, but I'm sure it was a threat seen through a few times. It's such a clear memory; I don't think I've imagined it. I remember having some fun with him one day. It was a sort of fête, or something. A school fête, I suppose...

You see, he is now regarded as a freedom fighter. People are proud of him now. But forty years ago, when I was growing up, he was a terrorist. You couldn't even talk about him. And the two things, terrorist and freedom fighter, are very different. Climates have changed. He has done exactly the same things, but when people talk of my father now, they talk of him as a man who fought for freedom. Do I do feel proud of him? Yes, I suppose so, but not as a dad... But I'm not embarrassed by him and what he's done. Never have been, never will be. The Welsh were second-class citizens. They're not now, and much of that is thanks to him'

What were Rhodri's thoughts on his father's orchestration of the MAC campaign? He replied earnestly:

'My father was a genius at what he did. Bringing in the splinter cell system and all that... well, the IRA took it up, didn't they? But I think he was a genius because when he actually got caught, they weren't tumbling like dominos. It stopped at him [and Alders], so that cell system which he brought in seemed to work. But I also think that if my father was planning to do what he did, he should *not* have started a family. But over the years, I've been able to see past that. Maybe he started a family and *then* decided to do what he did – which is possibly the way it worked. But whatever way it happened, our family was ripped apart. It was ripped apart so much that there were no family connections, really, for me and my brother. And it's all a consequence of his [John's] "untimely truancy", shall we call it? His untimely going away.

I was six years old. My brother was barely aged ten. And to begin with, we were left in the care of our mother, and I don't think he [John] realised how bad that was. How incapable she was of parenting. She just wasn't suitable. But I don't think my father realised, because he asked me a couple of years ago, "What was wrong, then?" I didn't have the heart to tell him. I had had enough of my mother's baloney, bullshit and self-centredness for years. Yet, I kept quiet when he asked. To be quite honest with you, I don't think my mother should have had children. She was a poor grandmother too, until I drew a line under it. It's one of those things, I suppose, but I haven't spoken to her for about fifteen years. My brother hasn't spoken to her for years either. I went to live with my mother's parents, Victor and Beryl, eventually, and my relationship with them was great. My brother was more inclined to rely on my father's parents, Tom and Minnie.'215

Have the two brothers been able to discuss the events of their childhood, if only as a means of supporting one another to make clearer sense of what transpired? 'We don't talk about the past at all, me and my brother,' Rhodri replied intently; adding:

'We're not close. We don't mention anything about what happened after he went down. It's best forgotten. But I think Vaughan got along with them [Tom and Minnie] pretty well. My school days were OK. I went to a Welsh school and they looked after me. In fact, one teacher used to pay for me to go on school trips to Tresaith and Llangrannog. I was never bullied by teachers or other pupils. I could look after myself. I enjoyed school, but I did get expelled a couple of times. I was just defending myself. I just don't like bullies. Never have. The fights were nothing to do with my father. But it was my home life which was tough – school was a doddle. I don't want to dwell on what went on during my childhood. I'd prefer to try and put it all behind me. But I will say this: after my father left, we had absolutely no money at all. Nothing. My mother was a drinker as well. She probably still is, and she is not a pleasant drunk. When we moved to Trelewis just after my father went to prison, we would go on holidays, but we never had any money at home. I remember the electric being turned off all the bloody time. And we didn't have a bed. Very basic things like that which we had to go without.

I don't remember any of my mother's wider family helping out financially, but I do remember a lot of arguing going on between Beryl and my mother because of the situation. In the end, I went to live with Beryl and Victor. But it took a while before that happened. Before that, when I was living with my mother, she took up with an ex-boxer. He was *very* unstable and very violent. Well, he and my mother had a daughter together. And one day, out of the blue, she just left! She'd been carrying on with this other man and she just buggered off. And so she left my half-sister, who was only a *dwt* [tot], and me in the care of this violent man. I wasn't even his son. My brother was living with us at the time, and it was nothing for this man to be violent towards us. It was nothing for him to say, punch us. Even to knock us out. And do you know what? He was a very enthusiastic man. He tried to provide a house for us all. He worked his socks off, fair play to him. But violence just came naturally to him. That's the way he had been treated by *his* father. The way he had been brought up didn't coincide with good parenting, but he didn't know any different. He was very unstable and my mother just buggered off and left us all. And that is the height of selfishness. I don't know many parents who would do that.

I could say more, but I'm not going to give any more examples from when I was young. It was terrible. I don't think my mother is a bad person. It's not vindictive. She can be very sentimental. She just always makes the wrong decisions. If she has two options, she will always choose the bad one. I can't even say that she became a bad mother after our father went inside. I wouldn't say that she was *ever* a good mother, ever a good parent. But once my father was gone, everything just fell apart.'

Had he ever discussed his father's actions in MAC with any of his mother's family? 'It was never discussed,' Rhodri responded matter-of-factly.

'But they hated it. You just knew that they hated what he had done. It was never mentioned between me and my uncles, me and my aunts, or between me and my grandparents. It was just swept under carpet. I think they were embarrassed by it. My mother knew *nothing* at all about what he was doing with MAC.'

Had Thelma's family, nonetheless, looked up to John, until his arrest and conviction? 'Yeah, possibly,' Rhodri replied, before chuckling:

'I remember them [Beryl and Victor] babysitting for me and my brother as youngsters, when my father and mother went out – and we were buggers to them. I remember that... We didn't half give them the runaround! But during those days before his arrest, I think they quite respected him.'

Did he enjoy a good relationship with the formidable Minerva, his father's mother? 'Well,' Rhodri began pensively:

'Do you remember Lou Beale [cantankerous matriarch] in *EastEnders*? Well, Minerva is Lou Beale! She ran the family, and what she said went! Her husband Tom was scared to move! When my father came out of prison – so what was he, in his mid-forties? – well, I have seen her banging his and Keith's heads together. Two grown men! She was that type of person. Both Keith and my father would run from her! But she kept the family together. You didn't dare do anything that she wouldn't like. I really don't know what she thought of my father's campaign. It's something we never spoke about. I wouldn't say it was the "elephant in the room". Just nobody ever spoke about it. I wouldn't say that Minnie was proud of my father. I would say it was more embarrassment. No – it was more *regret*. Regret that he had gone. You know: her little boy was locked up. Her baby was locked up. Tom never said a thing. You never had any emotion off Tom at all. Tom thought what Minnie told him to think! He was a lovely guy. He was very slight and very strong. He used to carry bags of coal on his back all the way from Gelligaer [Penybryn] to Trelewis for us.'

Had the relationship between him and his father developed when John was released from prison in July 1976? 'Yes,' Rhodri affirmed, before continuing:

'I was looking forward to him coming out. And when he did, I would see him on Sundays and we would go to his parents' home in Penybryn. And in the summer, we used to go for nice walks together – up to Capel Gwladys, for instance. It was the first bit of bonding, I suppose, for me. And I treasured it.'

Asked to sum up both his father's character and his devotion to Welsh nationalism, Rhodri declared:

'Well, I don't think there are even headstones on my grandparents' [Tom and Minerva] graves. I was attending a funeral at Gelligaer church, and after the service I went to where Tom is buried – this was a few years after he died – and there wasn't a headstone on it. So, I phoned my father straight away and said, "Do you know that there's no headstone on Grampy's grave?" And he said, "Yes." My father is not a sentimental man at all. Yet he seems so emotive about Welsh nationalism, and nothing else, really. I only found out that my father was illegitimate and adopted when I was in my late twenties and needed a new passport. He'd never mentioned it. I eventually found out when I received a copy of his adoption record – which states the name of his biological father... but I can't remember the name now. And I've since lost the adoption record, what with moving, and have no reason to reapply for it. Did my father's illegitimacy, and the fact that he discovered he was illegitimate by way of this letter when he was aged just ten, later fuel his campaign with MAC? I don't know. I am really not qualified to say. But I didn't dare ask Minnie about my father's illegitimacy. Perhaps my father is like his mother. Minnie wasn't one to show her affection. The only time I ever saw her show any physical affection towards my father was at Tom's funeral. My father was crying and she put her arms around him. And it was, like, half a minute. She seemed a bit uncomfortable... embarrassed. While she was the one you could rely on, I don't think she could show affection at all... The only thing I saw her show any sentiment for was her father's old snuff or twist box. This little brass box, which had on it the address of their family home in Cottrell Street in Aberfan. He must have taken it to work with him. He was a "banksman" in the pit. It was he who operated the cage up and down, containing the men and the coal... It was a responsible position.'

Encouraged to sum up his life as the son of John Jenkins, in terms of both its practical and emotional legacy, Rhodri Jenkins paused in quiet reflection before stating:

'Well I'm engaged to be married, in 2020. A little unofficial ceremony at Capel Gwladys. And so I'm happy and settled. But for years, despite having the money to buy a flat, I've preferred to house share. To come home after work [as a heating engineer] to company. I'm not one to complain, but... I am the son of a terrorist. I am monitored by the authorities. Not so much in Wales any more, but certainly when I go to London. It happened again recently when me and my fiancée went up there. We were so obviously being followed. It was ridiculous. One of these surveillance guys even came up to us and gave me directions! In London!

But I will say this: my father is a hero to some people. The last time he was here in Cardiff, we went to a concert at the Motorpoint Arena – my father was playing drums with the Cambria Band there. And the guy who books everything at the venue made a beeline for him. "Are you John Jenkins?" You know? He was thrilled to meet him. So proud of him. He was shaking his hand and saying, "It's such a pleasure to meet you." I was just standing there, watching this. It was quite emotional really. I realised then that some people hold him in great esteem. But I have to say, I was also thinking: "OK, mate. But where was he forty years ago [when I needed him]?" You know?'

Rhodri Jenkins' testimony provides a fascinating insight into life as John Jenkins' son. It is as tragic as it is compelling. Of less significance than the appalling treatment that Rhodri and Vaughan suffered at the hands of Thelma's partner after their father was incarcerated is Minerva's uneasy and disconcerted reaction to John 'sobbing in her arms' at the funeral of Tom Jenkins, which contradicts John's account of what transpired. But so too perhaps, does Rhodri's amusing, if startling, anecdote of witnessing

Minerva banging John and Keith's heads together when the two men were in advanced adulthood. Despite the story's mirthful quality, it does stand *somewhat* at odds with John's portrayal of Minerva as having a vigorous, 'not to be messed with', but controlled and measured temperament during their childhood. A disposition, John maintains, not given to violent outburst. Yet, Rhodri's account also provides an intriguing indication that Minerva may have harboured a lifelong affection for her father and may have regretted the apparent total breakdown of their relationship when she fell pregnant with John – certainly if the manner in which she appears to have valued her father's brass snuff box is anything to go by. It also begs the question of how the heirloom came to be in Minerva's possession. Might it be that Minerva was handed the snuff box by a sibling, following their father's death?

Whatever the truth surrounding these events, Rhodri suggests that another person whose life was negatively affected by the MAC campaign was his uncle, Peter – Thelma's brother. Prompted to elaborate on this supposition, Rhodri continued that until his father's arrest, Peter Bridgman's police career had been progressing steadily. But having been promoted to the rank of sergeant, any further progress was 'stunted' as a result of his brother-in-law's actions. 'Despite Peter having gone so far in such a short time, he was immediately classed [within police circles] as a terrorist's brother, I think,' Rhodri claimed, adding:

'The feeling was, "We can't sack him, but as a policeman that close... why didn't he suss it out?" He was his brother-in-law, you know? The Prince was under threat from MAC, and this man, John Jenkins; and the brother-in-law, a policeman, should have known about it. But he failed to spot it. The police may *even* have suspected that Uncle Peter provided my father with information, but I'm sure he didn't.'

Speaking in 2017, a close associate of Vaughan Jenkins' concurred with Rhodri's account of things. Their mother, it was sombrely declared, 'was as mad as a hatter'. Maybe not during the years the family cohabited, but certainly after John Jenkins was 'taken' from them. 'What people don't realise,' it was resolutely stated, 'is the effect of these things [the militant protest] on the people left behind.' Because John had been assigned an Army house in Wrexham, the boys and their mother were effectively made homeless. They were forced to move to the south and start from scratch.

The house they moved to in Trelewis was an end-of-terrace house on an estate. It is almost certain that 'locals would have heard' who their father was, 'as people talk'. But 'the police would have made sure of it anyway' – although neither Vaughan nor his brother has any idea how John was, or is, regarded in the communities of his youth. To her credit, Thelma had *perhaps* tried to provide for Vaughan and Rhodri. But it was 'hopeless'. The house had lacked furniture, including beds, and owing to the fact that 'there was no food in the house', Vaughan and Rhodri 'went to school for some dinner'. Thelma liked her alcohol and socialising too much. Having married an ex-Army serviceman from Trelewis, it was during an evening out that Thelma met an ex-boxer, who was a drummer on the local Valleys club circuit. Despite being 'a nasty piece of work', it quickly developed into a relationship. Having 'gone off the rails', including some minor trouble with the police, Vaughan was eventually taken into care and later adopted. He 'hated school and he hated people'. The trials and tribulations of his childhood and adolescence, including being adopted, did however prove 'an education' for Vaughan, and one 'that he would not have changed for the world'. It left him believing that 'some people take it all [life] for granted'. They take everything 'at face value' and know 'nothing' about *real* life'. Vaughan believes that he has seen a lot of life, but there are some people who have seen far more than he has. Whether sadly or not, such experiences have made Vaughan 'very questioning and cynical'. Even today, owing to the fact that his father was 'away' when he needed him most, during his childhood and teenage years, Vaughan refuses to call his father 'Dad'.[216]

Perhaps another more 'emotional' legacy of the MAC campaign is that John Jenkins is convinced that several close personal contacts and associates are 'frightened' of him. This includes his sons and his long-term companion, Peter. At a loss to understand why, John declared:

> 'They seem to be under the impression that I am some sort of – well, I don't know what they think. I really would like to know. But they have all said that they're frightened of me – and I can't understand why. What have I done? I've never threatened anybody. I've never said I can do this, or I can do that. Never. And yet they say they're scared of me. Perhaps they just misunderstand what the MAC protest was about and how I went about reining the more hot-headed individuals in.'

But whatever the truth, it is undeniable that the testimony provided by Rhodri and Vaughan Jenkins' associate is very uncomfortable. But if John's ability as a father and grandfather has been called into question, including by John, it should be noted that he is held in high regard by his niece Siân, who, speaking in 2018, described him as a 'pleasant and kind uncle' when she was growing up. The same goes for Katell Keineg, Judith Pritchard's daughter, who during the early 1980s would routinely meet John when their visits to Vaughan, his partner and her son would often inadvertently coincide. 'He was always nice,' Katell remarked of John – even if the relationship between John and Vaughan, although functioning, 'was not particularly affectionate'.[217] But perhaps, cynically speaking, John could afford to be nice to Siân and Katell. After all, he had no responsibility to either, and could walk away at the end of the day, secure in the knowledge that pleasantries would suffice.

Another person who has suffered as a result of the MAC protest is George Taylor's daughter, Jennie. Asked to outline how the militant campaign and the death of her father in Abergele on the eve of the Investiture have affected her life, Jennie declared:

'We used to have graffiti written on the walls of our house. It was just filth, really. People would also shout disgusting, vile comments at us in the streets. We even had dead rats pushed through the letter box. I remember, in a pitiful attempt to protect us children, my mother put up seven net curtains on the windows. It was done to stop people peering in, but they still tried to. My father was just a family man, who was much loved by his family. He was my hero. My mother lived with my father for many years. She loved him – and I know she would have tried to stop him. I can remember quite clearly my mother saying to me, "I can't believe George was involved" [in MAC]. I also remember he would come in and ruffle my hair when he got home. Afterwards, I would still look for my father. Former colleagues of my father's eventually came to the house and asked my mum, Mary, to have a word with me, as I would go to his workplace and ask them to help me look for my dad. I'd also ask the local firemen to help me look for him.

As a family, we had a terrible time. My mother suffered from depression; she couldn't work. She received a one-off widow's pension payment, but it didn't amount to much. They were hard times. Once I came home and found my mother on the floor, unconscious. I ran to get help from a neighbour, and it was found that my mother was suffering from malnutrition. I wasn't a naughty child, but I received a hiding from mother for stealing 12 sachets of powdered soup. She even took me to the police; and back to the shop to return the soup. The shopkeeper, who tried to stop her handing them back, said, "She took soup, Mary, not sweets." But my mother believed that by stealing, I'd discredited my father's name. My mother was the *real* hero, not those whom John Jenkins speaks of. She died at 60, and would often say towards the end, "I just want to go to Dad".'

Had school, by providing an opportunity to immerse herself in her studies, provided a temporary means of escape from the abuse her family was being subjected to? By way of reply, Jennie continued:

'I had an awful time in school. It was horrendous. Every year, at the time of Investiture, or when a new teacher or pupil arrived, I was made to stand on a chair in the classroom. The headmaster would then say that my father had tried to kill the Prince. One year I refused. I swear that I ran away and was caught, taken to the gym, tied to a wooden ladder and whipped with a cane across my legs. He kept saying to me, "You're a bad apple, Jennie Taylor, just like your father." He said, "I *will* make you cry." I said, "You won't." I didn't cry, but I did wet my knickers. The blood was running down my legs. A teacher ran to our house and told my mum. She even told mum that she would probably get the sack for doing so, but that she had to come, as I was getting caned so badly. When my mother arrived, I'd managed to slip past her and make it home. She went to the headmaster's office and he was sat in his chair. On the table in front of him was the cane, which was smeared with my blood. My mother said, "I hope that isn't my daughter's blood." And he said, "That girl needs breaking, Mary." So my mother hit him across the face with the cane. She later called the police, who said that if *she* pressed charges, then the headmaster had told them that he would do likewise against my mother. I don't know if the police thought that the matter might escalate against her, but they then said to her, "They've already lost one parent, Mary." So she was forced, out of fear of what might happen, to drop it. For weeks later, nurses attended to my injuries. I had cuts which wouldn't heal across the top of my legs.

I should say that other teachers were more sympathetic. Some were very kind. But I was then sent to a Special School in Colwyn Bay, because of the bullying from the other children. With the other children at the school in Colwyn Bay, I would recite 'One Man and his Dog', over and over again. Can you imagine how this felt to somebody who had been forced to leave their school because of bullying, and not because of learning difficulties? It was awful. So when I came home, my mother would set me sums and give me reading lessons to keep me up to speed. On one occasion, Prince Charles came to open an annexe at the school in Colwyn Bay, and I was asked to stay home. My mother said there was "no way" I was staying at home. But unlike all the other children, I was asked not to make cakes and bring them in. And do you know, while the Prince was inspecting the school and declaring this annexe open, I was locked in a cupboard. Ultimately, I left school and achieved a first-class honours degree in Social Policy. I'm a social worker.'

It is impossible not to be moved by the revelations of Rhodri Jenkins and Jennie Taylor. Such painful disclosures – especially when suffered at such a young age – bring sharply into focus the detrimental effect on families that a policy of militant activism routinely provokes. But for all Jennie's understandable anger at John Jenkins, few would accuse Jenkins of being untruthful. Asked to outline any regrets he may harbour, John replied candidly:

'Of course I have regrets. I have lots of regrets. Who hasn't? I regret very much that so many lives were ruined. For instance, the injuries suffered by that little boy [Ian Cox]. That's a great source of regret to me. I regret the fact that people were killed; the suffering of George Taylor's family; the suffering of my own family; the fact that Alders' marriage was ruined – or so I later heard. There are many things I regret. But then people keep saying to me, "Well, you can't have an omelette without breaking eggs," and so on. And I suppose that's true. You can't hope to upset the state without getting some scratches in the meantime.

You see, while I'm prepared to talk about regrets, I've also been asked what more we [MAC] could have done. Well, we could have done a lot more, but we were held back by our first function, which was putting together knowledge. The MAC campaign was not about attacking people or killing anybody. It was about getting the people of Wales to understand a bit more about who was walking on them and what it was really all about. We knew that we would *not* achieve that by upsetting them. So therefore, our terms of function were constrained by the fact that whatever we did, it had to go down well with the Welsh people. I will say this one more time:

the object of the exercise was to win "hearts and minds", and you don't do that by upsetting everybody.

And I am quite sure that we [MAC] did have a certain amount of acquiescence. I wouldn't call it direct support, though in some cases it was, but we did receive acquiescent support from the majority of the Welsh public. People understood what we were doing and, generally speaking, were acquiescent about it. As they were with the burning of the cottages. I heard it in pubs myself, many times: "Why should these wealthy buggers from England have two or three houses, and I'm living with my mother-in-law because we can't get a house?" That's what we tried to tap into with MAC: to show the Welsh people that they *did* have the ability to apply a sanction when it became clear that all the normal approaches didn't work. And why? Because the Government – for its own political reasons – didn't *want* them to work. And if the law was applied to change the situation in the favour of Wales, then the Government would simply change the law to suit its own advantage. So, while I do have many reasons to be regretful, I *have* to believe I was right to do what I did. I couldn't live with myself if I thought I'd got it wrong. So, do I regret my involvement in the cause itself? No, I don't. I don't regret doing what I believe I *had* to do – and what I believe needed to be done. In that sense, I feel I achieved what I wanted to achieve. In a way, I started something off... something which has been ignored, of course, by all those "right thinking people", but it was done – and I can live with myself. I am at peace with myself. I could do no more; and I don't think you can ask much more of anybody.'

## Factors the MAC campaign lacked compared to other protest movements

Yet, while John Jenkins may be correct to assert that *Mudiad Amddiffyn Cymru*'s campaign enjoyed a degree of 'acquiescent support' across Wales, it is also true that the green shoots of mass insurrection against the British state failed to materialise either before or after Jenkins' arrest and imprisonment. How does John account for this? 'I think there were a number of reasons,' Jenkins intoned. 'We were up against the British state's well-oiled propaganda machine for one thing – which the Welsh had been subjected to for centuries.' Jenkins continued:

'But also, importantly – unlike most underground organisations – MAC wasn't state-sponsored in the way that EOKA's campaign was. I mean, there were certain similarities between EOKA's position and MAC's position, in one sense. But there were also huge differences. EOKA was supported by a state – Greece, of course. And Greece provided all the information and equipment and experience which EOKA needed. MAC didn't have that. We also lacked the mass support that Martin Luther King and his campaign of passive resistance enjoyed in the States. We lacked that mass support because of the fact that we were unable to propagandise whatever we were doing. Each explosion, as it were, had to speak for itself. We couldn't speak. We couldn't give interviews, other than the single interview we gave in May 1968. And so, while I did have respect for Martin Luther King and the way he remained committed to pacifism, I was never able to compare King's approach with *our* approach.'

## John Jenkins today as he contemplates the MAC offensive, his legacy and mortality

The extent to which the MAC campaign has been forgotten by the general public was brought home to John in the summer of 2017. Hospitalised in Wrexham having suffered a broken hip in a fall at his home in Johnstown, Jenkins was referred to a mental health support team, following concerns that he was hallucinating. With it stated on his medical records that John had served in the military, it was decided that Jenkins' confused and delusional belief pattern might be related to combat stress sustained during a British military engagement. Asked to throw light on how events unfolded, a gaunt-faced Jenkins declared: 'They knew nothing about MAC, or even the Sixties. Yet again, I found myself dealing with people who hadn't done their homework.' Encouraged to elaborate, John added wearily:

'It all began when I told the staff nurses that I was feeling increasingly anxious, and that things were turning over and over in my mind. I then mentioned this to a doctor who visited me, and he said, quite sensibly enough, "It sounds like we should have a look at the mental health situation. Because that is usually – not always, but that is *usually* the cause of things like this. People who are, or have been, under a lot of stress – domestic stress, or stress in work or whatever – well, their mind starts taking over. It's too much for them to deal with all together, and so they start hallucinating. Don't worry," he said, "once we find out what's caused it, it usually goes away." And fair enough, shortly after, I was visited by this support team. Having orchestrated the MAC bombing campaign, I told them that I believed that I was showing signs of combat stress. And so they asked me if I'd served in Korea and places like that. They then informed me that when you are sent out to deal with an enemy that you don't see, or when you are wounded by an enemy that you can't see, that it can lead to combat stress. They thought my stress was related to a more conventional, military sense of conflict. I replied that I meant that I was suffering with the stress of command. Which is a different thing altogether from *their* understanding of combat stress, and all that bloody thing.

Well, they just stared at me blankly. So I said, "From Tryweryn." One said "Tryweryn?" I said, "You know about Tryweryn, don't you?" No, they knew nothing about anything, and they were there to question me about combat stress. So I said to them, "Read it up, and then come back and we'll have a chat about it." I thought Christ, some analysis this is going to be! So off they went. And then some time later, this very senior mental health person came to see me, who apparently was more specialist in these things, and he wanted to talk about it. But again, he knew *nothing* at all about it. I mean, I'm trying to explain these events which happened in the Sixties, and he knew nothing about the Sixties and what happened, other than what he'd read in the history books. It's like talking to someone about the reasons for the First World War, starting on the first day of the war, and yet they know *nothing* about what preceded it. And so I tried to explain that you cannot analyse the situation unless you are aware of the context in which it is situated – and if you are not aware of the context, and you know nothing about what happened before or since, then how the hell are you supposed to analyse it?'

So was Jenkins able to explain to the mental health care professional the significance of Cwm Tryweryn being flooded? He continued:

'Well, having eventually got him to understand about the flooding of Cwm Tryweryn and that it was a cause for anger, he said, "Why was that, then? Why did you feel that the Government wasn't listening?" I then realised that he had interpreted my comments about leading protest over the issue as a few clodhoppers who were protesting about the flooding from a local agricultural perspective. These people knew absolutely nothing! I said, "I can't really sit here and explain the developing situation in south Wales in the early Sixties, unless you know something about it." "Well, er, I wasn't working here then," he said. I don't think they were trying to trip me up, but they should be aware of the situation and they should have enough knowledge to be *able* to trip me up if necessary. But none of the people I spoke to knew anything about MAC, or about the MAC campaign. They seemed to know that I had done time, but they couldn't vaguely understand what for! That is what annoys me so much. I don't care if they know, or if they don't know what I did; or if they care about what I did, or if they *don't* care about what I did. But if they are there to analyse the situation, then they should at *least* be aware of the situation, and of the conditions which caused the situation. How can such so-called analysts and experts even attempt to make sense of a situation within a mental health framework when they have no understanding of the reasons for it? I mean, if they are not interested, they are not interested – but then don't expect me to sit down and explain it all to them. That is not my job. It is *their* job to come prepared.

But to go back to these hallucinations. They weren't about MAC or the campaign, but that's not to say that they won't come back – and that's the trouble. They were about situations which never developed, or which never came about, but which seemed at the time to be absolutely real. But I no longer want to discuss these matters with the so-called "experts" in order to analyse the situation, because I realised that it was the "experts" who were causing me bloody stress! I told them in the end that I was fine and feeling much less anxious! You know, if the MAC campaign had happened in London, it would be far better known, but because it didn't happen in London, or in the south east of England, it never happened. And *that* is what annoys me so much. It is the root of the whole bloody situation. And as I've said, it was coming to pass. We were beginning to realise that we would *have* to hit harder and harder, and target that area, in order to get people to understand what the whole situation was about.'

It is unclear what underpinned John's psychological condition in the summer of 2017. Were the reasons for John's confusion physiological: the body's shock reaction to the breaking of a bone? Or was Jenkins exhibiting feelings of repressed guilt or anger? Might his hallucinations have been a manifestation of a subconscious fear with regards how an escalation in the MAC campaign might have developed? Whatever the truth, in autumn that year, having recovered fully from the effects of the broken hip, John Jenkins was transferred from the hospital in Chirk to a care home in Johnstown. There, in the summer of 2018, an initially sanguine John was asked how he accounted for his fresh face and healthy demeanour, not to mention his emotional clarity. 'It must be the quiet life I've led,' Jenkins replied with typical wry amusement. Was he happy? 'Happy? What's happy?' he responded, smiling, before adding thoughtfully:

'I'm content. I'm well looked after. It's a much less strict regime than hospital. There you'd be woken by the noise and movement of the staff arriving for their shift at 6.30 a.m. or whatever, and then would follow the hustle and bustle and getting you up, and all that. Here, staff leave you to your own devices if they're assured you're OK and want time and space to yourself. I like it. Peter comes to see me every day too, which is nice of him. As for the staff, they know I'm a bit "noted", as it were, because I keep getting phone calls and letters and things like that, you know. And of course, they don't miss much, so they know something's going on. But they don't know what – and they don't like to ask and be too direct. I'd tell them if they asked. I've got nothing to hide. I mean, I've been here a while now; long enough for them to have got to know *me*, before they know who I am. And in the end, that's what counts. But I'm not going to volunteer information. Why on earth should I assume that anyone is interested in me and my life?

That said, sometimes past events reappear as a talking point. For instance, when I was visiting a health centre recently, a doctor was studying my file, and as she read, she asked, "So what was your profession?" I replied I'd been in the Army and was also a retired social worker. "Oh yes," she said. "We know about that, but there is a big gap. Where were you before that, then?" "Well," I replied, "I was in prison doing ten years for terrorist offences." "What!" She nearly fell off her bloody chair! But she was alright though – once she realised that I wasn't going to bite her! She was highly educated after all – and an Irish Catholic. And in my experience, such educated people tend to be less judgemental and open to reason. I explained that I had opposed the Investiture on the grounds that it was a celebration of our conquest as a nation. She was neither critical nor condoning – just what I would expect from someone of her standing. Finally she said, smiling, "So I've got to write down 'retired terrorist'?" I said, "That's it." So yeah.

It's nice here. It's peaceful. I have more time and privacy to read and to listen to informative programmes on the radio. I also spend my time contemplating and thinking, particularly of my childhood in recent months. I've been amazed to find myself remembering Welsh songs that I learned in the nursery school in Treharris – one called, I think, *'Hob Y Deri Dando'*; and another I've been singing is a tale of a little bird. How on earth am I able to remember them – and the name of the boy who lived next door when I was aged 3? I haven't thought about these things in over 80 years! Yeah, I'm OK...

That said, increasingly these past months, I've been having nightmares in which spectres appear. They're nearly always children. Or at least they have been for a while now; and they're appearing more frequently – in the daytime too. For instance, I walked into my room here with one of the staff a few days ago, and as I turned the door handle and entered the room, I stopped chatting and said to her, "What are all these kids doing in here?" The room was full of them. On coming in behind me she said, "What kids? There's no one in here." They're easily distinguishable. They look completely lifelike. They can't speak, and they don't smile. They're expressionless... and I don't recognise them, nor the adults. They don't hurt me, but if I move my hand to gently pat one of the children, my hand goes straight through them. I realise that they're ghosts. It's not reality. But I can be sat in a room with say five people, three of whom are children, and each one will look a solid person to me. But I'm now aware that the three children are ghosts.'

## How John would like to be remembered

John was asked in winter 2018 if he was 'prepared' for his passing. 'Oh yes,' he replied laconically, adding:

'I'm more than ready. I have been for some time... I would welcome it. I know life is going to go on as usual, whether I'm here or whether I'm not here, so it doesn't bother me that much. I feel I've done all the worrying and pondering and thinking required of my life. I've had enough of it – and of trying to work other people out. I came in, I summed up the situation, and I did what I feel I had to do... and so I'm quite happy. I'm prepared. I'm ready for the next chapter, as it were. There is that hymn which says: "It is well, it is well with my soul!"[218]... I mean, I've been no better and no worse than other guys, but the one thing that I haven't been guilty of is being a hypocrite. Look at the hypocrites who litter politics, the world of celebrity, even the Church...

That said, as I consider my mortality in view of my involvement in MAC, the psychological stuff has come back and bitten me on the backside. It's as though they are all in the background laughing. Well, not laughing, but almost saying, "Told you so." In the sense that if you bear a burden long enough, it begins to wear you out – and it does, there's no doubt about it. When I started off in MAC, I was one thing. By the time it ended, I was another thing. I was a different person, because I'd been subjected to a series of pressures which I wasn't used to. I'd never experienced such pressures before, so there was no precedent as to how I was supposed to deal with it. So I had to create a precedent – which I did. The trouble is, while it has its rewards, it also has its bills, and one of the bills returned to me again recently in the form of this psychological pressure... I do have regrets, as I've said. But in *specific* relation to the MAC protest, I have no problem with facing judgement for my deeds and actions. None whatever... I don't think so. Look, there was never a time when what I was doing was perfect. If I was perfect, I would have been crucified as well.'

Does he have hymns and Bible readings in mind for his funeral service? 'No, I'm not bothered about that,' Jenkins declared frankly, before continuing:

'When I'm gone, I'm gone. That's the end of it, as far as I'm concerned. I know it could be a celebration of a different sort, and people there with guns and God knows what. But nothing's been arranged, as far as I know – there again, it's Wales: nothing ever is arranged! These things just happen. It wouldn't surprise me at all if someone fires a gunshot over my grave, but it's a pity they couldn't have thought of it a few years earlier, when they could have actively joined in [the protest]. Because people firing over your grave is a just a signal that you're recognised in certain areas as being crucial to the movement. Well, that's nice, but it would have been better if those people had joined MAC at the time. It's a bit late in the day for all that. But they [those organising the funeral service] can just get on with it.'

In view of such comments, perhaps John's attitude towards his parents' headstones can be traced to the lack of importance he places on his own funeral service and remembrance. But how would he *like* to be remembered? Jenkins replied trenchantly:

'As one of those people who kept our flag flying over the Investiture. Our flag. To show that we weren't all delighted to have been conquered. That not all of us were pleased that the descendants of those people who slaughtered our Royal Family were now flaunting themselves here and expecting us to bow on bended knee.'

The extent to which the MAC protest sent a chill wind along the corridors of power, and caused ministerial and indeed monarchical concern, was revealed in the summer of 2016. It was finally admitted that following the Investiture, the Queen stayed in bed for a week suffering from 'nervous exhaustion' – the only recorded instance of it in the Queen's long reign.[219] In 1969, royal doctors devised a more tactful description of her indisposition, declaring that all engagements in the week following the Investiture were being cancelled owing to a 'feverish cold.'[220] Prompted to read the item and respond, John read aloud: "'The Investiture of the Prince of Wales provided the Queen with one of the worst few days in her long reign. Welsh nationalists were setting off bombs to protest and the event became so stressful that the monarch returned to London and took to bed for a week with what palace officials now admit was 'nervous exhaustion'.'" Having momentarily pondered the disclosure, John declared:

'Well, there's not many who can say that! I don't think they [the establishment] were very pleased about it... Actually, I feel no sense of achievement – because we lost a lot to get the Queen to stay in bed for a week. We lost two dead men and one little boy was grievously injured, and for that we put the Queen in bed for a week. So, no. I don't think it was worth it for that.'

Does the fact that his name was omitted from a list published in 2004 and entitled 'the all-time 100 Welsh heroes' cause Jenkins irritation, particularly in view of the fact that Cayo Evans, the leader of the Free Wales Army, featured at number 33? 'Ah yeah, the all-time 100 Welsh heroes,' John remarked disparagingly, before adding:

'How is it that this fella Cayo Evans appears in this list when he didn't do a bloody thing? But there again, it just confirms what I've been saying: the public don't understand what our [MAC's] basic functions were. His basic function was to get in the bloody papers. Mine was to keep out of the damn things; not to be seen in the papers under any circumstances! Well, only for what we, as a group, were trying to achieve. As for this list, or any other, I don't feel any private sense of frustration. I wouldn't say that I wouldn't *want* to be [included in such a list]. It would be nice, I suppose. But it means nothing to me. I'm not saying that it fills me with delight to see Cayo's name appear somewhere on the list, but it doesn't mean that much. Public approbation is like anything else: it comes and it goes.'[221]

Nonetheless, asked what he would like this epitaph to read, Jenkins thought for a moment and declared: *'Don't listen to what the Old Man of Pencader said. But listen to what the quiet man of Penybryn did*. That sentence,' Jenkins intoned, 'puts into perspective my idea about those who think, and those who do; and those who talk, and those who don't mean a damn thing.[222] 'Or perhaps,' John then stated: *'Home at last, but what a journey!* No – wait!' Jenkins declared, pausing momentarily to lend the comment perfect dramatic timing, 'What about: *Here lies John Jenkins. He made the Queen go to bed for a week.'* It seems fitting enough.

## Will the identity of those in MAC ever be revealed?

Despite many years as a heavy smoker – though he gave up the habit some ten years ago on doctor's advice, following a mild heart attack – John has enjoyed good health throughout his life. Along with having inherited his mother's robust constitution, one possible reason for John's continued vigour is a lifelong aversion to alcohol. A renowned teetotaller, Jenkins' avoidance of alcohol stems from an enduring lack of interest in it; and more recently, from the fear that under its intoxicating influence, MAC's former operational director might inadvertently reveal names and details of the group's campaign. Information 'which even today', Jenkins maintains, the police would consider of 'significant interest'. To reveal such information, Jenkins opines, would be nothing less than a betrayal. 'For what they did,' John declared with typical impactful flair, 'the MAC boys deserve my silence.'

Nonetheless, as a lover and respecter of history, what does Jenkins think of the idea of recording for posterity the names of MAC operatives, for future historians and readers of Welsh history? In response to the suggestion that their names should be written on a sheet of paper and placed within a sealed envelope until 1 July 2029, to coincide with the 60th anniversary of the Investiture, John replied enigmatically, 'I'll think about it.' Pausing momentarily, he continued:

> 'The only person who knows who was in MAC is me. I have never divulged their names to anyone. It is a credit to the fact that our security was so good that nobody knows who was in MAC. And that is why the police are afraid to move too fast, too far; because they don't know who was in MAC either, in spite of all their talk about information having been received. No information has *ever* been received. And Wales' reputation of being a place where you can't keep a secret has taken a bit of a dive, because we can keep a secret and we have kept it for a long time. And it is still there. I am under oath myself not to divulge names until they are dead. That's what I told them when they first joined. "In terms of your identity being revealed, you are safe. I will say nothing to anybody until you are dead." And I am not just talking about the front-line activists. I am talking about the assistants: those who provided financial support; the ladies who cooked a meal; those ladies around Wales who also said, "I have a spare room in the front, they [activists] can sleep in there for the night if they need to." *All* these people were in MAC. And I will never divulge their names while they are alive.'

## John Barnard Jenkins – will there ever be another, and is MAC still a force to be reckoned with as Wales looks to the future?

Asked to sum up both his personality in relation to militant activism and whether Wales is ever likely to see a similar character emerge, Jenkins stated intently:

> 'I am by nature unassuming. I function best as an *éminence grise*: the person who operates behind the throne, pulling the strings. That's where I feel most comfortable: on the outskirts. Where I'm able to influence events, but not be directly involved with them. It is then that I can look at things objectively and see what needs doing. And so I don't believe that I actually led MAC. I just pulled the elements together. Well, perhaps I did lead it. I don't know. But I pulled the elements together and so made MAC into a cohesive, effective, working force, which did what it promised. We said that we would change the nature of the activities of the Investiture, and we did just that. Despite what our detractors said, that "MAC failed

because the Investiture went ahead." Yes, it went ahead, but under *very* different conditions than that which was originally planned. And I would do it again if the occasion arose. I can't do it presently, because I am, of course, not unknown. But I am sure that there are others out there who would be equally able to get on with things. There is nothing unusual about me. I just push on when perhaps most people would stop. But I can't be on my own – there must be others. In fact, I know there are.'

But does MAC still pose a threat? Jenkins nodded approvingly, and continued:

'And all they are waiting for, presumably, is a flashpoint to arise – where there is a complete change of heart for many people. Would they still be made of the same stuff as the 1960s? Oh yes. I think so – as was evidenced when *Meibion Glyndŵr* were active. They are still there, and I know they are still reliable. The term we used, "healthy", still applies. The dependability and ability of these people in Wales can still be relied upon. Because how many people have come forward since my jail term with information about anything? None – and that is the best pat on the back that I could ever have got from anywhere. But I am sure of one thing: because of what we did in the Sixties, they [Whitehall] will never presuppose us again and implement something without first considering our reaction to it.'

Perhaps John Jenkins is correct, but the controversy surrounding the renaming of the second Severn crossing in 2018, when – against considerable online protest in Wales – the bridge was renamed the Prince of Wales Bridge, might suggest that the voice of Wales is *still* being ignored. Nonetheless, what of the future? What will the census figures to be published in 2021 reveal in relation to Wales? Will they highlight a similar pattern to those published in 2011, when it was recorded that those who speak Welsh had fallen by 1% since 2001 and that 26% of those living in Wales were born outside it – of which the overwhelming majority were born in England? It is a situation which, not surprisingly, 'troubles' John Jenkins, although it should be noted that John displays a degree of exasperation with the parochialism sometimes displayed by a number of his compatriots, and in keeping with more progressive attitudes, dismisses notions of Wales as a mystical, modern-day Shangri-La. However, those in Wales with more hard-nosed attitudes are rigid in their assessment that a deliberate policy of cultural and political dilution, akin to that adopted by the Chinese in Tibet, has been enacted in Wales. This in part, they maintain, has been achieved with the connivance of the British state: through media coverage outlining the affordability of property in Wales, in conjunction with the splendour of the landscape and the country's safe living environment. Asked to comment on whether he believes that such a policy has been promoted by sections within the UK intelligence community, John replied pensively:

'It's a tough one. But it would appear from all the evidence we have that they would have been trying to do that. But the point is, you can't blame the English people themselves. Why would they not want to leave, when they can sell up in England and move to Wales with God knows how much in their bank accounts to buy anything they like here? Mind you, I will say this: in recent years we've seen the uproar in England over the immigration issue. It featured significantly in the Brexit debate. "Something must be done to stop all these Bulgarians and Poles from coming to England!" Not to mention the so-called "white flight" phenomenon. Yet, if we [Welsh] take a similar view in response to the thousands upon thousands of English people moving here, we are branded as racist! But the fact remains that the only people you can blame are the Welsh who sold to them. What they [English incomers] have done is perfectly legal, normal and natural. I can only conclude that this has been a policy never denied. Perhaps it wasn't pushed, but it wasn't stopped either. The situation could be rectified to some degree, through the Welsh Government adopting a counter-policy, which insists that anyone moving to Wales – from anywhere – has to agree to receive lessons in the Welsh language and the nation's history and culture. That would at least ensure a more successful assimilation. But the Welsh Government would never do such a thing. In fact, I now believe that by the time we gain our independence, due to the lack of affordable housing, further cultural dilution and uncontrolled inward migration, it won't be the Wales we want anyway!'

How will the Investiture of Prince William as Prince of Wales be recognised? Is it correct to assume there exists the prospect of an investiture ceremony with all the grandeur afforded to Prince Charles in 1969, guaranteed to enrage vehement Welsh nationalists? Or will the occasion pass without issue or incident – the cost alone perhaps ensuring that such a spectacle is not repeated, not to mention the supposed intention across the political divide for a more sensitive and understated offering? Prompted to outline his thoughts on the matter, John declared:

'I doubt very much they would be foolish enough to have a ceremony, but they might try to. They have obviously been spending a lot of time in the last couple of years trying to promote him [William] in some future role. He's already been appointed Vice Royal Patron of the Welsh Rugby Union! But I doubt if they would be idiotic enough to attempt another investiture… No, I doubt it. I think it would be a very stupid thing for them to do, because it would be waving a red rag to a bull again. Put it this way: the red dragon still has teeth. Even if he *is* sitting in the dentist's chair, and they look like getting pulled.'

What of the ever-contentious subject of Welsh water? Has the issue been resolved with the announcement in November 2017 by Alun Cairns, the Welsh Secretary of State, that the authority to make water-related decisions will be shared by the UK and Welsh Governments?[223] It is a development dismissed facetiously by Jenkins as 'tokenism'. How else can it be described, Jenkins added, 'when there is so much [power] on one side and so little on the other? It certainly isn't a chat between equals.' Apart from that, Jenkins concluded deridingly, 'Cairns has his own agenda; and one which doesn't have a great deal to do with Welsh independence!'

Yet will any of these situations provide the flashpoint which sees direct action adopted once again to protect Welsh cultural or political interests? Only time will tell, although it may be doubtful whether, in this age of widespread CCTV camera surveillance, 'prevent thinking' strategies and 28-day detention of suspects under anti-terrorist legislation, a campaign of militant activism would ever be so sustained as MAC's under Jenkins' direction.[224] Even John concedes that in view of the technical and judicial advances now available to the state, only a 'miracle' would ensure another MAC. But it should also be acknowledged that following the conviction of John Jenkins: an intelligent, articulate and highly respected member of Her Majesty's Forces, everyone became a possible suspect, irrespective of age, gender or social status. It is a shift in attitude, admitted a former senior police officer, born of the fact that 'never again will they [the authorities] make that mistake' – of accepting at face value the view that such figures were pillars of patriotic moral rectitude. That one such as John Jenkins would engage in such activity was deemed incomprehensible. But for all the lessons learned, surely political discourse and common sense should determine any future policy affecting Wales; leaving Welsh political violence – and its appalling litany of death, injuries and emotional trauma – to be consigned to the history books.

## History's judgment of MAC and John Jenkins

So how will the campaign of *Mudiad Amddffyn Cymru* and its protagonists be viewed by history? Will the protest by MAC be dismissed as an irrelevance? Will it be denounced as a campaign of violence undertaken by a group of cowardly, romantic, marginalised desperadoes and hotheads, whose protest of hopeless idealism warrants the merest mention as a footnote in the historical record? Or might those drawn to undertake action in the name of MAC be viewed more warmly? Is it possible that MAC activists will be considered a dedicated and able band of patriots, driven to act in the defence of Wales after witnessing their proud home nation suffer repeated humiliation at the hands of a detached, mute and unhearing political elite?

Perhaps more pertinently, how will John Jenkins be viewed by future generations? As a charismatic and masterful tactician, who against overwhelming military and financial odds proved a worthy opponent to the British state? Will the perception be that John was a courageous man of strong principle and conviction, who, as Gwynfor Evans opined, 'sacrificed much for a cause he believed in'? Or will Jenkins' deeds be rejected as the actions of a feckless reactionary, a deluded cynic and a self-absorbed, malcontent firebrand? Might John Jenkins be held in the same regard as Welsh history's most celebrated freedom fighter, Owain Glyndŵr? It is, of course, impossible to know. But as Jenkins is '*convinced* that the MAC campaign was an essential part of Wales' devolution journey', which resulted in the creation of the Welsh Assembly, it is intriguing to speculate.

As the militant protest of *Mudiad Amddffyn Cymru* evokes such contrasting emotions, it is perhaps unsurprising that opinion of MAC – and of John Jenkins – is still divided and heartfelt. 'I didn't like that,' declared a former mid-Wales police officer in 2017, when discussing the MAC offensive. 'It was nasty. A nasty campaign.' Contacted to give his opinion of John Jenkins and his legacy, Jenkins' former MAC associate

David Walters was unequivocal. 'It's a pity,' he remarked, 'but that guy should have been treated as a hero in Wales. Instead of that he's been totally ignored.' It is an opinion with which *some* in Wales are likely to concur. But whatever the truth, it is perhaps fitting that the closing words belong to John Barnard Jenkins. Asked to sum up the militant campaign of *Mudiad Amddiffyn Cymru*, MAC's flawed and brilliant strategist replied, somewhat curtly: 'I'm proud of what I achieved. Particularly with what I had to work with. But I wish it hadn't been necessary.' Perhaps, despite his obvious pride in and the moral justification he feels for his cause, John Jenkins really is the Reluctant Revolutionary.

# Notes

1.   John Jenkins: 'The failure to tell me specifically where I was born may have been to protect my feelings.'
2.   The Salvation Army Home, Northlands, 202 North Road, Cardiff, opened in 1922. It could accommodate 18 mothers and 12 babies.
3.   John Jenkins: 'The letter was tucked away in a chest of drawers in my mother's bedroom, amongst her bottles of perfume and make-up.' Born in 1904, Minerva had the same birthday as John.
4.   The official witnesses to the marriage were Minerva's brother, William J Barnard, and Tom's father, Thomas Jenkins.
5.   Before the business became Dodington's Stores in the early 1930s, it was known as F J Allwoods family grocery store, which was established in the 1890s. On being sold by the Dodingtons in the 1940s, it was acquired by Thomas and Evans Ltd, who ran the business until the 1950s. *Cardiff Yesterday*, Volume 30; also, *Western Mail* (Cardiff Directory), 1937.
6.   When looking through his late mother's correspondence, John discovered two photographs of Minerva. One had been taken while she was working in the Land Army in Llanrhystud, near Aberystwyth, during the closing stages of, or immediately following, World War I; and in the other photograph she was wearing 'a sort of maid's uniform' while in the employ of the Dodington family. The photographs have since been mislaid.
7.   According to the 1931 Census, a family by the name of Dodington had moved to Cardiff from Dorset at some point since the previous census was taken in 1921.
8.   In 1886, the Guardianship of Infants Act (Section 5) empowered the court to make a custody or access order on the application of a child's mother, and legislation (Section 3) subsequently provided that the court could order a father to pay the mother weekly or other periodical sums by way of maintenance. *Children – The Modern Law*, 4th Edition (Jordan Publishing Ltd, 2013), p.416.
9.   John Davies, *A History of Wales* (Penguin, 1993), p.489.
10.   According to Professor Brinley Thomas, 'the Welsh patriot should sing the praises of industrial development', for 'the Welsh language was saved by the redistribution of a growing population brought about by industrialism.'
11.   John is unsure if Minerva's parents still lived on Cottrell Street at the time of the disaster, as the Jenkins family, and more specifically Minerva and John, rarely spoke of her parents.
12.   Keith Jenkins: 'My father was a lovely man, but he was what you might call today a little backward.'

[13] John Jenkins: 'Once she married, my mother never worked outside the family home again. It was the tradition of the South Wales Valleys at that time: a married woman's place was in the home.'

[14] John Jenkins: 'She was not named Minerva, the Roman goddess of wisdom, for nothing.'

[15] John Jenkins: 'Although "indoor" in one sense, the toilet was accessed by walking through a passageway which ran alongside the house. Being in places exposed to the elements, if we had a heavy fall of snow, we had to dig our way to get to the damn place!'

[16] *Daily Mail*, 15 February 2019; also, Gwyn Alf Williams, *When Was Wales* (Penguin, 1985), p.249; John Davies, *A History of Wales* (Penguin, 1993), p.492; Trevor Herbert (ed.), *Wales 1880–1914: Welsh History and its Sources*. (UWP, 1988). Historian Guy Walters refutes 'the mythology as propagated by the hard-Left' that Winston Churchill ordered troops to fire on striking miners. He claims that on the second day of disturbances, a miner (Samuel Rhys) received a heavy blow to the head from which he died days later, but that the fatal injury was inflicted by battle-charging Metropolitan police rather than Rhys being shot by a soldier of the 18th Hussars. The latter had yet to arrive in Tonypandy to quell the unrest, which included striking miners looting 'nearly every shop' in the town. Being 'extremely reluctant' to deploy the Hussars, Churchill showed 'restraint' in requesting that police deal with the disturbances, before finally agreeing to deploy the troops. As such, Walters maintains, Churchill was no 'villain' and 'would always regret his decision'. Furthermore, the manner in which events unfolded and the way Churchill's actions have been misrepresented is 'bad history'. Yet, unsurprisingly, the episode appears far from clear. G A Williams states that there was 'a selective sacking of the town'. J Davies adds that 'there was a pattern and a meaning to the protest' and that while 'the soldiers were prudently deployed, there were occasions (with their deployment in the area lasting months) that they were in confrontation with protestors'; and 'thus it is not myth that Churchill used soldiers against strikers' and that 'their presence... deprived the miners of victory'. Moreover, T Herbert reports that when speaking in Cardiff during the General Election campaign of 1950, an apparently contrite Winston Churchill declared: 'When I was Home Secretary in 1910, I had a great horror and fear of having to become responsible for the military firing on a crowd of rioters and strikers. Also, I was always in sympathy with the miners...'

[17] About 30 years ago, John returned to the pit village of Penybryn and was saddened by how much the area had changed. With the pits all closed down and the area subject to economic decline, little of what John remembered from his happy childhood remained.

[18] *Rarebit* was broadcast from Cardiff by the BBC between February 1940 and December 1944. The show's most lasting legacy remains its closing song, *We'll Keep a Welcome (in the Hillsides)*. It started as a monthly 30-minute feature in the BBC's Forces Programme to entertain armed forces personnel, especially those

from Wales, but *Welsh Rarebit* quickly gained widespread popularity and from June 1941 also featured periodically in the schedules of the BBC Home Service. It was primarily a variety show, but also included regular features like *Tommy Troubles* and *Dai's Letter to the Forces*, which was a sentimental reflection of life in Wales. The programme attracted 12 million listeners at its peak, and is still one of the most popular entertainment shows ever to have been produced in Wales. *Welsh Rarebit* returned in the BBC Light Programme on Saint David's Day 1948, and ran until July 1951. A final 'Christmas Special' edition was broadcast in December 1952.

[19]  The other was Allan Rogers, MEP for SE Wales, 1979–84 and Labour MP for Rhondda, 1983–2001. Rogers was the Opposition Spokesman on Defence,1987–92, and Foreign Affairs, 1992–94; he later became a member of the ISC (Intelligence and Security Committee), a cross-party committee of MPs and peers who oversee the work of the intelligence and security agencies. Beti Jones, *Welsh Elections 1885–1997* (Y Lolfa, 1999), pp.134, 203.

[20]  Combining all of John's growing interests of travel, history, culture, science and nature, it is little wonder he enjoyed reading *The National Geographic*, which the Jenkins family 'received through a monthly subscription'.

[21]  The supply teacher, Alfred T Evans, was later returned as the Labour MP for Caerphilly at the by-election in July 1968. He represented the constituency until the General Election in 1979. Beti Jones, *Welsh Elections 1885–1997* (Y Lolfa, 1999), pp.114, 129, 188.

[22]  Revd Francis Kilvert, the renowned Victorian diarist, noted that St Harmon in Radnorshire 'was reputed to be the oldest Christian Foundation in the County, having been founded in the early fifth century.'

[23]  In 314, just a year after Emperor Constantine granted Christians freedom of worship throughout the Roman Empire, a Church Council was held in Arles in France. It was attended by three British bishops: Eborius, Bishop of York; Restitutus, Bishop of London; and Adelfius, probably Bishop of Caerleon (Gwent).

[24]  Written by Venerable Bede in about 731, The *Ecclesiastical History of the English People* (*Historia Ecclesiastica Gentis Anglorum*) states that Augustine arrived in Britain in 597, having been sent by Pope Gregory to convert the Anglo-Saxons to Christianity. The *Historia* is considered one of the most important original references on Anglo-Saxon history and has played a key role in the development of an English national identity. The native Britons, whose Christian Church survived the departure of the Romans, earn Bede's ire for refusing to help convert the Saxons. By the end of the *Historia*, the English and their Church are dominant over the Britons.

[25]  John Jenkins: 'I went back quite recently to have a look at Bargoed Grammar School, and there is just a heap of rubble there. They knocked it all down.'

[26]  British troops liberated the Bergen-Belsen Nazi concentration camp on 15 April 1945, and Dachau was liberated two weeks later on 29 April.

27    Unable to recall which election this was, it is likely that John is referring to the 1945 General Election, held 5 July 1945, when he was 12. In his home constituency, Rhondda East, the Labour Party won with 16,733 votes (48.4%), the Communist Party came second with 15,761 votes (45.5%) and Plaid Cymru came third with 2,123 votes (6.1%). At the 1950 General Election, the Labour Party consolidated its position, winning with 26,645 votes (75.9%). Beti Jones, *Welsh Elections 1885–1997* (Y Lolfa, 1999), pp.90, 94.

28    John Jenkins: 'All these discussions about what qualifications were needed to do this or that sort of job just didn't bother me. Besides, I was far too busy with outside interests, such as trying to learn more about Welsh history – which wasn't easy, as so little was available.'

29    On 8 August 1945, representatives of the US, UK, the Soviet Union and France signed what became known as the London Charter. This established a charter for the setting up of an international military tribunal to try those members of the Axis Powers accused of being war criminals, but whose crimes were not confined to a single country.

30    Between 20 November 1945 and 1 October 1946, the Nuremburg tribunal met 216 times before delivering its verdict. Of the 24 Nazis charged with war crimes, one committed suicide during the trial, another was judged unfit to stand trial on the grounds of severe dementia, 3 were acquitted and 19 were found guilty. Of those found guilty, 7 received prison sentences and the remaining 12 were sentenced to death by hanging. Martin Bormann was found guilty in his absence and Hermann Goering committed suicide on the eve of his execution. The remaining 10 were hanged on 16 October 1946.

31    John Jenkins: 'Although we only lived two or three miles apart, the only way to get from her house to mine directly was to walk. There were roads, but the road sort of circled around at other angles. To go straight from the one to the other in the shortest possible time meant walking across. And ordinarily, that's what we used to do. We'd meet at the halfway point.'

32    *Two Men Went to War* (Ira Trattner Productions, 2002).

33    John Jenkins: 'I don't keep in touch with my former colleagues, nor do I attend the reunion dinners, etc. They didn't have any such get-togethers until I wrote a letter to the depot saying it was a shame that, "Here we are, scattered all throughout the world, and we don't get these marches like other people do." No "Freedom of the City" and all that sort of stuff. And so, why couldn't they put something on for us? And they did. They then said that people could come back to the depot in Aldershot and – well, sergeants anyway – have a couple of weeks there.'

34    Terry Burrows, *History of the Modern World* (Carlton, 1999), p.228. The aim of the Festival of Britain was to 'demonstrate Britain's contribution to civilisation, to stimulate trade and to encourage creative effort in British national life'.

35    In February 1953, confectionery rationing ended. Seven months later, sugar rationing ended, and on 4 July 1954, meat and all other food rationing ended in Britain.

36    John Jenkins: 'The rabbi did *not* think this was a place for celebration. The effect on me of visiting Dachau concentration camp [where barbaric medical 'experiments' were carried out on living prisoners and the bodies of over 30,000 people were burnt in the crematorium] was profound.'

37    Gwynfor Evans, *Welsh Nation Builders* (Gomer, 1988), p.204.

38    *Liverpool Daily Post*, 22 December 1955.

39    Social Enquiry Report Concerning John Barnard Jenkins, 26 February 1970.

40    John Jenkins: 'I didn't know much about Nelson Mandela until later – and it wasn't enough to make an impact.'

41    The Atomic Weapons Establishment (AWE – formerly the Atomic Weapons Research Establishment) at Aldermaston is where the UK designs and manufactures Trident missiles, and where decommissioned and redundant nuclear weapons are dismantled. The first Aldermaston March in April 1958 saw around 3,000 protesters march from London to Aldermaston over four days, with a total attendance of 12,000 at the establishment's gates on arrival.

42    Israel, France and the UK intended to regain Western control of the Suez Canal and to remove Egyptian President Gamal Abdel Nasser from power. In the event, Nasser's position was strengthened.

43    Peden, G C, 'Suez and Britain's Decline as a World Power', *The Historical Journal*, (Cambridge University Press, December 2012), pp.1073–1096.

44    Both Thelma and John were two years into their three-year nurse training course when they married and moved to Cyprus. Having both failed to quality as General Nurses, did Thelma resent John, or regret the decision not to complete the course? 'I have no idea,' Jenkins answered. 'I never discussed it with her.'

45    *The Mail on Sunday*, 15 July 2018.

46    Terry Burrows, *History of the Modern World* (Carlton, 1999), p.256.

47    *The Mail on Sunday*, 15 July 2018; also, BBC news, 23 January 2019. Papers lodged at the High Court allege that during the Cyprus insurgency, British colonial forces raped a 15-year-old girl, committed murder and tortured civilian detainees with beatings and mock hangings. Efforts by appalled Army servicemen to report their complaints to superior officers were allegedly suppressed. The UK Government, having denied that any wrongdoing occurred during the EOKA uprising and maintaining that the settlement is not 'any admission of liability', is to award £1m damages to 33 Cypriot pensioners.

48    Archbishop Makarios was depicted by the British press as a crooked Cypriot priest and viewed with suspicion by the British authorities. When Makarios died of a heart attack in August 1977, his funeral was interrupted by a rainstorm, unheard of in Cyprus at that time of year. A Greek-Cypriot newspaper said that this proved an old Greek proverb: 'When a good man is buried, even the Heavens shed tears'.

49    See Christopher Andrew, *The Defence of the Realm. The Authorised History of MI5* (Penguin, 2009), pp.465–66 for more information regarding the UK Government's concern that Makarios 'was about to torpedo the negotiations' to end the conflict in Cyprus. For information concerning the blackmailing of Makarios, see Rupert

Allason, (a.k.a. Nigel West) *The Friends: Britain's Post-War Secret Intelligence Operations* (Weidenfeld and Nicolson, 1988), p. 78; also Stephen Dorril, *MI6: Inside the Covert World of Her Majesty's Secret Intelligence Service* (Touchstone, 2000), p.556.

[50] Following a campaign of insurgency in which terrorist tactics were used, British troops left Aden on 29 November 1967. 'Gone Away – No Milk, No Papers' was the message scrawled by a soldier on the wall of Aden's empty prison. Having ruled the province since 1839, it summed up the indecent haste of Britain's departure. When UK forces left, the independent People's Republic of South Yemen was proclaimed.

[51] Rhys Evans, *Gwynfor Rhag Pob Brad* (Y Lolfa, 2005), p.222.

[52] Defending solicitor Elystan Morgan subsequently became an MP, a Circuit Judge and Member of the House of Lords.

[53] Dr Phil Williams came third in the 1964 election, polling 3,956 (11%) of the votes cast in the Caerphilly constituency. Beti Jones, *Welsh Elections 1885–1997* (Y Lolfa, 1999), p.108.

[54] In 1892, the National Institutions Bill had sought to establish a Secretary of State for Wales. The Bill failed, but the notion received renewed support between 1918 and 1922. In 1946, D R Grenfell led a deputation to the Government, advocating the establishment of such an office. The Labour Party's endorsement of the creation of a Secretary of State for Wales, as first outlined in its 1959 Election manifesto, was only possible following Aneurin Bevan's acceptance that Wales should receive a political office which was solely responsible for some of the nation's political needs.

[55] In 1969 health and agriculture were devolved to the Welsh Office, followed by education in 1970.

[56] John Jenkins: 'It [the Welsh Office] has done a lot of good, but it could have done a damn sight *more* good. But there again, that was never the intention. It was a political gesture, done to demonstrate a 'loosening of the reins' and a 'freedom to breathe', yet without ever taking the reins away. The horse would never be allowed to gallop. No way. I mean they were shouting and bawling in the seventies and eighties about the possibility of oil being found in Welsh waters, and I said then, "If that ever happens, we've lost all chance of any bloody thing." We would have been ignored. They would have grabbed it; and that would be it. It would have gone the same way as Scottish oil.'

[57] One indication of the British Army's English orientation, Jenkins believed, was provided by the noticeboard at the Bielefeld camp entrance, which stated *Englische Kaserne* or 'English Barracks'.

[58] Able to infiltrate the television frequency, Radio Free Wales aired immediately after television programmes ended for the night and was often broadcast from Garth Newydd, a Plaid Cymru activist commune in Merthyr Tydfil where Harri Webb, Meic Stephens and others lived. A primary objective was to highlight the proposal by the National Broadcasting Council for Wales to allow a series of local

party broadcasts, including provision for Plaid Cymru, which was vetoed – with the connivance of the Labour Party – by the Government in 1955. It decreed that a political party must contest 50 Parliamentary seats before it could be granted airtime. As there were 36 seats in Wales, a solely Welsh party did not qualify to broadcast. Plaid Cymru's first political broadcast was in 1965. By 1970, the rule over contesting 50 seats was removed.

[59] On 15 October 1962, having broken two locks to gain access, Owain Williams, Robert Wyn Williams and Edwin Pritchard raided the explosives magazine at Crofts Quarries, Llithfaen. They stole nearly 4,000 detonators and 15 fuses. In court at Blaenau Ffestiniog on 7 May 1963, Robert Wyn Williams was fined £25 and Edwin Pritchard was fined £40. Owain Williams was already in custody over the explosions at the Tryweryn reservoir site in February 1963 and for targeting with explosives an electricity pylon at Gellilydan, Maentwrog, Trawsfynydd in March 1963. Having pleaded guilty to all three charges, Williams was sentenced to 12 months' imprisonment at Ruthin Assizes on 1 July 1963.

[60] Jenkins later confirmed that collier Alf Williams, Dave Pritchard and Trefor Beasley were among the MAC trainers. Jenkins also revealed that he attended Alf Williams' funeral, declaring: 'I only ever went to funerals of people who, as far as I was concerned, counted, in my terms... People such as Alf, Dave Pritch, Trefor and Dafydd y Dug [Dafydd Burns].'

[61] *The Guardian*, 8 October 1965; *Western Mail*, 18 October 1965; *Wrexham Leader*, 28 August 1964. On 2 August 1960, work began to prepare Cwm Tryweryn for flooding as the construction site became operational. With water first dammed at the site on 1 September 1964, the newly-named Llyn Celyn was full to capacity by August 1965. It was, proclaimed the *Wrexham Leader*, 'a new wonder of Wales'.

[62] Speaking in 2018, Pritchard's former wife, Judith, declared, 'I didn't know that Dave was involved in the protest, although I was one of those who purchased a small amount of land at the Clywedog site. It cost about £100, I think. I still have the map here with my little plot on it. We hoped it would prevent the valley being drowned, but nothing came of it, of course. They just ignored us and pushed it through Parliament. I don't know if we ever had the money back!'

[63] 6.5 inches (170 mm) of rain fell in the Aberfan area in the first three weeks of October 1966, nearly half of which was in the third week. Tony Austin, *Aberfan: The Story of a Disaster* (Hutchinson, 1967), p.10.

[64] There were seven spoil tips on the slopes above Aberfan. Tip 7, which slipped onto the village, was begun in 1958 and stood 111 feet (34 m) high at the time of the disaster. Approximately 140,000 cubic yards (110,000 m³) of debris covered the village in just minutes.

[65] Tragically, the children arrived to begin lessons at 9 a.m., and the half-term holiday was due to start at 12 p.m.

[66] 'No one was brought out alive after 11 o'clock.' Chief Constable of the County Borough of Merthyr Tydfil, T K Griffiths. *Merthyr Express*, 28 October 1966.

[67] Sir Tasker Watkins' private papers. Transcript of police interview with John Jenkins, 11 November 1969.

[68] Lord Robens, *Ten Year Stint* (Cassell, 1972), p.251.

[69] *The Sunday Times*, 30 October 1966.

[70] *Merthyr Express*, 28 October 1966.

[71] Ian McLean and Martin Johnes, *Aberfan: Government and Disasters* (Welsh Academic Press, 2000), p.29.

[72] Edmund Davies, *Report of the Tribunal Appointed to Inquire into the Disaster at Aberfan on October 21st 1966.* (Her Majesty's Press, 1967), p.33.

[73] Ibid, p.34.

[74] As a protest against what he regarded as the Labour Government's cynical response to the Aberfan disaster, S O Davies boycotted the ceremony at which Harold Wilson, then Prime Minister, was given the Freedom of the Borough of Merthyr Tydfil in 1970. Alun Roberts, *Welsh National Heroes* (Y Lolfa, 2002), p.103.

[75] Lord Robens was informed of the disaster during an NCB board meeting that morning. Following discussions with the NCB's Director-General of Production and its Chief Safety Engineer, it was agreed [as per policy] that they should inspect the situation, and so left for Aberfan immediately. In his autobiography, Robens stated that the decision for him not to go was because 'the appearance of a layman at too early a stage inevitably distracts senior and essential people from the tasks upon which they should be exclusively concentrating.' Instead of visiting the scene that Friday evening or the next day, Robens attended a ceremony to invest him as the Chancellor of the University of Surrey, where he was photographed smiling proudly in grand robes. Responding to criticism over her husband's actions, Lady Eve Robens has maintained that in private her husband was greatly affected by the disaster, the stress of which may have instigated the strokes he later suffered.

[76] McLean & Johnes, *Aberfan: Government and Disasters*, p.13.

[77] TNA, COAL 73/2.

[78] *Western Mail*, 31 August 1967.

[79] Interview between Neil ap Siencyn (formerly Jenkins) and Wyn Thomas, 22 October 2006.

[80] Asked if the Queen had ever put a foot wrong, Lord Charteris – the Queen's former Private Secretary – responded by way of a single word: 'Aberfan.' *Sunday Express*, 28 April 2002. The decision, the Queen quietly acknowledged, to simply issue a press release and send the Duke of Edinburgh the following day, rather than visiting herself, was incorrect. *The Guardian*, October 2002. Speaking on the 50th anniversary of the disaster, the Queen paid tribute to the 'indomitable spirit' of the people of Aberfan. *Daily Mail*, 22 October 2016.

[81] Sir Tasker Watkins' private papers. Transcript of police interview with John Jenkins, 11 November 1969.

[82] TNA, ASSI 84/577. Undated witness statement by Thomas Jones. Interviewed by police following the explosion, T Jones, the owner of Arllwyn, the house

which overlooked the pipeline and which suffered 'some broken windows' in the explosion, stated that he and his family visited his father in Borth 'one weekend in every three or four'; and that consequently, he 'felt sure' his movements 'would be known to many of the local people'.

83 *Western Mail* and *Liverpool Daily Post*, 2 October 1967.

84 Lord Snowdon had been appointed Constable of Caernarfon Castle and requested to organise the pageant of the Royal Investiture of Prince Charles.

85 *Herald of Wales*, 7 October 1967.

86 *The Sun*, 9 October 1967.

87 *Town* Magazine, December 1967.

88 *Broadsheet*, University College of Wales, Cardiff periodical. Autumn 1967.

89 Tony Bunyan, *The Political Police in Britain* (Julian Friedmann, 1976), p.149; also, *Planet*, June/July 1972.

90 *Western Mail*, 6 January 1968.

91 In August 1968, Owain Williams was arrested at Birmingham airport. At his trial at Caernarfon Assizes some ten weeks later, Williams was acquitted of unlawful possession of explosives.

92 *Western Mail*, 25 March 1968.

93 *The Observer*, 29 October 1967. While at Aberystwyth, it was intended that the Prince should study 'the history, language and problems of Wales'.

94 TNA, ASSI 84/577. Witness statement by Harold Pendlebury, 5 December 1969; also Ian Skidmore, 17 December 1969.

95 David John Underhill [a.k.a. Dafydd y Dug and Dafydd Burns] was later arrested (along with members of the FWA and figures within the anti-Investiture movement) before being acquitted on all charges after spending three months in custody prior to the Investiture.

96 It was later confirmed that Trefor Beasley was a MAC activist and that Harri Webb had utilised his position within Plaid Cymru to garner support for MAC.

97 George Thomas was appointed Secretary of State for Wales on 5 April 1968, replacing Cledwyn Hughes, who had succeeded James Griffiths in the post on 5 April 1966.

98 *Western Mail*, 26 May 1968. Thomas added: 'The anonymous cowards who slunk away this morning are a disgrace to the Welsh people.'

99 Further damaging to Thomas' reputation were claims made in 2014 that he had been involved in child sexual abuse in the 1960s. Following the conclusion of a public inquiry, it was announced that from 1 September 2017, the George Thomas Hospice in Cardiff was changing its name to City Hospice, partly to distance the hospice from 'any negative connotation' associated with the former Lord Tonypandy. It should be noted that George Thomas, a popular and long-standing constituency MP who died in 1997 aged 88, was never charged with, let alone convicted of, any crime.

100 *Wrexham Leader*, 9 February 1968. The 7-storey building cost £100,000 to construct.

101 *Daily Mirror*, 29 June 1968. 'Charles faces jeering crowd'

102 *North Wales Chronicle*, 18 July 1968. Informal visit of Lord Snowdon and Prince Charles to Caernarfon Castle.

103 Beti Jones, *Welsh Elections 1885–1997* (Y Lolfa, 1999), pp.112, 114, 117, 118. In the 1970 General Election, Dr P Williams came second, polling 11,505 (28.5%) in the Caerphilly constituency and H V Davies also came second, polling 3,528 (14%) in Rhondda West.

104 Rhys Evans, *Portrait of a Patriot* (Y Lolfa, 2008), p.279.

105 Anonymous, interview with Wyn Thomas, November 2016.

106 *Wrexham Leader*, 22 November 1968. Coinciding with the announcement that forthwith Caernarfon Castle was to be 'lit up like a prison' to stop 'extremists' daubing slogans on its exterior walls was the disclosure that 'research' indicated that while 'Welsh people deplore extremists; they don't want Prince Charles to be Prince of Wales'. Though one respondent declared: 'The Queen, so I would imagine, would rather bequeath her son a polo pony than an ingrate nation such as ours.'

107 John Jenkins: 'We never used gunpowder; and what would we be doing down there in an Air Force station, for God's sake? A government building, yes – but nothing to do with the Investiture, or anything else of interest to us.'

108 John Jenkins: 'I didn't fear that a member of MAC was operating outside my authority. They [MAC activists] were dreamers and too impractical to... I felt, owing to the erratic nature of the hits, that it was someone acting alone; who didn't belong to an organisation.'

109 A few examples are: Wylfa Power Station, 5 April 1968; Wrexham Railway Staff Association Club, 28 November 1968 and Bangor Post Office, 1 July 1969.

110 *Wrexham Leader*, 2 July 1968. Despite 'several' people throughout north Wales being interviewed by Special Branch and Crime Squad officers, Det. Chief Supt. Arthur Benfield, head of Cheshire CID, conceded that inquiries had led 'nowhere'.
    *Wrexham Leader*, 2 August 1968. 'Several people were interviewed'; 'one man questioned for eight hours' and flats and an office in Wrexham were searched in previous days. Police made no arrests. This happened 'fairly often'; and while it was 'likely the office was *Cymdeithas yr Iaith*'s', John 'was careful not to make enquiries, because that would have been a pointer'.

111 Interview between Judith Pritchard and Wyn Thomas, 19 February 2018. 'Along with my then husband, Paol Keineg, I was a founding member of the UDB (*Unvaniezh Demokratel Breizh*). It was a nationalist group, but much more socialist than Plaid Cymru. I know it was trying to make political connections with other groups – including Sinn Féin. But I can't recall the UDB wanting to launch a militant movement, or ever discussing blowing things up. As for the MAC protest, I cannot remember it *ever* being on the news in Brittany.'

112 On 1 July 1969, Julian Cayo Evans and Dennis Coslett were imprisoned for 15 months and Keith Griffiths (aka Gethin ap Gruffydd) for 9 months.

[113] The person holding this position – in 1969, Bernard Fitzalan-Howard, the 16th Duke of Norfolk – is responsible for all state ceremonial involving the monarchy.

[114] *Western Mail*, 12 April 1969. The information was received following a public appeal. John Jenkins: 'I now suspect it was Alders' ex-fiancée, Ann Woodgate, who informed the authorities anonymously.'

*Western Mail*, 22 April 1969. Two cottages in Llangollen were searched for explosives following a tip off. Nothing was found.

[115] Jennie Taylor: 'I *wish* my father had kept a diary – it might have proved this claim of Jenkins' to be rubbish.'

[116] John Jenkins: 'It's a myth: invented by the media because it makes good copy.'

[117] *Cheshire Chronicle*, 23 July 2013. A verdict of accidental death was recorded at the inquest into the deaths of Alwyn Jones and George Taylor in October 1969.

[118] BBC Radio Cymru, *Manylu*, 22 March, 2010. A former Special Branch officer added that while Alwyn Jones was 'suspected of being involved in at least one bombing incident', George Taylor 'was not on their radar'. Other former police officers, however, believe Taylor had no reason to join Jones unless actively involved.

[119] Email correspondence between Jennie Taylor and Wyn Thomas, June 2018.

[120] Interview between John Jenkins and Wyn Thomas. Also, interview between Trevor Fishlock (*The Times'* correspondent in Wales at the time) and Wyn Thomas, 18 November 2002. Fishlock remarked: 'It was speculated that maybe the holdall bag in which the bomb lay bumped against a wall or a knee; perhaps the device had been pre-set and the clock tipped over; the sweating nitro-glycerine might have needed very little to detonate it.'

[121] Part-time fireman George Taylor was linked to the explosion when attending fire crew informed police that he had inexplicably failed to answer the bell which had sounded earlier at the Taylor residence – the signal for Taylor to contact the Abergele fire station and receive further instructions. Some two hours after the blast, members of the Shrewsbury Unit arrived at the Taylor home.

[122] Anonymous interview with Wyn Thomas, June 2018. In response to being informed of the family's campaign to clear George Taylor's name, he continued: 'I would say that if it is correct that George Taylor was *not* on the police radar and that judging by the condition of the bodies, he appears to have been standing *some* distance back from Alwyn Jones when the device activated, the family does indeed have cause to consider that an alternative series of events may have occurred – thus providing them the grounds on which to challenge the official account.'

[123] Anonymous interview with Wyn Thomas, August 2018. 'I know it isn't nice to say this, but I would say that the general feeling at the time was that they'd got what they deserved.'

[124] *Daily Telegraph*, 2 July 1969.

[125] *Regimental Records of The Royal Welch Fusiliers* (Vol VI). (The Royal Welch Fusiliers, 2001) p.417.

[126] John Jenkins: 'Well, the "security alarm" was nothing to do with MAC. It may

have been nothing more than a disgruntled local being questioned by an Army serviceman, or the police who were patrolling the area, and being told that he couldn't walk on a public footpath or through a field running near Vaynol Hall. I'd be surprised if the local was told the Queen was staying there. But whether informed of this or not, a verbal confrontation may have ensued, which resulted in it being recorded as a "security alarm". You see, people today might imagine that the locals were fully in support of the Investiture, but we were being told that often this was not the case, and that in fact, there was some animosity felt towards it – particularly at a local level.'

127  Informed of the RWF's officer's name, John Jenkins declared, 'I personally recruited all members of MAC who undertook active protests, and that is not a name that means anything to me. He may, of course, have used another name to get in. But no, I don't think so. I don't believe that any member of the Royal Welch Fusiliers joined MAC, nor for that matter, a serviceman from any other regiment in the British Army. Well, not to my knowledge.'

128  Mike Lewis: 'Mr Jenkins must be getting on a bit now. He's aged 86? Well, good luck to him.'

129  John Jenkins: 'Owing to the degree of police and Special Branch surveillance, you couldn't get two minutes to place a decent bomb anywhere! It was extremely difficult to do any damn thing.'

130  Anonymous interview with Wyn Thomas, January 2018. A former Caernarfon resident, who knew where the device was placed and was in the town during the Investiture, declared: 'It's some distance from the processional route, and had it activated on Investiture Day, what with all the cheering, if heard at all, I think most people would have dismissed it as a car backfiring.'

131  NLW, MS 22816-19.

132  *Western Mail*, 21 April 1970.

133  John Jenkins: 'They also asked me to visit this hotel in Bargoed and report back any suspicions. I didn't go... They wanted to make me worried, so that I would go and tell people to keep their heads down; they'd then monitor the reaction.'

134  John Jenkins: 'For reasons of strategy and security, I always did everything regarding MAC with two things in mind. So in between these 'eating the leek' ceremonies, I met Owain... I was dressed in the full regimental, pre-1914 regalia of the Royal Welch Fusiliers, which comprised a bright scarlet tunic with black collars and cuffs, with all the leek and things, black trousers and a gleaming white canvas leg protector to protect against the guy rope attached to the drum. I don't think I was wearing the ceremonial headdress... I'm quite sure this encounter in Loggerheads proved a turning point in the campaign.

135  NLW, MS 22816-19. At the time of Jenkins' arrest, he received an approximate wage of £19 p/w, of which £2.15s.0d. per week was paid to the Army in accommodation fees.

136  Jenkins' and Alders' detention ensured they missed a concert at Earls Court the

following weekend at which the band of the Royal Welch Fusiliers cadets were invited to perform.

137 John Jenkins: 'The Risley library was the life saver. I read six books a day in my cell. With one hour of exercise, and so 23 hours to kill, what else was there to do?'

138 Ernie and Rowena Alders were married 18 October 1969. John Jenkins acted as Alders' best man.

139 *Liverpool Daily Post*, 10 April 1970.

140 John Jenkins: 'I pleaded not guilty to all charges, despite the wealth of evidence against me, because apparently, all lawyers or barristers urge their clients to plead not guilty – so my counsel, Peter Thomas QC, advised me to.'

141 *Liverpool Daily Post*, 16 April 1970; also TNA, ASS 84/577.

142 John Jenkins: 'Perhaps I expected too much of him. I expect too much of people, anyway.'

143 *Western Mail*, 14 April 1970.

144 John Jenkins: 'I was angry with him for saying so much; and I'm sure the authorities were angry that I managed to stop the trial and shut him up – because they were doing alright with Ernie.'

145 *Liverpool Daily Post*, 21 April 1970.

146 For a thorough and comprehensive analysis of the MAC, FWA and other anti-investiture campaigns, and their detection, police questioning and trials, see: Wyn Thomas, *Hands Off Wales: Nationhood and Militancy* (Gomer), 2013.

147 The Treason Act 1795 continued to make a capital offence of treason, which was defined as to 'compass, imagine, invent, devise or intend death or destruction, or any bodily harm tending to death or destruction, maim or wounding, imprisonment or restraint, of the person of ... the King.' By section 36 of the Crime and Disorder Act 1998, the maximum punishment for high treason became life imprisonment.

148 *Liverpool Daily Post*, 21 April 1970.

149 Anonymous interview with Wyn Thomas, July 2017.

150 John Jenkins: 'During an interview with police, Thelma told them about the bomb in Llandudno, having apparently overheard me talking in my sleep.'

151 NLW, MS 22816-19. In a letter to Sir Michael Adeane, the Queen's Private Secretary, Jenkins reiterated the degree to which Charles had been in danger and castigated the police for having missed the device, commenting that the Chief Supt. assigned to escort Charles from the Royal Yacht was promoted shortly afterwards.

152 NLW, MS 22816-19; *Western Mail*, 16 July 1976; also, interview between John Owen Evans (former Assistant Chief Constable) and Wyn Thomas, 5 July 2009.

153 NLW, MS 22816-19.

154 NLW, MS 22816-19. A fund orgainsed by Welsh nationalist sympathisers to assist the Jenkins family over Christmas 1970 raised over £500.

155 Prof. Richard English [talking about his own research with IRA volunteers]:

'The IRA did adopt a cellular structure in the 1970s. I came across no reference suggesting that they got the idea from MAC.'

[156] Prof. Richard English [talking about his own research with IRA volunteers]: 'None of my interviewees ever mentioned John Jenkins at all.'

[157] Christopher Andrew, *The Defence of the Realm. The Authorised History of MI5* (Penguin, 2009), p.623, recounts Joe Cahill's arrest on 28 March 1975 on board the *Claudia*; which, having been tracked by a British surveillance operation, was intercepted off the coast of County Waterford by the Irish Navy while carrying five tons of arms, ammunition and explosives from Libya. John Jenkins: 'I don't recall us discussing it.'

[158] Micky Gaughan died on hunger-strike at Parkhurst Prison on 4 June 1974, aged 24. *An Phoblacht/Republican News*, 14 June 1990, p.12; also, Jenkins, *Prison Letters*, p.91.

[159] *Western Mail*, 21 November 1972. [Editorial] 'Despite these affinities [of Welsh nationalist claims that Wales was being treated unfairly within the UK political union] these doom-laden prophecies of another Irish situation in Wales are, thankfully, too remote to gain credence.'

[160] On 31 October 1973, three Provisional IRA volunteers escaped from Mountjoy Prison in Dublin aboard a hijacked Alouette II helicopter, which briefly landed in the prison's exercise yard.

[161] John Jenkins: 'Each cell had an internal phone, which you'd use to ask to be let out to go to the toilet, but when you remember how many were imprisoned there, you might have to wait perhaps an hour before it was your turn.'

[162] On 9 December 1968, Norman Richard Bassett was convicted of murdering his mother, Eileen Nellie Bassett, on 5 September 1968. Arriving at the home they shared, police discovered written in her blood on her bedroom wall: 'You who were once my mum, how lost am I.' Released in 1982, Bassett was convicted in 2014 of attempted murder, which he carried out in 2004. Questioned regarding this offence, Bassett claimed to have been 'instructed to carry out the attack by the head of MI5 special branch, because the victim was an android alien.'

[163] On 10 October 1969, John Proud Elliot and Anthony Christopher Gill were convicted of murdering Larry Alfred King, aged 16, on 18 May 1969. Elliot and Gill attacked King with an axe and a sheath knife when a scooter, which the three had purloined earlier, malfunctioned.

[164] Later in 1972, Thelma married Stephan Banner, from Trelewis.

[165] John Jenkins: 'I was always accompanied by two prison officers when attending these court hearings, and we'd travel by approved prison transport, like an official car, because prisoners are not permitted to travel on public transport. On the way back to Albany, we'd stop at a government installation, like RAF Lyneham in Wiltshire, to use the toilet. It amounts to them keeping you away from the public, because it would have been bad for members of the public to see a man accompanied by two prison officers whilst handcuffed.'

[166] John Jenkins: 'I had a reasonable enough relationship with Thelma's mother, even

after I was convicted. She was on my side; and she was disgusted by her daughter's disloyalty. The father was in-between. I am *not* saying that Beryl Bridgman supported MAC – she wouldn't have understood the political situation. But she certainly didn't support the way her daughter was behaving either. Thelma's mother was an old-fashioned Valleys type; she was from the coalfields and as far as she was concerned, as a husband and father, I should be looked up to and cared for, and all the rest of it. They had some ferocious arguments about it, apparently. I even heard that Beryl threw a stone through Thelma's window, so angered was she at the way Thelma was carrying on.'

167  Letter from John Jenkins to Paol and Judy Keineg, dated 30 March 1972; also, 8 March 1974. Thelma's 'mere suspicions' that he was having an affair resulted in her confronting Jenkins 'with a knife' a 'number of times'. In Germany, Jenkins maintained, on seeing him wink at his secretary – the Colonel's daughter – Thelma had 'flung everything in the place' at John, 'including the ashtray'.

168  Viscount Colville was a staunch supporter of Prime Minister Edward Heath, and as the situation in Ulster worsened in the early 1970s, was tasked by Heath to state in the House of Lords the Government's position in tackling the escalating terrorist threat in the province.

169  NLW, MS 22816-19.

170  Letter from John Jenkins to Paol and Judy Keineg, dated 22 January 1973. John Jenkins: 'The UK was eventually ticked off by Strasbourg.'

171  Letter from John Jenkins to Judy Keineg, dated 18 February 1974. John was officially informed that he could not receive copies of *Le Peuple Breton* 'because it is not being sent to me by a distributor or newsagent in the UK'.

172  *John Jenkins: Prison Letters* (Y Lolfa, 1981 – reprinted 2019).

173  NLW, MS 22816-19; also, *John Jenkins: Prison Letters* (Y Lolfa, 1981).

174  John Jenkins received a A for his essay entitled 'Discuss the value of the Mooney Problem Check List in the assessment of maladjustment'; and another A for his essay entitled 'Does the impulse to scorn women or to be cynical about them enrich Elizabethan love poetry?' He was informed by the tutor that, against her protestations, she was asked to 'mark down' Jenkins' essays, as it looked like he was being 'favoured'.

175  Letter from John Jenkins to Judy Keineg, dated 8 March 1974.

176  The 5p and 10p coins were introduced 23 April 1968 and the 50p coin introduced 14 October 1969.

177  Whether a consequence of supporting John Jenkins or not, Tom Ellis' winning votes increased from 28,885 at the 1974 General Election, to 30,405 in 1979, although Ellis' percentage share of the vote fell from 51.1% to 49.2%. Beti Jones, *Welsh Elections 1885–1997* (Y Lolfa, 1999), pp.126, 130.

178  TNA, J 82/4263. His barrister informed the court that despite securing employment, John had 'suffered the difficulties which all long-term prisoners suffer [on being released].'

179  A conditional discharge is an order made by a criminal court whereby an offender

will not be sentenced for an offence unless a further offence is committed within a stated period.

180 In 2018, John Jenkins dismissed as 'pathetic' and 'inaccurate, as it only happened once' the online allegation contained in *ENIGMA 2000* article – *The Smokey Dragon – Part 2*, which claims that the 'homosexual' Jenkins had 'convictions for importuning males'; claimed in the piece to be 'a far cry from freedom fighting!'

181 An article featuring the interview with Jenkins later appeared in weekly Welsh-language newspaper *Faner*. The *Meibion Glyndŵr* arson protest, during which over 200 homes and businesses across Wales and England were targeted, is thought to have ended in 1992. It was principally undertaken to draw attention to the fact there existed in Wales some 30,000 second homes and a council house waiting list of over 50,000.

182 At the Old Bailey on 4 November 1968, 37-year-old Douglas Britten, an RAF Signals Intelligence Specialist, was sentenced to 21 years' imprisonment for passing secrets to the KGB.

183 Interview between John Owen Evans (former Assistant Chief Constable) and Wyn Thomas, 5 July 2009. 'The police believed that Jenkins was involved in the *Meibion Glyndŵr* arson campaign.'

184 *Western Mail*, 1 April 1980.

185 *Y Cymro*, 2 December 1980. Eurig ap Gwilym was charged with 'conspiracy to cause criminal damage' and also with 'having in his custody certain items, intending without lawful excuse, to use them to damage property'. He was remanded into custody from his arrest in March until sentenced at Mold Crown Court to two years – with a third taken off for time already served. It was thought that ap Gwilym was a member of *Cadwyr Cymru* and that the group had links to the IRA and ETA. *Cadwyr Cymru* ('the Keepers of Wales') were one of four movements thought responsible for the arson attacks, along with *Meibion Glyndŵr*, the Welsh Army for the Welsh Republic (WAWR) and MAC.

186 John admitted that not all potential employers were so understanding, with a manager of a children's home in Cardiff angrily declaring in the days before Jenkins' placement ended, 'If I'd known who you were, you would not have put one foot inside here.'

187 Jenkins attended preliminary hearings at Cardiff Stipendiary Magistrates Court on 2 July, 5 August, 2 September and finally 15 November 1982, when the case was sent to trial at Cardiff Crown Court.

188 During the court hearing, a transcription of Jenkins' *Nationwide* interview was read out.

189 For more information, see John Osmond, *Police Conspiracy?* (Y Lolfa, 1984). Jenkins was charged with assisting an offender, contrary to Section 4 (1) of the Criminal Law Act, 1967.

190 Speaking of Minerva Jenkins in November 2018, John's long-term companion Peter declared with affection, 'She was a good friend to me.' Thomas Jenkins had

passed away (aged 76) on 15 October 1986 and was interred on 21 October. Keith Jenkins passed away (aged 80) on 18 May 2017 and was interred alongside his parents on 1 June.

191 For further information see: AACAP and D Pruitt, *Your Child: Emotional, Behavioral, and Cognitive Development from Infancy through Pre-Adolescence* (William Morrow, 1998); Elizabeth Berger, *Raising Children With Character: Parents, Trust, and the Development of Personal Integrity* (Jason Aronson), 1999); Erik Erikson, *Childhood and Society* (W W Morton & Company, 1994).

192 John feels that his suspicions were confirmed when he later read, in the pages of British historical accounts, Owain Glyndŵr's depiction as a 'rebel' rather than a patriot and freedom fighter, which the youthful Jenkins considered a worthier description.

193 TNA, ASSI 84/577; also, *LDP*, 21 April 1970.

194 Anonymous interview with Wyn Thomas, August 2018. A close female acquaintance of Thelma Jenkins during 1969 described her as 'a lovely person' and said 'he [Jenkins] had what he wanted from her.'

195 John Jenkins: 'I'm proud that my sons and their offspring speak Welsh.'

196 TNA, J 82/4263.

197 During her research, Dr Lewis concluded that most, if not all, of the inmates she worked with had been abused as children, or had experienced or witnessed potentially traumatic events, including violence… and that in many cases the children who received the strictest discipline became the most violent.

198 Maladaptive behaviours inhibit a person's ability to adjust healthily to particular situations. In essence, they prevent people from adapting to or coping well with the demands and stresses of life.

199 Email correspondence between Baron Morgan (Kenneth Owen Morgan) and Wyn Thomas, 1 October 2013. 'As an academic historian; a Welsh-speaking Welshman; and republican who strongly supports devolution – and has often spoken on it in the Lords – I am very pleased that this miscellaneous bevy of youthful, violent crackpots [MAC] had only a minimal impact on Welsh history. It is all to the good that Wales resembles Ireland hardly at all in this respect.'

200 Christopher Andrew, *The Defence of the Realm. The Authorised History of MI5* (Penguin, 2009). Andrew does state on p.696, however: 'in 1982, the weekly [MI5] Directors' Meetings spent more time discussing the terrorist threat in Britain from Welsh extremists (for which it had the lead role) than that from the Provisional Irish Republican Army (for which it did not).'

201 Prof. Richard English, *Does Terrorism Work? A History* (Oxford, 2016). See FN 48, in which Prof. English states: 'Wyn Thomas's impressive study of Welsh militancy [*Hands Off Wales: Nationhood and Militancy* (Gomer, Llandysul, 2013)] argues that Welsh terrorism perhaps achieved some lesser progress: but his account makes equally clear that the central goal of independence has remained utterly distant in Wales.'

202 Dr Nicholas Brooke, *The Dogs That Didn't Bark: Political Violence and Nationalism*

*in Scotland, Wales and England.* A Thesis Submitted for the Degree of PhD at the University of St Andrews, 2016. See pp.41–88.

203 Benedict Anderson, *Imagined Communities* (2nd revised edn., Verso, 1991), p.6.

204 Ernest Gellner, *Thought and Change* (Weidenfeld & Nicolson, 1964), p.169. The term 'nationalism' coincided with the demise of the monarchical principle in Europe. It was first used in print in 1789 by the anti-Jacobin French priest Augustin Barruel and acquired an immediate political overtone as groups were classified as 'nationalists'. The Revolutionary and Napoleonic Wars (1792–1815) caused the spread of 'nationalism' through much of continental Europe.

205 E J Hobsbawm, *Nations and Nationalism since 1780* (Cambridge University Press, 1990), p.91.

206 Peter Scott, *Knowledge and Nation* (Edinburgh University Press, 1990), p.168.

207 *Reflections on the Philosophy of History of Mankind*, Frank E. Manuel (ed.), (University of Chicago Press, 1968).

208 Ernest Gellner, *Nations and Nationalism*, p.44; Eric Hobsbawm, *Nations and Nationalism Since 1780*, pp.58–61; Anthony D Smith, *Nations and Nationalism in a Global Era* (Polity, 1995), p.66.

209 Karen A Mingst & Ivan M Arreguín-Toft, *Essentials of International Relations* (6th revised edn., W W Norton & Company, 2014), pp.278, 279, 446, 452, 455.

210 David Rapoport, *The Four Waves of Modern Terrorism*, (Georgetown University Press, 2004 – also published online).

211 Jeffrey Kaplan, *A Strained Criticism of Wave Theory*, (published online, 2015: https://www.tandfonline.com/doi/abs/10.1080/09546553.2015.1112279)

212 Jeffrey Kaplan, *Terrorism's Fifth Wave: A Theory, a Conundrum and a Dilemma*, (published online, 2008: http://www.terrorismanalysts.com/pt/index.php/pot/article/view/26)

213 Closed files relating to the MAC campaign stored at The National Archives. File reference number: DPP 2/5992; DPP 2/5991; DPP 2/5990; DPP 2/5989, all closed for 78 years. Record opening date 1 January 2049. ASSI 84/578, closed for 94 years. Record opening date 1 January 2065.

214 Closed files relating to the WAWR campaign stored at The National Archives. File reference number: DPP 2/7817; DPP 2/7814; DPP 2/7839; DPP 2/7838; DPP 2/7834; DPP 2/7829; DPP 2/7827; DPP 2/7825; DPP 2/7822; DPP 2/7819; DPP 2/7815; DPP 2/7840; DPP 2/7841; DPP 2/7828; DPP 2/7820; DPP 2/7816; DPP 2/7836; DPP 2/7830; DPP 2/7824; DPP 2/7823; DPP 2/7818; DPP 2/7837; DPP 2/7835; DPP 2/7833; DPP 2/7826; DPP 2/7831; DPP 2/7832; DPP 2/7821, all closed for 88 years. Record opening date 1 January 2074. File reference number: J 82/4263. Record opened 19 August 2014.

215 Vaughan Jenkins: 'I'll tell you a story which sums up my grandmother. I was in my early/mid-teens, and one afternoon when I entered her lounge, she had her head down and was knitting something. So I said, quite nicely, "So what books did you read when you were in school?" She just stared at me, so I added, "You know – when you were in school, what sort of books did you read?" Well, she

continued to stare at me for a moment, and then she said, "Don't be so stupid." And that was the end of that conversation! She put her head down and started knitting again!'

[216]  John confirmed that Vaughan refuses to call him 'Dad'.

[217]  Vaughan Jenkins lived on the Swansea Road estate in Merthyr Tydfil with his wife, her son and 'Screwy', Katell's boyfriend at the time.

[218]  https://www.hymnal.net/en/hymn/h/341

[219]  *Daily Mail*, 7 June 2016.

[220]  *Daily Mail*, 9 June 2016.

[221]  Culturenet Cymru, *100 Arwyr Cymru/Welsh Heroes*, 2004, p.80; also, *Western Mail*, 14 July 2004. It was apparently alleged by the former IT Manager of Culturenet Cymru that the poll was rigged to prevent Cayo Evans from appearing in the top 20. Neither John Jenkins nor George Thomas appeared in the poll. For the interview including this allegation, see: http://walesontheweb.blogspot. com/2004/09/culturenet-not-quite-right.html.

[222]  In Pencader, a memorial commemorates the reply the Old Man of Pencader allegedly gave to Henry II in the twelfth century, when asked if he thought Welsh opposition to England would last: "This nation may now be harassed, weakened and decimated by your soldiery, as it has so often been by others in former times; but it will never be totally destroyed by the wrath of man... I do not think that on the Day of Direct Judgement any race other than the Welsh, or any other language, will give answer to the Supreme Judge for all this small corner of the earth."

[223]  BBC News, 16 November 2017. The agreement was announced in November 2017 and intended to come into force five months later. The new arrangement, declared Alun Cairns, the Welsh Secretary of State, shows 'how far we have come from the events... which resulted in the flooding of the Tryweryn Valley'. The agreement, he continued, 'puts cross-border arrangements for water on a footing for the twenty-first century and underlines what can be achieved when two governments work together for Wales' future prosperity.' The Welsh Secretary added that the new accord reflected 'the significance of the flooding of Capel Celyn'.

[224]  *Sunday Times*, 22 April 2018. In a leaked and published document, it was reported that a new Government strategy will enable counter-terrorism investigators to warn other agencies – government departments, councils, devolved administrations and local police forces – about lower priority terrorist suspects on their radar *before* they are considered dangerous enough to be placed under MI5 surveillance. MI5 has information on more than 23,000 'subjects of interest', but only 3,000 are under active investigation. Designed to combat the threat from both domestic and international terrorism, the Government hopes that the move (which will grant the police and security services greater powers) will provide better intelligence at an early stage of a planned attack.

# Bibliography

## Primary Sources

### Newspapers

*Cardiff Yesterday*, Volume 30; also, *Western Mail* (Cardiff Directory), 1937; *Daily Mail*; *Liverpool Daily Post*; *The Mail on Sunday*; *The Guardian*; *Western Mail*; *Wrexham Leader*; *Merthyr Express*; *The Sunday Times*; *Sunday Express*; *Herald of Wales*; *The Sun*; *The Observer*; *Daily Mirror*; *North Wales Chronicle*.

### Welsh-language publications

*Faner*; *Y Cymro*; *Y Ffrynt*.

### Periodicals

*Planet*; *Town* Magazine; *Broadsheet*, UCW, Cardiff; *An Phoblacht/Republican News*.

### Oral testimony

John Jenkins; Trevor Fishlock; John Owen Evans; Neil ap Siencyn; Jennie Taylor; Keith Jenkins; Rhodri Jenkins; Vaughan Jenkins; Peter Cridland; David Walters; Judith Pritchard; Mike H L Lewis; Margaret Roberts; Emrys Roberts, *plus others who insisted upon remaining anonymous.*

### Post/email correspondence

Raymond Kendall; Professor Richard English; Jennie Taylor; Dr Dorothy Otnow Lewis; Baron Morgan (Professor Kenneth Owen Morgan).

### The National Archives

COAL 73/2; ASSI 84/577; J 82/4263.

### National Library of Wales

MS 22816-19.

### John Jenkins private papers

John Jenkins Open University degree (Social Sciences) essays.

**Judith Pritchard private papers**

Letters from John Jenkins to Paol and Judy Keineg.

**Sir Tasker Watkins private papers**

Social Enquiry Report Concerning John Barnard Jenkins, 26 February 1970.

Transcript of police interview with John Jenkins, 11 November 1969.

## Secondary Sources

AACAP and Pruitt, D, *Your Child: Emotional, Behavioral, and Cognitive Development from Infancy through Pre-Adolescence* (New York, William Morrow, 1998).

Allason, R, *The Friends: Britain's Post-War Secret Intelligence Operations* (London, Weidenfeld and Nicolson, 1988).

Anderson, B, *Imagined Communities* (2nd revised edn.) (London, Verso, 1991).

Andrew, C, *The Defence of the Realm. The Authorised History of MI5* (London, Penguin, 2009).

Austin, T, *Aberfan: The Story of a Disaster* (London, Hutchinson, 1967).

Bainham, A, Gilmore, S, *Children – The Modern Law*, 4th Edition (Bristol, Jordan Publishing Ltd, 2013).

Berger, E, *Raising Children With Character: Parents, Trust, and the Development of Personal Integrity* (Lanham, Jason Aronson, 1999).

Brooke, N, *The Dogs That Didn't Bark: Political Violence and Nationalism in Scotland, Wales and England* (A Thesis Submitted for the Degree of PhD at the University of St Andrews, 2016).

Bunyan, T, *The Political Police in Britain* (London, Julian Friedmann, 1976).

Burrows, T, *History of the Modern World* (London, Carlton, 1999).

Davies, E, *Report of the Tribunal Appointed to Inquire into the Disaster at Aberfan on October 21st 1966* (London, Her Majesty's Press, 1967).

Davies, J, *A History of Wales* (London, Penguin, 1993).

Dorril, S, *MI6: Inside the Covert World of Her Majesty's Secret Intelligence Service* (New York, Touchstone, 2000).

English, R, *Does Terrorism Work? A History* (Oxford, Oxford University Press, 2016).

Erikson, E, *Childhood and Society* (London, W W Norton & Company, 1994).

Evans, G, *Welsh Nation Builders* (Llandysul, Gomer, 1988).

Evans, R, *Gwynfor Rhag Pob Brad* (Talybont, Y Lolfa, 2005).

Evans, R, *Portrait of a Patriot* (Talybont, Y Lolfa, 2008).

Gellner, E, *Thought and Change* (London, Weidenfeld & Nicolson, 1964).

Herbert, T (ed.), *Wales 1880–1914: Welsh History and its Sources* (Cardiff, University of Wales Press, 1988).

Hobsbawm, E J, *Nations and Nationalism since 1780* (Cambridge, Cambridge University Press, 1990).

Jenkins, J, *Prison Letters* (Talybont, Y Lolfa, 1981 – and reprinted in 2019).

Jones, B, *Welsh Elections 1885–1997* (Talybont, Y Lolfa, 1999).

Lord Robens, *Ten Year Stint* (London, Cassell, 1972).

Manuel, F E (ed.), *Reflections on the Philosophy of the History of Mankind* (Chicago, University of Chicago Press, 1968).

McLean, I, Johnes, M, *Aberfan: Government and Disasters* (Cardiff, Welsh Academic Press, 2000).

Mingst, K A, & Arreguín-Toft, I M, *Essentials of International Relations* (6th revised edn.) (London, W W Norton & Company, 2014).

Osmond, J, *Police Conspiracy?* (Talybont, Y Lolfa, 1984).

Peden, G C, 'Suez and Britain's Decline as a World Power', *The Historical Journal* (Cambridge University Press, December, 2012).

Rapoport, D, *The Four Waves of Modern Terrorism* (Washington, Georgetown University Press, 2004).

*Regimental Records of The Royal Welch Fusiliers*, Vol VI (Uckfield, The Royal Welch Fusiliers, 2001).

Roberts, A, *Welsh National Heroes* (Talybont, Y Lolfa, 2002).

Scott, P, *Knowledge and Nation* (Edinburgh, Edinburgh University Press, 1990).

Smith, A D, *Nations and Nationalism in a Global Era* (Cambridge, Polity, 1995).

Thomas W, *Hands Off Wales: Nationhood and Militancy* (Llandysul, Gomer, 2013).

Williams, G A, *When Was Wales* (London, Penguin, 1985).

## Video, Television and Radio Material

*Two Men Went to War* (Ira Trattner Productions, 2002).

BBC News.

*Manylu* (BBC Radio Cymru).

## Websites accessed

*ENIGMA 2000 article – The Smokey Dragon – Part 2* (published online, 2004: http://www.cvni.net/radio/e2k/e2k025/e2k25article.html)

https://www.tandfonline.com/doi/abs/10.1080/09546553.2015.1112279)

Jeffrey Kaplan, *A Strained Criticism of Wave Theory*, (published online, 2015: https://www.tandfonline.com/doi/abs/10.1080/09546553.2015.1112279)

Jeffrey Kaplan, *Terrorism's Fifth Wave: A Theory, a Conundrum and a Dilemma*, (published online, 2008: http://www.terrorismanalysts.com/pt/index.php/pot/ article/view/26)

https://www.hymnal.net/en/hymn/h/341

http://walesontheweb.blogspot. com/2004/09/culturenet-not-quite-right. html

# Index

Also from Y Lolfa:

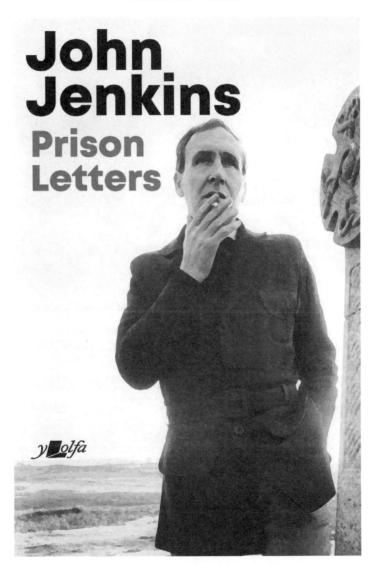

# John Jenkins
## Prison Letters

*y* **l**olfa

£9.99